Lecture Notes in Computer Science   2617

Edited by G. Goos, J. Hartmanis, and J. van Leeuwen

Springer
Berlin
Heidelberg
New York
Barcelona
Hong Kong
London
Milan
Paris
Tokyo

Hajo A. Reijers

Design and Control of Workflow Processes

Business Process Management for the Service Industry

 Springer

Series Editors

Gerhard Goos, Karlsruhe University, Germany
Juris Hartmanis, Cornell University, NY, USA
Jan van Leeuwen, Utrecht University, The Netherlands

Author

Hajo A. Reijers
Technical University of Eindhoven
Department of Technology Management
Den Dolech 2, P.O. Box 513, 5600 MB Eindhoven, The Netherlands
E-mail: H.A.Reijers@tm.tue.nl

Cataloging-in-Publication Data applied for

A catalog record for this book is available from the Library of Congress.

Bibliographic information published by Die Deutsche Bibliothek.
Die Deutsche Bibliothek lists this publication in the Deutsche Nationalbibliografie;
detailed bibliographic data is available in the Internet at <http://dnb.ddb.de>.

CR Subject Classification (1998): H.4.1, H.5.3, K.4.3, J.1, H.2

ISSN 0302-9743
ISBN 3-540-01186-2 Springer-Verlag Berlin Heidelberg New York

Springer-Verlag Berlin Heidelberg New York
a member of BertelsmannSpringer Science+Business Media GmbH

http://www.springer.de

© Springer-Verlag Berlin Heidelberg 2003
Printed in Germany

Typesetting: Camera-ready by author, data conversion by Boller Mediendesign
Printed on acid-free paper   SPIN: 10872920   06/3142   5 4 3 2 1 0

Foreword

This monograph is a beautiful mixture of rigorous scientific research and very practical experiences. The monograph provides several new insights in the field of business process modeling and analysis. The term "workflow process" is used instead of "business process" to express the focus on the handling of a flow of cases in an organization. In the last decade the process view has become the dominant way to structure organizations. Although many books promote this view, they seldom provide a scientifically sound approach to modeling and analyzing business processes.

There are two important aspects of a business process: its correctness and its efficiency. The first aspect concerns the correct handling of cases, i.e., without logical errors, and the second concerns the throughput time for cases and the effort required to execute them. The monograph provides new results for analyzing these two aspects, but there are also new results for the redesign of processes. Two approaches are offered: heuristics to redesign an existing process and a derivation method to develop a process given a specification of the desired output of the process.

The research for this monograph was conducted by Hajo Reijers during the last five years while he was working halftime for Deloitte & Touche as a management consultant and halftime as a Ph.D. student at the Eindhoven University of Technology. It was a great pleasure for me to be both his thesis advisor at the university and his supervisor in the consulting firm. The unique combination of scientific work at the university and real practice as a consultant turned out to be very fruitful. Many ideas for this research popped up during consultancy work and several scientific results were successfully applied in industry.

The monograph contains many interesting results that are worth applying in practice, while it is also a source of new and intriguing questions for further research.

Kees van Hee
National Director of Consultancy, Deloitte & Touche
Professor of Computer Science, Eindhoven University of Technology

Preface

The motivation behind the conception of this monograph was to advance scientific knowledge about the design and control of workflow processes. A workflow process (or workflow for short) is a specific type of business process, a way of organizing work and resources. Workflows are commonly found within large administrative organizations such as banks, insurance companies, and governmental agencies. Carrying out the tasks of a workflow in a particular order is required to handle one type of case. Examples of cases are mortgage applications, customer complaints, and claims for unemployment benefits. A workflow used in handling mortgage applications may contain tasks for recording the application, specifying a mortgage proposal, and approving the final policy. The monograph concentrates on four workflow-related issues within the area of Business Process Management; the field of designing and controlling business processes.

The first issue is how workflows can be adequately modeled. Workflow modeling is an indispensable activity to support any reasoning about workflows. Different purposes of workflow modeling can be distinguished, such as system enactment by Workflow Management Systems, knowledge management, costing, and budgeting. The focus of workflow modeling in this monograph is (a) to support simulation and analysis of workflows and (b) to specify a new workflow design. The main formalism used for the modeling of workflows is the Petri net. Many existing notions to define several relevant properties have been adopted, such as the *workflow net* and the *soundness* notion.

The second issue addressed in this monograph is the design or redesign of a workflow. Redesigning business processes has received wide attention in the past decade. Until this day, it has been seen as one of the major instruments available to companies for improving their performances. The monograph presents the Product-Based Workflow Design (PBWD) method, which derives a workflow design from the characteristics of the product it supports. This concept is well known in manufacturing where an assembly line may be determined on the basis of a Bill-of-Material, but is rather unorthodox in administrative settings. The method allows us to use context-specific design targets, such as cost reduction or responsiveness improvement, to determine the final design. Aside from its methodological and technical foundation, practical experiences are presented within a large Dutch bank and a social security agency with PBWD. In addition, the monograph contains about 30 redesign heuristics. These heuristics are derived from both existing literature and practical experience. They can be used to redesign business processes in a more conventional, incremental way. A case description is added to illustrate the application of these heuristics.

The third issue is the performance evaluation of workflow processes. A new stochastic version of the Petri net is presented that addresses both the structural characteristics of workflows and its typical timing behavior. Two techniques are described that can be used to determine the stochastic behavior of a workflow design as measured in its throughput time. The throughput time of a single case is defined as the amount of time that passes from the start of its processing to its completion. Both techniques may help the designer of a workflow to determine whether the design targets will be achieved by the new design. The first technique uses basic building blocks and a well-known synthesis technique to construct a workflow model that can subsequently be analyzed exactly. The Fast-Fourier Transform is used to improve the efficiency of the analysis. The second technique can be applied to the subclass of sound, free-choice, and acyclic workflow nets to determine lower and upper bounds for the throughput time distribution of the respective net. An important restriction of both techniques is that they abstract from resource constraints.

The fourth and last issue addressed in this monograph is how to sensibly allocate resources in an operational workflow. Once again, the performance indicator focused on is the throughput time. A familiar approach used in industry is to add extra resources at bottle-necks within the business process, i.e., the classes of resources that are pressed the hardest, to reduce the throughput time. This approach is critically assessed and its limitations are presented. An alternative method for *marginal allocation* is presented. Its optimality is proven for a subclass of stochastic workflow nets with resource constraints. To derive an inductive feeling of its effectiveness outside this class, a workbench of workflow nets has been developed. Simulation techniques have been used to test the method of marginal allocation on this workbench, which has led to cautious but positive conclusions.

The common feature of the treatment of the four issues is an attempt to provide scientific support for Business Process Management and the management of workflows in particular.

February 2003   Hajo A. Reijers

Contents

References

van der Aalst, W.M.P. (1992): Timed Coloured Petri Nets and Their Application to Logistics. PhD thesis. Eindhoven University of Technology, Eindhoven

van der Aalst, W.M.P. (1993): Interval Timed Coloured Petri Nets and their Analysis. In: Marsan, M.A. (ed.): Application and Theory of Petri Nets 1993. Lecture Notes in Computer Science, Vol. 691. Springer-Verlag, Berlin, 453-472

van der Aalst, W.M.P. (1994): Using Interval Timed Coloured Petri Nets to Calculate Performance Bounds. In: Haring, G., Kotsis, G. (eds.): Proceedings of the 7th International Conference of Modelling Techniques and Tools for Computer Performance Evaluation. Lecture Notes in Computer Science. Vol. 794. Springer-Verlag, Berlin, 425-444

van der Aalst, W.M.P. (1996): Three Good Reasons for Using a Petri net-based Workflow Management System. In: Navathe, S., Wakayama, T. (eds.): Proceedings of the International Working Conference on Information and Process Integration in Enterprises (IPIC'96), 179-201

van der Aalst, W.M.P. (1998): The Application of Petri Nets to Workflow Management. The Journal of Circuits, Systems and Computers, $8(1)$, 21-66

van der Aalst, W.M.P. (1999): On the Automatic Generation of Workflow Processes Based on Product Structures. Computers in Industry, $39(2)$, 97-111

van der Aalst, W.M.P. (2000a): Workflow Verification: Finding Control-Flow Errors Using Petri net-based Techniques. In: van der Aalst, W.M.P., Desel, J., Oberweis, A. (eds.): Business Process Management. Lecture Notes in Computer Science, Vol. 1806. Springer-Verlag, Berlin, 161-183

van der Aalst, W.M.P. (2000b): Reengineering Knock-out Processes. Decision Support Systems, $30(4)$, 451-468

van der Aalst, W.M.P. (2001): How to Handle Dynamic Change and Capture Management Information: An Approach Based on Generic Workflow Models. International Journal of Computer Systems, Science, and Engineering, $16(5)$, 295-318

van der Aalst, W.M.P., Berens, P.J.S. (2001): Beyond Workflow Management: Product-Driven Case Handling. In Ellis, S. (ed.): International ACM SIGGROUP Conference on Supporting Group Work (GROUP 2001). ACM Press, New York, 42-51

van der Aalst, W.M.P., de Crom, P.J.N., Goverde, R.R.H.M.J., van Hee, K.M., Hofman, W.J., Reijers, H.A., van der Toorn, R.A. (2000a): ExSpect 6.4: An Executable Specification Tool for Hierarchical Colored Petri Nets. In: Nielsen, M., Simpson, D. (eds.): Application and Theory of Petri Nets 2000. Lecture Notes in Computer Science, Vol. 1825. Springer Verlag, Berlin, 455-464

van der Aalst, W.M.P., Desel, J., Oberweis, A. (eds.) (2000b): Business Process Management. Lecture Notes in Computer Science, Vol. 1806. Springer-Verlag, Berlin

van der Aalst, W.M.P., van Hee, K.M. (1996): Business Process Redesign: A Petri net-based Approach. Computers in Industry, $29(1-2)$, 15-26 van der Aalst, W.M.P., van Hee, K.M. (2002): Workflow Management: Models, Methods, and Systems. MIT Press, Cambridge

van der Aalst, W.M.P., van Hee, K.M., Reijers, H.A. (2000c): Analysis of Discrete-Time Stochastic Petri Nets. Statistica Neerlandica, **54**(2), 237-255

van der Aalst, W.M.P., van Hee, K.M., van der Toorn, R.A. (2002): Component-Based Software Architectures: A Framework Based on Inheritance of Behavior. Science of Computer Programming, **42**(2-3), 129-171

van der Aalst, W.M.P., ter Hofstede, A.H.M. (2000): Verification of Workflow Task Structures: A Petri-net-based Approach. Information Systems **25**(1), 43-69

van der Aalst, W.M.P., Odijk, M.A. (1995): Analysis of Railway Stations by means of Interval Timed Coloured Petri Nets. Real-Time Systems, **9**(3), 241-263

van der Aalst, W.M.P., Reijers, H.A., Limam, S. (2001): Product-driven Workflow Design. In: Shen, W. (ed.): Proceedings of the Sixth International Conference on Computer Supported Cooperative Work in Design 2001. NRC Research Press, Ottawa, 397-402

Agostini, A., De Michelis, G. (2000): A Light Workflow Management System Using Simple Process Models. Computer Supported Cooperative Work **9**(3), 335-363

Aldowaisan, T.A., Gaafar, L.K. (1999): Business Process Reengineering: An Approach for Process Mapping. Omega **27**(5), 515-524

Al-Mashari M., Zairi, M. (2000a): Creating a Fit between BPR and IT Infrastructure: A Proposed Framework for Effective Implementation. International Journal of Flexible Manufacturing Systems **12**(4), 253-274

Al-Mashari M., Zairi, M. (2000b): Revisiting BPR: A Holistic Review of Practice and Development. Business Process Management **6**(1), 10-42

APDST (1995): Academic Press Dictionary of Science and Technology. Academic Press, London

Asmussen, S., Nerman O., Olsson, M. (1996): Fitting Phase-type Distribution via the EM Algorithm. Scandinavion Journal of Statistics **23**(4), 419-441

Baets, W. (1993): IT for Organizational Learning: Beyond Business Process Engineering. Business Change and Reengineering **2**(2), 32-40

Balbo G., Silva, M. (eds.) (1998): Performance Models for Discrete Event Systems with Synchronisations: Formalisms and Analysis Techniques. Kronos, Zaragoza

Barlow, R.E., Proshan, F. (1975): Statistical Theory of Reliability and Life Testing. Hold, New York

Baskett, F., Chandy, K.M., Muntz, R.R., Palacios-Gomez, F. (1975): Open, Closed and Mixed Networks of Queues with Different Classes of Customers. Journal of the ACM **22**(2), 248-260

Basten, T. (1997): Parsing Partially Ordered Multisets. International Journal of Foundations of Computer Science **8**(4), 379-407

Belmonte, R. Murray, R. (1993): Getting Ready for Strategic Change: Surviving Business Process Redesign. Information Systems Management, summer, 23-29

Berg, A., Pottjewijd, P. (1997): Workflow: Continuous Improvement by Integral Process Management. Academic Service, Schoonhoven (In Dutch)

Bergstra, J.A., Klop, J.W. (1984): Process Algebra for Synchronous Communication. Information and Control **60**(1-3), 109-137

Berthomieu, B., Diaz, M. (1991): Modelling and Verification of Time Dependent Systems using Timed Petri Nets. IEEE Transactions on Software Engineering **17**(3), 259-273

Berthomieu, B., Menasche, M. (1983): An Enumerative Approach for Analyzing Timed Petri Nets. In: Mason, R.E.A. (ed.): Information Processing: Proceedings of the IFIP congress 1983. IFIP congress series 9. Elsevier Science Publishers, Amsterdam, 41-46

Bhatt, G.D. (2000): Exploring the Relationship between Information Technology, Infrastructure and Business Process Re-engineering. Business Process Management 6(2), 139-163

Bin Lee, H., Woo Kim, J., Joo Park, S. (1999): KWM: Knowledge-based Workflow Model for Agile Organization. Journal of Intelligent Information Systems 13(3), 261-278

Bond, T.C. (1999): Systems Analysis and Business Process Mapping: a Symbiosis. Business Process Management Journal 5(2), 164-178

Bradley, S. (1994): Creating and Adhering to a BPR Methodology. Gartner Group Report, 1-30

Brand, N., van der Kolk, H. (1995): Workflow Analysis and Design. Kluwer Bedrijfswetenschappen, Deventer (In Dutch)

Bricon-Souf, N., Renard, J.M., Beuscart, R. (1999): Dynamic Workflow Model for Complex Activity in Intensive Care Unit. International Journal of Medical Informatics 53(2-3), 143-150

Bruss, L.R., Roos, H.T. (1993): Operations, Readiness, and Culture: Don't Reengineer without Considering Them. Inform 7(4), 57-64

Burke, G., Peppard, J. (1993): Business Process Redesign: Research Directions. Business Change and Reengineering 1(1), 43-47

Buzacott, J.A. (1996): Commonalities in Reengineered Business Processes: Models and Issues. Management Science 42(5), 768-782

Calvert, P. (1994): An Advanced BPR Methodology with Integrated, Computer-based Tools. In: Glasson, B.C. (ed.): Business Process Re-engineering: Information Systems Opportunities ad Challenges. Elsevier Science, Amsterdam, 161-170

Carlier, J., Chretienne, P. (1988): Timed Petri Net Schedules. In: Rozenberg, G. (ed.): Advances in Petri Nets 1988. Lecture Notes in Computer Science, Vol. 340. Springer-Verlag, Berlin, 62-84

Carr, D. Johansson, H. (1995): Best Practices in Reengineering. McGraw-Hill, New York

Casimir, R.J. (1995): Gaming in Information Systems Development. PhD thesis. Katholieke Universiteit Brabant, Tilburg

Champy, J. (1995): Reengineering Management. Harper Collins, London

Chao, X., Miyazawa, M., Pinedo, M. (1999): Queuing Networks: Customers, Signals, and Product Form Solutions. Wiley & Sons, Chichester

Chiola, G., Dutheillet, C., Franceschinis, G., Haddad, S. (1990): On Well-formed Coloured Nets and Their Symbolic Reachability Graph. In: Rozenberg, G. (ed.): Proceedings of the 11th International Conference on Applications and Theory of Petri Nets. Paris, 387-411

Chretienne, P. (1983): Les Réseaux de Petri Temporisés. PhD thesis. Université Paris VI, Paris

Cormen, T. H., Leiseron, C.E., Rivest, R.L. (1990): Introduction to Algorithms. The MIT Press, Cambridge

de Crom, P.J.N., Reijers, H.A. (2001): Using Prototyping in a Product-driven Design of Business Processes. In: D'Atri, A. (ed.): Proceedings of the Open Enterprise Solutions: Systems, Experiences, and Organizations Conference. Luiss Edizioni, Rome, 41-47

Cumani, A. (1985): Esp – a Package for the Evaluation of Stochastic Petri Nets with Phase-type Distributed Transition Times. In: Proceedings of the International Workshop on Timed Petri Nets. IEEE-CS Press, 144-151

Davenport, T.H., Short, J.E. (1990): The New Industrial Engineering: Information Technology and Business Process Redesign. Sloan Management Review, 31(4), 11-27

Dehnert, J. (2002): Non-controllable Choice Robustness Expressing the Controllability of Workflow Processes. In: Esparza, J., Lakos, C. (eds.): Application and Theory of Petri Nets 2002. Lecture Notes in Computer Science, Vol. 2360. Springer-Verlag, Berlin, 121-141

Dellarocas, C., Klein, M. (2000): A Knowledge-Based Approach for Designing Robust Business Processes. In: van der Aalst, W.M.P., Desel, J., Oberweis, A. (eds.): Business Process Management. Lecture Notes in Computer Science, Vol. 1806. Springer-Verlag, Berlin, 50-65

Deiters, W. (2000): Information Gathering and Process Modeling in a Petri Net Based Approach. In: van der Aalst, W.M.P., Desel, J., Oberweis, A. (eds.): Business Process Management. Lecture Notes in Computer Science, Vol. 1806. Springer-Verlag, Berlin, 274-288

Desel, J., Erwin, T. (2000): Modeling, Simulation and Analysis of Business Processes. In: van der Aalst, W.M.P., Desel, J., Oberweis, A. (eds.): Business Process Management. Lecture Notes in Computer Science, Vol. 1806. Springer-Verlag, Berlin, 129-141

Desel, J., Esparza, J. (1995): Free Choice Petri Nets. Cambridge Tracts in Theoretical Computer Science 40. Cambridge University Press, Cambridge

Dutheillet, C., Haddad, S. (1989): Regular Stochastic Petri Nets. In: Proceedings of the 10th International Conference on Applications and Theory of Petri Nets, Bonn, 43-62

Duffy, D. (1994): Managing the White Space (Cross-functional Processes). Management, April, 35-36

Dyer, M.E., Proll, L.G. (1977): On the Validity of Marginal Analysis for Allocating Servers in M/M/c Queues. Management Science 21, 1019-1022

Ellis, C.A. (1979): Information Control Nets: A Mathematical Model of Office Information Flow. In: Proceedings of the Conference on Simulation, Measurement and Modeling of Computer Systems. ACM Press, Boulder, 225-240

Ellis, C.A. Nutt, G.J. (1993): Modelling and Enactment of Workflow Systems. In: Marsan, M.A. (ed.): Application and Theory of Petri Nets. Lecture Notes in Computer Science, Vol. 691. Springer-Verlag, Berlin, 1-16

Evarts, H.F. (1964): Introduction to PERT. Allyn & Bacon, Boston,

Florin, G., Natkin, S. (1982): Evaluation Based upon Stochastic Petri Nets of the Maximum Throughput of a Full Duplex Protocol. In: Girault, C., Reisig, W. (eds.): Application and Theory of Petri Nets. Informatik Fachberichte 52. Springer-Verlag, Berlin, 280-288

Flores, G., Graves, M., Hartfield, B., Winograd, T. (1988): Computer Systems and the Design of Organizational Interaction. ACM Transactions on Office Information Systems 6(2), 153-172

Fox, B. (1966): Discrete Optimization via Marginal Analysis. Management Science 13, 210-216

Galliers, R. (1997): Against Obliteration: Reducing Risk in Business Process Change. In: Sauer, C., Yetton, P. (eds.): Steps to the Future: Fresh Thinking on the Management of IT-Based Organizational Transformation. Jossey-Bass, San Fransisco, 169-186

Gerrits, H. (1994): Business Modeling Based on Logistics to Support Business Process Re-Engineering. In: Glasson, B.C. (ed.): Business Process Re-engineering: Information Systems Opportunities ad Challenges. Elsevier Science, Amsterdam, 279-288

Ghezzi, C., Mandrioli, D., Morasca, S., Pezze, M. (1991): A Unified High-level Petri Net Formalism for Time-critical Systems. IEEE Transactions on Software Engineering 17(2), 160-172

Goldratt, E.M., Cox, J. (1984): The Goal. Gower, Aldershot

Grefen, P., Aberer, K., Hoffner, Y., Ludwig, H. (2001): CrossFlow: Cross-organizational Workflow Management in Dynamic Virtual Enterprises. International Journal of Computer Systems, Science, and Engineering 15(5), 277-290

Grint, K., Wilcocks, L. (1995): Business Process Re-engineering in Theory and Practice: Business Paradise Regained. Blackwell, Oxford

Grinter, R.E. (2000): Workflow Systems: Occasions for Success and Failure. Computer Supported Cooperative Work 9(2), 189-214

Grover, V., Jeong, S.R., Kettinger, W.J., Teng, J.T.C. (1995): The Implementation of Business Process Reengineering. Journal of Management Information Systems 12(1), 109-144

Gruhn, V. (1995): Business Process Modeling and Workflow Management. International Journal of Cooperative Information Systems 4(2-3), 145-164

Gulden, G.K., Reck, R.H. (1991): Combining Quality and Reengineering for Operational Superiority. Perspectives on the Management of Information Technology 8(1), 1-12

Guo, D.L., DiCesare, F., Zhou, M.C. (1992): A Moment Generating Function Based Approach for Evaluating Extended Stochastic Petri Nets. IEEE Transactions on Automatic Control 38(2), 321-327

Hall, G., Rosenthal, J., Wade, J. (1993): How to Make Reengineering Really Work. Harvard Business Review, november-december, 119-131

Hammer, M. (1990): Reengineering Work: Don't Automate, Obliterate. Harvard Business Review, july-august, 70-91

Hammer, M., Champy, J. (1993): Reengineering the Corporation: A Manifesto for Business Revolution. Harper Business, New York

Hansen, G. (1994): Automating Business Process Re-engineering: Using the Power of Visual Simulation Strategies to Improve Performance and Profit. Prentice Hall, New York

Harrington, H.J. (1991): Improving Business Processes. TQM Magazine, 39-44

van Hee, K.M. (1994): Information System Engineering: A Formal Approach. Cambridge University Press

van Hee, K.M., Reijers, H.A. (1999): An Analytical Method for Computing Throughput Times in Stochastic Workflow Nets. In: Horton, G., Möller, D., Rüde, U. (eds.): Proceedings of the 11th European Simulation Symposium. Society for Computer Simulation International, Delft, 635-643

van Hee, K.M., Reijers, H.A. (2000): Using Formal Analysis Techniques in Business Process Redesign. In: van der Aalst, W.M.P., Desel, J., Oberweis, A. (eds.): Business Process Management. Lecture Notes in Computer Science, Vol. 1806. Springer-Verlag, Berlin, 142-160

van Hee, K.M., Reijers, H.A., Verbeek, H.M.W., Zerguini, L. (2001): On the Optimal Allocation of Resources in Stochastic Workflow Nets. In: Djemame, K., Kara, M. (eds.): Proceedings of the Seventeenth UK Performance Engineering Workshop. Print Services University of Leeds, Leeds, 23-34 van Hee, K.M., Somers, L.J., Voorhoeve, M. (1989): Executable Specifications for Distributed Information Systems. In: Falkenberg, L.J., Lindgreen, P. (eds.): Proceedings of the IFIP TC 8 / WG 8.1 Working Conference on Information System Concepts: An In-depth Analysis. Elsevier Science Publishers, Amsterdam, 139-156

Hofacker, I., Vetschera, R. (2001): Algorithmical Approaches to Business Process Design. Computers & Operations Research **28**(13), 1253-1275

Holliday, M.A., Vernon, M.A. (1987): A Generalised Timed Petri Net Model for Performance Analysis. IEEE Transactions on Software Engineering **13**(12), 1279-1310

Hupp, T., Polak, G., Westgaard, O. (1995): Designing Work Groups, Jobs, and Work Flow. Jossey-Bass, San Fransisco

Hutchison, A. (1994): CSCW as Opportunity for Business Process Re-engineering. In: Glasson, B.C., (ed.): Business Process Re-engineering: Information Systems Opportunities ad Challenges. Elsevier Science, Amsterdam, 309-318

Jablonski, S., Bussler, C. (1996): Workflow Management: Modeling Concepts, Architecture, and Implementation. International Thomson Computer Press, London

Jackson, J.R. (1957): Networks of Waiting Lines. Operations Research **5**, 518-521

Jackson, J.R. (1963): Jobshop-like Queuing Systems. Management Science **10**, 131-142

Jackson, S.E., Randall, S. (1985): A Meta-analysis and Conceptual Critique of Research on Role Ambiguity and Role Conflict in Work Settings. Organizational Behavior and Human Decision Processes **36**(2), 17-78

Janssens, G.K., Verelst, J., Weyn, B. (2000): Techniques for Modeling Workflows and Their Support of Reuse. In: van der Aalst, W.M.P., Desel, J., Oberweis, A. (eds.): Business Process Management. Lecture Notes in Computer Science, Vol. 1806. Springer-Verlag, Berlin, 1-15

Jarzabek, S., Ling, T.W. (1996): Model-Based Support for Business Re-engineering. Information and Software Technology **38**(5), 355-374

Jensen, K. (1992): Coloured Petri Nets. Basic Concepts, Analysis Methods and Practical Use 2. EATCS monographs on Theoretical Computer Science. Springer-Verlag, Berlin

Joosten, S. (2000a): Calculus with Language. Informatie **42**(6), 26-31 (In Dutch)

Joosten, S. (2000b): Why Modellers Wreck Workflow Innovations. In: van der Aalst, W.M.P., Desel, J., Oberweis, A. (eds.): Business Process Management. Lecture Notes in Computer Science, Vol. 1806. Springer-Verlag, Berlin, 289-300

Kallio, J., Saarinen, T., Salo, S., Tinnilä, M., Vepsäläinen, A.P.J. (1999): Drivers and Tracers of Business Process Changes. Journal of Strategic Information Systems **8**(2), 125-142

Kaplan, R.S., Atkinson, A.A. (1989): Advanced Management Accounting. Prentice-Hall, Englewood Cliffs

Kaplan, R.S., Murdoch, L. (1991). Core Process Design. The McKinsey Quarterly **2**(1), 27-43

Kettinger, W.J., Teng, J.T.C., Guha, S. (1997): Business Process Change: A Study of Methodologies, Techniques, and Tools. MIS Quarterly **21**(1), 55-80

Kiepuszewski, B., ter Hofstede, A.H.M., van der Aalst, W.M.P. (2001): Fundamentals of Control Flow in Workflows. QUT Technical report, FIT-TR-2001-01. Queensland University of Technology

Klein, M. (1995): 10 Principles of Reengineering. Executive Excellence 12(2): 20

Knolmayer, G., Endl, R., Pfahrer, M. (2000): Guidelines for Business Process Modeling. In: van der Aalst, W.M.P., Desel, J., Oberweis, A. (eds.): Business Process

Management. Lecture Notes in Computer Science, Vol. 1806. Springer-Verlag, Berlin, 16-29

Koulopoulos, T. (1995): The Workflow Imperative: Building Real World Business Solutions. Van Nostrand Reinhold, New York

Kobielus, J.G. (1997): Workflow Strategies. IDG Books, Foster City

Lawrence, P. (ed.) (1997): Workflow Handbook 1997, Workflow Management Coalition. John Wiley and Sons, New York

Lazcano, A., Alonso, G., Schuldt, H., Schuler, C.: The WISE Approach to Electronic Commerce. International Journal of Computer Systems, Science, and Engineering 15(5), 345-357

Lee, R.M. (1992): Dynamic Modeling of Documentary Procedures: A CASE for EDI. In: Proceedings of the Third International Working Conference on Dynamic Modeling of Information Systems

Levin, R., Kirkpatrick, C. (1966). Planning and control with PERT/CPM. McGraw-Hill, New York

Leymann, F., Altenhuber, W. (1994): Managing Business Processes as an Information Resource. IBM systems journal 33(2), 326-348

Lin, C., Marinescu, D.C. (1987): On Stochastic High-Level Petri Nets. In: Proceedings of the International Workshop on Petri Nets and Performance Models. IEEE Computer Society Press, Madison, 34-43

Lowenthal, J.N. (1994): Reengineering the Organization: a Step-by-Step Approach to Corporate Revitalization. ASQC Quality Press, Milwaukee

MacSweeney, G. (2001). Traveling the Long Road to End-to-end Processing. Insurance & Technology 26(10), 30-34

Manganelli, R., Klein, M. (1994a). The Reengineering Handbook: a Step-by-step Guide to Business Transformation. American Management Association, New York

Manganelli, R., Klein, M. (1994a). Should You Start from Scratch? Management Review 83(2), 45-47

Marsan, M.A. (1990): Stochastic Petri Nets: An Elementary Introduction. In: Rozenberg, G. (ed.): Advances in Petri Nets 1989. Lecture Notes in Computer Science, Vol. 424. Springer-Verlag, Berlin, 1-29

Marsan, M.A., Balbo, G., Bobbio, A., Chiola, G., Conte, G., Cumani, A. (1985): On Petri Nets with Stochastic Timing. In: Proceedings of the International Workshop on Timed Petri Nets. IEEE Computer Society Press, Ohio, 80-87

Marsan, M.A., Balbo, G., Conte, G. (1984): A Class of Generalised Stochastic Petri Nets for the Performance Evaluation of Multiprocessor Systems. ACM Transactions on Computer Systems 2(2), 93-122

Marsan, M.A., Balbo, G., Conte, G. (1986): Performance Models of Multiprocessor Systems. MIT Press, Cambridge

Marsan, M.A., Balbo, G., Conte, G. (1995): Modelling with Generalized Stochastic Petri Nets. Wiley series in parallel computing. Wiley, New York

Marsan, M.A., Chiola, G. (1987): On Petri Nets with Deterministic and Exponentially Distributed Firing Times. In: Rozenberg, G. (ed.s): Advances in Petri Nets 1987. Lecture Notes in Computer Science, Vol. 266. Springer-Verlag, Berlin, 132-145

Martin, J. (1991): Rapid Application Development. MacMillan, New York

Merlin, P. (1974). A Study of the Recoverability of Computer Systems. PhD thesis. University of California, Irvine

Merlin, P., Faber, D.J., (1976): Recoverability of Communication Protocols. IEEE Transactions on Communications **24**(9), 1036-1043

Meyer-Wegener, K., Böhm, M. (1999): Conceptual Workflow Schema. In: Proceedings of the Fourth IFCIS International Conference on Cooperative Information Systems. IEEE Computer Society Press, Ohio, 234-242

Merz, M., Moldt, D., Müller, K., Lamersdorf, W. (1995): Workflow Modeling and Execution with Coloured Petri Nets in COSM. In: Billington, J., Diaz, M. (eds.): Proceedings of the Workshop on Applications of Petri Nets to Protocols within the 16th International Conference on Application and Theory of Petri Nets, 1-12

Michelis, G.D., Grasso, M.A. (1994): Situating Conversations within the Language/Action Perspective: The Milan Conversation Model. In: Proceedings of Computer Supported Cooperative Work. ACM Press, Chapel Hill, 89-100

Min, D.M., Kim, J.R., Kim, W.C., Min, D., Ku, S. (1996): IBRC: Intelligent Bank Reengineering System. Decision Support Systems **18**(1), 97-105

MIS (1993): Behind the News: Re-engineered 1 and Re-engineered 2. Managing Information Systems **1**(8), 16-17

Moder, J.J., Philips, C.R. (1964): Project Management with CPM and PERT. Reinhold, New York

Moldt, D., Valk, R. (2000): Object Oriented Petri Nets in Business Process Modeling. In: van der Aalst, W.M.P., Desel, J., Oberweis, A. (eds.): Business Process Management. Lecture Notes in Computer Science, Vol. 1806. Springer-Verlag, Berlin, 254-273

Molenaar, T. (2002). Effectivity Study Workflow Systems. Computable **34**(3):7 (In Dutch)

Molloy, M.K. (1981). On the Integration of Delay and Throughput Measures in Distributed Processing Models. PhD thesis. University of California, Los Angeles

Morasca, S., Pezzè, M., Trubian, M. (1991): Timed High-Level Nets. The Journal of Real-Time Systems **3**(2), 165-189

Morgan, G. (1986): Images of Organization. Sage Publications, Newbury Park

Murata, T. (1989): Petri Nets: Properties, Analysis and Applications. Proceedings of the IEEE **77**(4), 541-580

Neuman, K., Steinhardt, U. (1979): GERT Networks. Lecture Notes in Economic and Mathematical Systems, Vol. 172. Springer-Verlag, Berlin

Neuts, M.F. (1981): Matrix-Geometric Solutions in Stochastic Models: An Algorithmic Approach. John Hopkins University Press, Baltimore

Nissen, M. E. (2000): An Experiment to Assess the Performance of a Redesign Knowledge System. Journal of Management Information Systems **17**(3), 25-43

O'Neill, P., Sohal, A.S. (1999): Business Process Reengineering: A Review of Recent Literature. Technovation **19**(9), 571-581

Oberweis, A, Schätzle, R., Stucky, W., Weitz, W., Zimmerman, G. (1997): INCOME/WF – A Petri net Based Approach to Workflow Management. In: Krallmann, H. (ed.): Wirtschatsinformatik '97. Springer-Verlag, Berlin, 82-101

Orlicky, A. (1972): Structuring the Bill of Materials for MRP. Production and Inventory Management, december, 19-42

Orman, L.V. (1998): A Model Management Approach to Business Process Reengineering. Journal of Management Information Systems **15**(1), 187-212

Ott, M., Nastansky, L. (1998): Groupware Technology for a New Approach to Organization Design Systems. In: Chismar, W. (ed.): Proceedings of the Thirty-First Hawaii International Conference on System Sciences. IEEE, Los Alamitos, 562-571

Pagnoni Holt, A. (2000). Management-Oriented Models of Business Processes. In van der Aalst, W.M.P., Desel, J., Oberweis, A. (eds.): Business Process Management. Lecture Notes in Computer Science, Vol. 1806. Springer-Verlag, Berlin, 99-109

Pallas Athena (1997): PROTOS User Manual. Pallas Athena BV, Plasmolen

Peppard, J., Rowland, P. (1995): The Essence of Business Process Re-engineering. Prentice Hall, New York

C.A. Petri (1962). Kommunikation mit Automaten. PhD thesis. Institut für instrumentelle Mathematik, Bonn

Petrozzo, D.P., Stepper, J.C. (1994): Successful Reengineering. Van Nostrand Reinhold, New York

Platier, E.A.H. (1996): A Logistical View on Business Processes: Concepts for Business Process Redesign and Workflow Management. PhD thesis. Eindhoven University of Technology, Eindhoven

Poyssick, G., Hannaford, S. (1996): Workflow Reengineering. Adobe press, Mountain View

Pritsker, A.A.B., Happ, W.W. (1966): GERT: Graphical Evaluation and Review Technique, Part I: Fundamentals. Journal of Industrial Engineering 17(5), 267-274

Pritsker, A.A.B., Whitehouse, G.E. (1966): GERT: Graphical Evaluation and Review Technique, Part I: Probabilistic and Engineering Applications. Journal of Industrial Engineering 17(6), 293-303

Ramamoorthy, C.V., Ho, G.S. (1980): Performance Evaluation of Asynchronous Concurrent Systems Using Petri Nets. IEEE Transactions on Software Engineering 6(5), 440-449

Ramchandani, C. (1973): Performance Evaluation of Asynchronous Concurrent Systems by Timed Petri Nets. PhD thesis. Massachusetts Institute of Technology, Cambridge

Razouk, R.R., Phelps, C.V. (1984): Performance Analysis Using Timed Petri Nets. In: Yemeni, Y. (ed.): Proceedings of the 1984 International Conference on Parallel Processing. IEEE Computer Society Press, Ohio, 126-128

Reisig, W., Rozenberg, G. (eds.) (1998a). Lectures on Petri Nets I: Basic Models. Lecture Notes in Computer Science, Vol. 1491. Springer-Verlag, Berlin

Reisig, W., Rozenberg, G. (eds.) (1998b). Lectures on Petri Nets II: Applications. Lecture Notes in Computer Science, Vol. 1492. Springer-Verlag, Berlin

Reijers, H.A. (1994): The Design of BASIC: A Descriptive Approach for the Specification and Application of Communication Systems. Master's thesis. Eindhoven University of Technology, Eindhoven (In Dutch)

Reijers, H.A., van der Aalst, W.M.P. (1999): Short-Term Simulation: Bridging the Gap between Operational Control and Strategic Decision Making. In: Hamza, M. (ed.): Proceedings of the IASTED International Conference on Modelling and Simulation. ACTA Press, Pittsburgh, 417-421

Reijers, H.A., Goverde, R.H.J.J.M (1998): Resource Management: A Clear-Headed Approach to Ensure Efficiency. Workflow Magazine 4(6), 26-28 (In Dutch)

Reijers, H.A., Goverde, R.H.J.J.M (1999a): Smooth Cases: An Application of Product-Based Design. Deloitte & Touche Bakkenist report. Deloitte & Touche Bakkenist, Diemen

Reijers, H.A., Goverde, R.H.J.J.M (1999b): Functional Limitations on Workflow Management Systems. Workflow Magazine, 5(4):11-13, 1999b. (In Dutch)

Reijers, H.A., Goverde, R.H.J.J.M, Remmerts de Vries, R.N. (1999): Functional Limitations on Workflow Management Systems. Workflow Magazine **5**(3), 24-27 (In Dutch)

Reijers, H.A., Voorhoeve, K. (2000): Optimal Design of Process and Information Systems: A Manifesto for a Product Focus. Informatie **42**(12), 50-57 (In Dutch)

Reijers, H.A., van der Toorn, R.A. (2002): Application Development under Architecture within the Context of BPR. In: Terano, T., Myers, M.D. (eds.): Proceedings of the Sixth Pacific Asia Conference on Information Systems 2002. JASMIN, Tokyo, , 659-673

van Reijswoud, V.E., Mulder, H.B.F., Dietz, J.L.G (1999): Communicative Action-based Business Process and Information Systems Modelling with DEMO. Information Systems Journal **9**(2), 117-138

Rolfe, A. (1971): A Note on Marginal Allocation in Multiple-Server Service Systems. Management Science **17**, 656-659

Ross, S.M. (1996): Stochastic Processes. John Wiley and Sons, New York

Rupp, R.O., Russell, J.R. (1994): The Golden Rules of Process Redesign. Quality Progress **27**(12), 85-92

Sackett, G.P. (1978): Observing Behaviour; Vol II: Data Collection and Analysing Methods. University Park Press, Baltimore

Sarker, S., Lee, A.S. (1999): IT-enabled Organizational Transformation: A Case Study of BPR failure at TELECO. Journal of Strategic Information Systems **8**(1), 83-103

Schäll, T. (1996): Workflow Management Systems for Process Organisations. Lecture Notes in Computer Science, Vol. 1096. Springer-Verlag, Berlin

Scheer, A.W. (1994): Business Process Reengineering: Reference Models for Industrial Enterprises. Springer-Verlag, Berlin

Seidmann, A., Sundararajan, A. (1997): The Effects of Task and Information Asymmetry on Business Process Redesign. International Journal of Production Economics **50**(2-3), 117-128

Sharp, A., McDermott, P. (2001): Workflow Modeling: Tools for Process Improvement and Application Development. Artech House Publishers, Boston

Sierhuis, M. (2001): BRAHMS: a Multiagent Modeling and Simulation Language for Work System Analysis and Design. PhD thesis. University of Amsterdam, Amsterdam

Sifakis, J. (1977): Use of Petri Nets for Performance Evaluation. In: Beilner, H., Gelenbe, E. (eds.): Proceedings of the Third International Symposium IFIP W.G. 7.3., Measuring, modelling and evaluating computer systems. Elsevier Science Publishers, Amsterdam, 75-93

Sifakis, J. (1980): Performance Evaluation of Systems using Nets. In: Brauer, W. (ed.): Net Theory and Applications: Proceedings of the Advanced Course on General Net Theory, Processes and Systems. Lecture Notes in Computer Science, Vol. 84. Springer-Verlag, Berlin, 307-319

Simison, G.C. (1994): A Methodology for Business Process Re-engineering? In Glasson, B.C. (eds.): Business Process Re-engineering: Information Systems Opportunities ad Challenges. Elsevier Science, Amsterdam, 61-69

Sommerville, I., Sawyer, P. (1997): Requirements Engineering: A Good Practice Guide. Wiley, London

Stoddard, D.B., Jarvenpaa, S.L. (1995): Business Process Redesign: Tactics for Managing Radical Change. Journal of Management Information Systems **12**(1), 81-107

Szyperski, C. (1998): Component Software - Beyond Object-Oriented Programming. Addison-Wesley, Boston

Talwar, R (1993): Business Re-engineering – a Strategy-driven Approach. Long Range Planning **26**(6), 22-40

Taylor, F.W. (1947): Scientific Management. Harper Collins, London

Thomasian, A.J. (1969): The Structure of Probability Theory with Applications. McGraw-Hill Book Company, New York

Trajcevski, V. Baral, C., Lobo, J. (2000): Formalizing and Reasoning About the Specifications of Workflows. In: Proceedings of the 7th International Conference on Cooperative Information Systems, 1-17

Valette, R. (1979): Analysis of Petri Nets by Stepwise Refinements. Journal of Computer and System Sciences **18**(1), 35-46

Verbeek, H.M.W., Basten, T., van der Aalst, W.M.P. (2001): Diagnosing Workflow Processes using Woflan. The Computer Journal **44**(4), 246-279

Verbeek, H.M.W., van der Aalst, W.M.P. (2000): Woflan 2.0: A Petri net-based Workflow Diagnosis Tool. In: Nielsen, M., Simpson, D. (eds.): Application and Theory of Petri Nets 2000. Lecture Notes in Computer Science, Vol. 1825. Springer-Verlag, Berlin, 475-484

Verster, K. (1998): Appendix: Administrative Logistics Methods and Techniques. In: Rodenburg, K.J., van den Berg, M.J.F. (eds.): Administrative Logistics. Brinkman Uitgeverij, Amsterdam (In Dutch)

Voorhoeve, M. (2000): Compositional Modeling and Verification of Workflow Processes. In: van der Aalst, W.M.P., Desel, J., Oberweis, A. (eds.): Business Process Management. Lecture Notes in Computer Science, Vol. 1806. Springer-Verlag, Berlin, 184-200

van der Wal, J. (1997): Flexibility. Notes to the Applied Probability Course. Eindhoven University of Technology, Eindhoven (In Dutch)

Wang, S. (1997): A Synthesis of Natural Language, Semantic Networks, and Objects for Business Process Modeling. Canadian Journal of Administrative Sciences **14**(1), 79-92

Weber, R.R. (1980): On the Marginal Benefit of Adding Servers to G/GI/m Queues. Management Science **26**: 946-951

Winograd, T. (1987): A Language/Action Perspective on the Design of Cooperative Work. Human-Computer Interaction **3**(1), 3-30

Wirtz, G., Weske, M., Greise, H. (2000). Extending UML with Workflow Modeling Capabilities. In: Etzion, O, Scheuermann, P. (eds.): Proceedings of the 7th International Conference on Cooperative Information Systems. Lecture Notes in Computer Science, Vol. 1901. Springer-Verlag, Berlin, 30-41

Wong, C.Y., Dillon, T.S., Forward, K.E. (1985): Timed Places Petri Nets with Stochastic Representation of Place Time. In: Proceedings of the International Workshop on Timed Petri Nets. IEEE Computer Society Press, Ohio, 96-103

Zampetakis, H. (1994): Survey Re-engineering and Rightsizing – Magic Bullet Often Misses the Target. Financial Review, february, 38

Zapf, M., Heinzl, A. (2000): Evaluation of Generic Process Design Patterns: An Experimental Study. In: van der Aalst, W.M.P., Desel, J., Oberweis, A. (eds.): Business Process Management. Lecture Notes in Computer Science, Vol. 1806. Springer-Verlag, Berlin, 83-98

Zenie, A. (1985): Coloured Stochastic Petri Nets. In: Proceedings of the International Workshop on Timed Petri Nets. IEEE Computer Society Press, Madison, 262-271

Zisman, M.D. (1977): Representation, Specification and Automation of Office Procedures. PhD thesis. University of Pennsylvania Wharton School of Business, Philadelphia

Zuberek, W.M. (1980): Timed Petri Nets and Preliminary Performance Evaluation. In: Proceedings of the 7th annual Symposium on Computer Architecture. Quarterly Publication of ACM Special Interest Group on Computer Architecture **8**(3), 62-82

1 Introduction

In the late eighties, the idea of process thinking emerged in industry. This was the time that major American companies such as IBM, Ford, and Bell Atlantic saw the benefit of focusing on cross-functional business processes. This contrasted with the traditional focus on typical functional business areas such as procurement, manufacturing, and sales. Process thinking should enhance the service to clients by extending beyond ad hoc, local decision making that pays little attention to the effectiveness across the process.

The focus on business processes in organizing and managing work may seem quite straightforward today, but this was not always the case. In Figure 1.1, this historical development is given.

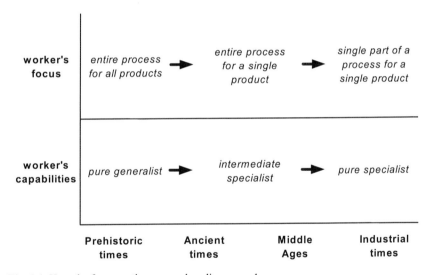

Fig. 1.1. How the focus on the process has disappeared

In prehistoric times, people supported themselves by producing their own food, tools, and other items. In other words, people executed their own production processes, which they knew thoroughly. In ancient times this generalist work form evolved into an intermediate level of specialism. People started to specialize themselves into the art of delivering one specific type of goods or services, culminating in the guilds of craftsmen of the Middle Ages. Not only did a craftsman barter or

H.A. Reijers: Design and Control of Workflow Processes, LNCS 2617, pp. 1-29, 2003.
© Springer-Verlag Berlin Heidelberg 2003

sell his own goods, he also mastered the skills to perform all the necessary operations to produce them. In other words, the process of delivering one type of good was totally executed by the craftsman himself.

This higher degree of specialism started to shift into a form of pure specialism during the Industrial Revolution. In the mid-eighteenth century, the operations to produce a specific product were meticulously studied and unraveled. In factories, pure specialists were trained to carry out a single operation, which they worked on during their entire work period. The execution of their work was only one of the many steps in producing the entire product. This industrial way of organizing work resulted in a large boost in productivity. Not only in industry, but also in administrative settings it became the dominant organization form. It required the rise of a professional bureaucracy to manage the various specialists. The simplest way of differentiating responsibilities among the managers was to create within the company functional departments in which people with a similar focus on part of the production process were grouped. This type of organization dominated the work place for the greatest part of the nineteenth and twentieth century. The process, by now, was scattered over the functions within a company. It was also out of view for organizers and decision makers.

Today, the focus on the process is back. Everywhere around the world, in almost every industry, business processes are being fine-tuned, downsized, reengineered, value-added and re-aligned. On a more operational level, even more frequent process-centered decisions are made. These may concern specific orders, clients, people and machines. However, regardless of the decision-making level, many decisions are put in motion without an accurate picture of the expected earnings beforehand, but rather on a "gut feeling". There may be a well-understood positive effect of a decision on, for example, the production cost, but a reliable quantitative estimate or qualitative rationalization of the intended effect is often lacking. Taking the cost and time that is involved with these decisions, there is a need for more answers in this field.

Arguably, there is a practical interest in business processes. The scientific interest is raised because managing business processes is notoriously difficult. There are, for example, no general and clear-cut answers about the best way to organize the work in a bank, insurance company, or hospital. However, some ways are better than others, which raises the question why. On closer inspection, managing business processes can be much like solving a mathematical optimization problem. There often is – but not always – a clear target function, the essential aspects of a business process may also be suitable for representation in the form of a formal model, and the answer is not straightforward as there are many degrees of design freedom with their own consequences. There is an intellectual challenge in thinking of methods to optimize the way in which business processes are managed.

Although knowledge from different disciplines is available on the subject of managing business processes, there are large gaps in this body of knowledge. Knowledge about organizing work has been documented for centuries, especially in a military context. The Romans mastered the organization of human resources for one of their major activities – conquest – by distinguishing decuriae, centuriae, cohortis and legionis. During Napoleon's time the triage concept was invented, which can be found back as a business process construct within many contemporary organizations (see also Section 6.1). Organizing work as a research topic really took off during the Industrial Age. At the end of the 19th century, Frederick Winslow Taylor started to use stopwatch timing as the basis of his observations of the cutting of metal and the shoveling of coal. These timings were further broken down into smaller elements to reorganize the work. Taylor referred to his time studies and resulting standards as scientific management (Taylor, 1947).

Nowadays, Management Science, with supporting fields of study such as (Production) Logistics and Operations Research, is an established scientific discipline focusing on the subject of organizing work, usually within an organizational context. Especially in manufacturing – the production of physical goods – there is a strong exchange between practice and research. With the rise of popularity of the computer in the twentieth century and the increasing role information processing plays as a supporting or even primary part of business processes, the importance of Computing Science as a research field for organizing work has grown. The crossover field of study between Management and Computing Science involving business processes is nowadays commonly referred to as Business Process Management.

The purpose of this monograph is to present the results of the author's research, which has taken place within the field of Business Process Management over the last five years. More specifically, the central issues in this monograph are the modeling, design, and analysis of workflow processes. Workflow processes are typically found within large administrative organizations, such as banks, insurance companies, and government. Examples of workflow processes are the handling of loan applications, the registration of new clients, or the issuing of building permits. The main questions that are addressed in this monograph are as follows:

- How to make a model of a workflow process.
- How to design or redesign an effective and efficient workflow process in practice.
- How to determine the performance of a workflow process.
- How to allocate resources in an operational workflow process.

Much of the inspiration for this monograph was derived from practice. The author has been involved in several information technology projects as a management consultant. Projects in which he participated involved the implementation of workflow management systems, the analysis and redesign of business processes, and the building of information and decision support systems. Parts of this monograph will be illustrated with this practical experience.

In this introductory chapter, we will examine the concept of a business process. As may have become clear by now, this is a vital concept within this monograph. We will introduce the terminology to be used throughout the chapters in describing characteristics of business processes. We will subsequently identify the field of business processes management and present an overview of its most popular contemporary branch, the redesign of business processes. Next, we will focus our discussion of business processes on workflow processes. We will discuss the characteristics of this type of process in comparison to other business processes. Also, workflow management technology will be discussed, which is commonly associated with supporting workflow processes. Based on the characteristics of workflow processes, we will discuss the applicability of existing knowledge – particularly from the field of production logistics – to the field of managing workflows. Finally, we will specify the purpose of this monograph and give an overview of its structure, building upon the terminology and concepts introduced.

1.1 The Business Process

The concept of a business process has been defined by Davenport and Short (1990) as "a set of logically related tasks performed to achieve a defined business outcome". This general outline has become widely adopted in the literature on the design and management of business processes. Hammer and Champy (1993) essentially say the same thing, but they also stress the client-centered aspect of a business process: "a collection of activities that takes one or more kinds of input and creates an output that is of value to the customer". We will not try to extend or refine this definition as many others have proposed, but informally explore the commonly distinguished ingredients of a business process.

1.1.1 Products and Business Processes

The "business outcome" or "output" of a business process can often be described more explicitly as the product, which is created by the process. A common distinction is the one between goods – which have a physical manifestation – and services – which do not. Examples of goods are buildings, wafer-stepping machines, and clothing. A strategic piece of advice, an insurance, or criminal jurisdiction are examples of services. Business processes producing goods are known as manufacturing processes. A business process that delivers services is often referred to as a workflow, service or administrative process. We will come back to a more specific interpretation of the term "workflow" in Section 1.4.

For many business process concepts, there is a subtle but important distinction between their conceptual and actual manifestation. To start with, the sort of product produced by a business process should be differentiated from actual instances of the product. We can say, for example, that a business process is intended to produce the DVC – 235 video camcorder, which has a 400 times zoom and a 3,5" liquid crystal display. In this sense, we refer to an abstract product concept, also known as a product type, class, or family. Only with an instance or specimen of this type of video camcorder, it is possible to shoot a movie. In this monograph, from the context of the term "product" it should be clear which interpretation is meant.

A similar distinction exists for the concept of a business process itself. We use the term "business process" to refer to a conceptual way of organizing work and resources. In this sense, a business process is not tangible. However, product instances are produced by executing or instantiating the business process. A business process execution involves real people, materials, clients, machines, computers, and delivers one or more actual products. In this sense, the execution is the actual manifestation of a business process.

The relations between the concepts we discussed are depicted in the UML entity-relationship model in Figure 1.2.

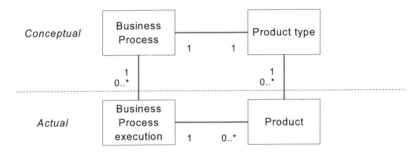

Fig. 1.2. Relations between business process and product

In such a model relevant entities are depicted as named boxes. Relations may hold between entities. It is common to give the cardinalities of these relations using the symbols '0', '1' and '*'. For example, between the business process and a business process execution a 1 on 0..* relation is in effect. The first direction of the relation expresses that there can be zero or more executions for one business process (0..*). In the other direction of the relation, for each business process execution there is exactly one business process it belongs to (1). Another example is the 1-on-1 relation between the business process and the product type: for each business process there is exactly one product type, and vice versa.

Note that an execution of a business process may deliver one or more instances of a certain product. More than one delivery of a product at a time by a single process execution is known as batch production. A process execution may also fail for some reason, so that no product instance is delivered at all.

Not graphically depicted in Figure 1.2 is the integrity constraint that the product that results from executing a specific business process is an instance of the product type that the business process is intended to produce.

The execution of a business process passes through several stages in producing products. It often is convenient to distinguish the state of a business process execution. For example, to inspect whether a deadline will be met in producing a certain item, its current state of completion is relevant. Distinguishing an execution state is often done by referring to the operations that are already executed, the parts that still need to be constructed, or other milestones that are reached during the execution. As there may be many concurrent executions of a business process, we can refer to the state of a complete business process as the collection of states of its individual executions.

Finally note that the business process as a way of organizing work is a static concept; the state of a business process as a collection of business process execution states is dynamic. These distinctions will prove to be of the utmost use in considering the different problems in managing business processes.

1.1.2 Performance Targets

With the introduced terminology, we can describe the main purpose of a business process as a way to organize how specimens of one type of product are produced. On top of this, companies will try to accomplish additional performance targets in executing and managing the business process (see e.g., Hammer and Champy, 1993; Sharp and McDermott, 2001). These targets may take on various forms. For example, a company may attempt to manufacture a product at the lowest possible cost with a marginally acceptable product quality. Another company may produce a similar product, but with as its most important characteristic that it is specifically tailored to the wishes of the client – regardless of cost. One might say that both companies produce the same product but with totally different performance targets. Commonly, performance targets combine specific interpretations of the four main dimensions of cost, time, quality and flexibility (Brand and Van der Kolk, 1995). A very important performance target in many industries involves the throughput time (see Schäll, 1996; Van Hee and Reijers, 2000), also known as flow, response, cycle or sojourn time. One of our interests in this monograph involves algorithms to determine this quantity (see Chapter 4).

1.1.3 Clients

Another key ingredient of business process definitions is the client. As we already stated in our introduction, a better service to the client was the driver behind focusing on business processes in the first place. Products are produced to satisfy an existing or future demand of a client, being either a person or an organization. A client can be external to the system that hosts the business process, but the client can also be part of it. An example that illustrates the latter form is a manufacturing department that requests an overhaul from the maintenance department of the same company. The client may also be rather abstract, like in many governmental business processes. For example, some business processes of the Department of Justice or Defense are not performed for one specific client, but rather aimed at servicing the community.

1.1.4 Orders and Triggers

Clients may explicitly place an order for a product or service. For some business processes, the receipt of an order is the start event of each of its executions. For other processes, the start event may be different. For example, the production of a book may start before there any orders. Events that start a process are commonly referred to as triggers (e.g., Moldt and Valk, 2000). However, the term "trigger" is not exclusively used for events starting entire processes. A trigger may also be required to start a smaller part of the process. For example, the processing of financial transactions may incorporate an automatic check, which is scheduled to be performed during a batch operation at midnight. Even if all other processing has taken place, handling of the transaction is postponed until this time event takes place.

1.1.5 Organization

A concept that we have already mentioned is the organization that hosts the business process. Commercial organizations are referred to as enterprises or companies. Non-commercial organizations may be known as agencies or institutes. An organization is commonly divided into departments on a functional, geographic, or product-oriented basis, for example: "Procurement", "Europe, Middle East, and Africa (EMEA)", "Fiscality". Combinations of these criteria are often seen as well. Each department or function of an organization may be divided into even smaller units. The exact web of divisions, departments, units and sub-units within an organization is often expressed in the form of an organigram.

The basis for considering the boundaries of an organization usually is juridical. An organization comprises all the activities, assets, and means that fall within the responsibility of a legal body. Historically, processes were mostly found within the confinement of a single organization as such. Nowadays, business processes easily span these boundaries. Different parts of a business process may be executed by different parts of different organizations. If the client is kept unaware of the (legal) boundaries between the partners of the business process, this is called a virtual organization.

1.1.6 Resources

The product of a business process is delivered by the commitment of resources, also known as "means of production". A resource is a generic term for all means that are required to produce a product within the settings of a business process. The effort to distinguish resources is made, because most of them are scarce. Their distinction makes it possible to handle them sensibly. Characteristically, consumable resources are mostly consumed when they are applied. Raw materials and semi-manufactures are the prime examples of consumable resources. For example, in producing a gardening tool, the wooden grip is a consumable resource. Reusable resources can be committed for a long period of time and wear out only gradually. Within the context of a medical operation process, a surgeon and an anesthetist may be distinguished as reusable resources. The operation room and the medical information system can also be seen as reusable resources, as their existence is essential for an operation to be performed and they may be used time and again. Human resources, as a specific type of reusable resources, are also known as agents, participants or users. Reusable resources that are non-human are also referred to as the infrastructure, for example in the sense of a "technical infrastructure". Note that resources in combination with the earlier mentioned triggers form the "inputs" that Davenport and Short mention in their business process definition.

It often is convenient to classify resources with similar characteristics into resource classes or resource types. This facilitates a more efficient and robust way of organizing the responsibilities and authorizations in a business processes. For example, instead of assigning certain individuals to a specific task, it is specified that any resource from a certain class may perform it. In general, two main dimensions are used to define resource classes: a functional and organizational one. A resource class based on functional characteristics is known as a role, function or qualification; for example, the resource class "mechanic" or "senior acceptor". An organizationally oriented resource class is often based on criteria already in use to distinguish different parts of an organization, such as departmental, geographic, or product divisions. Resource classifications are mostly used to classify human resources.

1.1.7 Tasks and Subprocesses

By now we have repeatedly mentioned "parts of the process" as a frame of reference. In many approaches and definitions of business processes it is indeed very common to decompose a business process into smaller parts (e.g., the definition of Hammer and Champy (1993)). One way of decomposition is to distinguish subprocesses, also known as subflows. Any part of a business process can be seen as a subprocess. Subprocesses are distinguished to divide the complexity of business processes into a hierarchic or network relation.

The smallest distinguishable part of a process is often referred to as a task, but also as a step, activity or action. Within a business process that delivers bicycles, two separate tasks may be: (1) the painting of the frame and (2) the assembly of the wheels onto the frame. A task is a complete specification of a part of work to be accomplished. The "term" task resembles the term "business process" in the sense that it is abstract and not tangible: it is a way of organizing a small piece of work and its required resources. The boundaries of a task are often chosen such that each task is a logical unit of work. Typically, a potential transfer of work from one type of resource to another indicates a boundary of a task. Other aspects that determine the proper unit size are, for example, the involved location of the work, the expected time span to execute the task, all kinds of regulations, and the number of involved parties in executing the work. The so-called ACID properties (atomicity, consistency, isolation, and durability), derived from transaction processing, can also be used to define a logical unit of work.

Dependencies may exist among the tasks within a business process. A common use of imposing a dependency between tasks is to express an execution order that is to be respected. For example, a dependency may be used to express the fact that the assembly of the wheels on a bicycle frame must be executed only after the frame has been painted. Dependencies may have various other semantics, expressing for instance an information exchange or control dependency.

In the same spirit as in our discussion of the business process, it is possible to distinguish structural and dynamic manifestations of tasks. A task that has to be executed in the production of a specific product can be referred to as a work item. If a task has been executed for this product, the work item is completed. If a resource is actually executing a work item in the context of a business process execution we speak of an activity. Note that in contrast to some other authors we reserve this latter term exclusively for this specific, dynamic manifestation of a task.

The different manifestations of tasks within a business process are summarized in Figure 1.3.

Structural	Dynamic
task a specification of a part of work within a business process	***work item*** a task to be executed for a specific product ***activity*** a task being executed for a specific product by a specific resource

Fig. 1.3. Structural and dynamic manifestations of work

1.1.8 Categorizations

Aside from the aspects of a business process discussed above, it is possible to categorize business processes in different ways. We already distinguished manufacturing from administrative processes. Another common classification is based on the execution frequency of the business process and its level of standardization as follows (see Van der Aalst and Van Hee, 2002):

1. *Customized process, ad hoc process or project*: the business process is intended to be executed only once and it is tailored specifically to the demands of the

client. Examples: building of a communication satellite, defense of a client in court, writing a paper for a scientific journal.

2. *Mass-customization or production process*: the business process is commonly executed with a high frequency (dozens to thousands of times a year); the process incorporates a limited bandwidth of variation to satisfy the client's specific preferences. Examples: building houses within the same plan, handling requests for loans, issuing insurance policies.

3. *Mass-production or transaction processing*: the business process is executed at an extremely high frequency (thousands to millions of times a year) and the process is fully standardized; there is no room for specific client demands. Examples: handling of financial transfers, making telephone connections, issuing driver's licenses.

This classification will prove to be of use when we discuss the technology supporting the execution and management of business processes in Section 1.4.

Another common classification of business process takes as distinctive criterion the place of the business process within the hosting organization(s). The different classes of business processes are as follows:

1. *Primary or production processes*: the business processes of a company that realize the goods or services targeted at external parties. These processes usually generate the revenues for profit companies. For not-for-profit companies, these processes generate the products that implement their reason of existence. Examples: approving loans within a bank, electricity generation within an energy production company, building a block of apartments within a construction company.

2. *Secondary or support processes*: the business processes that are there to support or maintain the primary business processes. A large part of the secondary processes is aimed at maintaining the means of production. Human resource and financial management processes are also secondary processes. Examples: purchasing of raw materials within a manufacturing company, house cleaning within an insurance company, expertise center within a government agency.

3. *Tertiary or managerial processes*: the business processes that direct and coordinate the primary and secondary business processes. The former processes impose business targets on the latter. The management of tertiary processes is accountable to the owners of the organization or to higher authorities on their performance. Examples: plan and control cycle, project management, and board meetings.

The primary reason to consider a business process, its products, performance targets, clients, triggers, organization, resources, tasks and relations between them, is to support a decision of some kind. Three criteria can be used to distinguish between decision-making levels within an organization (Van der Aalst and Van Hee, 2002). The first is the frequency of decision making. The second factor is the range of the decisions taken, which we make operational as the time period in which the effect of the decision can be experienced. The third and last factor concerns the question whether the dynamic state of the process or the static structure of the process is more relevant. We distinguish a hierarchy of four different levels of decision making as follows:

1. *The real-time level*
   Decisions are taken with a high frequency (intervals ranging from microseconds to hours), but the impact of the decision is felt for only a very short period. The dynamics of the process are extremely relevant to take the decision, where the static process is only relevant on a task level. A real-time decision may involve the operation of a single task by handling a computer or machine.

2. *The operational level*
   Decisions are taken with a considerable frequency (from hours to days) and their impact is limited. The dynamics of the process are very relevant to take the decision. The structure of the process is relevant in so far as it concerns one or several related tasks. An operational decision may involve how the manufacturing of a specific product must be continued.

3. *The tactical level*
   Decisions are made periodically (from days to months) and their impact ranges from limited to considerable. The structure of the complete process tends to be as important as condensed or aggregated views on the dynamic state of the business process. A tactical decision may involve the allocation of resources to tasks within a business process.

4. *The strategic level*
   Decisions are made only once or no more than every couple of years, and the effects are felt for a long period of time, possibly years. The dynamic state of the process is typically of no importance. A strategic decision may involve the restructuring of the complete process.

Note that with respect to the previous classifications, the above levels of decision making can be distinguished within primary, secondary, and tertiary processes, as well as within mass-customization and mass-production processes. However, with respect to a customized process, strategic decision making may be limited.

1.2 Business Process Management

The focus of this monograph is the field of Business Process Management (BPM). Before we can formulate the purpose of this monograph in Section 1.6, we will explore the BPM subject in some more detail. Although it is a popular term in both business practice as in the sciences, there is no agreement on its meaning. Rather, there are topics with respect to business processes that are commonly gathered under this term, notably the design, analysis, modeling, implementation and control of business processes (Schäll, 1996; Van der Aalst et al., 2000b; Dellarocas and Klein, 2000; Sharp and McDermott, 2001; Van der Aalst and Van Hee, 2002).

We adopt a view on Business Process Management as put forth by Leymann and Altenhuber (1994). They distinguish two fundamental aspects, namely the build time aspect and the run time aspect of managing business processes. The build time aspect focuses on the creation of the business process; the run time aspect focuses on its execution. Using this distinction we regard BPM as the field of designing and controlling business processes. We will briefly discuss the two dimensions – design and control – in this section. The distinction of the two has also become very common in the field of the so-called Workflow Management Systems for discussing their main functionality, see e.g., Jablonski and Bussler (1996); we will discuss this technology in Section 1.4.

Within the spectrum of different decision-making levels (see Section 1.1), the design of business processes – the first dimension of our BPM definition – is traditionally seen as a strategic issue. Typical examples of strategic decisions that are relevant from a BPM view are decisions on the restructuring of a business process, decisions on the organization that will be involved in executing the business processes (with as a strategic alternative outsourcing), and decisions on financial, logistic, quality, and other objectives for business processes. However, there are many strategic decisions that do not fall within the scope of BPM. The question which products should be continued and which products should be abolished (product life cycle), the markets that should be conquered or abandoned, the preferred corporate and brand image, and the financial funding of the organization are not typically BPM issues. The examples indicate a part of strategic decision making that focuses on the products and the existence of the organization as a whole, rather than on the business processes that are hosted by this organization.

The other dimension of our BPM definition, the control of business processes, focuses more on decisions that are taken on the real-time, operational, and tactical levels of decision making (see Section 1.1). Activities that typically take place on these levels are, for example, production planning, resource assignment, budgeting, and exception handling. To take resource assignment as an example, it is clear that to decide on the best way of assigning scarce resources to the business process, relevant variables include the following:

- The number of already committed resources.
- The expected size of the work.
- The number of orders within the process.
- The required skills for doing the work.

There is an essential similarity and an essential difference between the design of a business process on the one hand and its control on the other. For decision making in both domains, a clear understanding of the static view of a business process is highly relevant. After all, if the process structure for a decision is not relevant it falls outside the scope of BPM by definition. However, for the design of a business process the dynamic view on the process in question is not relevant, while it is highly relevant for its control. (As stated before in Section 1.1, the static view involves the structure of the process and the dynamic view the state during execution.) Consider, for example, the relevant variables we listed for deciding on the best way to assign scarce resources that involve static elements (the expected size of the work and the required skills) and dynamic elements (the number of committed resources and the number of orders).

We would like to make two comments with respect to the above observation. The first is that the scope of decision making on a run-time level within a business process typically is constrained by a single task (see the distinction of different decision making levels in Section 1.1). Issues that involve the execution of a single task hardly require a view on larger parts of the business process most of the time, let alone the total process. Therefore, run-time decision making, i.e., the proper execution of a single task, is not commonly treated as a BPM issue. In this monograph we will totally abstract from decision making on this level.

The second and more important remark is that by the rapid technological developments the supposedly sharp distinction between design and control issues is fading. Good examples on this note are the so-called ad hoc workflow management systems that provide capabilities to the end-user to change the structure of the business process during its run-time execution. Section 7.1 includes a case description that also supports the narrowing of the gap between strategic decision making and operational control. This case has been described earlier by Reijers and Van der Aalst (1999).

In summary, the design and control of business processes are defined as the elementary parts of BPM. Accordingly, they will be the driving subjects of the chapters in this monograph. Although there is a strong conceptual difference between the two BPM dimensions, one should be cautious in using this distinction too rigorously. Because the design dimension of BPM has received the widest attention of the business and science community alike in the past twenty years, we will elaborate on the developments in this field in the following section. It will clarify the maturity state of research in the BPM field, which in its turn is relevant to understand the purpose of this monograph.

1.3 Business Process Redesign

Historically, the focus of BPM has been on the strategic level of decision making; in particular, on the design and redesign of business processes. The driver behind this phenomenon is the extreme importance of the way that corporate work is organized as overall business processes for the profitability, effectiveness, and efficiency of organizations. Hammer (1990) and Davenport and Short (1990) were the first to report on more or less systematic approaches to produce radical performance improvement of entire business processes. Their major vehicles were the application of information technology and the promotion of changing the structure of the process. This approach was coined with the terms "Business Process Reengineering" by Hammer (1990) and "Business Process Redesign" by Davenport and

Short (1990). Their ideas were embraced by industry. It was also a first, gentle wave in the later flood of literature that arose on this subject.

Hammer and Champy (1993) subsequently stressed the extreme nature of re-design and additionally identified the intended outcome. They promoted it as the "fundamental rethinking and radical redesign of business processes to achieve dramatic improvements in critical measures of performance, such as cost, quality, service, and speed". Over the years, different authors have made variations on the original terms, e.g., Business process improvement (Harrington, 1991), Core proc-ess redesign (Kaplan and Murdoch, 1991), Business process transformation (Burke and Peppard, 1993), and Business process management (Duffy, 1994). De-spite the variations, the concepts behind these approaches are essentially so similar that it has led practitioners to effortlessly substitute one term for the other. We will refer to the general concept with "BPR".

1.3.1 Popularity

The popularity of BPR in industry has grown to a considerable level since its in-troduction, although the penetration of BPR differs. An Australian software ser-vice company conducted a client poll of 107 Australian and Asian companies and reported that 50 % of them were already undertaking or planning to undertake BPR initiatives (MIS, 1993). In 1994 the CSC Index Survey of US and European Companies was conducted by Champy (1995). In this study, 621 American and European companies with revenues of at least US$ 500 million per year were sur-veyed. More than 69 % of these companies had already adopted BPR as a means to improve their business operations. As many as 88 % of the American compa-nies were using BPR or were about to start BPR projects. In a similar study in the UK Grint and Wilcocks (1995) reported a percentage of 59 %. A recent study of Kallio et al. (1999), which included 93 large and medium-sized Finnish compa-nies, showed that 41 % of these companies conducted one or more BPR projects. These and many other studies seem to suggest that BPR is more popular among larger companies. Zampetakis (1994) suspects that unlike North American com-panies – which take on BPR as a way to demonstrate they are taking action in their quarterly reports – companies in other parts of the world (e.g., Australia) are slower to reengineer and, as such, also have a lower rate of failure. In practice, BPR is usually applied to competitive, client-facing business processes with as most common examples order delivery, marketing and sales processes (Kallio et al., 1999).

The drivers behind the popularity of BPR are manifold. In the first place, com-panies feel the increasing pressure of a globalizing market (Hammer, 1990; Van Hee and Reijers, 2000). Cost reduction has become prevalent to survive. High po-tential benefits have tempted companies to adopt BPR, as several success stories on BPR have shown 70 % savings in time and cost (e.g., Belmonte and Murray, 1993).

A second driver is that the historically strong position of suppliers in many mar-kets is becoming less dominant compared to that of the client (Hammer and

Champy, 1993; Van Hee and Reijers, 2000). Clients today are characterized by their relentless demands in quality, service and price; take for example their willingness to act on default of contract and by their disloyalty (O'Neill and Sohal, 1999). To win clients' repeated business, companies have to please them by shortening their production time, increasing their product quality and showing flexibility in handling the changes in the client's preferences. BPR is generally seen as a means to improve on all of these factors.

The third and last major change driver is technology. Information technology is considered to be the most important enabler for BPR (Kallio et al., 1999). Information technology offers a wide variety of new possibilities to manage the business process better, while increasing their flexibility (Van Hee and Reijers, 2000). The widespread application of Enterprise Resource Planning Systems (Scheer, 1994) and Workflow Management Systems (Van der Aalst and Van Hee, 2002) in industry is a strong example on this note. Also, computer-aided software engineering (CASE) and object-oriented programming has helped simplify systems' design around business processes (Baets, 1993; Petrozzo and Stepper, 1994). Hutchison (1994) recognizes groupware applications as stimulating and supporting the re-engineering of business processes. In summary, the availability of new information technology makes companies perceive the expected gain of a BPR project as attractive and its associated risk as more acceptable.

Sharp and McDermott (2001) conjecture that "process thinking" and BPR by now have become main-stream thinking in industry. They suppose that this explains why the focus of research and management literature has shifted away from BPR in recent years.

1.3.2 Risks and Challenges

Notwithstanding the popularity of BPR, different studies have indicated that a large number of BPR programs fail. Some failure estimates are up to 70 % (e.g., Bradley, 1994; Champy, 1995). The interpretation of such a figure, however, is troublesome. Falling short of the intended objectives is an obvious mark of failure, but it is conceivable that in many cases no clear objectives have been formulated at all. This is a reason for Van der Aalst and Van Hee (2002) to insist on formulating clear and measurable objectives, as well as establishing the so-called null measurement at the start of a project. A null measurement establishes the score of the performance targets just before the redesign is carried out. Such a measurement makes an ex-post evaluation possible. It is also noteworthy that in spite of reported failure rates of BPR projects, the presence of BPR success stories in literature exceeds the number of failure cases by far. Although this is a natural phenomenon – what is there to gain for a company to report on a failed BPR project? – it also indicates the difficulty of correctly estimating the success/failure ratio of BPR projects. Finally, Peppard and Rowland (1995) put the failure rate of BPR projects within the context of the general tendency of most large-scale projects, which fail to achieve all the targets set for them at the starting point.

Although recent, complete and unambiguous figures on BPR success are lacking, it is evidently so that BPR projects may indeed fail or come up short of expectations. The risks that cause failure or shortcoming are usually divided into two categories: technical and organizational. These categories are related to the common view of a BPR initiative as a twofold challenge, as follows (e.g., Manganelli and Klein, 1994a; Carr and Johansson, 1995; Galliers, 1997):

1. *A technical challenge*, which is due to the difficulty of developing a process design that is a radical improvement of the current design.
2. *A sociocultural challenge*, resulting from the severe organizational effects on the involved people, which may lead them to go against those changes.

Apart from these challenges, project management of a BPR initiative itself is also named as a common field of risk (e.g., Grover et al., 1995). Project management is concerned with managing both the technical and sociocultural challenge throughout the BPR initiative. The components of a BPR initiative are depicted in Figure 1.4.

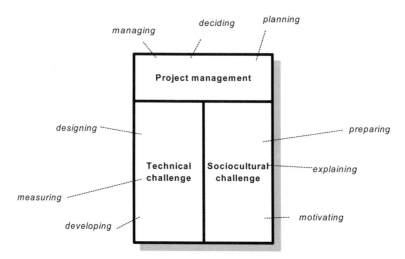

Fig. 1.4. The components of a BPR initiative

Most literature on the risks involved with BPR initiatives identify the organizational risks as the greatest, followed by the project management risk (e.g., Bruss and Roos, 1993; Carr and Johansson, 1995; Galliers, 1997; O'Neill and Sohal, 1999; Kallio et al., 1999). Commonly perceived organizational risks are, for example, resistance to the change, lack of motivation, and improper communication. Commonly perceived project management problems spots, for example, include time schedules, required resources, and budgets. The technical risks, such as a bad design, identification of the wrong process and the unreliability of information technology (IT), are usually perceived as less severe. However, it is clear that the various risks are related. For example, implementing a bad design is likely to cause strong opposition from the people who are forced to use it.

The apparently settled classification and prioritization of BPR risks might very well explain the focus that a major part of the BPR literature has. The work that has been produced over the past ten years can roughly be divided into two categories. On the one hand, there is literature concerned with promoting BPR, case-based descriptions of BPR and overviews of the BPR literature. This type of literature is predominantly of a descriptive nature. It is often amusing and sometimes informative, but not much good for someone who wants to execute BPR himself. On the other hand, there is prescriptive literature explaining how to execute BPR as a whole, or parts of it. This latter type of literature is dominated by the treatment of project and change management issues of BPR projects (e.g., Stoddard and Jarvenpaa, 1995) – the sociocultural or project management side – instead of how to design a new business process – the technical side.

Prescriptive literature is sometimes advertised as "a step-by-step guide to business transformation" (e.g., Manganelli and Klein, 1994a) suggesting a complete treatment of the organizational and technical issues involved in BPR. However, work like this seems to be primarily aimed at impressing a business audience. At best it gives some directions to manage organizational risk, but usually lacks actual technical direction to redesign a business process. Even the classic work of Hammer and Champy (1993) devotes only 14 out of a total of over 250 pages to this issue, of which 11 pages are used for the description of a case. Gerrits (1994) mentions: "In the literature on BPR, examples of successful BPR implementations are given. Unfortunately, the literature restricts itself to descriptions of the 'situation before' and the 'situation after', giving very little information on the redesign process itself." As Sharp and McDermott (2001) commented very recently: "How to get from the as-is to the to-be [in a BPR project] isn't explained, so we conclude that during the break, the famous ATAMO procedure is invoked – And Then, A Miracle Occurs".

In conclusion, we can establish that despite of the popularity of BPR as a field of research and application the developments in this field have not reached a mature state yet, especially with respect to technical issues. Rather than on the technical art or science of redesigning business processes, the focus in recent BPR literature is on the following:

- Case studies, e.g., by Sarker and Lee (1999).
- Rehashing existing BPR literature, e.g., by O'Neill and Sohal (1999) and Al-Mashari and Zairi (2000b).
- Boundaries of BPR, e.g., by Al-Mashari and Zairi (2000a) and Bhatt (2000).

Without a rigorous presentation of the maturity of BPM as a whole, we claim that the field of study is still in its infancy. Especially the technical side of BPR is severely underexposed, although a good process design is nothing less than the cornerstone of any successful BPR project. Because the field of BPM is too large to approach within the setting of this monograph, we will focus on a specific kind of business process: the class of workflow processes.

1.4 Workflows

The *workflow process* or simply *workflow* is a special kind of business process. Often the use of the terms "business process" and "workflow" is mixed up, either in the sense that they are explicitly used as synonyms (e.g., Van der Aalst and Van Hee, 2002) or that they are presented side by side without any distinctive comments (e.g., Knolmayer et al., 2000). Another popular interpretation, already mentioned in Section 1.1, is to see a workflow as an administrative business process, i.e., as a business process that delivers services or informational products (e.g., Van der Aalst and Berens, 2001). The term "workflow" is also used to exclusively refer to the control dimension of a business process, i.e., the dependencies among tasks that must be respected during the execution of a business process (Dellarocas en Klein, 2000; Sharp and McDermott, 2001). A final and empirical interpretation is to consider those business processes as workflows that can be supported by Workflow Management Systems (Deiters, 2000). We already mentioned this type of system already in the previous section as an example of a technology driver for BPR. Although we are not enthusiastic about defining conceptual terms by characteristics of actual technology, it is worthwhile to explore workflow management technology in some more detail before discussing the essential characteristics – in our view – of workflows.

1.4.1 Workflow Management Systems

The main purpose of a workflow management system (WfMS) is to support the definition, execution, registration and control of business processes (Van der Aalst, 1998). This complex of tasks is considered to be the domain of workflow management or alternatively office logistics. In principle, workflow management can be executed without the use of technology; in particular without a WfMS. In fact, this traditionally was the case before workflow management technology was developed at all – and probably still is in most practical business settings.

In practice, a WfMS takes care of delivering the right piece of work to the right resource at the right time. Each time an essential piece of work has been completed during a business process execution, the WfMS determines how the business process execution is to be continued by delivering the next piece of work to one or more resources that are capable of executing it. The WfMS can do this on the basis of a model of the business process, also called a workflow definition. In this workflow definition, all the tasks within the business process are distinguished, as well as their dependencies. The workflow definition also incorporates the information on the type of resources that are required for the execution of each task (see Section 1.1). In this way, the WfMS can address the right resource – usually a person or a computer system – at the right moment. Human resources are usually using electronic equivalents of post boxes to communicate with a WfMS, in particular for the purpose of accepting new work from the WfMS and notifying that work has been completed to the WfMS.

In handing out work, WfMS's are able to integrate with other types of information technology, such as databases, document management systems and transaction systems. This is efficient and it has many ergonomic advantages. For example, along with a piece of work to be executed all relevant information can be handed to the human resource that will be carrying it out. Also, the WfMS can invoke the proper information system to execute an automated task.

All actions of the WfMS are recorded by it. As a result, all sorts of historical management information on business process executions can be derived from the WfMS. Popular figures are, for example, the number of products produced, the work accomplished by personnel in specific periods, the number of rejections of a certain type of proposal, etc.

Of the current business process executions under control of the WfMS, the system also maintains a detailed real-time administration of each of its states. This dynamic administration is required for the WfMS to operate at all. After all, it would be very inefficient for the system to ignore steps already executed. The WfMS therefore offers a valuable window on the operational state of the process. Typical operational information harvested from a WfMS consists of the number of current business process executions and the length of queues of work items.

The first WfMS's as generic software packages became commercially available in the early 1990s (Jablonski and Bussler, 1996). Workflow management functionality could be distinguished within other software packages before this time. It could not, however, be separated from other functionality concerning the content of the work to be supported (e.g., specific calculations, storage and retrieval functionality, etc.). In this sense, it is relevant to distinguish between the generic software with which business processes can be managed – the WfMS – and a system that is used to manage a specific business process – a workflow system (Van der Aalst and Van Hee, 2002). Clearly, WfMS's can be used to build workflow systems. However, any system that incorporates knowledge about how the business process is executed logistically can be used for a workflow system. Today, Enterprise Resource Planning (ERP) and Customer Relation Management (CRM) systems are incorporating more and more workflow functionality. Also note that a workflow system does not execute any tasks of the business process itself. It focuses on the logistics of the work – not its content.

WfMS's are typically used within the setting of mass customization (see Section 1.1; Van der Aalst and Van Hee, 2002). This is related to the alleged advantages of WfMS's. As there are many possible viewpoints in discussing their merits, we will restrict ourselves to two of the most outspoken ones, which are as follows:

1. *Flexibility*
   In separating the logistics of the work, to be managed by a WfMS, from the content of the work, which still is to be executed by humans and computers systems, it is in principle easier to change and manage the logistics of the process independently from the content of the tasks (and the other way around).

2. *Optimization*
   By using a dedicated automated system for the logistic management of a process, the process is executed faster and more efficiently.

These advantages must be set off against other IT solutions or against executing and managing business processes manually. The support of document management systems and imaging facilities strongly intensify these advantages. Furthermore, both types of advantages are more strongly felt in settings where there is a high frequency of business process executions that require some sense of responsiveness to a client's preferences, i.e., a situation of mass customization (see Section 1.1).

Despite these advantages and the high expectations concerning WfMS's in the beginning of the 1990s as the "technology of the 21st century", the application of this type of technology has not caught on as was expected. Technological as well as change management issues are seen as major reasons for this. Reijers et al. (1999), Reijers and Goverde (1999b), Grinter (2000), Agostini and De Michelis (2000), and Joosten (2000) explore some of the reasons for this disappointing development. It is not a subject of this monograph.

1.4.2 Workflow Characteristics

A workflow as a special kind of business process has some distinctive characteristics that set it apart from other business processes. Also, there are some characteristics that workflows typically share, although they are not essential. We will successively discuss both categories.

Essential Characteristics

Essential for a workflow is that it is a case-based and a make-to-order business process. The case-based character of a workflow refers to the case concept. A case is defined as the subject of operations in a business process execution. Examples of cases are subscription requests, mortgage applications, and hospital admissions. A business process is case-based if during its execution each activity can be attributed to one single, discrete case. The singularity of the case means that it is uniquely distinguishable from all other cases. The workflow case is discrete in the sense that there is a clear moment of the case coming into existence and a clear moment of completion of the case. Neither of these two aspects – singularity and discreteness – are universally present in actual business processes. Within mass-production processes (see Section 1.1) there is often no clear distinction of cases during their execution. For example, it is not always known beforehand which two actual subassemblies will be assembled in the end to produce a specific final product. The discrete character of a case is violated in processes that have no clear start or end.

The make-to-order characteristic of a workflow means that the trigger starting a process execution is an order. A workflow cannot be executed to produce a good or service in advance of the actual order (make-to-stock). As we have discussed in Section 1.1, an order is a common but in general not the only possible way of starting a business process. The order and case concepts are highly related in workflows. More precisely, there is one order for each case; there is one workflow execution for each case. For example, an order may be a specific application for a mortgage. The receipt of this order is a unique trigger. This trigger initiates the creation of a unique case: a mortgage application. The handling of the case in the form of calculations, tenders and decisions is performed as a specific execution of the mortgage workflow. When the application has been completely handled (the case is complete), the workflow execution ends and a product is possibly delivered. Obviously, one order may simultaneously involve any quantity of products of various types.

The most common end-state of a business process is the completion of the case in the form of a product. This is, however, not the only possibility. In many workflow processes, there are ways of ending its execution while not delivering a product. For example, a mortgage application may not be acceptable for a bank given the financial situation of the applicant or applicants. Alternatively, the client may revoke the order halfway through the workflow execution. Either way, the application will not result in closing the mortgage, i.e., the actual product. A workflow execution may therefore lead to no or exactly one product.

Combining the essential characteristics of a workflow with the general business process relations as depicted in Figure 1.2, we come up with the relations depicted in Figure 1.5.

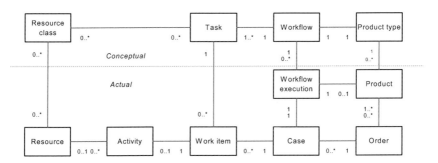

Fig. 1.5. Relations between the workflow concepts

For the sake of completeness, the concepts of tasks, work items, activities, resources, and resource classes discussed earlier are also included in the model. In doing this, the relations between the most important concepts for this monograph are present. We will briefly discuss the relations not treated before.

In Figure 1.5 we see that a workflow consists of one or more tasks (see Section 1.1). A tasks occurs in one workflow only. Resources are grouped into resource classes, which in turn can be used to specify who is both capable and authorized to perform a task. For each task, this may be a number of resource classes. An individual resource itself may be a member of several resource classes.

Both types of dynamic manifestations of tasks – activities and work items – are also included in the model (see Section 1.1). A work item is a task that has to be performed for a specific case. In the depicted model, an activity is a work item that is executed by a specific resource. If no resource is required, i.e., it is automatic, no resource is required.

It should be clear that the depicted model is a simple approach to structure the important workflow concepts. More complex situations can be imagined. For example, the same task may occur in more than one workflow, i.e., it is shared. Also, the given model expresses that several resource classes may be assigned to a task, although only one resource at a time will actually work on a work item. In reality, more than one resource at a time may work on a work item. Take, for example, a medical team that carries out an operation. The model is not complete either. As we remarked in Section 1.1, all kinds of dependencies may be in effect between tasks, e.g., precedence relations, and the same holds for resource classes, e.g., hierarchical relations. Not graphically depicted either are the constraints for each cycle within the entity relationship. Obviously, relations between the same instances are expressed. However, the model is useful to indicate the scope of the topics addressed in each of the chapters to follow.

Common Characteristics

Next to the essential characteristics there are others, usually found with workflow processes. To start with, many workflow processes mostly incorporate administrative or informational operations – calculating, writing, storing, deciding, communicating – and these processes often deliver services – advices, loans, permits. The reason for this phenomenon is that specific information about the case plays an important role during the business process execution from the start. It is this information that has to be processed and compared, leading to the creation of other information with similar processing steps as result. For example, in a workflow process that handles requests for construction permits, all the following information is relevant before the process may start: the size of the intended building, its purpose, its exact location, the construction method, the building period, etc. Unlike many manufacturing processes it is not possible to anticipate the exact case characteristics by producing a variety of products in advance. For example, a stock of construction permit rejections makes no sense.

The informational character of a workflow, however, is not essential. There are workflow processes that incorporate physical operations. For example, conditional to the issuing of a mortgage, Dutch banks demand a physical copy of the contract of sale. In addition, banks are required by the Dutch Bank Law to physically archive these for a certain period. Also, it is perfectly possible – although not always the most productive way – to produce goods in a make-to-order and case-based way.

Another common but not essential characteristic of workflows is the fact that humans form a large part of the required resources for its execution. This in contrast to many manufacturing and mass-production processes where most of the operations are automated. Workflows typically involve decision-making steps that cannot be totally formalized, because they require a human value judgment or interpretation. An example of this decision can be found in how Dutch social security agencies decide on granting unemployment allowances. The judgment whether the applicant is to blame for his discharge is highly relevant within this context. If there are conflicting statements of different parties, a specialist has to make a judgment weighing the credibility of these statements. Another example is the decision of a bank whether the purpose of a loan is commercially attractive to support. Many factors determine this attractiveness in practice, but there is no algorithmic way of combining these factors into a standardized decision-making task.

The human factor in workflow processes, however, is not essential. It is easy to imagine practical workflows that require no human interference at all. In fact, many organizations that host workflows are considering measures to fully automate these processes, so that they can be offered to clients via the Internet. Common terms for this trend are Straight-Through-Processing and Unattended Workflow (MacSweeney, 2001). As will be shown in the GAK case of Chapter 7, it often is possible to automate many steps within a workflow that were formerly performed by humans. Even if completely automated processing is not possible, large categories of cases may be identified that do not require human judgments.

A final, common characteristic of a workflow is that the business process in question is often repetitively executed (e.g., Schäll, 1996). The workflow structure may be changed once in a while, but after each change it is used as the basis for delivering multiple products. We already established that a considerable part of the resources in a workflow are human, indicating that workflows usually are not fully standardized. Using the presented classification based on the execution frequency of the business process and its level of standardization in Section 1.1, it is therefore fair to say that workflows are mostly of the mass-customization type. Less frequently, workflows are used for high-volume transaction processing. This requires the tasks in the workflow to be fully automated. Although it is much more infrequent, it is also possible to use a workflow as a customized process, i.e., for the production of only one product. A concern that may cause one to prefer this alternative despite the cost is that complete control of the process execution is required. An example would be the construction of a large infrastructural work that is to be delivered under tight quality procedures.

Discussion

Having discussed the characteristics of workflows, we return our attention to the definitions of workflows as special business processes in the introduction of this section. As discussed, the interpretation of a workflow as an administrative process is slightly narrow. However, the empirical interpretation of workflows as business processes that can be supported by WfMS's makes some sense. WfMS's are founded on the concept of unique, discrete cases and they do recognize orders as starting triggers of the process (see Van der Aalst and Van Hee, 2002).

We must be cautious, however, in identifying workflows as those processes that can be supported by WfMS's. We name three reasons for this. The first is that there are workflows that cannot be easily supported by WfMS's, because their structure is unclear or very complex. The issuing of a permit in a corrupt country may be difficult to support because of the lack of transparency in the process.

Also, the decision-making process during the weekly meeting of a board may be too difficult to capture in a workflow definition.

The second reason is more empirical. In their treatment of workflow modeling Jablonski and Bussler (1996) explicitly distinguish between system-related and unrelated perspectives on workflows. This indicates that there are perspectives on a workflow that are more and less related to the characteristics of a WfMS.

Thirdly, it is interesting to note that there are other types of systems such as ERP, CRM and case-handling systems – of which the vendors claim that they are essentially different products from WfMS's – that do focus on the support, definition, control and execution of workflows. This phenomenon allows us to state that workflows include those processes that can be supported by WfMS's, but that processes outside this arena also may qualify as workflows.

Finally, at the beginning of this section we also considered the notion of a workflow as the control dimension of a business process. In Section 2.2 we will return to this specific interpretation when we discuss the different conceptual aspects of a workflow model. We will see that this view coincides with a narrow interpretation of one of the components of a workflow model that we will distinguish.

1.5 Workflow and Logistic Management

The science of Business Process Management has particularly evolved itself in the field of manufacturing processes. As a consequence of the essential and practical characteristics of workflows (see Section 1.4), we will discuss the applicability of logistic concepts applied in manufacturing processes for the management of workflows.

A large part of the manufacturing theory focuses on the design and management of stock, such as its proper geographical and logical location, the proper stock level, the speed of stock replenishing, etc. Because a workflow essentially is a make-to-order process, this theory is largely inapt for workflows. Some of its concepts and terminology are, however, still usable. For example, if larger business processes are composed as chains of subsequent workflows, decoupling points can be distinguished between the end of a workflow and the start of the next. Take, for example, the goods flow of a production company in Figure 1.6. Despite the decoupling points "raw materials" and "end products", the receipt, assemble, and dispatch steps may be treated as separate workflows.

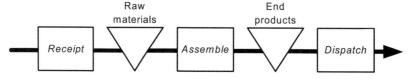

Fig. 1.6. Goods flow of a production company

In addition, an in-process inventory is created during the execution of workflows, so the concept of stock is not totally absent in workflows. The work in progress may be a significant figure, especially with respect to the performance measurement of workflows.

The practical aspects of workflows – in contrast with their essential characteristics – usually determine the applicability of other manufacturing theory. A rough comparison between manufacturing processes and workflows is as follows. In a manufacturing process, physical objects are produced like cars, clothing, construction materials, computers, etc. Principal resources in manufacturing are machines, robots, humans, conveyor belts and trucks. These resources are typically involved with assembling, inspecting, processing, and transporting materials. In a workflow, products are often – but not necessarily – informational. Moreover, in workflows some tasks may be executed completely by computer applications, but a substantial part of the work in administrative processes involves human experts. As a result, the common form of workflows differs from a manufacturing process from a logistic point of view in some subtle aspects (Van der Aalst et al., 2001), as follows:

- *Making a copy is easy and cheap.* In contrast to making a copy of a product like a car, it is relatively easy to copy a piece of information, especially if the information is in electronic form.
- *There are no real limitations with respect to the in-process inventory.* Informational products do not require much space and are easy to access, especially if they are stored in a database.
- *There are less requirements with respect to the order in which tasks are executed.* Human resources are flexible in comparison with machines; there are few technical constraints with respect to the lay-out of the administrative process.
- *Quality is difficult to measure.* Criteria to assess the quality of an informational product are usually less explicit than those in a manufacturing environment.
- *Quality of end products may vary.* A manufacturer of goods usually has a minimal number of components that any product should incorporate. However, in an administrative process it might be attractive to skip certain checks in producing the informational product to reduce the workload. For example, in checking a tax declaration the inspection of deductible loans may be skipped; a specific car must contain an air bag for the driver.
- *Transportation of electronic data is timeless.* In a network information travels almost at the speed of light; in a manufacturing environment, the transportation of parts is an essential share of the total lead-time.

In spite of these subtle differences, there also are many similarities between manufacturing processes and administrative processes (Platier, 1996). In both domains, managing the process focuses on the routing of work and the allocation of work to resources. There also is a common notion of a process as a set of tasks that have to be executed in an order that is fixed at some level and incorporates some degree of flexibility as well. Additionally, the performance of both types of processes is measured in highly similar ways with indicators such as throughput time, waiting time, client satisfaction and utilization. For example, management in both domains is concerned with the delivery of their product to their clients in the right amount of time. Concepts that originate from manufacturing to affect the performance of a process are frequently seen to be applied in workflows as well. For example, in manufacturing, different policies have emerged to order the flow of similar work items from the perspective of the resources, like First-In-First-Out (FIFO) and Earliest Due Date (EDD). These concepts have now been integrated in WfMS's (Van der Aalst and Van Hee, 2002).

There is one more difference between manufacturing processes and most workflows worth mentioning. Within manufacturing, the relation between the product and the process is very explicit in the process itself. This is much less so in most workflow processes. We will exploit this gap to consider a new way of designing workflows, as described in Chapter 3.

1.6 Objective of the Monograph

Based on the presented concepts so far we can express the objective of the research that underlies this monograph as follows:

to advance scientific knowledge of Business Process Management
by providing methods and techniques for the design and control of workflows.

Because of the extent of the BPM field of study, we will focus on four areas, which are the following:

– How to make a model of a workflow process.
– How to design or redesign an effective and efficient workflow process.
– How to analyze the performance of a workflow process.
– How to sensibly allocate resources in a workflow process.

In this section, we will give an overview of the content of this monograph. We will describe the various chapters and classify them with respect to the above areas.

1.6.1 Modeling: Chapter 2

For many process design and process control decisions it is necessary to have a clear idea of the business process or workflow at hand. A convenient way of reasoning about business processes or workflows is to capture the relevant ingredients in the form of a model. Throughout this monograph we will often turn to a model of the workflow at hand. In Chapter 2 we will present the conceptual aspects of a workflow model. We will also introduce the Petri net formalism that is the basis for the modeling of these aspects. The new contribution of this chapter is an abstract classification of the components of a workflow model and a specific timed version of the workflow net.

1.6.2 Design: Chapter 3

Arguably, the design of business processes is the area within BPM that has received the widest attention over the past two decades. This is understandable as the way in which business processes are structured has a large impact on the cost, speed, and quality of the products produced with it. As we have discussed in Section 1.3, the technical side of designing business processes is rather undeveloped. In Chapter 3 we will address this strategic issue by presenting an approach to design workflows that is inspired by manufacturing principles.

1.6.3 Performance Analysis: Chapter 4

The analysis of a future workflow is essential for build-time decision making – the subject of Chapter 3. Before such a newly designed workflow is put into practice, it is desirable to predict whether the set of performance targets will be met in practice. It will facilitate the choice between different designs. In Chapter 4, we will present two new analytical methods that can be used to analyze workflows. The methods that are presented focus on determining a specific type of performance target, namely the throughput time. This is a common and popular performance target in practice (see Section 1.1).

1.6.4 Resource Allocation: Chapter 5

An important tactical issue in the field of BPM is how to allocate resources within an existing business process in the most effective way. The strategic issue of redesigning a new business process is also involved. Usually, a new business process is designed by first deciding on a new structure for the process – which typically involves the definition of tasks and their dependencies – and secondly the allocation of resources to these tasks. In Chapter 5 we will present a new allocation method that yields optimal results with respect to minimizing the throughput time for a specific class of workflows. It will be compared to an existing approach as it is applied in manufacturing. Simulation experiments are used to investigate the effectiveness of the allocation method for classes of workflows for which optimality could not be proven.

1.6.5 Redesign: Chapter 6

There is various fragmentary knowledge available in the form of heuristics about organizing work within business processes at a micro-level. An example of such a heuristic is that small subsequent tasks that require similar skills are best combined. This kind of knowledge is often applied to justify decisions on several levels of decision making, particularly concerning the strategic issue of designing a new process. The contribution of Chapter 6 is that it gives an overview of this body of knowledge. We will also illustrate the effectiveness of some of these heuristics with a realistic example.

1.6.6 Systems and Experiences: Chapter 7

A substantial part of the approaches, techniques, methods, and theory that is presented in this monograph has been applied in practice, as we mentioned in the introduction of this Chapter. In fact, practice was the origin of most of the presented approaches. In Chapter 7 we will present our practical experiences by applying BPM concepts in the design and control of workflows.

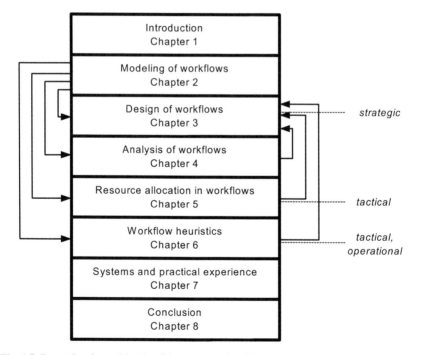

Fig. 1.7. Dependencies and levels of the monograph subjects

The relations between the subjects of the various chapters are presented in Figure 1.7. Each chapter is depicted as a black box. Each arrow leading from a box to another means that the former subject can be used to support the subject of the latter. For example, knowledge about allocating resources is useful in for the design of new workflows. Knowledge about modeling workflows is applicable to all other subjects. Some subjects are not only subordinate to others, but are also directly applicable to support decision making. In such a case, the appropriate decision-making level is on the right hand side of the box.

Note that Chapter 7 contains case descriptions where the various pieces of knowledge and techniques of the other chapters are applied. Chapter 8 includes an evaluation of the presented material and directions for further research.

2 Workflow Modeling

For the purpose of process-oriented decision making it often is convenient to use a model of a workflow. A workflow model is a simplified representation of a past, actual or future workflow process. The focus on workflow models as supporting decision making is prevalent in this chapter, but it should be realized that workflow modeling in general has a wider purpose. For example, a workflow model may be used to familiarize new personnel with daily operations. We will briefly consider in Section 2.1 the various applications of workflow models. In particular, we will regard the application of a workflow model to parameterize a Workflow Management System.

In Section 2.2 we present our view on the conceptual parts of a workflow model. We will distinguish four basic workflow components and the types of data that can be used for modeling the various components.

Next, in Section 2.3, we will briefly highlight some of the techniques that are used in modeling workflows. We will discuss the backgrounds of the various techniques, their application and some of their limitations.

We will end this chapter with the presentation of the Petri net. Its basic notions will be presented, as well its specific application to the modeling of workflows. We will devote special attention to the modeling of time in Petri nets and the definition of a timed workflow model.

A considerable part of this chapter contains already existing theory, such as the various modeling techniques (Section 2.3) and Petri net concepts (Section 2.4). The knowledgeable reader may want to skip these and focus on the three new contributions, which are as follows:

- The overview of workflow modeling purposes (Section 2.1).
- The conceptual workflow meta-model with its four components (Section 2.2).
- The stochastic workflow net (Section 2.4).

The basic workflow net and its stochastic variant form the heart of this chapter. These notions will be used in most of the following chapters. They formalize the aspects of the business process with respect to workflows, as discussed in the previous chapter.

H.A. Reijers: Design and Control of Workflow Processes, LNCS 2617, pp. 31-59, 2003.
© Springer-Verlag Berlin Heidelberg 2003

2.1 Modeling Purposes

As we have pointed out in Section 1.1, it is essential to the notion of a business process in general and a workflow in particular that work is not carried out at random. Instead, all kinds of procedures and structures are in effect. These involve the order of the work, the responsibilities of the staff, the interaction between the resources, the exchange of information, etc. The goal of modeling a workflow is to incorporate all relevant aspects of a workflow, while abstracting from irrelevant others.

Obviously, what is relevant for one type of decision may be irrelevant for the other. For example, in Chapter 1 we made a distinction between strategic decision making on the one side and tactical, operational, and real-time decision making on the other. We established that the build time structural aspect of a workflow is relevant for both types of decisions, while the run time dynamic aspect of a workflow is required for tactical, operational, and real-time decisions only. Also, strategic decision making generally requires a less detailed view on a workflow than the other types of decision making, although its scope may be broader.

In this monograph, we approach workflow modeling primarily as a means to support decision making within the context of Business Process Management (see Section 1.2). However, workflow models can have various other purposes. It can be easily imagined that the way in which a workflow is modeled is strongly driven by its specific purpose. Without claiming completeness, we present an overview of these different purposes.

2.1.1 Training and Communication

Workflow models may be used to introduce new employees with the overall structure of the business process they will take part in, the products that are delivered by it, and the dependencies with other parts of the company (see Sierhuis, 2001). Changes in existing procedures may also be communicated within a company by distributing updated workflow models.

2.1.2 Simulation and Analysis

An executable specification of a workflow can be used to simulate the behavior of the workflow under different circumstances. This application is a typical example of decision support in matters as BPR (see e.g., Hansen, 1994) and operational control (see e.g., Reijers and Van der Aalst, 1999). Various qualitative and quantitative analytical methods have been developed to assess the effectiveness of existing or new workflows. The development of some of these algorithms is the subject of Chapter 4. The application of simulation for tactical decision making is the subject of Chapter 5.

2.1.3 Costing and Budgeting

Many contemporary costing and budgeting approaches are based on the Activity Based Costing (ABC) method (Kaplan and Atkinson, 1989). The goal of ABC is to measure and then price out all the resources used for activities that generate goods and services for clients. A workflow model – more specifically its listing of the different tasks and their interdependencies – can be used a basis for ABC.

2.1.4 Documentation, Knowledge Management, and Quality

A workflow model can be used as a backbone for work instructions on each of its tasks. Such instructions can be consulted by the resources responsible for their execution. When knowledge is incorporated into the model about, for example, exceptions and involved regulations the model is extended into an operational knowledge base.

Workflow models can also support the implementation of Total Quality Management (TQM). TQM emphasizes the importance of business process codification as a means to reduce role conflict and ambiguity, thereby increasing work satisfaction and reducing feelings of alienation and stress. For a review, see Jackson and Randall (1985). A documentation purpose of workflow models also worth mentioning is the recording of a BPR outcome, a new workflow design (see Chapter 3).

2.1.5 Enactment

On the basis of a workflow model, a workflow can be managed and controlled in real-time by an enterprise system such as a WfMS or Enterprise Resource Planning System. As we have mentioned in Section 1.4, such a workflow model is often referred to as a workflow definition. In actual WfMS's, the modeling of the logistical structure of a workflow and the modeling of the types of resources has been divided into separate models.

2.1.6 System Development

A workflow model may be used as input for system development activities, specifying functional requirements for the supporting systems that have to be modified or build (see e.g., Bond, 1999; Reijers and Van der Toorn, 2002). Especially when a workflow has been redesigned, the new layout and the specific content of newly engineered tasks may require a different support from information systems. Sharp and McDermott (2001) claim that a redesign of a workflow is hardly ever executed without application development being a large part of the effort.

2.1.7 Organization Design

A workflow model may be the first step in the design of an organization (see e.g., Ott and Nastansky, 1998). From the tasks in a workflow model the qualifications of the required personnel can be derived, which in their turn may be used to define job descriptions. The structure of the workflow may also help to identify how resources are efficiently grouped into departments, case teams, etc. Quantitative analysis of a workflow model may help to determine the number of different types of personnel required to deliver a desired level of performance (see Chapter 5).

2.1.8 Management Information

A workflow model may be used to identify and specify the key mile stones within a workflow from a manager's perspective (see e.g., Van der Aalst, 2001). Actual information on work progress with respect to these mile stones may be generated from a WfMS that enacts the particular model or may be determined by manual count.

It is clear that workflow models that serve different purposes will also vary in content and detail. For example, a workflow model that is used for system development will focus much more on an information-oriented description of the tasks in a workflow than is the case for a work instruction. A model that is used for the simulation of a workflow will incorporate the interaction behavior of a client, although this will be left out in a workflow enactment model where real clients place orders, respond to inquiries, etc. Finally, the level of detail of a model that is used to communicate a change in a workflow will not necessarily incorporate financial information, although this is a must for a model that is used for ABC costing.

Within this monograph, we clearly focus on workflow modeling (a) to support the purposes of simulation and analysis and (b) as a means of documenting a BPR design. In Chapter 7, we will briefly return to the specific purposes of a workflow model to support system development activities. In the next section we will distinguish the conceptual parts of a workflow model. These parts may be appropriately shaped with respect to the modeling purpose.

2.2 Workflow Components

Various authors have considered the essential parts of a workflow model, e.g., Koulopoulos (1995), Kobielus (1997) and Sharp and McDermott (2001). The most thorough and detailed view is by Jablonski and Bussler (1996), who have presented the Mobile workflow model. Within Mobile different perspectives are distinguished. Perspectives are different, orthogonal views one can have on a workflow model. The recognition of various perspectives does justice to the various deployment areas of workflow models and the resulting differences. Jablonski and Bussler make a first principal distinction between factual and systemic perspectives. A factual perspective exists independently from the characteristics of the actual WfMS that may enact the workflow model. Systemic perspectives come into view because of a special form of enactment, i.e., the specific, mostly technical properties of the system that takes care of the workflow enactment. The focus of the Mobile model is on factual perspectives, because of their more generic nature. Jablonski and Bussler further categorize these into five "fundamental" factual perspectives as follows:

1. *The function perspective*, which describes the (recursive) composition of a workflow out of its subflows and tasks.
2. *The operation perspective*, which describes for each part of the workflow (i.e., the subflows and tasks) which operations it supports and which applications implement these operations.
3. *The behavior perspective*, which defines the execution order of the workflow parts (subflows and tasks) of a workflow.
4. *The information perspective*, which describes which data is consumed and produced by the workflow.
5. *The organization perspective*, which specifies which resource is responsible for each of the tasks in the workflow.

In addition, they distinguish six more perspectives, which respectively focus on the reasons of executing a workflow (causality), the constraints that have to be fulfilled (integrity), the time and cost dimension of the workflow (quality), the history of the workflow executions (history), the authorizations within a workflow (security) and independency aspects (autonomy).

The attractiveness of the Mobile framework is its explicit goal to be extensible with other perspectives. The orthogonality of the perspectives should allow for this. Jablonski and Bussler deliberately present Mobile as not exhaustive, because "the deployment area of workflow management is pervasive and new perspectives or extensions to existing perspectives will most probably be encountered". Yet, each of the perspectives is clearly focused on the role of a workflow model as a basis for workflow enactment. This is one of the modeling purposes we distinguished in the previous section. As a result of the enactment-orientation, Mobile seems to be too fine-grained for analysis-oriented purposes, while at the same time the fundamental perspectives are too limited for supporting all the purposes of our modeling efforts. As our interest is in workflow modeling within the context of BPM, we present a simpler but more focused view on the conceptual parts of a workflow model.

We distinguish four basic functions that together can capture both the build time and the run time aspects of a workflow model. We will refer to these functions as workflow components. We will distinguish the case, routing, allocation and execution components.

2.2.1 Case Component

The case component in a workflow model describes which cases exist, how new cases are created and what each case looks like. Cases are specific instances of the "thing" that the workflow in question can handle, like tax forms, insurance claims, service complaints, production orders, etc (see Section 1.4). Most of the time, a workflow is capable to process one type of case; between each case slight variations may exist in their properties. The case component addresses what is to be handled by the workflow.

Within the Mobile framework, the case component is absent. This can be explained by the fact that a WfMS does not need a component to create cases, as this is performed by its environment. For simulation and analysis purposes, the case component is indispensable. Moreover, the notion of cases is needed to describe the behavior of the other components.

2.2.2 Routing Component

The routing component determines how cases are routed through the workflow. When considering a workflow, we are usually interested in a breakdown of it into smaller parts: primarily its tasks and possibly its subflows (see Section 1.1). Although a workflow in itself is structured, it can be flexible in the sense that one case will be handled differently from another. For example, when a case is more complex, more parties have to take a look at it. The routing component will fix for each case, depending on its properties, which set of tasks within the workflow are to be carried out and in what order.

The routing component can be seen as a condensed version of the function, operation, behavior and information perspectives of Mobile. Depending on the specific purpose of the workflow model, accents of all of these perspectives may appear in the routing component. For example, the exact manipulation of information may be very important for a systems development purpose, but less so for a workflow performance analysis. Note that additional information on the cost and time associated with the workflow execution (Mobile's quality perspective) are also part of the routing component. Also note that the strict interpretation of workflows as being control flows (see Section 1.4) refers only to the routing workflow component.

2.2.3 Allocation Component

The allocation component specifies which classes of reusable resources exist, being either human or non-human (e.g., machines), and which of these will take care of which work items. A work item in a workflow consists of a task that has to be performed for a specific case (see Section 1.1). Depending on the workflow, the allocation of work to resources can be driven by very different circumstances. For example, rush orders are handed out to a specific class of resources. The allocation component addresses the issue of who will be performing the work during execution of a workflow.

The allocation component coincides with the organizational perspective within Mobile.

2.2.4 Execution Component

Finally, the execution component determines when the resources will actually execute the work that has been allocated to them. The existence of this component stresses the difference between the decision to whom work is assigned – specified by the allocation component – and the decision to really perform it – taken by the execution component. As we will see, in some workflows resources themselves decide upon the order in which they execute the work that is assigned to them. Circumstances may also result in work being postponed.

A comparable perspective in Mobile is not present. This can be explained from the fact that the behavior of resources is not part of a workflow specification for a WfMS, the major aim of the Mobile model. A critique as put forth by Sierhuis (2001) is that precisely the execution behavior of humans is often inadequately modeled in workflow models. Especially, the "off-task behavior" of resources and their multi-tasking is omitted. These aspects can be modeled within the execution component, although it should be clear that adding this detailed execution behavior in fact serves the modeling purpose.

By now we have identified the case, routing, allocation, and execution components and discussed how they respectively address the what, how, by whom, and when questions (see Table 2.1). Other views on the conceptual parts of a workflow model focus primarily on the routing and allocation components. For example, Kouloupoulos (1995) and Kobielus (1997) describe a workflow as distinguishing routes, roles, and rules. Sharp and McDermott's (2001) variation is by distinguishing roles, responsibilities and routes.

Table 2.1. How each of the components addresses one of the basic process questions

What?	*How?*	*By whom?*	*When?*
Case	**Routing**	**Allocation**	**Execution**

Adequate modeling of each of these components with respect to the purpose of the model is the basis for each workflow model throughout this monograph. Note that a component involves the distinction, the structure, and the behavior of various entities. In Chapter 7 we will give a detailed example of the modeling of the workflow components in a practical setting of operational control support.

2.3 Modeling Techniques

For the modeling of a workflow, a multitude of modeling techniques – also known as languages – has been proposed. A few examples are data processing spheres, case plans, life-cycle diagrams, process algebra's, flowcharts, structure charts, business rules, Petri nets, activity diagrams, speech acts, PERT networks, and data flow diagrams. For wider and motivated enumerations, see e.g., Leymann and Altenhuber (1994) or Schäll (1996). The various existing techniques differ in the modeling constructs they offer, their notation, ease of use, and other aspects. The presentation of more suitable, expressive or intuitive modeling techniques is a beloved – and probably non-exhaustive – topic of research. We can broadly distinguish two reasons for the variety in modeling techniques, respectively related with the purpose of the workflow model and the characteristics of the workflow to be modeled.

2.3.1 Purpose of the Workflow Model

Just as the purpose of a workflow model will be of influence on the desired content of the model, the content of the model itself will make one type of modeling technique more suitable for the occasion than another. We will discuss a few characteristic relations between the purpose of the model and the suitability of the technique.

Communication

The first situation we distinguish concerns the situation when a workflow model is used primarily as a communication means among practitioners of various background within a company. In this case, the ability of the modeling technique for graphical expression is valued. The swim lane diagram of Sharp and McDermott (2001) is a typical example of a highly graphical type of model. Merz et al. (1995) call the graphical aspect as an important advantage of a modeling technique. However, the trap of communicative pictures is their lack of a precise meaning. This is why Van der Aalst (1996) also stresses the importance of a formal semantics of the modeling technique. A typical example of a business process modeling technique that lacks a complete and precise semantics is the Event-Driven Process Chains (Scheer, 1994).

Enactment

A second characteristic situation concerns the modeling of a workflow with an explicit enactment purpose. One effect of this purpose is that modelers often turn to the proprietary modeling technique that is provided by the WfMS. This is understandable as it minimizes the translation effort of a workflow model into an enactable model. It may, however, seriously impede the validation of the model with naive end-users. Porting a workflow model from one WfMS to another also becomes cumbersome (Meyer-Wegener and Böhm, 1999). If workflow models are built with an enactment purpose, modeling techniques that simplify their maintenance are valuable. After all, workflow models that are used for enactment will be subject to frequent updates due to changes in organizational structures and procedures. Bin Lee et al. (1999) propose, for example, knowledge representation schemes which enable a fast propagation of changes in their models.

Due to the enactment purpose of workflow models substantial attention in research is paid to the incorporation of information modeling capabilities into workflow modeling techniques. After all, the exchange and control of all types of information by a WfMS with other systems is crucial (see Jablonski and Bussler, 1996). Both Wirtz et al. (2000) and Moldt and Valk (2000) propose extensions of the process modeling capabilities of Petri nets with object oriented concepts for structuring information objects and their relations.

Analysis

The last situation we discuss concerns the analyzability of the model. If attractive analysis theories or techniques exist that can be used within the analysis purpose of the workflow process, a modeling technique that corresponds with the analysis framework is clearly advantageous. Van der Aalst (1996) and Oberweis et al. (1997) identify the existence of theoretically proven analysis techniques as one of the main reasons for selecting a corresponding modeling technique. Merz et al. (1995) also name the possibility to carry out simulations and verifications on a workflow model as a benefit for its modeling technique. An illustration of this phenomenon is the language Aw, which was developed by Trajcevski et al. (2000). It explicitly aims at exploiting existing action theories on reasoning about robot control programs and logical formalization of active databases in analyzing workflows.

2.3.2 Properties of the Workflow

The second main reason for the debate on techniques for workflow modeling concerns the properties of the object itself, the workflow process. We will give a few examples to illustrate this effect too.

Complex Routing

Clearly, a workflow process with a complex routing behavior including concurrent tasks, repetitions and branching will require a more expressive modeling technique than workflow processes that only incorporate linear sequences of tasks. For example, the very popular flowchart modeling technique does not support the modeling of concurrent behavior.

Structure

Similarly, the degree of structure in a workflow is of a great importance for the fit of the modeling technique. Probably the clearest watershed in workflow modeling techniques is between the task-oriented view on workflow processes and the language/action approach. In a task-oriented view, a workflow is considered as a set of interrelated tasks with process inputs and outputs. Examples of modeling techniques within this tradition are by e.g., Ellis and Nutt (1993), Gruhn (1995), and Van der Aalst (1998). The language/action approach focuses on the conversations and negotiations between workflow participants (Flores et al., 1988; Michelis and Grasso, 1994; Van Reijswoud et al., 1999). The task-oriented view seems more appropriate for modeling structured workflows, while the language/action approach has merits for modeling unstructured workflows (Schäl, 1996; Bin Lee et al, 1999). The watershed is also present in WfMS's: Staffware and Cosa follow the task-oriented view, Action Workflow follows the language/action approach (see e.g., Van der Aalst and Van Hee, 2002)

Specific Properties

Very specific properties of a workflow may influence the modeling technique too. Bricon-Souf et al. (1999) describe the proprietary modeling approach of the PLACO system. It is used within the setting of medical intensive care units within hospitals. It explicitly distinguishes the urgency of the matter in determining the authorization of a resource to perform a task.

    In the next section we will explain our choice for the Petri net formalism as the basis for our modeling technique.

2.4 Petri Nets

In this monograph we will use Petri nets as the basis for modeling workflows. Since Zisman (1977), who used Petri nets to model workflows for the first time, several authors have modeled workflows in terms of Petri nets, amongst which Ellis (1979), Lee (1992), Ellis and Nutt (1993), Merz et al. (1995) and Van der Aalst and Van Hee (1996).

    The choice for Petri nets is consistent with a task-oriented view on workflows (see previous section). This view is in our opinion best suited for the purpose of BPM. A strong argument for this is the orientation of BPR, one of the most influential fields within BPM (see Section 1.3). The founders of BPR, Davenport and Short (1990) and Hammer and Champy (1993), explicitly use the task distinction as a primary ordering concept for business processes and not – which would have suited a language/action approach – on the participants within a workflow and their conversational behavior. As a consequence, we have to accept that our approach may be less suitable for the modeling of less structured workflows (see previous section). In fact, Pagnoni Holt (2000) suggests as a basic condition for Petri nets to be useful for workflow modeling that all workflow parts can be described as well-defined pieces of reality.

Another attractive feature of the Petri net modeling technique is that it allows for a clear distinction between the structure of a workflow and its dynamic state. Like we have explained in Section 1.2, for different types of decisions structural and/or dynamical aspects of a business process are of importance. The use of Petri nets makes it possible to use the same modeling technique of workflows for these decisions. As we will see in the formal treatment of Petri nets in Section 2.4, the distinction between the structure and the dynamics is one of its basic properties. Van der Aalst (1996) also recognizes this as an important advantage of Petri nets.

Additional benefits of the Petri net modeling technique are: their formal semantics (Merz et al., 1995; Van der Aalst, 1996), their graphical notation (Merz et al., 1995), support for complex process constructions – in particular concurrency (Oberweis et al., 1997), and the availability of many analysis techniques (Merz et al., 1995, Van der Aalst, 1996; Oberweis et al., 1997).

Petri nets in their basic form, however, lack the expressive power to model a complete workflow model, covering all the workflow components in detail which we have discussed in Section 2.2. One obvious shortcoming is the lack of powerful data modeling capabilities. It can be imagined that these capabilities are required to specify the exact operations that take place within a workflow task. This need has been partially satisfied by the introduction of High-Level Petri Nets and, more specifically, the addition of color to Petri nets (e.g., Jensen, 1992; Van Hee, 1994). As stated before, both Wirtz et al. (2000) and Moldt and Valk (2000) also have proposed object-oriented extensions to improve the data modeling capabilities of Petri nets. Another shortcoming is that Petri nets do not explicitly distinguish resources. In Chapter 5, we will nonetheless show how their availability and behavior can be incorporated in Petri nets. Finally, the timing of the model – which is importance for performance evaluation purposes of workflow models – is not part of the basic Petri net.

In summary, we appreciate Petri nets as a good modeling technique, especially of the workflow routing component and – slightly less graceful – of the workflow allocation component. We will explicitly mention in each chapter where we apply Petri nets how the relevant components for the purpose of the chapter can be modeled at the appropriate level of detail, possibly using additional Petri net and other concepts. In the next sections, we formally describe the basic Petri net notions and their extensions with workflow concepts. We end this section with a wider debate of the modeling of time in Petri nets. This timed workflow net is crucial for the subject of Chapter 4.

2.4.1 Preliminaries to Petri Nets

For the definition and application of Petri nets for workflow modeling we use the basic notions of bags, relations, and sequences.

Bags

A *bag* is defined as a finite multi-set of elements from some alphabet A. A bag over alphabet A can be considered as a function from A to the natural numbers $\mathbb{N}$ such that only a finite number of elements from A is assigned a non-zero function value. For some bag X over alphabet A and $a \in A$, $X(a)$ denotes the number of occurrences of a in X, often called the cardinality of a in X. The set of all bags over A is denoted $\mathcal{B}(A)$. The empty bag, which is the function yielding 0 for any element in A, is denoted **0**. For the explicit enumeration of a bag, a notation similar to the notation for sets is used. Square, double brackets are used instead of curly brackets and superscripts are used to denote the cardinality of the elements. For example, $[\![a^2, b, c^3]\!]$ denotes the bag with two elements a, one b, and three elements c. For any bag X over alphabet A and element $a \in A$, $a \in X$ iff $X(a) > 0$. The sum of two bags X and Y, denoted $X \uplus Y$, is defined as $[\![a^n \mid a \in A \wedge n = X(a) + Y(a)]\!]$. The difference of X and Y, denoted $X \setminus Y$, is defined as $[\![a^n \mid a \in A \wedge n = (X(a) - Y(a)) \max 0]\!]$. Bag X is a subbag of Y over A, denoted $X \subseteq Y$, iff for all $a \in A$, $X(a) \leq Y(a)$.

Bags will be used in the definition of stochastic Petri net version as discussed later on in this section.

Relations

A relation R on a set A is a subset of the Cartesian product $A \times A$. We use the following notations for some special relations:

- $\mathrm{id}_A = \{(a, a) \mid a \in A\}$ is the identity relation,
- $R^{-1} = \{(b, a) \mid (a, b) \in R\}$ is the inverse of R,
- for $k \in \{1, 2, 3, \ldots\}$, R^k is inductively defined by $R^1 = R$ and, for $k > 1$:
   $R^k = \{(a, c) \mid (a, b) \in R^{k-1}$ and $(b, c) \in R$ for some $b \in A\}$,
- $R^+ = R^1 \cup R^2 \cup R^3 \cup \ldots$ is the transitive closure of R,
- $R^* = \mathrm{id}_A \cup R^+$ is the reflexive and transitive closure of R, and
- $(R \cup R^{-1})^*$ is the symmetric, reflexive, and transitive closure of R.

Relations will be used in the definition of stochastic Petri net version as discussed later on in this section.

Sequences

Let A be a set. A finite *sequence* on A is a mapping $\{1, \ldots, n\} \rightarrow A$, including the mapping $\epsilon: \varnothing \rightarrow A$, called the empty sequence. We represent a finite sequence $\sigma: \{1, \ldots, n\} \rightarrow A$ by the string $a_1 a_2 \ldots a_n$ of elements of A, where $a_i = \sigma(i)$ for $1 \leq i \leq n$. The length of σ is n, and the length of ϵ is 0. If $\sigma = a_1 a_2 \ldots a_n$ and $\tau = b_1 b_2 \ldots b_m$ are finite sequences then the concatenation of σ and τ, denoted by $\sigma\tau$, is the sequence $a_1a_2...a_nb_1b_2...b_m$ of length $n+m$. A sequence σ is a prefix of a sequence τ if either $\sigma = \tau$ or $\sigma\sigma' = \tau$ for some sequence σ'. We will denote with $\sigma|_B$ the restriction of the sequence to the set B. It can be recursively defined by $\epsilon|_B = \epsilon$ and

$$(a\sigma)|_B = \begin{cases} a(\sigma|_B) & \text{if } a \in B, \\ \sigma|_B & \text{if } a \notin B. \end{cases}$$

2.4.2 Petri Net Basics

The Petri net was invented by Carl Adam Petri (1962). The basic notions we present in this section are mostly derived from Desel and Esparza (1995). The interested reader is referred to their work for a rigorous treatment of many classical Petri net concepts.

Definition 2.1   (Petri net). A *Petri net* is a triplet (P, T, R):
- P is a finite set of places,
- T is a finite set of transitions (P $\cap$ T = $\varnothing$),
- R $\subseteq$ (P $\times$ T) $\cup$ (T $\times$ P) is a set of arcs (flow relation).

A place p is called an *input place* of a transition t iff there exists a directed arc from p to t. Place p is called an *output place* of transition t iff there exists a directed arc from t to p. We use $\bullet t$ to denote the set of input places for transition t. The notations $t\bullet$, $\bullet p$ and $p\bullet$ have similar meanings, e.g., $p\bullet$ is the set of transitions sharing p as an input place.

Definition 2.2   (Node, path, connected, strongly connected). For a Petri net PN = (P, T, R), any element $x \in$ P $\cup$ T of is called a *node*. A *path* of PN is a nonempty sequence $x_1...x_k$ of nodes which satisfies $(x_1, x_2),..., (x_{k-1}, x_k) \in$ R. A path $x_1...x_k$ is said to lead from x_1 to x_k. We denote $path(x_i \rightarrow x_k)$ iff there is a path from x_1 to x_k. PN is called *weakly connected* (or just connected) if every two nodes x, y satisfy $(x, y) \in (R \cup R^{-1})^*$. PN is *strongly connected* if $(x, y) \in R^*$, i.e., for every two nodes x, y there is a path leading from x to y.

Definition 2.3   (Cluster). Let x be a node of a Petri net PN = (P, T, R). The cluster of x, denoted $[x]$, is the minimal set of nodes such that:
- $x \in [x]$,
- if a place p belongs to $[x]$ then $p\bullet$ is included in $[x]$, and
- if a transition t belongs to $[x]$ then $\bullet t$ is included in $[x]$.

A Petri net can be used to expresses the structure of a system, process, or procedure. Its dynamic state is expressed with the marking of a Petri net.

Definition 2.4   (**Marking**). A *marking* of a Petri net (P, T, R) is a mapping M: $P \rightarrow \mathbb{N}$. A marking is represented by the vector $(M(p_1)...M(p_n))$, where $p_1, p_2, ..., p_n$ is an arbitrary fixed enumeration of P. A place p is marked at a marking M if $M(p) > 0$. A set of places R is marked if some place of R is marked.

In graphical depictions of Petri nets, places are mostly represented by circles and transitions by boxes. At any time a place contains zero of more *token*s, drawn as black dots. The marking of a Petri net is the allocation of tokens over places. As a marking is a bag, we will represent a marking as follows: $[\![p_1, p_2^2, p_4]\!]$ is the marking with one token in p_1, two tokens in p_2, 1 token in p_4 and no tokens in other places. In Figure 2.1, a Petri net is depicted. Note that the places of a Petri net are used to determine the state of the system.

The allocation of tokens – the dynamic state of the system which is modeled with the Petri net – may change during the execution of the net. Transitions are the active components in a Petri net: they change the marking of the net according to the following *firing rule*. The firing rule specifies that a transition is enabled if all its input places are marked. It can fire then, consuming a token from each of its input places and producing a token for each of its output places.

Definition 2.5   (**Firing rule**). A marking M of Petri net (P, T, R) enables a transition $t \in T$ if it marks every place in $\bullet t$. If t is enabled at M, then it can fire, and its firing leads to the successor marking M' (written $M \xrightarrow{t} M'$) which is defined for every place $p \in P$ by

$$M'(p) = \begin{cases} M(p) \text{ if } p \notin t\bullet \text{ and } p \notin \bullet t, \text{or } p \in \bullet t \text{ and } p \in t\bullet \\ M(p) - 1 \text{ if } p \in \bullet t \text{ and } p \notin t\bullet \\ M(p) + 1 \text{ if } p \notin \bullet t \text{ and } p \in t\bullet \end{cases}$$

A marking M is called *dead* if it enables no transition of the net.

Definition 2.6   (**Firing sequences, reachable markings, alphabet**). Let M be a marking of Petri net (P, T, R). If $M \xrightarrow{t_1} M_1, M_1 \xrightarrow{t_2} M_2, ..., M_{n-1} \xrightarrow{t_n} M_n$ are transition firings then $\sigma = t_1 t_2 ... t_n$ is a firing sequence leading from M to M_n. The set $\{ t_1, t_2 ... t_n \}$ is called the alphabet of σ, denoted $\mathcal{A}(\sigma)$. We write $M \xrightarrow{*} M'$, and call M' reachable from M, if $M \xrightarrow{\sigma} M'$ for some firing sequence σ. The set of all markings reachable from M is denoted by $[M\rangle$.

Definition 2.7   (**Conflict**). If a marking M of Petri net (P, T, R) enables transitions t and u, and firing of either of these transitions would disable the other, both transitions are said to be in *conflict*.

The integrating concept of a Petri net structure with a state is called a system. For Petri net systems, various properties have been defined which are useful in their analysis.

Definition 2.8   (Petri net system, initial and reachable markings). A Petri net system (or just a *system*) is a pair (PN, M_0) where:
- PN is a connected Petri net having at least one place and one transition, and
- M_0 is a marking of PN called the *initial marking*.

A marking is called *reachable* in a system if it is reachable from the initial marking.

Definition 2.9   (Liveness). A system is *live* if, for every reachable marking M and every transition t, there exists a marking $M' \in [M\rangle$ which enables t.

Definition 2.10   (Boundedness, safeness). A system is *bounded* if for every place p there is a natural number b such that $M(p) \le b$ for every reachable marking M. The bound of a place p in a bounded system (N, M_0) is defined as: max $\{ M(p) \mid M \in [M_0\rangle \land p \in P \}$. A system is called b-bounded if no place has a bound greater than b. A system is called *safe* iff it is 1-bounded.

Definition 2.11   (Free-choice). A Petri net (P, T, R) is free-choice iff for every two transitions t and u either $\bullet t \cap \bullet u = \varnothing$ or $\bullet t = \bullet u$.

Definition 2.12   (Acyclic net). A Petri net (P, T, R) is *acyclic* iff there is no path – except for the empty path – with node $t \in P \cup T$ as both its start and its end.

To conclude the general Petri net notions, we present a general theorem will be of use in the coming chapters, especially in Chapter 4.

Theorem 2.1   (Exchange Lemma). Let PN = (P, T, R) be a Petri net and U and V disjoint subsets of T, satisfying $\bullet U \cap V\bullet = \varnothing$. Let σ be a (finite or infinite) sequence of transitions such that $\mathcal{A}(\sigma) \subseteq U \cup V$. Then:

1. If $M \xrightarrow{\sigma} M'$ is a finite firing sequence, then $M \xrightarrow{\sigma|_U \sigma|_V} M'$.
2. If $M \xrightarrow{\sigma}$ is an infinite firing sequence and $\sigma|_U$ is finite, then $M \xrightarrow{\sigma|_U \sigma|_V}$.
3. If $M \xrightarrow{\sigma}$ is an infinite firing sequence and $\sigma|_U$ is infinite, then $M \xrightarrow{\sigma|_U}$.

Proof. See Desel and Esparza (1995). □

2.4.3 Workflow Nets

The workflow net was defined by Van der Aalst (1998). The following definitions and results are derived from his work.

Definition 2.13   (Workflow net). A Petri net PN = (P, T, R) is a workflow net if and only if:
- PN has two special places: i and o; place i is a source place, i.e., $\bullet i = \varnothing$; place o is a sink place, i.e., $o \bullet = \varnothing$,

– if transition t^* would be added to the set of transitions T $(t^* \notin$ T) and the arcs (o, t^*) and (t^*, i) would be added to the flow relation R of PN, the resulting net is strongly connected.

The first requirement in the definition of a workflow net reflects the typical begin and end of a workflow: a typical start situation can be established, after which the workflow is carried out in such a way that a desired end situation is reached. The second requirement in the definition ensures that there are no dangling transitions or places. By modeling tasks in a workflow as transitions, it is ensured that tasks which do not contribute to the processing are not considered in the model.

If a workflow net PN is extended in the sense of the second part of this definition we refer to it as the *extended workflow net* PN. Similar to the Petri net jargon, we call a workflow net with a marking a *workflow net system*.

In Figure 2.1 an example workflow net system is depicted, which is a condensed version of an example by Van der Aalst (1998). The workflow net depicts the routing component of a workflow that is used to process complaints. The tasks *register, notify, check, manual, time-out, process, automatic, finalize*, and *return* have been modeled as transitions. To model the states between the tasks, places have been added. For example, if place $c2$ is true (i.e., it contains a token), then the complaint is ready to be checked.

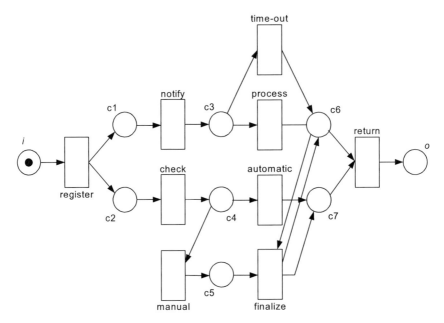

Fig. 2.1. An example workflow net system

Using the introduced notions, we make a few observations about the depicted workflow net system as follows:

– The workflow net marks i, which exclusively enables the *register* task.
– Marking $[\![c_3, c_5]\!]$ is a reachable state that – in particular – does not enable the *finalize* task.
– Marking $[\![o]\!]$ is a reachable and dead state.
– The workflow net system is not live, but the extended workflow net marked at $[\![i]\!]$ would be.
– The workflow net system is safe (and therefore also bounded).
– The workflow net is not free-choice and not acyclic; by, for example, removing the flow relations between $c6$ and the finalize task the remaining net is free-choice and acyclic.

A workflow net can be seen as the life-cycle of a single case. In general, there can be many cases which are handled according to the same workflow net. Each of these cases corresponds to one or more tokens. If tokens of multiple cases reside in the same Petri net, then these tokens may get mixed. For example, transition *return* may consume two tokens which correspond to different cases. Clearly, this is undesirable. There are two ways to solve this problem. First of all, it is possible to use a High-level Petri net where each token has a value (color) which contains information about the identity of the corresponding case (case identifier). Transitions are not allowed to fire if the case identifiers of the tokens to be consumed do not match, i.e., a precondition inspects and compares token values.

Another way to solve this problem is the following. Each case corresponds to a unique instance of the Petri net. If there are n cases, then there are n instances of the Petri net. One can think of such an instance as a layer. If these layers are put on top of each other, it is possible to see the cases in the same diagram. The latter is interesting from a decision making point of view, because one gets an overview of the state of the workflow. For example, if a place contains a lot of tokens, this might indicate a bottleneck.

In the remainder of this paper, we consider Petri nets which describe the life-cycle of a single case in isolation. In this way, we can use the classical Petri net notions. A great advantage of using the classical Petri net in modeling is that standard analysis techniques can be applied directly (Van der Aalst, 1998).

One way to handle the interpretation of the correctness of a workflow net is the soundness property. The soundness property expresses the desirable situation of a workflow process that it can be continued under all circumstances to a desirable end situation. This specific end situation is the state of the net where the sink place is marked, but no tokens are left in other places.

Definition 2.14   (Soundness). A workflow net W = (P, T, R) is sound if and only if:
– for every marking M reachable from marking $[\![i]\!]$, there exists a firing sequence leading from marking M to $[\![o]\!]$. Formally:

$$\forall_M \left([\![i]\!] \overset{*}{\longrightarrow} M \right) \Rightarrow \left(M \overset{*}{\longrightarrow} [\![o]\!] \right), \text{(completion option)},$$

- $\llbracket o \rrbracket$ is the only reachable marking from $\llbracket i \rrbracket$ with at least one token in place o.
  Formally: $\forall_M \left(\llbracket i \rrbracket \xrightarrow{*} M \wedge M(o) \geq 1 \right) \Rightarrow \left(M = \llbracket o \rrbracket \right)$ (proper completion), and
- there are no dead transitions in (W, $\llbracket i \rrbracket$). Formally:

  $\forall_{t \in T} \exists_{M,M'} \llbracket i \rrbracket \xrightarrow{*} M \xrightarrow{t} M'$.

The soundness property prohibits, for example, the undesirable situation where a workflow comes into a deadlock. Another banned situation is that the end situation is reached multiple times. For example, if the end situation represents the state where a single payment order has been successfully executed, multiple tokens are undesirable.

In general, the soundness property can be used in two ways. It is a check for modeling an existing workflow whether it is modeled correctly, as operational business processes are unlikely to be not sound. The second check is for a new design, when a designer can easily introduce an error – especially if the model is large.

The following theorems give the relation between some general Petri net properties on the one hand and the specific soundness property for workflow nets on the other hand.

Theorem 2.2   (Soundness equals liveness and boundedness). A workflow net W is sound if and only if the extended system ($\underline{W}$, $\llbracket i \rrbracket$) is live and bounded.
Proof. See Van der Aalst (1998). □

Theorem 2.3   (Safeness of sound, free-choice workflow nets). If the workflow-net W is sound and free-choice, then the system ($\underline{W}$, $\llbracket i \rrbracket$) is safe.
Proof. See Van der Aalst (1998). □

On the basis of Theorem 2.2 we can establish that the workflow net depicted in Figure 2.1 is sound. We can also see that the already established safeness and free-choice property of this net is consistent with Theorem 2.3.

For the composition of a workflow net, the following results are of interest. They have been derived from Van der Aalst (2000a). In Chapters 3 and 4, the so-called synthesis step will be used to compose complex workflow nets from simpler ones.

Definition 2.15   (Synthesis step). Let $PN_1 = (P_1, T_1, R_1)$ and $PN_2 = (P_2, T_2, R_2)$ be two workflow nets such that $T_1 \cap T_2 = \varnothing$, $P_1 \cap P_2 = \{i, o\}$ and $t^+ \in T_1$. The *synthesis step* of replacing transition t^+ in PN_1 by PN_2 yields the workflow net $PN_3 = (P_3, T_3, R_3)$ with:
- $P_3 = P_1 \cup P_2$,
- $T_3 = (T_1 \setminus \{t^+\}) \cup T_2$, and
- $R_3 = \{(x, y) \in R_1 \mid x \neq t^+ \wedge y \neq t^+\} \cup$
    $\{(x, y) \in R_2 \mid \{x, y\} \cap \{i, o\} = \varnothing\} \cup$

$\{(x, y) \in P_1 \times T_2 \mid (x, t^+) \in R_1 \wedge (i, y) \in R_2\} \cup$
$\{(x, y) \in T_2 \times P_1 \mid (t^+, y) \in R_1 \wedge (x, o) \in R_2\}.$

Theorem 2.4   (Compositionality). Let $PN_1 = (P_1, T_1, R_1)$ and $PN_2 = (P_2, T_2, R_2)$ be two workflow nets such that $T_1 \cap T_2 = \varnothing$, $P_1 \cap P_2 = \{i, o\}$ and $t^+ \in T_1$. If $PN_3 = (P_3, T_3, R_3)$ is the workflow net obtained by a synthesis step of replacing transition t^+ in PN_1 by PN_2, then for PN_1, PN_2 and PN_3 the following statements hold:

1. If PN_3 is free-choice, then PN_1 and PN_2 are free-choice.
2. If $(PN_1, [\![i]\!])$ is safe and PN_1 and PN_2 are sound, then PN_3 is sound.
3. $(PN_1, [\![i]\!])$ and $(PN_2, [\![i]\!])$ are safe and sound iff $(PN_3, [\![i]\!])$ is safe and sound.
4. PN_1 and PN_2 are free-choice and sound iff PN_3 is free-choice and sound.

Proof. See Van der Aalst (2000a). □

From this result, it follows that this specific replacement procedure which is described in this theorem ensures the preservation of many important Petri net properties for workflow nets and systems.

2.4.4 Modeling Time

The concept of time was intentionally avoided in the classical Petri net as introduced by Petri (1962), as timing constraints may prevent certain transitions from firing. Since the early seventies there has been a discussion within the Petri net community on the addition of time. From an analysis viewpoint, timing constraints undermine the attractive property that all possible behavior of a real system is represented by the structure of the Petri net. More theory-oriented researchers oppose or simply ignore timing issues. However, over the course of years, timing has been recognized by more application-oriented researchers as crucial to examine the efficiency of real applications in areas like computer architecture design, communication protocols, manufacturing, logistics, software system analysis, and workflow redesign, e.g., Van der Aalst (1992), Jensen (1992), Van Hee (1994), Van der Aalst and Van Hee (1996).

Many different ways of incorporating time in Petri nets have been proposed. This is due the fact that different trade-offs can be made between the analyzability of the Petri net on the basis of the underlying net structure and the user's wish to adequately represent real-life phenomena. In the next sections, we will discuss the different aspects of incorporating time in Petri nets.

Location of the Delay

As described in this section, a Petri net consists of places and transitions connected via arcs. Therefore, time can be associated with places, transitions, or arcs. In most timed Petri net models, transitions determine time delays. In only a few models, time delays are determined by places and/or arcs. Although traditionally time is associated with transitions, authors such as Sifakis (1977, 1980) argue that it is more convenient to associate time to places since this leaves the original firing rule intact: enabling and firing are instantaneously. For high-level Petri nets with colored tokens (i.e., tokens carry a data value), it is most natural to attach time-stamps to tokens, as done by Jensen (1992), Van der Aalst (1993) and Van Hee (1994). The timestamp indicates the time a token becomes available for consumption. In the models presented by Jensen (1992), Van der Aalst (1993) and Van Hee (1994) transitions set the timestamps of produced tokens, i.e., time delays are determined by transitions.

Type of Delay

Independent of the choice where to put the delay (i.e., transitions, places, or arcs), several types of delays can be distinguished. We can make a distinction between deterministic, non-deterministic, and stochastic delays. Many of the early timed Petri net models by authors such as Ramchandani (1973), Sifakis (1977), Zuberek (1980), Wong et al. (1985), and Van Hee et al. (1989), use deterministic delays. This means that the delay assigned by a transition, place, or arc is fixed. Deterministic delays allow for simple analysis methods but have limited applicability. In real applications, delays correspond to the duration of activities which are typically variable. Therefore, fixed delays are often less appropriate. There are two ways to describe intrinsic variability in delays: non-deterministic and stochastic delays. Non-deterministic delays are specified using constraints, for example: it takes less than 15 minutes to type a letter. Stochastic delays are sampled from probability distributions.

Most of the models handling non-deterministic delays use time intervals to specify the duration of the delay. Merlin (1974, 1976) introduced such a model in the early seventies. Other models using interval timing have been proposed by Berthomieu and Menasche (1983), Berthomieu and Diaz (1991), Van der Aalst (1993, 1994), and Van der Aalst and Odijk (1995). However, most of the timed Petri net models use stochastic delays. In these models each delay is described by a probability distribution. To make analysis tractable, typically, only a restricted set of probability distributions is allowed. In the SPN model by Florin and Natkin (1982), only exponential delays (i.e., delays sampled from a negative exponential probability density function) are allowed. The widely used GSPN model by Marsan et al. (1984) allows for both immediate transitions (i.e., transitions with no delay) and timed transitions (i.e., transitions with exponential delays). Other types of probability distributions may only be applied if the topology of the net conforms to strict conditions, see Marsan et al. (1985).

Preselection and Race Semantics

Adding time to Petri nets requires a redefinition of the enabling and firing rules. In a classical Petri net the following statements holds: a transition is enabled if each of the input places contains enough tokens (typically one), only enabled transitions can fire, and firing is instantaneously (i.e., the moment tokens are consumed from the input places, tokens are added to the output places). Transitions are said to be in conflict if they share input places. Note that firing a transition in conflict with other transitions may disable some or all of these transitions. The choice between several enabled transitions in conflict with each other is resolved in a non-deterministic manner.

When adding time to a Petri net the enabling and firing rules need to be modified to specify how conflicts are resolved (i.e., the relation between enabling and firing) and whether firing is instantaneous or not (the semantics of the firing rule). Clearly, these two issues are related. Assume that transitions determine the delays. If firing is instantaneous (i.e., it does not take any time), then it is necessary to associate time to the enabling of a transition. But then, there is no need to explicitly define how conflicts are resolved. After all, enabled transitions "race" against each other and the one that is scheduled to fire first will fire. This firing/enabling semantics is called the race semantics. In Figure 2.2 the race semantics is illustrated.

In each of the three depicted situations, transitions t and u become enabled at the moment of the first small vertical bar. Each transition is timed to fire at the time depicted by its second vertical bar. With a dotted line, the moment that a conflict arises between these two transitions is depicted. In the situations (i), (ii), and (iii) transition t becomes respectively enabled before, simultaneously with, or after transition u becomes enabled. According to the race semantics, in each of the situations transition t will fire, because it is scheduled to fire first.

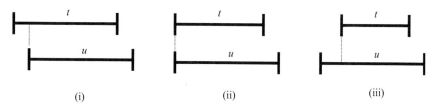

(i)   (ii)   (iii)

Fig. 2.2. The race semantics

It is also possible to specify the way conflicts are resolved more explicitly. This latter firing/enabling semantics is called the preselection semantics. For example, priorities or probabilities can be used to resolve conflicts. In the preselection semantics there is no race between enabled transitions: the moment transitions become enabled one of the enabled transitions is selected. Race semantics are typically combined with instantaneous firing, i.e., time is in the enabling of transitions. Therefore, we also use the term enabling delays to refer to these semantics. Preselection semantics are typically combined with holding times, i.e., tokens reside for some time inside a place or transition. Note that for race semantics the resolution of conflicts and the delay are handled by the same mechanism. For preselection semantics the mechanism to resolve conflicts is separated from the actual delay. Most of the stochastic Petri nets use race semantics, such as the nets by authors such as Florin and Natkin (1982), Marsan et al. (1984, 1985, 1986, 1995), Marsan (1990), and Balbo and Silva (1998). As established by Van der Aalst (1992), race semantics allow for a more direct translation to Markov chains.

Timed Petri nets using race semantics also are more expressive than timed Petri nets using preselection semantics. For example, race semantics allow for a compact representation of time-outs. Preselection semantics are more intuitive and easier to use. Therefore, most of the high-level Petri nets such as the ones described by Jensen (1992), Van der Aalst (1993) and Van Hee (1994) and support preselection semantics. Other authors such as Razouk and Phelps (1984) propose a mixture of race and preselection semantics.

For preselection semantics the delays (i.e., holding times) can be associated to the firing of a transition (e.g., Berthomieu and Diaz, 1991) or the minimal time a token spends in a place (e.g., described by Sifakis, 1980).

For race semantics the delays are associated to the enabling time. Note that an enabled transition can be disabled by another transition in case of a conflict. Such a transition loses the race and will not fire. If the transition becomes enabled again, a new race starts. In this new race there are several possibilities for the new enabling time of this transition. Authors such as Balbo and Silva (1984), Marsan et al. (1985, 1995) typically distinguish three so-called memory policies: age memory, enabling memory, and reset memory. For age memory, the remaining enabling time is frozen the moment the transition becomes disabled and is resumed the moment the transition becomes enabled again. For enabling memory, a new enabling time is sampled every time a transition becomes enabled, i.e., previously interrupted transitions have to start from scratch. For reset memory, a new enabling time is sampled every time a transition fires. This means that also transitions not in conflict with the transition that fired are interrupted and have to re-sample a new enabling time. It is interesting to note that for stochastic Petri nets with just exponential delays the three memory policies coincide. The memoryless property of the negative exponential probability density function makes the residual enabling time statistically equivalent to the originally sampled enabling time.

Capacity, Priority, and Queuing Policy

For timed Petri nets, the capacity of places and transitions is relevant. Places can have a limited capacity to restrict the number of tokens residing in a place at the same moment in time. Transitions can have a capacity to limit the number of concurrent enablings/firings of the same transition. Consider a transition with one input place containing three tokens. Is this transition enabled three times under race semantics? Can the transition fire concurrently with itself under preselection semantics? To answer these questions, we identify three types of capacity related semantics: single server semantics, multiple server semantics, infinite server semantics. For single server semantics the capacity of a place/transition is 1, for multiple server semantics the capacity of a place/transition is some integer k, and for infinite server semantics there are no capacity restrictions. Most timed Petri net models assume infinite server semantics.

Several timed net models allow for a priority mechanism. In other words, if multiple transitions compete for the same token, the transition with the highest priority fires. Note that the priority mechanism can be used for preselection purposes. In the widely used GSPN model by Marsan et al. (1984) immediate transitions (i.e., transitions with no delay) have priority over timed transitions.

Some Petri net models allow for the specification of queuing policies. However, since tokens in the same place (of the same color) are indistinguishable, it often does not make any sense to choose a queuing discipline. In general, priorities (i.e., not transition priorities but token priorities), random selection, and processor sharing are easy to handle in a stochastic Petri net, as established by Balbo and Silva (1984). State-dependent queuing disciplines such as first-come-first-served, last-come-first-served, longest-job-first, and earliest-due-date-first are more difficult to represent and analyze.

Network Topology

Another commonly applied trade-off that already has been mentioned previously is to restrict the topology of the net in favor of its analyzability. For event graphs, a Petri net subclass, Ramamoorthy and Ho (1980) and Chretienne (1983) have shown how their time behavior can be efficiently analyzed. The CPM and PERT modeling techniques (Evarts, 1964; Moder and Philips, 1964; Levin and Kirkpatrick, 1966) suppose acyclic event graphs with infinite server semantics and deterministic timing. The PERT technique additionally allows for delays on the basis of the beta distribution. With its successor, GERT (Graphical Evaluation and Review Technique) (Pritsker and Happ, 1966; Pritsker and Whitehouse, 1966; Neuman and Steinhardt, 1979), it is possible to model a wider variety of stochastic networks, using many different logical relations for the input and output sides of the nodes. The GERT technique extends the range to nets with (limited) parallel behavior, with specific types of cycles, and with arbitrary distributions. This subclass is called the STEOR network. GERT also supposes an infinite-server semantics.

2.4.5 Stochastic Workflow Nets

In this monograph we will use a stochastic workflow net model, as presented in this section. It is based on our definition of a Stochastic Petri net, which itself is a restricted version of the general Petri net model by Van Hee (1994). There are some important differences between the Stochastic Petri net model as defined in this paragraph and other timed Petri net models which we have discussed in the previous sections. These differences involve the following:

1. The resolution of conflicts.
2. The characterization of the delays.
3. The domain of the delay probability distributions.

In our Stochastic Petri net model a preselection semantics is used for the resolution of conflicts on the basis of the weights of the enabled transitions (see part c. of 0). This in contrast to the race semantics applied in, for example, the GSPN model. A race semantics is not very appropriate in applications such as the modeling of workflows for two important reasons, which are as follows:

1. Activities in a workflow are often performed by human resources whose work typically cannot (or will not) be cancelled upon completion of other activities.
2. Time is mostly not the argument on which conflicts are settled/choices are made; rather, conflicts are resolved on the basis of e.g., explicit properties of the work at hand.

The second important difference is that our Stochastic Petri Net model allows for arbitrary instead of merely negative exponential probability distribution functions in the GSPN model. The latter restriction is not very appropriate in settings such as workflows, where work is performed by both human resources and machines. As a result, the time patterns of the performed activities may be capricious. Approaches do exist to approximate general distribution functions with a combination of negative exponential probability distribution functions, the so-called Phase-Type distributions (e.g., Cumani, 1985). This approach requires the logical net structure to be adapted to reflect an approximately correct time behavior of the system. Our approach has the advantage that the analysis model can also be used to validate its complete behavior with naive users. This application of the process model is important in the redesign of workflows, the subject of Chapter 3.

Finally, the domain of the stochastic delay for each transition is discrete instead of continuous, unlike in most other timed Petri net models. In other words, delays will be measured in discrete units. The motivation is one of numerical and notational convenience. More specifically, the presented computational approaches in Chapter 4 can be illustrated and applied with more ease. The computations to be presented are, however, fundamentally the same for continuous and discrete time domains. In practice, the choice for a discrete time domain is never a limitation. It is always possible to use a fine-grained discrete time domain to approximate a continuous time domain, although this may have computational drawbacks. Whenever this is convenient, we will uniquely specify the probability density function ft by giving its related probability distribution function Ft.

Note that the definition of our Stochastic Petri net does not take resource constraints on the firing of transitions into account. We say that the Stochastic Petri net has an infinite server semantics. The (un)availability of resources is in general an important factor in the total time that is required to handle a case with an actual workflow. Within this model, the focus is on the intrinsic quality of the workflow by not regarding resources. In Chapter 5 we will extend the presented model to investigate the optimal allocation of resources.

Another, minor observation that can be made is that there are no priorities used in the definition of our Stochastic Petri net. It is not hard to extend the model in this direction, but the need does not arise for our purpose. Finally, it is noteworthy that tokens are uncolored. The firing of a transition is possible if each of its input places is filled with an indistinct token. As stated earlier in this section, this will not obstruct the analysis of workflows as each case will be treated separately.

Definition 2.16 (Stochastic Petri Net). A Stochastic Petri net is a tuple (P, T, R, W, f):
- (P, T, R) is a Petri net (see Definition 2.1),
- W: T → $\mathbb{N}^+$ (weight function),
- f: T → ($\mathbb{N}$ → [0,1]) (delay function) such that for $t \in$ T, f_t is a probability density function over $\mathbb{N}$.

A transition $t \in$ T is called *timed* if $f_t(n) > 0$ for some $n > 0$, $n \in \mathbb{N}$. A transition $t \in$ T is called *immediate* if $f_t(0) = 1$.

The weight function W is added to the standard Petri net to resolve conflicts during the execution of a Stochastic Petri net, as will be shown in Definition 2.19. The delay function f will be used to sample transition delays that represent the service time of actual task executions. Timed transitions may impose delays, while immediate transitions always have a zero delay. There is no formal distinction between these types of transitions with respect to conflict resolution, priority, etc., but for computation purposes their distinction will prove to be convenient.

In Figure 2.3 an example Stochastic Petri net is depicted. Recall that timed transitions may impose a positive delay; they are depicted as transparent blocks labeled with their identity. Places are also labeled with an identifier. Immediate transitions are depicted as black bars and are usually not labeled. Alongside a transition, its weight is given. Weights that equal 1 are usually omitted from a figure.

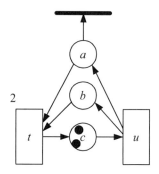

Fig. 2.3. A Stochastic Petri net example

A central notion to characterize the dynamic behavior of a Stochastic Petri net is its timed state. A timed state gives for each place the number of tokens it contains. Each token carries its own time stamp.

Definition 2.17 (Timed State). For a Stochastic Petri net SP = (P, T, R, W, f) the timed state space S: P → ($\mathbb{N}$ → $\mathbb{N}$) is defined. Any state of SP can be characterized with a timed state $s \in$ S. For any $p \in$ P, $s(p)$ is a finite bag (multi-set) of time labels over the alphabet $\mathbb{N}$.

The two black dots in place c of the example net in Figure 2.3 indicate a timed state with two tokens. We usually do not mention their labels in a figure. The availability of two tokens with time label 12 in place c for the example net can be represented by the state s with $s(a) = s(b) = \mathbf{0}$ and $s(c) = [\![12^2]\!]$.

Definition 2.18   (General initial timed state). For a Stochastic Petri net (P, T, R, W, f) with timed state space S, its *general initial timed state* $M_0 \in$ S is defined as:

$$\text{for } p \in \text{P, } M_0(p) = \begin{cases} [\![0]\!] & \text{if } p = i, \\ \mathbf{0} & \text{otherwise.} \end{cases}$$

The timed state M_0 represents the state of the system where the special source place i contains exactly one token, which carries the time stamp zero. As we will see, this is a convenient initial state for analysis purposes.

A timed state gives for each place of a Stochastic Petri net a specification of the number of tokens that reside in it, along with their time stamps. With the timed state, we can describe the stochastic process that a Stochastic Petri net brings forth.

Definition 2.19   (Stochastic Petri net behavior). A Stochastic Petri net (P, T, R, W, f) with time space S and initial timed state M induces a stochastic process SP = $\{ (X_n, Y_n, Z_n) \mid n = 0, 1, 2, \dots \}$. X_n is the timed state of the Stochastic Petri net after the n-th firing of a transition, Y_n is the transition that fires in timed state X_n, and Z_n is the delay that this transition imposes on the tokens it produces. The stochastic process SP is defined on an abstract probability space $(\Omega, \mathcal{F}, \mathbb{P})$ using the functions *first*, *time*, *fire* and g as follows:

1. The function *first* is an auxiliary function to identify for each place in a certain timed state the earliest time stamp of the (possibly many) tokens that reside in it: for $s \in$ S and $p \in$ P, $first(s(p)) = \min(\{ n \in \mathbb{N} \mid s(p)(n) \neq 0 \})$.

2. The function *time* gives for each timed state the first moment in time that a transition may fire:
   for $s \in$ S, $time(s) = \min_{t \in T} \max_{p \in \bullet t} first(s(p))$.

3. If a transition is a member of the set *fire(s)*, this indicates that it is a candidate for firing for a given timed state s:
   for $s \in$ S, $fire(s) =$
   $\{ t \in T \mid time(s) \in \mathbb{N} \land \max_{p \in \bullet t} first(s(p)) = time(s) \}$.

4. If a transition t fires, it removes from each of its input places one token with the earliest time stamp and it adds to each of its output places a token with a time stamp that equals the moment of firing added with a certain delay:

for $s \in S$, $t \in T$, $d \in \mathbb{N}$ and $p \in P$, $g(s, t, d)(p) =$

$$
\begin{cases}
s(p) & \text{if } p \notin \bullet t \text{ and } p \notin t\bullet, \\
s(p) - [\![first(s(p))]\!] & \text{if } p \in \bullet t \text{ and } p \notin t\bullet, \\
s(p) \uplus [\![time(s) + d]\!] & \text{if } p \notin \bullet t \text{ and } p \in t\bullet, \\
s(p) - [\![first(s(p))]\!] \uplus [\![time(s) + d]\!] & \text{if } p \in \bullet t \text{ and } p \in t\bullet.
\end{cases}
$$

For the stochastic process SP holds the following:
a. $X_0 = M$.
b. $X_{n+1} = g(X_n, Y_n, Z_n)$ for $n = 0, 1, 2, \ldots$.
c. The probability that a candidate transition fires is determined by its relative weight within the set of other candidates:

$$
\mathbb{P}[Y_n = t \mid X_n = s] = \begin{cases} \dfrac{w(t)}{\displaystyle\sum_{u \in fire(s)} w(u)} & \text{if } t \in fire(s), \\[2ex] 0 & \text{otherwise,} \end{cases}
$$

with Y_n, given X_n, independent of X_k, Y_k and Z_k for $k < n$.
d. The delay of a firing transition is independently sampled from the probability distribution that belongs to that transition:
$\mathbb{P}[Z_n = d \mid Y_n = t] = f_t(d)$, with Z_n given Y_n, independent of X_k, Y_k and Z_k for $k < n$.

Note that if for any timed state s holds that $time(s) = \infty$ then the Petri net has reached a dead state: no further firing of transitions is possible. After all, the set $fire(s)$ is empty. Also note that a stochastic Petri net is *eager*, i.e., if $time(s) < \infty$ then some transition t from $fire(s)$ will actually fire at $time(s)$. Although the firing of transitions is ordered, multiple transitions may fire at $time(s)$. For example, suppose that $g(s, t, d) = s'$ and $g(s', t', d') = s''$ then $time(s)$ may equal $time(s')$. Finally, note that SP is a discrete Markov chain.

Workflows

We will evaluate the performance of a workflow by analyzing a model of it in the form of a Stochastic Workflow Net.

Definition 2.20   (Stochastic Workflow net). A Stochastic Workflow net (SWN) is a tuple (P, T, R, W, f):
– (P, T, R) is a workflow net (see Definition 2.13),
– (P, T, R, W, f) is a Stochastic Petri net (see Definition 2.16).

Some important time notions can be defined on Stochastic Workflow nets.

Definition 2.21   (Marking time). If the SWN WF = (P, T, R, W, f) with general initial timed state M_0 induces the stochastic process $\{\ (X_n,\ Y_n,\ Z_n)\ |\ n = 0,\ 1,\ 2,\ \dots\ \}$, the random variable $\vartheta(p)$ for any place $p \in P$, the *marking time of p*, is defined as follows:

$$\vartheta(p) = \left(\min\ k, m \in \mathbb{N} : X_k(p)(m) \neq 0 : m \right).$$

If confusion can arise about the context of the marking time, we denote $\vartheta_{WF}(p)$.

The marking time is the earliest time that a certain place is marked. It evaluates to ∞ if the place is never marked.

We focus the performance analysis in this monograph on one of the most important performance indicators in industry, the *throughput time*. Although authors from different disciplines use different terminology for this concept such as *passage, response, sojourn, cycle, completion,* and *traversing time*, we stick to our term for reasons of popularity in the field of workflow management. The throughput time of a *specific case* is the total amount of time spent from the moment that the handling of the case started until the moment it is completed.

Definition 2.22   (Throughput time). For the sound SWN WF = (P, T, R, W, f) with general initial timed state M_0 that induces the stochastic process $\{\ (X_n,\ Y_n,\ Z_n)\ |\ n = 0,\ 1,2,\ \dots\ \}$, the random variable Γ – the *throughput time* of WF – is defined as the marking time of the sink place, $\vartheta(o)$. If confusion can arise about the context of the throughput time, we denote Γ_{WF}.

If an SWN is sound, then we know that eventually a dead state will be encountered on the basis of the general initial timed state. This dead state is the timed state where there is exactly one token in the sink place o with some time stamp. This is the throughput time that we are usually interested in.

The throughput time *of a workflow* is characterized by a distribution function that expresses the probability that an arbitrary case will require a certain throughput time.

Definition 2.23   (Throughput time distribution). For a sound SWN WF = (P, T, R, W, f) with initial timed state M_0 that induces the stochastic process $\{\ (X_n,\ Y_n,\ Z_n)\ |\ n = 0,\ 1,\ 2,\ \dots\ \}$, the *throughput time distribution* F_{WF} is defined as follows:

$$F_{WF}(n) = \mathbb{P}(\Gamma \leq n).$$

The throughput time distribution carries the complete information on the stochastic throughput time behavior of an SWN. Given a throughput time distribution F for some SWN, it is easy to compute throughput time characteristics such as expectation, variance, maximum, minimum, modus, etc. We end this paragraph with the definition of the throughput time density that at convenient places will be used instead of the throughput time distribution.

Definition 2.24 (Throughput time density). For a sound SWN WF = (P, T, R, W, f) with initial state M_0 that induces the stochastic process $\{ (X_n, Y_n, Z_n) \mid n = 0, 1, 2, \ldots \}$, the *throughput time density* f_{WF} is defined as follows:

$$f_{WF}(n) = \mathbb{P}(\Gamma = n).$$

This definition ends the introduction of the Petri net models used throughout this monograph for the modeling of workflows.

3 Workflow Design

In this chapter we will present a new approach for the design of a workflow, one of the main contributions of this monograph. The approach is product-based, which means that the characteristics of the product are pivotal for determining the structure of the workflow. It is in some sense similar to the approach used in manufacturing, where the Bill-of-Material of a product is used to arrange a production line. It is different from traditional workflow design approaches, which take an existing workflow as starting point and change it incrementally.

In general, designing a new workflow that aims at satisfying multiple, often conflicting performance targets is a complex job. To manage this complexity we will apply a separation of concerns. We adopt in this monograph the approach to first deal with distinguishing and specifying the tasks in a workflow and their interdependencies. In Section 2.2, we have called this the routing component of a workflow process, which can be seen as the structure of the workflow. Only then do we turn to the specification of the type of resources that will take care of carrying out the tasks, the exact responsibilities/functionality of these resources, and their availability. Confronted with real cases, the combined routing and allocation component determine the dynamics of the workflow.

The design of the structure of a workflow on the basis of product characteristics is the focus of this chapter, which is depicted as the thickly lined box in the top-right corner of Figure 3.1. The model describes the relevant entities in a workflow; it has been introduced in Section 1.4.

The particular order in designing the routing and allocation workflow components we propose cannot guarantee that the designed workflow is optimal from all viewing points. However, a simultaneous design is generally too complicated to handle, as the mutual influence of routing and allocation design decisions is large. For example, the shortage of one type of resource may influence the boundaries and ordering of tasks. Conversely, a specific structuring of tasks may make a specific type of resources obsolete. Although it can even be imagined that a reverse design order is followed – first specifying the resource quality, structure, and quantity and only then the task structure – it seems to be a more natural way to do it the other way around. In actual projects that we conducted (see Reijers and Goverde, 1999a; Van der Aalst et al., 2001; De Crom and Reijers, 2001) we practiced this approach.

H.A. Reijers: Design and Control of Workflow Processes, LNCS 2617, pp. 61-126, 2003.
© Springer-Verlag Berlin Heidelberg 2003

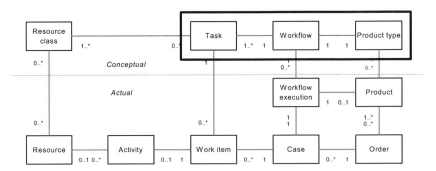

Fig. 3.1. Focus of chapter

Indeed, many documented BPR projects (e.g., Hammer and Champy, 1993) focus on redesigning the structure of the business process first. Note that approaches exist that mostly focus on redesigning the job profiles and responsibilities of resources, e.g., by Hupp et al. (1995). Typically, an existing routing component is then taken as the framework for such approaches. Such an approach may very well follow the task structure design approach that we propose in this chapter.

The workflow model as introduced in Chapter 2 will be used for specifying workflow designs throughout this chapter. One of the important phases in the overall method that we describe, is the thorough evaluation of a new workflow design (see Section 3.3). The performance evaluation algorithms of Chapter 4 can be used for this purpose. Chapter 5 can be seen as a logical sequel to the product-based design of the structure of a workflow, as the presented method can be used to assign resources to such a structure. Chapter 6 describes an alternative, heuristic way of redesigning workflows. In Chapter 7 we present case descriptions of the application of a product-based design in a Dutch social insurance company and a Dutch bank. These projects have been carried out by Deloitte & Touche Bakkenist in the years 1999 until 2001.

We start this chapter with a reflection on other business process design approaches. Next, we will discuss in Section 3.2 the essential idea behind a product-based design. In Section 3.3 the design method will be described in more detail. We end this chapter with Section 3.4, which is a review of the approach.

3.1 Process and Workflow Design

We have distinguished the actual design of a business process as the technical challenge of a BPR initiative (see Section 1.3). Although not each new process design takes place within a BPR project, it is the most common context for literature in this field. We include in this overview all methods that can be used for the diagnosis, redesign, modeling and evaluation of business processes. Most of the work does not explicitly focus on the design of workflows; we will explicitly mention it when this is the case.

We use the classification by Kettinger et al. (1997) who distinguish three levels of abstractions for methods with respect to business process design: methodologies, techniques, and tools. A methodology, the highest level of abstraction, is defined as a collection of problem-solving methods governed by a set of principles and a common philosophy for solving targeted problems. At the next level of abstraction, a technique is defined as a set of precisely described procedures for achieving a standard task. At the lowest, most concrete level a tool is defined as a computer software package to support one or more techniques. Obviously, methodologies, techniques, and tools can be linked in different ways. We will successively discuss tools, techniques, and methodologies.

3.1.1 Tools

There is much literature available devoted to the presentation and discussion of specific design tools, e.g., Hansen (1994), Jarzabek and Ling (1996), Min et al. (1996). The majority of the tools identified by Kettinger et al. (1997) focuses on the modeling of a business process, be it existing or new. A large number of tools is also available for the evaluation of business process models, in particular supporting the technique of simulation. An example is the tool ExSpect (Van Hee et al., 1989; Van der Aalst et al., 2000a). Fewer tools are available to structurally capture knowledge about the redesign directions or to support existing creativity techniques. Tools are often presented as "intelligent" or "advanced" (e.g., Calvert, 1994; Min et al., 1996), although they do not actively design business processes. The tool KOPeR-lite which generates alternative designs on the basis of a given business process model may be the exception; in some respects it even outperforms redesigns by humans with a novice BPR knowledge and experience (Nissen, 2000).

3.1.2 Techniques

With the survey conducted by Kettinger et al. (1997) a set of 72 techniques targeted at designing processes were identified. Among the encountered techniques for process diagnosis were e.g., fishbone diagramming, Pareto diagramming, and cognitive mapping. To support the activity of redesigning, creativity techniques like out-of-box-thinking, affinity diagramming, and the Delphi method (brainstorm) are available. For the modeling and/or evaluation of business processes, techniques are in use as flowcharting, IDEF, speech act modeling, data modeling, activity-based costing, time motion studies, Petri nets, role-playing, and simulation. Research in the field of developing new techniques is still very popular, as indicated by recent work of e.g., Janssens et al. (2000) and Sharp and McDermott (2001).

3.1.3 Methodology

According to Kettinger et al. (1997), design methodology is primarily the field of consulting firms who have developed proprietary BPR methods. Some researchers even question the need for or possibility of a design methodology, as they see process design as an inherent creative pursuit. Simision (1994) ridicules the development of a design methodology as follows: "To write a piano concerto, first take an HB pencil, select a key…". Hammer and Champy (1993) state: "Redesign [of a new process] is the most nakedly creative part of the entire reengineering process... it is not algorithmic and routine. There are no seven- or ten-step procedures that will mechanically produce a radical new process design." Research-oriented methodologies or initiatives for methodologies do exist, but there are relatively few of them. In saying this, we ignore mere listings of activities that should take place within a BPR project without describing in some detail: the activities themselves, the dependencies between these activities, the techniques that should be applied, and the deliverables of the activities.

We will use two criteria to further classify and discuss the technical BPR literature on design methodology. The first criterion is the starting point of a new business process design. The second criterion is the method of designing the process, which we see as the core of any BPR methodology. As we will see, dependencies exist between these criteria. Other but less distinctive comparison factors would be the way of strategy forming and process selection. These will not be discussed.

Starting Point

There are three possibilities for the developing of a new business process. One can do either of the following:

1. Take a *clean sheet* approach, i.e., the process is designed from scratch.
2. Take the *existing* process as a starting point.
3. Use a *reference model* as a template for the new process.

There is considerable discussion in literature on the choice between the first and second alternative (see e.g., O'Neill and Sohal, 1999). The opponents of the clean sheet approach identify four major drawbacks, leading them to advocate using the existing process as a starting point, which are as follows:

- There is the danger of designing another inefficient system (O'Neill and Sohal, 1999).
- The clean sheet approach fails to build on knowledge and experience which has been built up over time and risks mistakes of the past (Manganelli and Klein, 1994b; Peppard and Rowland, 1995; O'Neill and Sohal, 1999).
- Workers may be unable to relate to the new process as it bears little resemblance to the work that is being done (Peppard and Rowland, 1995).

– By designing a process completely from scratch the scope of the redesign problem is not appreciated (Manganelli and Klein, 1994b; Petrozzo and Stepper,
1994; O'Neill and Sohal, 1999).

On the other hand, Peppard and Rowland (1995) identify as a drawback from
taking the existing process as starting point that process innovations are less likely
to happen, although they are not impossible. Hammer and Champy (1993) are
very clear about their preference: "Reengineering is about beginning again with a
clean sheet of paper. It is about rejecting the conventional wisdom and received
assumptions of the past. Reengineering is about inventing new approaches to
process structure that bear little or no resemblance to those of previous eras". In
favor of the clean sheet approach, Gulden and Reck (1991) state that the secrets of
designing a process "lay not so much in intimately understanding the way it is performed today, but rather in thinking about how to reshape it for tomorrow". Peppard and Rowland (1995) identify the dangers of analyzing existing processes in
too great a depth and becoming constrained by them when trying to think of new
ways of working.

Taking the existing process as a starting point is in practice the most common
way of developing a new business process, as observed e.g., by Aldowaisan and
Gaafar (1999). Peppard and Rowland (1995) suggest that the clean sheet approach
has more attraction to Western companies, while Japanese manufacturers try to
work from the existing processes. This may be due to cultural and economic differences. They also note that it is common to see organizations occasionally start
the design of a new process from a clean sheet, after which they apply several
smaller improvement projects to the newly designed process, as a means of continuous improvement.

The third, possible start point for a new process design – which we have not
discussed so far – is a so-called reference model. The reference model serves as a
template for a business process design that can be subsequently refined to match
the specific demands or objectives on the business process. The MIT Center for
Coordination Science (Dellarocas and Klein, 2000) maintains a repository of this
kind of business process templates for specific fields of operations. Reference
models are usually derived from earlier process design outcomes and typically describe essential process ingredients on an abstract level. Therefore, a reference
model approach can be seen as a compromise between a clean sheet and an existing process approach. Existing processes are the inspiration for the redesign, although it may be radically new for the organization in question.

Method

Concerning the method of designing the process a possible classification of the existing BPR methodology is as follows:

1. *Participative*: based on involving and stimulating a group of experts in the design of a new business process.

2. *Analytical*: based on an explicit recognition of design parameters and degrees of freedom, using algorithms or logic to yield a new business process.

Obviously, these characteristics are not completely mutually exclusive. The common practice of designing business processes is to use a participative methodology. Reijers and Voorhoeve (2000) have observed this in practice, but it can also be concluded from the abundance of creativity techniques aimed at supporting a participative BPR methodology. In fact, Kettinger et al. (1997) list creativity techniques such as brainstorming and out-of-box-thinking as the only techniques available to support the redesign stage within a BPR project. A common, participative approach to design a new business process is that management consultants encourage specialists, employers and managers within the setting of a workshop to think of alternatives to the existing business process or to think of completely new processes. The role of the external consultants is to manage the workshop and to stimulate people to abandon the traditional beliefs they may have about the process in question. A well-chosen delegation of internal specialists and managers should ensure that all expertise is available that is required to make a process design. Sometimes, consultants or academics are also hired for their intrinsic knowledge of a specific field of operations. Both Peppard and Rowland (1995) and Sharp and McDermott (2001) describe such a workshop-centered approach to design business process.

An analytical methodology builds upon analytical techniques to come up with a new process design. Hansen (1994) argues that the complexity of BPR efforts requires scientific, analytical techniques, as non-analytical, informal approaches lead to many failures of BPR projects. He claims that business process behavior depends on many interrelated parameters, which cannot be dealt with in an informal way. However, most of the material that relates to analytical BPR methodology does not really qualify as mature methodology. Rather, these are technical principles or heuristics that may be used to render superior new business process. In this sense, they are sometimes close to BPR techniques. Hammer and Champy (1993) present technical BPR principles, for example: tasks in a business process should be combined into larger tasks, a case manager is appointed as a single point of contact, and the number of checks and controls in a process should be reduced. Similar principles are presented by the following researchers:

- Rupp and Russell (1994) who give a summary of 16 principles, e.g., avoid intra-organizational dependencies and shared responsibilities, create more multi-skilled workers, design activities to run in parallel paths.
- Peppard and Rowland (1995) who identify and break down four core groups of principles that must lead to the elimination, simplification, integration and automation of work.
- Berg and Pottjewijd (1994) who identify and illustrate six forms of process improvement: elimination, integration, broadening, parallelization, volume increase, and effectiveness increase.
- Poyssick and Hannaford (1996) who list 36 process improvement rules.

– Van der Aalst and Van Hee (2002) who list 15 heuristic rules for the redesign of workflows, e.g., initially ignore the existence of resources when designing, consider specialization of generalized tasks, let resources work on the same case as much as possible.

Most of these directions are characterized by the tacit assumption that an existing business process is taken as the starting point of a new design. By locally applying a reengineering principle, the performance of the total business process is boosted. The principles presented are often derived from experience gained within large companies or by consultancy firms with repetitive application of these principles in BPR engagements. For example, the rules as proposed by Peppard and Rowland (1995) are derived from the experiences of the Toyota Company. Generally, many of the BPR principles lack an adequate (quantitative) support, as noted by e.g., Van der Aalst (2000a). Buzacott (1996), Seidmann and Sundararajan (1997), Van der Aalst (2000b), and Zapf and Heinzl (2000) provide analytical or quantitative support for the superiority of some of the BPR principles available. Chapter 6 gives a more thorough overview of these principles.

Analytical Approaches

Approaches that exceed merely summarizing BPR principles and come close to an analytical design methodology are provided by Orman (1998), Aldowaisan and Gaafar (1999), Van der Aalst (2000b) and Hofacker and Vetschera (2001). We will discuss each of these and make a comparison with the product-based design approach presented in the remainder of this chapter.

Orman (1998) presents a so-called model management approach, which could be seen as the basis of an analytical BPR methodology. In this approach, business processes are seen as decision models. The purpose of a business process is to limit an initially wide search space until a decision can be made. Tasks in a business process reduce uncertainty as to which final decision should be made. For example, the tasks in a business process to decide whether a mortgage loan should be granted may involve checking whether an applicant is a homeowner and whether he or she has a sufficient salary. Only applicants that satisfy both criteria may be granted a mortgage loan. Based on a given set of tasks, each with a specific cost and an expected reduction rate of uncertainty, an optimal ordering of tasks can be given in terms of expected cost. The model management approach also incorporates the issue whether tasks within a business process should be shared across different processes. These results are less convincing, as Orman believes that sharing may lead to different orderings. This is not quite justified in the light of WfMS's (see Section 1.4). Note that the model management approach does not take an initial process structure as starting point.

Aldowaisan and Gaafar (1999) present an approach, that takes a process design structure as a set of logically related tasks on the one hand and resources that yield a certain output on the other. In the first phase of their approach, the heuristics of Hammer (1990) are used to eliminate, integrate, and automate tasks within an existing business process to create a better design. In the second phase it is assumed that the search space for a further improved design structure is defined by two parameters: the number of employee types and the number of process tasks. In their approach, all different mappings of tasks on resource types are evaluated, the so-called process mappings. They proceed to show how to find the optimal process structure by balancing a quantitative cost and qualitative profit interpretation. Cost is expressed as the amount of training required to let resources perform tasks for which they were not initially capable. Profit is measured in terms of a simplified resource structure (fewer resource types) and the degree in which the case manager principle can be implemented (as few persons as possible execute tasks for a specific case; see also Section 6.1). A final check on the feasibility of the process map is executed by checking whether a sufficient number of resources is available. Note that Aldowaisan and Gaafar follow the same route of designing the routing component first and successively the allocation component as we have proposed in the introduction of this chapter.

Van der Aalst (2000b) focuses on the design of a typical pattern found within many workflow processes in practice, a so-called knock-out process. A knock-out process consists of a set of tasks that are used to decide whether a specific case should be accepted or rejected. Each task may lead to a rejection – the knock-out – and only if all tasks have a positive result the case is accepted (see also Section 6.1). Van der Aalst gives a heuristic rule to order tasks within the same resource class to minimize the throughput time, given the rejection and failure rates of all tasks, as well as their average processing time. The applied model and optimization rule is similar to that of Orman (1998). Van der Aalst extends this heuristic to the case where different resource classes are available and an unbalanced occupation rate may affect the throughput time negatively. Heuristics are provided also when to combine tasks so that by reducing set-up times the average throughput time is minimized (see also Section 6.1). Finally, heuristic conditions are distinguished when tasks should be put in parallel, possibly yielding a shorter throughput time but also increasing the resource utilization (see also Section 6.1).

Hofacker and Vetschera (2001) approach a process design effort as the problem of selecting the right subset of tasks out of a set of potential tasks. In their basic model, a task consumes one input and produces one output. They refer to these inputs and outputs as "resources". At the start of a process design, an initial set of resources is available and another set of resources is desired as the global output of the process. A process design is a totally ordered subset of tasks, which is said to be feasible if (a) for each task its input is available when it starts (either because it is part of the initial set or because it is produced by a preceding task) and (b) all global outputs are produced by executing the tasks in the design. Three solution strategies are investigated for finding such a subset, respectively mathematical programming, direct branch and bound methods, and genetic algorithms. They show that the first two strategies deliver results with an acceptable performance for rather small models. Although the formalization of the problem in their approach is rather elegant, it is characterized by an overly simple structure of the optimization function. In particular, the specific ordering of the tasks does not affect this function; it only takes into account the membership of a task in the process design. So, for example, the effect of parallel executions of tasks on the speed of processing cannot be measured. Also, alternative paths cannot be processing cannot be measured. Also, alternative paths cannot be incorporated in their notion of feasible processes, which is a strict abstraction of real workflows.

The focus for the four described approaches differs. We will elaborate on these differences by using the phases in a BPR effort as distinguished by Van der Aalst and Van Hee (2002). Orman (1998), Van der Aalst (2000b), and Hofacker and Vetschera (2001) focus on deriving an optimal routing component. On the other hand, the main point of the approach by Aldowaisan and Gaafar (1999) is on determining an allocation component on the basis of a given routing component. In the view of Van der Aalst and Van Hee (2002), designing the process structure should precede the allocation of resources, so in this sense these two types of approaches are supplementary. Typical for all four described approaches is that a notion of tasks should exist before the approach is applied. Aldowaisan and Gaafar (1999) do allow for an initial phase where task elimination, integration and automation can take place and Van der Aalst (2000b) even gives guidance on the conditions when to combine tasks. However, the analytical framework does not incorporate the evaluation on what should be done: which tasks are relevant for successfully executing the business process. This is one of the major distinctive factors of the approach that we will present in the following sections. We argue that this aspect is required for any approach to be applied as a design methodology.

3.2 Product-Based Workflow Design

3.2.1 The Relation between Process and Product

The Industrial Revolution at the end of the eighteenth century called for a new type of organization: labor became divided into specialties. This principle allowed for a fantastic increase in production output on the factory floor. Soon afterwards, this principle was applied in the growing field of office work and with similar success. Product-Based Workflow Design (PBWD) is a workflow design methodology that also translates a typical manufacturing concept to office work – the common context of workflows. In Section 1.5 we already explored some of the differences and similarities between workflow and logistical management. A typical characteristic in manufacturing is that the structure of the product is used to derive the manufacturing process. This principle is illustrated in Figure 3.2.

The figure represents how the structure of a product is used to determine the steps that should be taken to manufacture it, i.e., the process. The product in Figure 3.2 is schematically depicted as a large box. This box consists of three smaller black, white and gray boxes, which are combined in a specific way. The depicted process to produce such a product first fits together the black and white box (step 1.), after which this subassembly is placed on top of the gray box (step 2.). It is clear that this simple production process indeed delivers boxes of the desired elements and composition. Note that without further restrictions it seems possible to design alternative production ways composing the same product, e.g., first fitting together the black and gray boxes and then placing the white box between them.

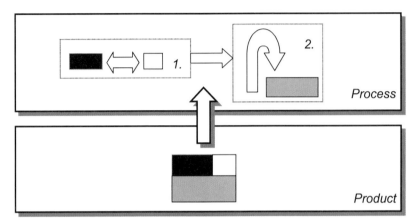

Fig. 3.2. The relation between product and process

The structure of the product in manufacturing is specified with a Bill-Of-Material (BOM) (Orlicky, 1972). The BOM is a tree-like structure with the end product as root and raw materials and purchased products as leafs. In the resulting graph, the nodes correspond to products, i.e., end-products, raw materials, purchased products, and subassemblies. The edges are used to specify composition relations (i.e., is-part-of relations). The edges have a cardinality to indicate the number of products needed. Figure 3.3 shows the simplified BOM of a car, which is composed of an engine and a subassembly. The subassembly is composed of four wheels and one chassis.

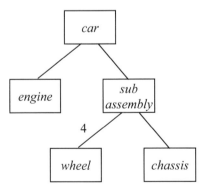

Fig. 3.3. The BOM of a car

If we take a look at, for example, Material Requirements Planning (often referred to as MRP-I), we see that it determines the production schedule based on the ordered quantifies, current stock, and the composition of a product as specified in the BOM. Contemporary Enterprise Resource Planning (ERP) systems such as SAP also take resource availability into account and use more refined algorithms.

The important observation here is that the manufacturing process is driven by *the structure of the product*. For example, in the production line for cars with a BOM like in Figure 3.3 the sub-assembly of the wheel and chassis will precede the final assembly step of the entire car.

In contrast to manufacturing, the product and the process have often diverged in actual workflow processes. Workflows found in banks and insurance companies for products like credit, savings and mortgages, damage and life insurance, etc. may well exist for decades. Since their first release, those processes have undergone an *organic evolution*. For example, historical problems in performing certain computations have resulted in the addition of calculatory checks. Another example is the effect that a historical case of fraud may have on a process. A very restrictive type of control may be added in answer. Aside from the evolutionary changes of the process, the state of technology of some decades ago has considerably influenced the structure of these workflows permanently. For example, it used to be laborious to make a copy of a client file. Therefore, in many actual workflows a highly sequential structure of tasks can be distinguished, where at most one person at a time works on an order. It is difficult to migrate from this original set-up of a workflow in an evolutionary way. In summary, the structure of an actual workflow may not be related to the product characteristics any more.

Clearly, for manufacturing process and workflows alike, there is a relation between the product and the process: the very justification of a workflow's existence is the generation of a specific type of product. As we have argued in Section 1.4 workflows are mostly of the mass-customization type. On the basis of a clear a priori notion of a standard product, product instances are delivered to clients, which may be slightly customized to the preferences of the client in question. The characteristics of the standard product are often described in administrative procedures, marketing material, internal regulations and product development materials. Mass customization is also accompanied by a high turnover volume. Financial institutions, utility companies, and government agencies are typical sectors that deliver mass customized products. The loose coupling between the product notion and the process structure in this setting is, at closer inspection, rather mysterious. We propose that analyzing the product specification may be a feasible and attractive starting point for designing workflow processes in this area. This is the fundamental idea behind PBWD.

To see how this would work, consider for example the processing of insurance claims. The product to be delivered on the basis of an actual claim is basically a decision: either the claim is accepted – followed by a payment – or the claim is rejected. (Note that this way of looking at a workflow as a knock-out process is similar to some of the design methodologies we presented at the end of the previous section.) All kinds of information elements may play a role in making this decision, like the amount of damage, the claim history of the claimant, and the coverage of the insurance. For example, one of the standard conditions of the insurance policy may specify that if the amount of damage is below a certain threshold, the claimant has not issued a claim for over a year and the damage is covered, then the claim is accepted and the damage paid. This hypothetical condition can be seen as a part of the insurance product specification. The information elements can be seen as raw materials or subassemblies for the production of a decision. The workflow process should "manufacture" the decision by distinguishing tasks to retrieve and asses the required information elements, while taking criteria such as average throughput time, service level, handling costs, and product quality into account. The latter are typically no characteristics of the product, but performance targets (see Section 1.1).

3.2.2 Characterization

PBWD is a prescriptive methodology that is concerned with the technical side of BPR. It is not a project management approach, nor does it pretend to cover the change management issues of innovations. (Note that the development of prototypes on the basis of PBWD deliverables may be an effective support of managing the change, see Section 3.3.4.) We defined the technical side of BPR in Section 1.3.2 as the issue of developing a process design that is a radical improvement of a current design. We identified the starting point and the method as distinguishing features of BPR methodologies in this field. Considering these features, PBWD takes a clean sheet approach; it explicitly does not take the existing process as a starting point. Furthermore, it is analytical in its approach in contrast to popular, participative approaches. Based on our literature survey (see Section 3.1), we conclude that it is one of the very few existing methodologies with these characteristics.

PBWD builds upon an idea as published by Van der Aalst (1999), where enhanced BOM's are described that allow for an automatic generation of workflows. Verster (1998) already described the decomposition of an informational product into data elements within the context of business process redesign. Although he proposes the structuring of this type of data for the purpose of simplifying the product and the process, no methodical derivation or optimization of the workflow from this structure is presented. These are specific characteristics of the PBWD design methodology, as will become clear from the following sections.

3.3 PBWD Methodology

In this section we will first outline the PBWD methodology. Then, we will discuss each of the phases in more detail, including a description of their deliverables. The phases that can be distinguished within a PBWD effort are as follows:

1. *Scoping*
   In this initial phase the workflow is selected that will be subject to the redesign. The performance targets for this workflow are identified, as well as the limitations to be taken into consideration for the final design.

2. *Analysis*

A study of the product specification leads to its decomposition into information elements and their logical dependencies. The existing workflow – if any – is diagnosed to retrieve data that is both significant for designing the new workflow and for the sake of evaluation.

3. *Design*

Based on the reengineering objectives, the product specification decomposition and estimated performance figures, several alternative workflow structures are derived. A workflow structure consists of tasks that retrieve or process information elements.

4. *Evaluation*

The alternative workflow structures are verified, validated with end-users and their estimated performance is analyzed in more detail. The most promising designs are presented to the commissioning management to assess the degree in which objectives can be realized and to select the most favorable workflow design.

These phases are presented in a sequential order, but in practice it is very plausible and sometimes desirable that iterations will take place. For example, the evaluation phase is explicitly aimed at identifying design errors, which may result in rework on the design. The focus of this section will be on the analysis and design phases of PBWD.

3.3.1 Scoping

Workflow Selection

An important aim for the scoping phase is to select the workflow that is to be designed or redesigned. More specific, it aims at identifying the product of which the corresponding workflow is to be designed.

The selection of a product-workflow combination can be made on various grounds (see Hammer and Champy, 1993; Hupp et al., 1995; Sharp and McDermott, 2001). If there is a new product developed by e.g., the marketing and product management departments, then the motivation for designing the workflow is clear. If an existing workflow is taken to be redesigned, selection criteria may be as follows:

- *Dysfunctionality of the workflow.* Typical symptoms of dysfunctional processes are: extensive information exchange, data redundancy, long throughput times, high ratio of controls and iterations, many procedures for exception handling and special cases, poor service quality and client satisfaction, and conflicts across departments. Benchmarks or experience may be used to decide on the seriousness of these figures.

- *Importance of the workflow.* A workflow may contribute more or less to the critical success factors of a company, its profitability, client satisfaction, market share, etc.
- *Feasibility of redesign.* A redesign effort is more likely to succeed when the workflow is directly linked to the needs of clients, when the scope of the workflow becomes smaller (but then the pay-off drops), when expected redesign costs become less, and when knowledge about the product, design approach and the existing workflow are available in larger quantities.

In practice, the various criteria for selecting a workflow to be redesigned are different for each company and even for each BPR effort.

Workflow Boundaries

After selecting the proper product/workflow combination it is important to fix the boundaries of the workflow to be redesigned. Important for these boundaries are the logical, locational, and client-centered viewpoints. We will briefly discuss each of these viewpoints. Note that in actual settings, other criteria may be more relevant.

In practice, what different departments may see as the logical start and end of a workflow may differ. For a sales person, the workflow for mortgage applications is ended when a signed contract is returned by the client. However, various operations in the back-office may be required to fulfill the mortgage offering. A logical start state and end state should be determined for the workflow that is to be redesigned prior to the design itself.

The second viewpoint for the boundaries concerns the location of the workflow. Similar existing workflows may be executed at different locations, e.g., in different offices or countries. The question should be solved for which locations the redesign will be effectuated. This issue will determine the types of systems that are incorporated, which kind of regulations are in effect, which performance is desirable, and which people are involved.

The last important viewpoint for the boundaries of a workflow concerns the client. Similar products may be offered to different types of clients. A typical distinction within a banking environment is to distinguish between well-to-do and other clients. Depending on the type of client, different procedures or product characteristics can be relevant.

Redesign Objectives

An important and often neglected activity during the scoping phase of a redesign initiative is to explicitly formulate the redesign objectives (see Van der Aalst and Van Hee, 2002). Aside from the performance targets such as throughput time, operational cost, and required labor hours that should be met by the newly designed workflow, the redesign initiative itself may have to be executed within a certain time, quality, and budget framework. Something that is even less frequently executed is so-called null measurement (see Van der Aalst and Van Hee, 2002). A null measurement establishes the score of the performance targets just before the redesign is carried out. Such a measurement enables the formulation of sensible target values and makes an ex-post evaluation possible.

Feasibility

The discussed elements of the scoping phase so far are general and applicable for all kinds of redesign efforts. To determine the feasibility of the PBWD approach to design a particular workflow it is of the utmost importance that there is a well-defined notion of the product to be delivered by this workflow. Actual manifestations of such a product notion are handbooks, internal regulations, procedure codifications, legislations, product specifications, etc. It is inevitable for a proper assessment of the feasibility of a redesign of PBWD that during the scoping phase a collection takes place of the materials that define the product specification.

Even if there is no physical manifestation of a product specification, it may very well be that the concept of a product does exist with e.g., marketers, product managers, or general management. It is important to check the maturity and concreteness of these notions. If they are sufficiently mature, it is required before the next phase of analysis starts that an explicit product specification is defined.

Black Boxes

Another specific aspect of the PBWD approach is found within the definition of the boundaries of the workflow. More specific, it is important to establish which existing information processing applications that support the current workflow are to be maintained in their existing form.

In many settings where the redesign of workflows is due, the workflow is primarily involved with information processing, aside from some limited physical operations (see Section 1.4.2). Therefore, computer applications may implement major parts of a workflow by carrying out specific tasks. As computer systems may be used in different workflows and also have a limited score on the maintainability scale, it often is considered unattractive to change existing systems as part of a redesign initiative. It is then important to distinguish the exact functionality that is to be preserved, the so-called black boxes. Distinguishing black boxes has its effect on the design effort. On the one hand a black box will simplify the analysis and design of the corresponding information processing part in the workflow. On the other hand, too many black boxes will obstruct a radical redesign of the workflow.

An example of a black box that we encountered during the redesign of a credit loan workflow was a system that was used to generate benchmarks on the basis of financial information on clients. This system was used in workflows for many other products, such as mortgages and insurances. The system was treated as a black box. Only its inputs and its outputs were analyzed.

A summary of the activities in the scoping phase is given in Figure 3.4. The deliverables of the scoping phase are as follows:

Scoping	
General	PBWD specific
Select workflow : *dysfunctionality, importance, feasibility*	Asses feasibility: *establish product specification*
Fix boundaries: *logical, locational, customers*	Fix boundary: *establish black boxes*
Determine performance targets: *zero setting, objectives*	

Fig. 3.4. The scoping phase

- A precisely demarcated workflow process to be designed.
- Performance targets for the new design.
- A product specification.
- Black boxes within the workflow.

3.3.2 Analysis

The Product Data Model

In the analysis phase, all distinguished materials that classify as product specification are analyzed to identify information elements, their dependencies, and the logic involved. For a proper representation of this information the traditional BOM found in manufacturing is not entirely suitable. This is due to several differences between informational products and physical products (see Section 1.5). These differences lead to two important updates of the traditional BOM. First, the same piece of information may be used to manufacture various kinds of new information. Therefore, also non-tree-like structures are possible. For example, the age of an applicant for a life insurance may be used to estimate both (a) the involved health risks and (b) the risks of work related accidents. Secondly, there are no physical constraints and therefore there are typically multiple ways to derive a piece of information. For example, health risks may be estimated using either a questionnaire or a full medical examination.

Before we present a formal product data model that incorporates the required information with the above observations, we present a graphical example of such a model in Figure 3.5. All nodes in this figure correspond to information elements that are may be used to decide whether a candidate is suitable to become a helicopter pilot in the Dutch Air force. We will refer to this model throughout this chapter as the Helicopter Pilot product data model. Arcs are used to express the dependencies between them. Unlike the BOM in Figure 3.3 there are no cardinal-ities. (The method does not fundamentally exclude cardinalities, so they may be added if required.) The meaning of the information elements is as follows:

- – *a*: suitability to become a helicopter pilot.
- – *b*: psychological fitness.
- – *c*: physical fitness.
- – *d*: latest result of suitability test in the previous two years.
- – *e*: quality of reflexes.
- – *f*: quality of eye-sight.

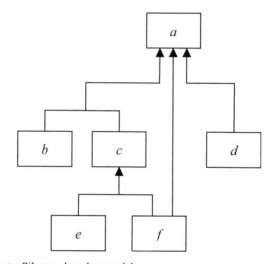

Fig. 3.5. Helicopter Pilot product data model

Each incoming arc of a node signifies an alternative way of determining a value for the corresponding information element. If outgoing arcs of multiple nodes are joined, this means that values of all of the corresponding information elements are required to determine a value for the information element the arrow leads to.
One of the things that is expressed in the figure is that there are three ways to de-termine information element *a*. The suitability of a candidate (*a*) can be deter-mined on the basis of either of the following:

1. The combined results of the psychological test (*b*) and the physical test (*c*).
2. The result of a previous suitability test (*d*).
3. The candidate's eye-sight quality (*f*).

In reality, these different ways may be applicable under different conditions. It can be imagined that if a pilot's eye-sight is extremely bad (*f*), then this directly gives a result that the candidate is not suitable (*a*). However, in a more common case, the eye-sight quality is one of the many aspects that are incorporated in a physical test (b), which should be combined with the outcome of the psychological test (c) to determine the suitability result (a). Also, not for each candidate that applies a previous test result (d) is available. But if there is one of a recent date, it can be used directly.

From the Helicopter Pilot product data model, it becomes clear how the dependencies between data may be used to derive a favorable design. For example, if the target is to minimize the cost it may be wise to check first whether there is a previous test result and next to check the eyes of the candidate. Only if these checks do not lead to rejecting the candidate, a full examination is additionally required. Obviously, the expected cost of all these activities really determine whether this is a good design.

Note that the figure resembles an AND/OR graph, as used in Artificial Intelligence research: a graph or tree structure describing the decomposition of a goal in terms of alternative subgoals (OR nodes) or combinations of subgoals that must all be satisfied (AND nodes) (APDST, 1995).

To formalize the model of related information elements, we introduce the product data model.

Definition 3.1   (Product data model). A product data model is a tuple $(D, C, pre, F, constr)$ with:

- D: a set of information elements, with a special top element:
  - $\underline{top} \in D$,
- C: a set of constraints; a constraint can be any Boolean function; the function that always yields *true* – denoted *true* – is part of C:
  - *true* $\in C$,
- the function *pre* gives for each information element the various ways of determining a value for it on the basis of the values of (different) sets of other information elements:
  $$pre : D \to \mathcal{P}(\mathcal{P}(D)), \text{ such that}$$
- there are no 'dangling' information elements and a value of a information element does not depend on itself:
  $$R = \{(p, c) \in D \times D \mid c \in \bigcup_{es \in pre(p)} es \} \text{ is connected and acyclic,}$$
- the top element cannot be used for determining the value of any other information element:
  $$\forall (p,c) \in R : c \neq \underline{top},$$
- if there is a set of information elements that can be used for the value of another, this set is not empty:
  $$\forall e \in D : \varnothing \notin pre(e),$$
- F: a set of production rules, based on the definition of *pre*, extended with 'empty' rules for elements that do not require values of other information elements:

$$F = \{\ (p,\ cs) \in\ D \times \mathcal{P}(D)\ |\ cs \in\ pre(p)\ \}\ \cup$$
$$\{\ (p,\ \varnothing)\ |\ p \in D \wedge\ pre(p) = \varnothing\},$$

- the function *constr* that associates a constraint to each production rule:

  constr : $F \to C$, such that

  - there are no constraining conditions on producing elements that do not require values of other information elements:

    $$\forall e \in D : pre(e) = \varnothing \Rightarrow constr(e, \varnothing) = true$$

The product data model identifies information elements, represented by the set *D*, and expresses the relations between them with the function *pre*. These relations are relevant for producing a value for the information element <u>top</u>. Determining a value for this element will be seen as the goal of the workflow to be designed. For analysis purposes it is convenient to identify a single top element, as will become clear. Note that it is always possible to distinguish exactly one information element <u>top</u>: if there is more information that should be available at the end of executing a workflow, an imaginary <u>top</u> information element may be distinguished that combines all this information. Note that in the example of Figure 3.5, information element *a* is the top element.

The *pre* function of the product data model yields for each information element *d* one or more ways to determine a value for *d*. If for information elements *d, e, f* $\in D$, we suppose that $\{e, f\} \in pre(d)$, then a value of *d* may be determined on the basis of values of *e* and *f*. We say that $(d, \{e, f\})$ is a *production rule* for *d*. We will consider *e* and *f* as *inputs* for a calculation of *output d*. Note that in the example of Figure 3.5, three production rules are in effect to determine a value for the top element *a*.

Note that each production rule for an information element *d* with $pre(d) = \varnothing$ is special. The information element *d* is called a *leaf*. Note that the information elements *b, e, f* and *d* in the example of Figure 3.5 are leafs. No other information elements are required to determine the value of a leaf. There are also no constraints to determine the value of a leaf. Leafs represent information elements of which the values cannot be produced from the values of other information elements that fall within the reengineering scope. Typically, these values have to be retrieved from a client or a third party. They may even already be available to the workflow owner.

Just as there can be different production rules for the same information element, the production rules may be applicable under different circumstances as well. For the rule $(d, \{e, f\})$, $constr(d, \{e, f\})$ yields a Boolean function. For example, supposing that the value of information element is a numerical, $constr(d, \{e, f\})$ may take on the form 'the value of *e* is larger than 5'. Only if this function evaluates to true when the production rule is attempted to be applied with real values of *e* and *f*, the rule $(d, \{e, f\})$ can indeed be applied. As in the example, typically aspects of other information elements play a role in this evaluation. Although in reality these dependencies may be very complex, we abstract from these dependencies by allowing only references in a constraint to values of the inputs of the respective production rule. Note that constraints are not depicted in the example.

The model as presented is the basic form of the product data model. Later in this section, we will discuss two types of extensions. The first is administrative by nature and facilitates the use of the product data model in a practical encounter. The second extension formalizes performance data involved with the application of the specific production rules (see Definition 3.2). This data is used for designing efficient workflows.

Note that for black boxes established in the analysis phase it is also required to distinguish their inputs and outputs. For example, within the project we conducted for a Dutch bank, there was a system in use for determining the market rate. This system was no subject to reengineering. Because of the valuable information it produced, the system's inputs had to be obtained as well.

Product Specifications

A product data model must be derived from the product specification that has been established in the scoping phase. Internal procedures at banks, insurance companies, and government agencies often already have as a feature that they have some structure. This is typically the field of the Administrative Organization / Internal Control. Although there are no guarantees, such a structure often implies that when an information element is mentioned for the first time either a procedure may follow shortly that explains how it is determined or a reference can be found to a definition elsewhere. This is especially the case in legal settings, where law books may be the actual product specifications. It is very important to stick as closely as possible to official documentation that expresses the workflow owner's policy. Obviously, experts may be consulted when there is difficulty in interpreting the product specification. This must be balanced against the risk of incorporating operational instead of factual information in the product data model.

Example 1

The following is an excerpt of the stipulations of a Dutch bank concerning medium length business loans:

The funds for a medium length loan that is made available to a client but which is not withdrawn by the client must be placed on the money market. If the funding cost of the loan is higher than the rewards of the temporary placing, this difference is the basis for the monthly disposal provision... The disposal provision amounts to half of this difference with a minimum of 1/12 % per month... The disposal provision should be part of the loan proposal.

In this excerpt, the "disposal provision" is defined as a relevant information element for bringing out a loan proposal to a client, which we take as the top element for the involved proposal process. Note that this element depends on other elements such as the "funding cost" and the "temporary placing rewards" which are not fully defined in this text.

Example 2

The excerpt that follows is part of article 17 of the Dutch Unemployment Law:

The right for an unemployment allowance arises for an employee if he has worked as an employee at least 26 weeks of the 39 weeks immediately preceding the first day of unemployment, and ...

If we assume the right for an unemployment allowance as an essential piece of information to determine the size of the unemployment allowance for an applicant, we gather a part of its definition from this excerpt. Other relevant information elements are: "employee", "first day of unemployment". Based on this excerpt, it is still an open question what kind of activity qualifies as "working".

When analyzing a product specification it is a good idea to distinguish the *top* information element first. Examples of typical top elements are as follows:

- For a banking process: the decision whether a loan should be granted to a company and - if so - under which conditions and for which amount.
- For a claim process of a social security agency: the decision whether an applicant should receive an unemployment allowance and - if so - for what reasons, for which period, and for which amount.
- For an intake process of an insurance company: the decision whether a family can be accepted as the holders of a health insurance policy.

Using the top element as the desired end result, it is a logical exercise to identify the information that can be used to directly render a value for the top information element. Obviously, this approach can be repeated for the newly found information elements. Instead of this backward analysis, it may seem attractive to start at the beginning of the existing process, for example by analyzing application forms, complaint forms, and request forms that are in use to start the process. This is *not* good practice as this may lead to the inclusion of superfluous information elements in the product data model. In a practical application of PBWD for a Dutch bank, we compared a posteriori the amount of information that was originally obtained in the business process and the information that was obtained in the final design. *This comparison showed that almost 30 % of the originally obtained information was superfluous* (see Section 7.3).

Administration and Selection of Information Elements

Distinguishing information elements and their dependencies is a start, but there is more to follow. Although not formally defined in the product data model, it is wise when applying PBWD to distinguish for each information element the following:

- An identifying *label*: this label simplifies searching the product data model and referencing to later documents, for example system specifications that may be developed to support the produced workflow design.
- A *name*: the name should be chosen such that it can be easily used by project members without being (too) ambiguous, for example: "periodic redemption sum", "reason for discharge", "trading name", etc.
- A short *description*: a verbal but unambiguous description of the information element, for example: "the total amount of directly available funds a client has at bank X and X's subsidiaries at the time of application".
- Its *type*, for example: date, free text, integer, real, Boolean, etc.; if the type of the information element is numerical, its *quantity* should be specified also (e.g., days, months, guilders, euros).
- The *range of possible values* (if known), for example the values of the information element "client's legal form" may be either "natural person" or "legal body".
- An explicit *reference* to the material where the definition of the information element can be found; this is extremely useful for keeping the product data model up to date and to justify its recognition at different times during the project.

The above information may not be required to make a workflow design, but its availability simplifies the use of the gathered data in a project team setting. After all, several people may want to consult and reference the same information during their analysis activity.

Another issue is how to pick the right information elements in a product data model. The following aspects are of relevance for this choice:

- An information element is chosen too large if different parts of it are used in different production rules; the information element should be broken up to enable the application of production rules without determining irrelevant information.
- Information elements should *not* be necessarily associated with their physical manifestation, nor is it necessary that physical information carriers have an information element counterpart (e.g., "intake form").
- Information elements may be atomic, for example a name, a credit score, etc. but they may be composite as well; examples are: all the members of a family, a listing of all the requested products with their characteristics, an overview of all the payment conditions that are in effect, etc.; the type of a composite in-

formation element is composed type, e.g., a set of numericals, free text, Booleans, etc.

Production Logic

The next step in completing the product data model is describing as accurately as possible the involved *production logic*. This step may either follow on the complete identification of all production rules, or as soon as a new production rule has been distinguished. The production logic specifies how the value of an output information element may be determined on the basis of the values of its inputs. (Note that some of the inputs may not actually be used in every calculation; they may be required for specific cases or to test the constraint.) The description of production logic may be given in *pseudo code* or any other semi-formal specification language. In several applications, we used a combination of Dijkstra's Guarded Command Language extended with first order predicate logic (see Example 3) or the functional language of ExSpect. Languages for a similar purposes are described by Wang (1997) and Joosten (2000). The most important criteria on any language for this purpose are univocality, expressiveness, and clarity.

A representation of the production logic for each production rule is valuable for at least four reasons, which are as follows:

1. Writing out the full specification is a direct *validation* on the distinguished inputs of the involved production rule: forgotten inputs or bad data types can be detected.
2. An analysis of the production logic is relevant for the *estimation* of performance characteristics when actually determining information with this production rule: labor/computer cost, speed, accuracy, etc. These characteristics are useful – as will be shown – in designing the workflow.
3. A representation of production logic that is of an algorithmic nature can be used as a *functional specification* for the information system that can execute this production rule. This is an important stepping stone for system development activities that may follow up the workflow redesign.
4. If the production logic is not totally algorithmic, it is likely that a human operator must execute it in practice. Then, the production logic is of use to develop *task instructions* for these operators.

The most accurate descriptions of production logic can be given when it involves an exact algorithm. In such a case, we will speak of a *formal* production rule. However, the production of many information elements in office settings is often not or not completely formal. It may be relevant, required or even the only option that a human passes a judgment without following a totally formalized decision making process. A typical example would be the question whether somebody is responsible for his or her own discharge. If there is a dispute, opposite explanations of different parties must be taken into account. A human should determine the plausibility of these explanations, as there are no known algorithms to do this. Another example is whether the purchase of some good is ethically admissible, which is a relevant piece of information in determining whether a loan should or should not be granted for this purpose. This decision may suppose a value system that is hard to describe formally. If a production rule is not of a formal nature it is important to at least check if all the required inputs are identified. As noted before, describing as precisely as possible how the output must be produced on the basis of its inputs also is a valuable step in determining working instructions for non-formal production rules. These working instructions can be provided to the people who will actually be responsible for determining the involved information in practice, that is to say: when the designed workflow is put into production. These rules may very well signal where *knowledge management systems* can be beneficial.

Although a *complete* univocal procedure may not exist for a production rule, it often is the case that – under specific circumstances – this decision is formal. For example, in determining whether someone qualifies for an unemployment allowance it is relevant to determine what the usual pattern of labor hours for this person was during a week. In general someone's actual labor pattern may be whimsical, e.g., due to a combination of different jobs or seasonal labor. So, determining the usual pattern is best done by using human interpretation. However, if the applicant has a steady pattern of working hours for a long period of time, e.g., eight hours per day from Monday to Friday over the last five years, determining the usual labor pattern is straightforward and can be described formally. Another example is the authorization function that must be performed to determine whether a loan proposal may be sent to a client. Generally, this function is a matter of human judgment that takes a large number of factors into account. On the other hand, if the loan sum is small, the client is a known client with sufficient coverage, *and* the purchasing goal is standard, the proposal can be accepted with no further inspection.

In cases where there is a mix of formal and non-formal logic, there are two specification options. The first option is that within the production rule a formal and a non-formal part are distinguished, of which their combined logic forms one specification. The other option is that both cases are converted into separate production rules, each with its own constraint identifying its domain of application. Splitting the logic up into separate production rules will simplify the exploitation of the differences in the workflow design. For example, the formal production rule may be applied as soon as the process starts because it is relatively cheap. However, if the gain is low in terms of shorter processing time or if the actual cases that correspond with the additional rule are scarce, the product data model becomes overly complex. This complicates finding an optimal workflow design.

We have had some good experiences with distinguishing separate production rules for determining the same information element, one of them being formal, the other informal. This was mainly because the field of application for the formal part proved to be relatively large. For example, for a workflow within a social security agency an important information element expressed whether the former employments of an applicant could be seen as consecutive from a legal and temporal point of view. The logic was hard to capture, as in some cases it had to be decided whether different jobs could be seen as logical successors within the same discipline. This required a human evaluation. However when an applicant never had more than one job at a time, temporally consecutive employments could be considered as legally consecutive jobs. In other words, under this condition the production rule could be described formally. Closer inspection indicated that in 85 % of all cases this formal rule could be applied. Applying this approach for all production rules indicated that 10 % of all cases could be handled by using formal procedures only. We will come back to determining such fractions later on in this section.

Example 3

If a client applies for a property-related loan, a bank will try to se-cure such a loan. The logic to determine the required types of secu-rities is partly formal and partly not. If the property is of a specific type, the required securities are fixed. Otherwise, a human judg-ment is necessary. The inputs for the presented production rule are the finance goal (fgl), the client's risk profile (rprf) and the desired credit product (cred). Below the semi-formal specification is given for the production rule required_securities to determine the securi-ties: the value of information element sec. The specification of the production rules for these inputs is not given here. For the sake of readability, not all data types have been formally defined (e.g., the "security list" is a set of 125 known security types).

```
proc     required_securities(fgl, rprf, cred, sec)
in       fgl: "purchase goal", rprf: N, cred: "product list"
out      sec: "security list"
```

sec :=   if *fgl* = "Register bound good"
                  then "Mortgage registration"
              elif *fgl* ∈ {"Company outillage", "Inventory", "Stock"}
                  then "Pawnage"
              else
                      "One or more securities should be picked from the security list such that a reasonable coverage may be expected taking into account the finance goal, the risk profile of the client and the credit product. Cov-erage by third parties is thereby allowed and a sur-plus value on the property may be used if a second mortgage registration is issued".
              fi
```
corp
```

Note that the black boxes that have been established in the analysis phase are explicitly no subject to extensive production logic analysis.

When all information elements, their inter-dependencies and the production logic have been described a final analysis step follows. This last step is required to

identify all the characteristics that are relevant to design a workflow that is efficient in terms of cost, reliability, speed, etc. The final analysis step consists of
three steps, which are as follows:

– A source analysis.
– A production analysis.
– A fraction analysis.

Source Analysis

The *source analysis* is aimed at identifying the sources of all leaf elements in the
product data model. As stated before, leaf values cannot be determined on the basis of other information elements. Therefore, they should be obtained from other
sources. Typically, multiple sources are available to obtain the same piece of information. For example, a record of historical grants of unemployment allowances
may be obtained from an applicant himself or from the agencies that have provided these allowances in the past. Another example is somebody's payable debt
position. In the Netherlands a bank may obtain this information from different
commercial (e.g., Experian, Equifax) and non-commercial credit scoring agencies
(e.g., Bureau Kredietregistratie).

Different ways of obtaining information may have different characteristics. A
client may be very willing to submit information about his own credit position, but
this information may not be very reliable. Similarly, local authorities may provide
correct domestic information at a very low cost, but their response time may be
considerable. Depending on the criteria that are identified in the scoping phase, it
is wise to first identify the possible sources for each leaf element and subsequently
score them on relevant points of comparison. Assuming general BPR goals like
improving efficiency, bringing back throughput time while maintaining (or improving) an existing quality level, relevant points of comparison for each leaf are:
cost of obtaining it, delivery *speed* of the information, *availability* of the specific
information and *reliability* of the provided information. We will come back to the
way this information is used in the description of the design phase.

Production Analysis

The *production analysis* focuses on the identified production rules with the aim to
estimate the involved cost, speed and quality of producing the new information.
As there may be different ways to obtain a piece of information, similarly different
production rules typically exist for the same piece of information. Designing the
workflow is for a large part concerned with selecting the right set and the right
execution order of production rules given a set of performance targets. From these
targets it becomes clear which optimization criteria are prevailing. For example,
suppose that an important performance target aims at a reduction of the labor cost.
If there is a formal and an informal production rule for the same piece of information, the first rule may be preferred. After all, the formal production rule may be
automated. Obviously, this efficiency gain should be set off against the cost and

time, which is involved with developing the software. The PBWD project that was conducted for the involved agency showed that 75 % of all production rules could be formalized (Reijers and Goverde, 1999a). Automating the execution of formal rules is therefore a major efficiency driver for designing workflows with PBWD.

For non-formal production rules the production analysis should yield as accurately as possible the involved *service time*. The service time is a good basis for determining the efficiency of a design. In combination with labor cost, it can also be used to determine the operational cost of the workflow execution. The required type of information on the service time is dependent on the optimization criterion. For example, if *average* cost should decrease, *average* service times suffice as basis information. More complex types of performance targets may require more information on the service times. For example, if 90 % of the products are to be delivered within a specific amount of time, the average service time is not sufficient. A complete distribution of the service time is then preferable. If possible, the causes for the fluctuation in the service time should be established as well. For example, higher service times for determining a proposed interest rate may be due to temporal turbulence on the money market. Many times the exact causes of a service time pattern are not known, but they will make the evaluation of a workflow design in following phases more reliable. Often, the service time pattern itself is not even known. Many companies do not have a detailed time registration of their business operations. Notable exceptions are those companies that use WfMS's for the management and execution of their workflows (see Section 1.4). A WfMS offers a wealth of information about business operation performance. (In Chapter 7 we will describe how this information can be used for operational control.) In most other companies, time information on an aggregated level of some sort does exist, mostly for planning purposes. It is the job of the analyst to decompose existing figures in these reports to their constituents. This can be done in cooperation with business professionals who are responsible for actually executing the work. An approach that we conducted in a project is to organize workshops with business professionals where they were asked individually to estimate minimal, normal, and maximal service times for individual business operations. Other approaches are interviews, surveys, observations in practice and time scoring by professionals during their daily activities (see e.g., Sackett, 1978).

It should be noted here that the production analysis is a very time-consuming part of the analysis phase, even more so when there is a poor tradition of operations measurement within the company at hand. The time that should be invested in obtaining reliable information should be balanced against the desired reliability of the quality estimates of the workflow design.

Fraction Analysis

The *fraction analysis* involves a study of the distribution of information element values. As we already explained, an information element may carry specific values. For example, the value of the information element "travel insurance required" may be either "yes" or "no". The figures on the likelihood of information elements taking on specific values are very relevant to design an efficient workflow. In combination with the figures from the production analysis (cost, speed, etc), favorable orderings of executing production rules may be determined. For example, suppose that there are two production rules for the same information element with different applicability domains, with very different input elements, but with a similar cost structure to obtain values for them. In such a case, it may be wise from a cost perspective to aim at executing the rule with the widest applicability first. Only if this production rule does not yield an outcome, applying the other rule may be tried.

In the discussion of the product data model, we already discussed the applicability domain of a production rule specified by constraints. The fraction analysis should yield an indication of the general probability that a production rule can be used for determining its corresponding information element. In other words, this is the probability that the constraint evaluates to true assuming that all information is available. Like in the case of the production analysis, reliable figures may be generally hard to obtain. In legal settings the legitimacy of decision masking may be such that there are detailed registrations of cases with all their specifics. This is an excellent source for information gathering. For situations where this type of registration is not available, a sample analysis may be executed. During a certain period of time all cases are observed and it is scored how many times the different production rules may be successfully applied.

In practice, the applicability of a production rule is often related to the value of another piece of information. Although it would be best to understand the exact situation when a production rule is applicable, it is generally not possible to fathom the dependencies between all the values of information elements. That is why the fraction analysis should focus on obtaining probability information as if these entities are *independent*.

Extended Product Data Model

At this point we will present an extended form of the product data model where information from the source analysis, production analysis, and fraction analysis is added to the basis product data model. This is not the only form a product data model may have in an actual BPR encounter. After all, the type and detail of information that is gathered – especially from the production analysis – depends on the chosen performance targets and optimization criteria. For example, if the design should be focused primarily on speed of the derived workflow, the cost of process execution may be less relevant and therefore no part of the product data model.

In the model that we present, we have added the ingredients for the design of a workflow model where three criteria are relevant: *cost*, *throughput time* and *quality*. We have chosen these criteria because of their popularity in actual BPR encounters (Hammer and Champy, 1993; Reijers and Goverde, 1999a; Sharp and McDermott, 2001). We will discuss later in this section how the information can be used to derive a favorable design.

Definition 3.2   (Extended product data model). The extended product data model is a tuple (D, C, *pre*, F, *constr*, *cst*, *flow*, *prob*):
- (D, C, *pre*, F, *constr*) is a product data model (Definition 3.1),
- a function *cst*, which gives the cost of using a production rule:
    $$cst : F \rightarrow \mathbb{N},$$
- a function *flow*, which gives the time it takes to use a production rule:
    $$flow : F \rightarrow \mathbb{N},$$
- a function *prob*, which gives the probability that a production rule will be successful when used:
    $$prob : F \rightarrow (0..1], \text{ such that:}$$
- if there are no constraints on using the production rule, then it will always be successful:
    $$\forall (p, cs) \in F : constr(p, cs) = true \Rightarrow prob(p, cs) = 1.$$

Because of the definition of the function *prob* and because there are no constraints on producing a value for a leaf (see Definition 3.1), a leaf value is always successfully obtained. Note that there may be costs associated with obtaining the value of a leaf – just as is the case for any other information element.

The events that determine whether production rules are successful are assumed to be *independent*. Because the probability of success for a rule can be less than 1, it is generally not ensured that the information element top can be determined for a given set of information element values. For example, suppose for the Helicopter Pilot product data model that for each of the three production rules for the top element there is a probability of 0,9 that it is successfully applied. Even if the values of the required information elements are all available, then there is still a probability of $(1-0,9)\cdot(1-0,9)\cdot(1-0,9) = 0,001$ that it cannot be determined whether someone is a suitable helicopter pilot. This somewhat odd assumption is caused by the fact that in practical situations interdependencies are generally not very well understood. We propose a practical use of the available information by treating these as independent. Obviously, if the real dependencies are known this information may be used in the derivation of actual process designs on the basis of the product data model. This kind of knowledge is not supposed in the further description of PBWD. Neither are the statistical techniques that may be used to identify significant dependencies.

Note that the specifications of the production rules are no part of the extended product data model. A formal specification of a language to express such specifications is beyond the scope of this chapter, but - as argued before - these specifications are of the utmost importance for validation, performance estimation, functional specifications and task instructions. However, the exact content of the production rules are not directly of importance to determine the best way of executing them. We will treat this subject in more detail in the a following part of this section.

We end this part with an extension of the product data model example that has been presented earlier. Associated with each production rule in the Helicopter Pilot product data model are the constraints, cost, throughput time, and probabilities.

The relations *constr*, *cst*, *flow*, and *prob* for each of the eight production rules of this example are as listed in Table 3.1. If x is an information element, the value of x is denoted with $*x$.

Table 3.1. Relations for testing a helicopter pilot candidate

Index	x	constr(x)	cst(x)	flow(x)	prob(x)
1.	$(a,\{\,b,\,c\,\})$	True	80	1	1,0
2.	$(a,\{\,d\,\})$	$*d \in \{$suit-able, not suit-able$\}$	10	1	0,1
3.	$(a,\{f\})$	$*f < -3,0$ or $*f > +3,0$	5	1	0,4
4.	$(b,\varnothing)$	true	150	48	1,0
5.	$(c,\{\,e,f\})$	true	50	1	1,0
6.	$(d,\varnothing)$	true	10	16	1,0
7.	$(e,\varnothing)$	true	60	4	1,0
8.	$(f,\varnothing)$	true	60	4	1,0

From this table it follows that in this example obtaining values for leafs is much more time-consuming than other values. This represents a common phenomenon that actions that involve communication with external parties take more through-put time than internal actions.

Furthermore, it can be concluded that if a candidate's eyes are worse than –3,0 or +3,0 dioptres this information can be used as a direct *knock-out* for the test re-sult, i.e., the execution of a task that establishes this information may be directly followed by a completion of the workflow. This is the production rule $(a, \{f\})$. The probability that this will happen for an arbitrary case is 0,4.

A summary of the activities in the analysis phase is given in Figure 3.6. The de-liverables of the analysis phase are as follows:

– An extended product data model.
– An information element administration, which is optional.

3.3.3 Design

By now we have described the first two phases of the PBWD methodology. The third is the design phase, which we describe in this section. Within the setting of a valid product data model, any successive execution of production rules that re-spects the dependencies within this model is a valid and feasible workflow design. As stated before, establishing a value of the top element is the ultimate goal of the execution of a workflow. An obvious way to connect the concepts of a workflow model with those of a product data model, is to regard a workflow design as a par-tially ordered set of tasks and each of these tasks as an ordered list of production

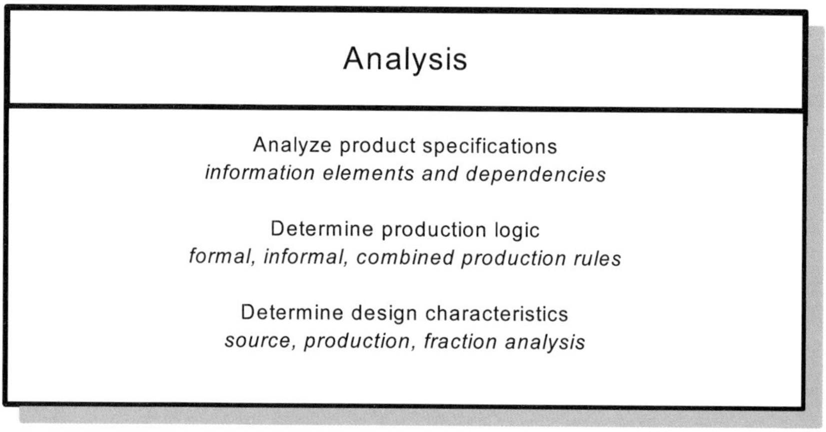

Fig. 3.6. The analysis phase

rules. If we say that for some case a task is executed, then we mean by this that all of the production rules that are part of this task are (attempted to be) executed. We will characterize the structure and behavior of a workflow with a workflow model based on Petri nets (see Section 2.4).

Until now, we left open what qualifies as a favorable design. Obviously, the choice for performance targets – which should be chosen by the process owner – determines for a large part which workflow designs are better than others. However, we have not discussed yet whether the evaluation of the best workflow execution should consider *a specific case* or a *common case*. Obviously, big differences may exist between the two. Handling a specific case in the way that is best fit to treat most members of a population may be inefficient or not very effective for this particular case. For example, suppose that an applicant for a loan commonly has only a modest capital. Then, the most sensible way of deciding whether someone can pay back the loan is to determine his capacity to earn the money in the near future in a profession. However, suppose that a millionaire applies for a loan, for example for fiscal reasons. Then the effort of the bank to determine his capacity of earning money by labor may be inefficient from the viewpoint of the bank and not service-minded from the viewpoint of the client. In general, different types of checks and information may be required for a specific case than in the common case.

In this section we will discuss two design approaches. The first and primary part of this section is aimed at deriving a workflow that is suitable for the common case. On average, i.e., taken a large number of cases in account, this approach will yield the best results. The approach means that at build time, before the execution of a process for a specific case starts, the exploration probabilities through the graph are limited to one or more preferred routes. Usually, figures are derived from a large population of cases to determine the best lay-out of this type of workflow.

The second approach is aimed at providing optimal flexibility in process execution for each single case. The largest possible space for exploration of the product data model is continuously offered, so that it can be decided *ad hoc* which next production rule is executed. The focus in describing this approach is not so much on the design of a workflow, but on the support of office workers by technology. We believe that a contemporary focus in industry on delivering specific, flexible service to individual clients (e.g., Sharp and McDermott, 2001) justifies a short discussion of this topic.

Our presentation of a workflow design approach that aims at servicing the common case is as follows. First, we will present a workflow model that specifies on an abstract level what the workflow looks like. This workflow model is used as an outline of the ordering pattern between production rules. Its attractiveness lies in its compact form and explanatory power to end-users. We will informally discuss its semantics. In Appendix A, we will show how the semantics of the net can be specified in a more formal way, using classical Petri nets. Then, we show how a favorable workflow model may be designed on the basis of a given extended product data model and specific performance targets. This approach includes a heuristic to limit the search space for a favorable design.

The Workflow Model

As stated in the introduction of this section, a workflow model is used as an outline of the ordering pattern of production rules in a workflow.

Definition 3.3   (Workflow model). A *workflow model* PM on an extended product data model $(D, C, pre, F, constr, cst, flow, prob)$ is defined by $(P, T, R, prod)$ where:

- (P, T, R) is a workflow net (see Definition 2.13),
- *prod*: $T \rightarrow F \cup \{ skip \}$, the production rule that may be applied in the task.

For the sake of simplicity, to each transition in a workflow model at most one production rule is assigned. Obviously, it is not hard to extend this notion to e.g., an ordered list of production rules. Although this extension will not increase the expressiveness of the model, it may decrease the size of a workflow model as measured in the number of transitions. After all, simple sequences of transitions may be combined into a single transition. Note furthermore that a transition t for which $prod(t) = skip$ does not attempt to apply a production rule. Such a transition is incorporated in the model for routing purposes, i.e., to ensure a proper flow.

To guarantee that some level of agreement exists between the product data model used and the workflow model that is derived from it, we present a correctness notion.

Definition 3.4   (Conformance). A workflow model $(P, T, R, prod)$ *conforms* to the extended product data model $(D, C, pre, F, constr, cst, flow, prob)$ if and only if:

1. a production rule can only be applied if all its inputs are available and these inputs - if not empty - can only be obtained by applying other production rules: for each firing sequence $\sigma = t_1t_2...t_k$ within (P, T, R) such that $[\![i]\!] \overset{\sigma}{\longrightarrow} M$ for some reachable marking M holds that

2. $\left[\forall 1 \leq i \leq k, (p,cs) \in F : prod(t_i) = (p,cs) \Rightarrow \right.$

$$\left. \left(\forall c \in cs : \exists 1 \leq j < i, ds \in \mathcal{P}(D) : prod(t_j) = (c,ds) \right) \right],$$

3. the top element may be produced by executing the workflow model: there is a firing sequence $\sigma = t_1t_2...t_k$ in (P, T, R) such that $[\![i]\!] \overset{\sigma}{\longrightarrow} M$ and $\exists 1 \leq i \leq k, cs \in \mathcal{P}(D) : prod(t_i) = (top, cs)$, and

4. the underlying workflow net is correct:
   (P, T, R) is a sound workflow net (see Definition 2.13 and Definition 2.14).

Note that due to the semantics of a product data model it is in general not ensured that all production rules are executed successfully in executing a conformant workflow. Also note that the second requirement makes the observation operational that it is no use to design a workflow that is incapable of reaching this goal. The third requirement is a general correctness notion for a workflow net. Soundness is in practice a very reasonable requirement for workflow nets (Van der Aalst, 1998). When soundness holds, many concepts can be defined on workflow nets that assume "normal" executions of a workflow net.

An example of a workflow model on the basis of the Helicopter pilot product data model introduced in this section earlier is given in Figure 3.7.

It is not hard to verify that the example workflow model conforms to the Helicopter Pilot product data model. After all, each task is associated with a production rule of which its inputs are produced by rules of preceding tasks, there is at least one production rule for the top element, and the workflow net is sound. Note that not each production rule of the product data model is present in the model, e.g., $(a, \{d\})$. Also note that to transitions t_1 and t_5 the same production rule is associated. We have yet to address the semantics of this double occurrence.

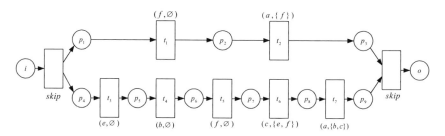

Fig. 3.7. Example workflow model

A workflow model specifies the order in which production rules are applied for a single case. The workflow model, however, leaves a couple of semantic questions unanswered. To start with, we have defined the extended product data model such that the application of a production rule may be limited. In the first place, required for the application of a production rule is that all its inputs are available. Secondly, the constraint for the production rule should evaluate to true. Only when both of these conditions are fulfilled, the production rule is *applicable*. But even then, there is a probability associated that influences the success of its application. So, even if a production rule is applicable, it may be either *successful* or not. In addition to the issues of applicability and success, the definition of the workflow model does not rule out that a production rule is associated with zero, one, or more transitions of the product data model. In the example of Figure 3.7, to transitions t_1 and t_5 the same production rule is assigned. This raises the question whether multiple applications of a production rule are allowed and – if so – whether they have the same applicability restrictions and whether they will deliver the same output values.

We will at this point informally answer these questions. If a transition in a workflow model fires to which a production rule (p, cs) is associated, this firing should be interpreted as an application of the production rule if at the time of firing all of the following is true:

–   The constraint for (p, cs) holds.
–   The values for each of the information elements in cs are known.
–   No value for p is already known.
–   No value for the information element <u>top</u> is already known.
–   No task to which the production rule (p, cs) is associated has already fired.
–   In all other cases, the production rule (p, cs) is *not* applied. In other words, although the transition fires, the production rule is skipped.

Furthermore, when a production rule *is* applied there is a probability of *prob*(p, cs) that it is successful, and a probability of 1- *prob*(p, cs) that it is not. If the production rule (p, cs) is successfully applied, a value for p becomes known. Initially, no values of information elements are known at all.

In Appendix A, a formal description of these semantics are given in the form of a so-called *bottom-level workflow model*. It is shown how this bottom-level workflow model can be derived from a workflow model as defined with Definition 3.3. The bottom-level workflow model is defined in Appendix A as an SWN (see Definition 2.20). It gives a more explicit semantics of actual executions of production rules than the workflow model it has been derived of. Although this is an advantage from the viewpoint of actually applying the design in practice or for analysis and evaluation purposes, a bottom-level workflow model quickly becomes quite large. This is why we prefer the use of the simpler workflow model for the sake of analysis and presentation in the remainder of this chapter.

An important notion for the rest of this chapter is the interpreted firing sequence.

Definition 3.5   (Interpreted firing sequence). Given a workflow model (P, T, R, *prod*) that conforms to the product data model (D, C, pre, F, constr, cst, flow, prob) and a firing sequence τ in the underlying workflow net $[\![i]\!] \xrightarrow{\tau} [\![o]\!]$, the *interpreted firing sequence* ρ = $(p_1, cs_1)(p_2, cs_2)...(p_m, cs_m)$, $m \in \mathbb{N}$, for $1 \leq j \leq m$ $(p_1, cs_1) \in F$, is the corresponding sequence of production rules that are successfully applied.

The interpreted firing sequence is closely related to the dynamics of the bottom-level workflow model of Appendix A, which also includes a formal definition of it. Crucial is that although a firing sequence of the workflow model may incorporate a number of transitions, the number of successfully applied production rules *may be much smaller*. After all, production rules may be skipped. The successful application of a production rule is an important determinant for the cost of a workflow execution, as will be discussed in the following sections.

This concludes the treatment of the used workflow model. We return our attention to the derivation of efficient workflow models on the basis of a product data model.

Limiting the Search by Cost Optimal Plans

In general, given a product data model there is an infinite number of conformant workflow models. In practice, it is not possible to investigate all workflow model designs on their suitability to implement the required performance targets. In this section we present a heuristic approach that limits the number of models to be investigated using so-called *plans*, subsets of the elements in the product data model. Within the confinement of an attractive plan, favorable designs of the workflow model are derived analytically.

For illustrating the plan heuristics we consider the following three design criteria: (1) *quality*, (2) *costs*, and (3) *time*. Costs and time are defined according to the functions *cst* and *flow*, as will be shown. Quality is defined as the probability that the value of the top element can be determined. This is obviously a rather restricted view of quality. Note that this interpretation depends on the structure of the product data model (i.e., the function *pre*) and the probability that a production rule leads to a value. To allow for a formal definition of these design criteria we formally introduce the notion of a *plan* first.

Definition 3.6   (Plan). Let (D, C, pre, F, constr, cst, flow, prob) be an extended product data model. Any subset S of D is called a plan.

One can think of a plan as a sub-graph of the graph denoting the product data model. The elements of the plan S are the information elements that should be produced. The set {a, d} is a plan corresponding to the product data model shown in Figure 3.5. In this plan the production rules (d, {∅}) and (a, {d}) are executed in some order. The set {a, e} is also a plan, although this plan will never lead to a value for information element a. For any given plan, we can determine the probability that a value for the top element is determined.

Definition 3.7   (Quality of a plan). Let $(D, C, pre, F, constr, cst, flow, prob)$ be an extended product data model. The quality of a plan $S \subseteq D$ is defined as $p\_quality(S) = q_{top}$, with q_d defined for all $d \in S$ as:

$$q_d = 1 - \prod_{(d,cs) \in F} \left(1 - \left(prob(d,cs) \cdot \prod_{e \in cs \cup \{\emptyset\}} q_e \cdot \delta(e) \right) \right),$$

where $\delta(e) = \begin{cases} 0, & e \notin S \wedge e \neq \emptyset \\ 1, & e \in S \vee e = \emptyset. \end{cases}$

The quality of a plan is the probability that the value of the top element can be determined successfully, assuming that *each* production rule with inputs and output in S is executed. Note that for any production rule $(p, cs) \in F$ holds that all elements in cs should be part of the plan in order to contribute to q_p.

Consider the product data model shown in Figure 3.5 and three plans $S_1 = \{a, d\}$, $S_2 = \{a, b, c, e, f\}$ and $S_3 = \{a, e\}$. For plan S_1 holds that the quality of this plan is $p\_quality(S_1) = q_{top} = q_a$. According to Definition 3.7, $q_a = 1- (1-prob(a,\{d\}).q_d.\delta(d))$ with $q_d = 1-(1-prob(d, \emptyset) \cdot q_\emptyset \cdot \delta(\emptyset)) = 1$. So, $p\_quality(S_1) = q_a = 0,1$ (see Table 3.1). Similarly, for plan S_2, $p\_quality(S_2) = 1$ and for plan S_3, $p\_quality(S_3) = 0$.

Another point to evaluate the performance of a plan is its cost.

Definition 3.8   (Costs of a plan). Let $(D, C, pre, F, constr, cst, flow, prob)$ be an extended product data model. The costs of a plan $S \subset D$ are:

$$p\_csts(S) = \sum_{(p,cs) \in F} cst(p,cs) \cdot \delta(p) \cdot \prod_{e \in cs \cup \{\emptyset\}} \delta(e)$$

The costs of a plan are simply given by the sum of all production rules costs relevant for the plan. Note that again it is assumed that production rule (p, cs) is executed if $\{p\} \cup cs$ is a subset of plan S. The costs of a plan can be interpreted as the maximum costs that are associated with the execution of a plan. Each production rule is assumed to be executed once, in accordance to the semantics of the workflow model.

Using the example of the Helicopter Pilot case again, the costs of plans $S_1 = \{a, d\}$, $S_2 = \{a, b, c, e, f\}$ and $S_3 = \{a, e\}$ are as follows. For plan S_1 the only relevant production rules are $(a, \{d\})$ and $(d, \emptyset)$. So, according to Definition 3.8, $p\_csts(S_1) = cst(a,\{d\}) \cdot \delta(a) \cdot \delta(d) \cdot \delta(\emptyset) + cst(d, \emptyset) \cdot \delta(d) \cdot \delta(\emptyset) = 20$ (see Table 3.1). Similarly, $p\_csts(S_2) = 405$ and $p\_csts(S_3) = 60$.

The last design criterion is the throughput time of a plan.

Definition 3.9   (Throughput time of a plan). Let $(D, C, pre, F, constr, cst, flow, prob)$ be an extended product data model. The throughput time of a plan $S \subseteq D$ is:

$$p\_through(S) = \sum_{(p,cs) \in F} flow(p,cs) \cdot \delta(p) \cdot \prod_{e \in cs \cup \{\varnothing\}} \delta(e)$$

With this notion of the throughput time, we focus on a worst-case scenario where all production rules of the plan are executed *once* in a sequential order. Note that this is in accordance with the presented semantics of a workflow model. Although several tasks with the same production rule can be incorporated, only one of these will be executed. The *actual* time required to produce all information elements of a plan depends on the order in which the production rules are executed. By executing some of the production rules of the plan in parallel, the actual throughput time can be reduced with respect to this worst-case scenario.

Consider again the helicopter example with plan $S_4 = \{a, b, c, d, e, f\}$. Assume that this plan is executed in the following order: $(d,\varnothing)$, $(a,\{d\})$, $(f,\varnothing)$, $(a,\{f\})$, $(e,\varnothing)$, $(c,\{e,f\})$, $(b,\varnothing)$, $(a,\{b,c\})$. Then the average worst case $p\_through(S_4) = flow(a, \{b, c\}) \cdot \delta(a) \cdot \delta(b) \cdot \delta(c) \cdot \delta(\varnothing) + flow(a, \{f\}) \cdot \delta(a) \cdot \delta(f) \cdot \delta(\varnothing) + flow(a, \{d\}) \cdot \delta(a) \cdot \delta(d) \cdot \delta(\varnothing) + flow(b, \varnothing) \cdot \delta(b) \cdot \delta(\varnothing) + flow(c, \{e, f\}) \cdot \delta(c) \cdot \delta(e) \cdot \delta(f) \cdot \delta(\varnothing) + flow(f, \varnothing) \cdot \delta(f) \cdot \delta(\varnothing) + flow(e, \varnothing) \cdot \delta(e) \cdot \delta(\varnothing) + flow(d, \varnothing) \cdot \delta(d) \cdot \delta(\varnothing) = 76$ time units. Now suppose that the production rule $(a, \{d\})$ leads to a value for a, then the $p\_through(S_4) = flow(a, \{d\}) \cdot \delta(a) \cdot \delta(d) \cdot \delta(\varnothing) + flow(d, \varnothing) \cdot \delta(d) \cdot \delta(\varnothing) = 17$ time units only. So, the average throughput time of a plan may be much smaller because a value for a information element can be obtained before all elements of the plan are derived.

From the definition of the introduced notions, it follows that it is easy to calculate for a plan S its quality $p\_quality(S)$, the associated costs $p\_costs(S)$ and the throughput time $p\_through(S)$. It is much more complex to calculate the actual throughput time of a workflow model, because of the effect of the orderings of tasks. Note that a plan is not a workflow model: it is merely a subset of information elements.

Different combinations of the formulated design criteria on plans can be made to restrict the search space for an attractive workflow design. The actual choice for these design criteria as well as their specific combination should obviously be chosen in an appropriate way for the project at hand. We will introduce a combined criterion based on the design criteria $p\_quality(S)$ and $p\_costs(S)$. Our heuristic allows for the definition of a so-called cost optimal plan, given a certain minimal quality level. The notion of a cost optimal plan enforces a common start requirement on the design of a workflow: costs should be kept down, but a minimal level of quality should be maintained. The tension between these characteristics is apparent and deliberately chosen. After all, aiming purely at a workflow with low cost will yield the empty workflow. This is obviously unattractive from a quality perspective.

Definition 3.10   (Cost optimal plan). Let $(D, C, pre, F, constr, cst, flow, prob)$ be an extended product data model and $q \in [0, 1]$ be a quality level. Plan $S \subseteq D$ is cost optimal if and only if

1. plan S attains the minimally required quality level:
   $p\_quality(S) \geq q$,
2. each other plan than S that minimally delivers the same quality is at least as costly:
   $\forall S' \subseteq D: p\_quality(S') \geq q \Rightarrow p\_csts(S') \geq p\_csts(S)$, and
3. no information elements are part of S that do not contribute to the quality of S:
   $\forall S' \subset S: p\_quality(S') < p\_quality(S)$.

We will illustrate the cost optimality notion with an example. Consider R the set of plans that can be derived from the product data model of Figure 3.5 to determine a top value. $R = \{S_1, S_2, S_3, S_4, S_5\}$ where $S_1 = \{a, d\}$, $S_2 = \{a, b, c, e, f\}$, $S_3 = \{a, e\}$, $S_4 = \{a,b,c,d,e,f\}$ and $S_5 = \{a, f\}$. Let the minimum quality to be obtained be defined as $q = 0{,}8$. We obtained the quality levels of plans S_1, S_2 and S_3 earlier: $p\_quality(S_1) = 0{,}1$, $p\_quality(S_2) = 1$, and $p\_quality(S_3) = 0$. It is easy to calculate the quality level of plans S_4 and S_5: $p\_quality(S_4) = 1$ and $p\_quality(S_5) = 0{,}4$. Only plans S_2 and S_4 fulfill the minimal quality requirement. For those plans, costs are $p\_csts(S_2) = 405$ and $p\_csts(S_4) = 425$. According to the definition of cost optimality, it appears that plan S_2 is the cost optimal plan.

A cost optimal plan gives the least costly subset of information elements that needs to be calculated to obtain a given quality level. Note that the costs associated to such a plan are the maximal costs, i.e., the costs that are made if all corresponding production rules need to be calculated.

Finding the Design

The best way to order the production rules is dependent – as stated before – upon the chosen performance targets for the workflow design. We have used notions of cost and time in evaluating plans, as they are often applied in practice (see e.g., the case description in Sections 7.2 and 7.3). Given these two specific criteria, there are two extreme ordering approaches for finding a favorable workflow design, which are as follows:

1. *Breadth-first.* Start with the leaf nodes in the plan and execute as many production rules in parallel as possible.
2. *Depth-first.* Start with the part of the plan that has the best quality/cost ratio, i.e., execute the production rules sequentially and start with the most promising branches first.

Assuming sufficient capacity the breadth-first approach optimizes the workflow with respect to throughput time but at high costs (in principle all production rules associated to the plan are executed). The depth-first approach minimizes the expected costs but may result in substantial longer throughput times.

We will present approaches for deriving both the breadth-first and the depth-first workflow model. A breadth-first workflow model can be easily generated on the basis of a product data model, as will be shown. To find the depth-first workflow model, a brute-force approach is proposed. We will indicate why a more efficient search for the depth-first workflow model is problematic.

The cost optimal plan as described can be used to make a first, heuristic shift in the production rules to be considered for either type of workflow model. It is, however, not obligatory to use the cost optimal plan. In what is to follow, we will simply refer to a "plan", which may be understood by the reader as the cost optimal plan or any subset of the information elements of the product data model. It will become clear that using the cost optimal plan is especially useful in a situation where a depth-first workflow model is sought for a large product data model.

Both the derivation of the breadth-first and the depth-first workflow model are based on the notion of a *solution*. A solution is a minimal set of production rules on the basis of which a value for an information element can be determined.

Definition 3.11   (Solution). Given a product data model $(D, C, pre, F, constr)$ and a plan S, the set of production rules $G \subseteq F$ is said to be a *solution* for an information element $d \in D$ – denoted $sol(G, d)$ – iff:

1. all inputs of a production rule can be produced by others:
$$\left[\forall (p,cs) \in G : \left(\forall q \in cs : \left(\exists ds \subseteq D : (q,ds) \in G\right)\right)\right],$$

2. a production rule adds value by either producing the desired information element or the input of another production rule:
$$\left[\forall (p,cs) \in G : p = d \vee \left(\exists (q,ds) \in G : p \in ds\right)\right],$$

3. there is at most one production rule for each output
$$\left[\forall (p,cs),(q,ds) \in G : p = q \Rightarrow cs = ds\right], \text{ and}$$

4. all production rules of the solution must be confined within the plan S:
$$\left[\forall (p,cs) \in G : p \in S \wedge \left(cs = \varnothing \vee cs \subseteq S\right)\right].$$

A simple way of deriving all solutions is to translate the product data model in a Petri net. Each information element that is part of the confining set, as well as the empty set should then be represented as a place. Each production rule should be included as a transition, with its input information elements as output places and its (single) output information element as an input place. Take, for example, the net as depicted in Figure 3.8. It represents a net that could be used to find the solutions of the top element for the Helicopter Pilot product data model, confined by the cost optimal plan $S_2 = \{a, b, c, e, f\}$.

Each firing sequence that leads from the marking of the top element place to a dead state gives a sequential ordering of a solution. For example, $(a, \{b, c\})(b, \varnothing)(c, \{e, f\})$ $(e, \varnothing)(f, \varnothing)$ is such a firing sequence, which is an ordering of the solution $\{(a, \{b, c\}), (b, \varnothing), (c, \{e, f\}), (e, \varnothing), (f, \varnothing)\}$. The firing sequence $(a, \{b, c\})(c, \{e, f\})(b, \varnothing)(f, \varnothing) (e, \varnothing)$ is also an ordering of this solution. The only other solution is $\{(a, \{f\}), (f, \varnothing)\}$.

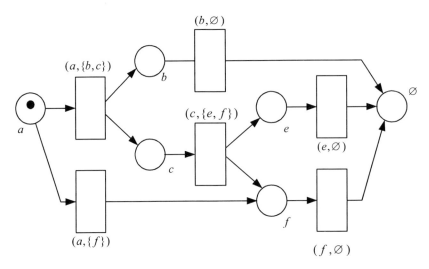

Fig. 3.8. Finding the solution for cost optimal plan S_2.

Note that although this type of Petri net has the structure of a workflow net, it is in general not sound.

On the basis of the solutions definition, we can define the notion of fulfillment. A fulfilling workflow model implements all solutions of a confined product data model in a correct way.

Definition 3.12   (Fulfillment). Given an extended product data model $(D, C, pre, F, constr, cst, flow, prob)$ a workflow PM = $(P, T, R, prod)$ model *fulfills* a plan $S \subseteq D$ if:
1. it is correct:
   PM conforms to $(D, C, pre, F, constr, cst, flow, prob)$ (see Definition 3.4), and
2. each production rule that is part of a solution for the top element *will* be attempted to be applied in executing the workflow:
   for each firing sequence σ in (P, T, R) such that $[\![i]\!] \overset{\sigma}{\longrightarrow} [\![o]\!]$ holds that
   $$\left[\forall G \subseteq F, n \in \mathbb{N} : sol(G, \underline{top}) \Rightarrow \right.$$
   $$\left. \left(\forall (p, cs) \in G : \left(\exists t \in \mathcal{A}(\sigma) : prod(t) = (p, cs) \right) \right) \right].$$

The second condition is very important, because all solutions together realize the quality of the plan that is used to confine the solution (see Definition 3.7). Especially when a cost optimal plan is used, it is reasonable to at least execute each production rule that follows from the cost optimal plan.

We will show in the following sections how to obtain the breadth-first and depth-first workflow model on the basis of a product data model.

Breadth-First Workflow Model

A breadth-first workflow models allows for the greatest degree of parallelism to achieve a value of the top element of the underlying product data model. We would like to make one remark before we start with the presentation of the derivation of such a workflow model. As follows from the definition of a workflow model (see Definition 3.3) we allow for several tasks to which the same production rule is associated. This may seem rather odd at first glance, but it is clear that one production rule may be part of different solutions. Even when a production rule appears more than once in a workflow model, it will be executed at run time at most once due to the specific semantics of the workflow model (see the discussion of the workflow model, earlier in this section).

The general principle that we will apply in the construction of a breadth-first workflow model is as follows. All solutions are determined on the basis of the product data model and a cost optimal plan or other plan. At the highest level of the breadth-first workflow model *each* of these solutions is pursued. On the highest level of the breadth-first workflow model, this can be seen as an equal number of parallel paths. Within each path, the involved set of production rules is subsequently unfolded, while respecting the dependencies from the product data model and maintaining the highest possible level of parallelism. In summary, *all* minimal combinations of production rules are executed in parallel that can possibly yield a value for the top element.

We will give a small, stylized example to illustrate the approach. We assume a product data model such as depicted in Figure 3.9, i.e., with a set of production rules $F = \{ (x, \{a, b\}), (a, \varnothing), (b, \{a\}), (b, \{c\}), (x, \{d\}), (c, \varnothing), (d, \varnothing) \}$ with top element x.

If we assume that the restricting (cost optimal) plan includes all information elements, then there are three solutions (Definition 3.11), which are as follows:

1. $\{ (x, \{a, b\}), (a, \varnothing), (b, \{a\}) \}$.
2. $\{ (x, \{a, b\}), (a, \varnothing), (b, \{c\}), (c, \varnothing) \}$.
3. $\{ (x, \{d\}), (d, \varnothing) \}$.

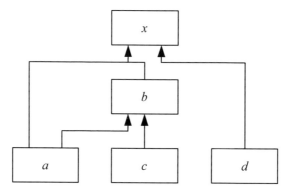

Fig. 3.9. Product data model example

Note that although there are two knock-outs, i.e., $(x, \{a, b\})$ and $(x, \{d\})$, there are three different solutions. After all, the inputs of production rule $(x, \{a, b\})$ can be obtained in two different ways.

For the creation of the breadth-first workflow model on the basis of the solutions of a top element we will use the two auxiliary workflow nets of Figure 3.10.

We will refer to the nets in the figure as auxiliary nets I and II. If we instantiate an auxiliary net, we call into existence a yet incomplete workflow model with unique identifiers and the structure of the respective auxiliary net. For each transition t of the workflow model that bears in the auxiliary net the label *skip*, its associated production rule will be *skip*, i.e., $prod(t) = skip$. For instantiating auxiliary net I, the number of parallel transitions n is of importance. We have to specify which production rules are associated with transitions with the labels $u_1, u_2, \ldots, u_n$ (for auxiliary net I) and v (for both auxiliary nets) to make it complete. Note that the execution of an instantiated auxiliary net I where $u_1, u_2, \ldots, u_n$ are associated with the *skip* production rule is equivalent from an interpreted firing sequence perspective (see Definition 3.5) to the execution of an instantiated auxiliary net II. In other words, the second auxiliary net is a specific case of the first. Its distinction will help to render small workflow models, as will be shown.

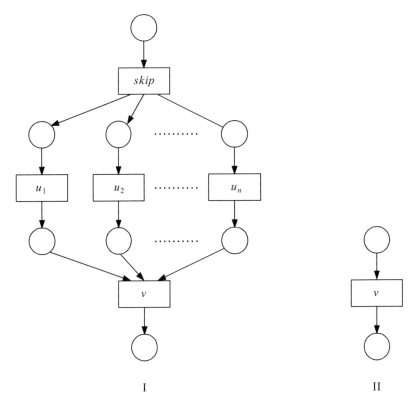

I   II

Fig. 3.10. Auxiliary nets for the construction of a breadth-first workflow model

Furthermore, for determining the breadth-first workflow model we use an auxiliary function *synth*. Suppose workflow models $WM_1 = (P_1, T_1, R_1, prod_1)$ and $WM_2 = (P_2, T_2, R_2, prod_2)$ such that $T_1 \cap T_2 = \varnothing$, $P_1 \cap P_2 = \{i, o\}$ and $t \in T_1$. Then $synth(WM_1, t, WM_2)$ yields the workflow model $(P_3, T_3, R_3, prod_3)$ where:

1. (P_3, T_3, R_3) is the workflow net obtained by a synthesis step of replacing transition t in PN_1 by the net PN_2 without its source and sink place (see Definition 2.15)
2. for $t \in T_3 \cap T_1$, $prod_3(t) = prod_1(t)$ and for $t \in T_3 \cap T_2$, $prod_3(t) = prod_2(t)$.

The auxiliary function *head* is defined on a product data model $(D, C, pre, F, constr)$ and $G \subseteq F$, $(p, cs) \in G$: $head(G) = (p, cs) \Leftrightarrow sol(G, p)$.

For any $(p, cs) \in F$ the auxiliary function *in* is defined as follows: $in(p, cs) = cs \cap D$. Note that for any $d \in D$, $in(d, \varnothing)$ yields $\varnothing$.

Finally we present the algorithm *create_bf*, which we have described as a procedure in pseudo-code. By calling this procedure and providing it with all solutions for the top element of the product data model, it recursively constructs a breadth-first workflow model using the auxiliary nets.

```
proc      create_bf(rule, PG, wm)
in        rule: F ∪ { skip }, PG : P(P(F))
out       wm: "workflow model"
local     G, G': P(F), j: ℕ, hm: "workflow model", PG': P(P(F))

   if PG = ∅ then
         "wm is the workflow model (P, T, R, prod) with unique identifiers on the basis of
          an instantiated auxiliary net II where prod(v) = rule"
   else
         "wm is the workflow model (P, T, R, prod) with unique identifiers on the basis of
          an instantiated auxiliary net I with n =| PG |, prod(v) = rule and for each 1 ≤ i ≤
          n, prod(uₙ) = skip";
         j := 1;
         while j ≤ n do
             G :∈ PG; PG := PG \ {G};
             PG' := { G' ⊆ G | d ∈ D ∧ sol(G', d) ∧ d ∈ in(head(G)) };        (*)
             create_bf(head(G), PG', hm);
             wm := synth(wm, uⱼ, hm);
             j := j + 1
         od
   fi
corp
```

The crucial part of this procedure is the statement that is marked with (*). On the basis of a solution $G \in PG$ for some $d \in D$ the set of solutions is determined for one of the inputs of the *single* production rule in G which has d as output. In other words, in a recursive fashion a solution of an information element is stripped into its subparts. The breadth-first workflow model can be found by calling the procedure *create_bf* as follows.

Definition 3.13 (Breadth-first workflow model). Given an extended product data model $(D, C, pre, F, constr, cst, flow, prob)$ and a cost optimal plan $S \subseteq D$, the breadth-first workflow model WF is derived by the procedure call *create_bf(*skip*, *top_solutions*, WF) with:

$$top\_solutions = \{\ G \subseteq F \mid sol(G, \underline{top})\ \}.$$

The set *top_solutions* incorporates all solutions for the top element of the product data model which stay within the confinements of the defined (cost optimal) plan.

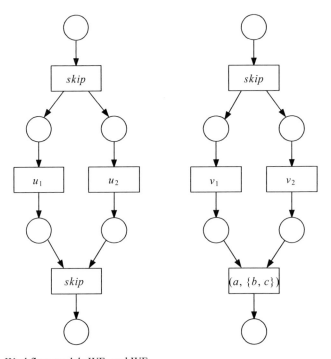

Fig. 3.11. Workflow models WF_1 and WF_2

We will demonstrate the derivation of a breadth-first workflow model on the basis of the Helicopter Pilot data model introduced earlier and cost optimal plan S_2 = $\{a, b, c, e, f\}$. We will use indexed variables for the multiple instances of the *create_bf* procedure, e.g., the set PG_2 represents the set PG in the second instantiation of the *create_bf* procedure. Successively created workflow models that arise because of a *create_bf* or *synth* operation, are numbered consecutively, e.g., WF_1, WF_2, etc.

Next, we assume – without loss of generality – that { $(a, \{b, c\})$, $(b, \emptyset)$, $(c, \{e,f\})$, $(e, \emptyset)$, $(f, \emptyset)$} is selected from PG_1. The second call of *create_bf* yields an intermediate workflow model WF_2 as depicted on the right-hand side of Figure 3.11.

Note that for notational convenience we label a transition with the associated production rule, as soon as it is clear which one it is. PG_2 consists of $\{(b, \emptyset)\}$ and $\{(c, \{e, f\}), (e, \emptyset), (f, \emptyset)\}$. Suppose that the former is selected first. The following call of the *create_bf* procedure yields the workflow model WF_3 as depicted on the left-hand side of Figure 3.12. PG_3 is empty because $(b, \emptyset)$ has no inputs that are part of D.

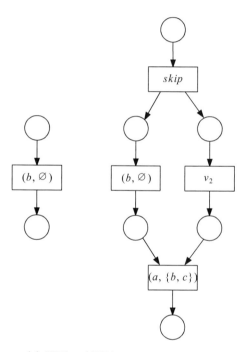

Fig. 3.12. Workflow models WF3 and WF4

The first synthesis step can now take place. It replaces transition v_1 in WF_2 with WF_3 without its sink and source place. The resulting workflow model WF_4 is depicted on the right-hand side of Figure 3.12.

The next iteration within the second instance of the *create_bf* procedure will take place on the basis of $\{(c, \{e, f\}), (e, \emptyset), (f, \emptyset)\}$. Successive creation and synthesis steps will yield workflow models WF_5, WF_6,…,WF_9. The latter – again without its source and sink place – will take the place of v_2 in the workflow model WF_4 resulting in a workflow model WF_{10}. WF_{10} in its turn will substitute transition u_1 in the workflow model WF_1, resulting in workflow model WF_{11}. WF_9 and WF_{11} are depicted in respectively the left-hand and right-hand side of Figure 3.13.

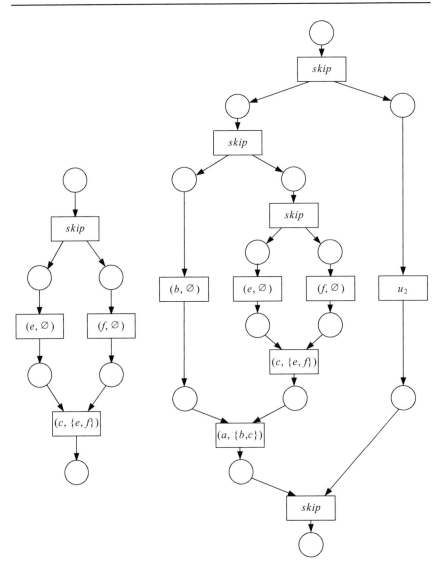

Fig. 3.13. Workflow models WF9 and WF11

The final creation and synthesis steps will yield workflow models WF_{12}, WF_{13}, and WF_{14}. Each of these models is a further specification of the behavior of the transition u_2 in workflow model WF_{11}. The final workflow model on the basis of the presented algorithm is WF_{15} such as depicted in Figure 3.14.

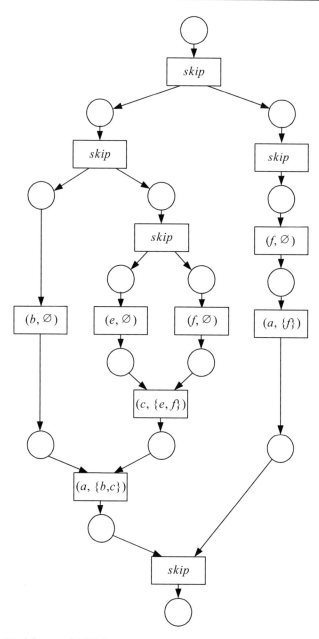

Fig. 3.14. Workflow model W15

From the product data model and the cost optimal plan S_2 it follows that there
are two different solutions to derive a value for the top element a. For each pro-

duction rule for *a*, there is exactly one solution (unlike the example of Figure 3.9). Both paths can be clearly seen in the workflow model as two concurrent branches. The inputs for both production rules – *b* and *c* for the one, *f* for the other – are placed in parallel. Note that to obtain a value for *c* the recursive nature of the algorithm ensures that input values for the production rule (*c*, {*e*, *f*}) are obtained in parallel.

Also note that the execution of W_{15} will enable simultaneously two transitions to which (*f*, ∅) is associated. Because of the semantics of the workflow model, the production rule will be executed *at most once* in any execution of the workflow.

The breadth-first workflow model yields the highest possible level of parallelism to obtain a value for the top element, regardless of cost. It is clear to see that a breadth-first workflow will always yield the fastest way to obtain a value for the top element. After all, each of the solutions for the top element within the scope of the plan is incorporated in it – including the fastest path for each particular case. A breadth-first workflow also fulfills the (cost optimal) plan that is used for confining the set of production rules of the used product data model.

Lemma 3.1   (Fulfillment of breadth-first workflow model). Given an extended product data model (D, C, *pre*, F, *constr*, *cst*, *flow*, *prob*) and a cost optimal plan $S \subseteq D$, the breadth-first workflow model WF = (P, T, R, *prod*) fulfills *S*.
Proof. We successively consider the two requirements of Definition 3.12, i.e., (i) the conformance and (ii) the inclusion of each production rule.

Ad (i). It is trivial that the workflow model created with the procedure *create* satisfies the first two requirement of the conformance definition (see Definition 3.4). Each workflow net with a structure of either of the auxiliary nets (see Figure 3.10) is free-choice and sound. Because the *synth* algorithm applies a synthesis step on the basis of Definition 2.15, soundness of the workflow net (P, T, R) follows directly from the compositionality result (Theorem 2.4).

Ad (ii). Each production rule that is part of some solution of the top element is associated with a transition. This is due to the definition of the *top_solutions* set in Definition 3.13 and the unfolding of each of its elements by the procedure *create*.
□

This concludes the treatment of the breadth-first workflow model. Note that the breadth-first workflow model not only delivers the fastest throughput time on average for an entire population, it also does so for each specific case. The depth-first workflow model that we will derive next is exclusively aimed at finding a workflow that *on average* will be optimal for a large population of cases.

Depth-First Workflow Model

A depth-first workflow model is a strictly sequential ordering of transitions to achieve at a low cost a value for the top element of the underlying product data model. In theory, there is an infinite number of sequential workflow models that fulfill the cost optimal plan of a given product data model. After all, multiple transitions may be added with the same production rule. From a practical point of view, all conformant permutations of production rules may be worth considering. After all, production rules will be applied at most once due to the semantics of the workflow model.

We distinguish two approaches to obtain a favorable member of this collection. The first approach, which we will present in some detail, is a rather brute-force generation of a finite set of sequential workflow models. All these models are subsequently evaluated, after which the best one is chosen. The second approach is a pragmatic variation of this approach. Depending on the specific content of the product data model it may be possible to find with relative ease the optimal path through the product data model. For example, if there are very few dependencies between production rules it may be easy to find such a smart ordering. As this approach is extremely dependent on the specific values of the product data model, we will not discuss it in this chapter. In Section 7.2, we will provide a case description of the design of a depth-first workflow that exploited the specific characteristics of the found product data model.

The brute-force approach also depends on the distinction of the solution and fulfillment notions (see Definition 3.11 and Definition 3.12). First all purely sequential workflow models are generated, each of which is ordered in an arbitrary sequential way. Next, all the permutations of these ordered solutions are considered. So, if there are n solutions, $n!$ orderings are considered. For each of these orderings, the expected cost is calculated. The one with the lowest expected cost is the depth-first workflow model we have been looking for. We will now describe how the production rules in a solution may be ordered.

Definition 3.14 (Ordering of solution). If $G \subseteq F$ is a solution of information element $d \in D$ within a product data model (D, C, *pre, F, constr*), then a sequence $\mu = (p_1, cs_1)(p_2, cs_2)...(p_m, cs_m)$ over F for some $m \in \mathbb{N}$ is an *ordering of G* iff:
1. the length of the sequence equals the size of the solution:
   $m = |G|$,
2. all production rules of the solution appear in the sequence:
   $\{ (p_i, cs_i) \mid 1 \leq i \leq m \} = G$, and
3. no production rules appear in the sequence of which the inputs are no outputs of previous rules in the sequence:
   $$\left[\forall 1 \leq i \leq m : cs_i \subseteq \{p_j \mid 1 \leq j < i\} \right].$$

In general many orderings are possible for a given solution of a information element d. Note that the first production rule of an ordering has no inputs and that its last production rule has d as output. Also recall the example of Figure 3.8, which shows how all ordered solutions can be found for a product data model.

The creation of all depth-first workflows on the basis of models is generated by using an auxiliary net as depicted in Figure 3.15.

Fig. 3.15. Auxiliary net for depth-first workflow models

We will simply refer to the net in the figure as the auxiliary net. If we instanti-ate it, we call into existence a (yet incomplete) workflow model with unique iden-tifiers and the structure of the auxiliary net. For instantiating the net, the number of sequential transitions n is of importance. We have to specify for an instantiated workflow model which production rules are associated with transitions with the labels $u_1, u_2, ..., u_n$ to make it complete.

We present the algorithm *create_df*, which we have described as a procedure in pseudo-code:

```
proc          create_df(PG, Pwm)
in            PG : P(P(F))
out           Pwm: "set of workflow models"
local         S: "sequence over F ", hm: "workflow model",
              PS, PS': "set of sequences over F ", G: P(F), τ: "sequence over F"
```

$PS := \varnothing;$
while $PG \neq \varnothing$ do
    $G :\in PG; PG := PG \setminus \{G\};$
    $\tau :\in \{\sigma \mid \sigma$ is an ordering of solution G cf. Definition 3.14$\};$ (*)
    $PS := PS \cup \{\tau\}$
od;
$PS' := \{\mu_1\mu_2... \mu_k \mid k = |PS| \wedge [\forall 1 \leq i \leq k : \mu_i \in PS] \wedge$
        $[\forall \sigma \in PS : (\exists 1 \leq i \leq k : \mu_i = \sigma)]\};$ (**)
while $PS' \neq \varnothing$ do
    $S :\in PS'; PS' := PS' \setminus \{S\};$
    "hm is the workflow model (P, T, R, *prod*) with unique identifiers on the basis of
        an instantiated auxiliary net with $n = |S|$ and for each $1 \leq i \leq$ n, $prod(u_n) = S(i)$"
od
corp

The procedure consists of four parts. In the first place, PG consists of all solu-tions for the top element. Secondly, for each solution $G \in PG$, an arbitrary order-ing is determined. The statement involved is marked with (*). Thirdly, all permu-tations of the ordered solutions are generated. The statement involved is marked with (**). Fourthly, all these permutations are subsequently used for the creation of all sequential workflow models. We can now give a formal definition of the creation of a set that contains the depth-first workflow model.

Definition 3.15   (Depth-first set). Given an extended product data model (D, C, *pre*, *F*, *constr*, *cst*, *flow*, *prob*) and a cost optimal plan $S \subseteq D$, the depth-first set of workflow models PWF is derived by the procedure call *create_df*(*top_solutions*, PWF) with:

$$top\_solutions = \{\ G \subseteq F\ |\ sol(G, \underline{top})\ \}.$$

Clearly, each workflow model that is part of the set that is generated by *create_df* has a purely sequential underlying workflow net due to the structure of the auxiliary net. It is trivial that each workflow model from this set is sound and that it fulfills the used (cost-optimal) plan. We claim that one of the members of this set of workflow models is the one that minimizes the average cost in servicing an entire population. Before we formalize this claim we want to consider the efficiency of the approach.

The depth-first set of Definition 3.15 can become quite large. Its number of elements can be expressed as *n*! where *n* is the number of elements of *top_solutions*. However, to appreciate the algorithm this figure should be compared with the number of different conformant permutations of *all* production rules that fall within the confinement of a (cost optimal) plan. These permutations could also be used to create a set of candidates for the depth-first workflow. This set is in general much larger. For example, take the Helicopter Pilot product data model and cost optimal plan $S_2 = \{a, b, c, e, f\}$. We already established that the set of solutions for this example consists of $\{\ (a, \{b, c\}), (b, \varnothing), (c, \{e,f\}), (e, \varnothing), (f, \varnothing)\}$ and $\{\ (a, \{f\}), (f, \varnothing)\ \}$. Therefore, our approach yields a set P*wm* of only two workflow models. Two workflow models that could be delivered by a call of the procedure *create_df*, based on the same, arbitrary orderings of the members of the solutions set, are depicted in Figure 3.16.

The number of permutations of the 6 different production rules that are used in the set of solutions is 6! = 120. Of these 120 permutations, 33 comply with the dependencies of the product data model. This is the number of workflow models that should be considered using the approach of ordering all production rules, in contrast to the two workflow models in our proposed approach.

At this point we return to the issue of finding the depth-first workflow model. We will only sketch how the expected cost may be determined for a specific workflow model, as it is a rather straightforward procedure. For each workflow model, each different combination of success probabilities of the production rules gives another interpreted sequence. The expected cost of a workflow model is the weighted sum of the cost of each interpreted sequence. The weight of an interpreted sequence is the product of the probabilities in effect. The process of determining the interpreted firing sequences and their associated cost is purely analytical and can be easily automated. The number of interpreted firing sequences one may expect at most on the basis of a workflow model that contains *n* different production rules is 2^n, taking into account for each production rule the possibility that it is successful or unsuccessful. Now consider the workflow models in Figure 3.16.

In both depicted models, 6 different production rules are in use. This means that there are at most $2^6 = 64$ interpreted firing sequences of each model. As follows from the extended product data model of the Helicopter Pilot example as introduced earlier this section, only production rule $(a, \{f\})$ will not always succeed. Therefore, the number of different interpreted firing sequences for each workflow model equals 2 at most. For the model on the right-hand side of Figure 3.16, only one interpreted firing sequence is of interest, as production rule $(a, \{f\})$ will never be executed. After all, $\{ (a, \{b, c\}), (b, \varnothing), (c, \{e,f\}), (e, \varnothing), (f, \varnothing)\}$ will *always* render a value for a. So, the expected cost of the workflow model on the left-hand side in the figure is 266 $(= 0,4 * 65 + 0,6 * 400)$; the cost of the right-hand side model 400. The workflow model on the left-hand side is therefore the depth-first workflow model.

At this point we will present our result for the depth-first workflow model we have derived.

Lemma 3.2   (Depth-first workflow model). The depth-first workflow model derived from the depth-first set (Definition 3.15) yields the lowest expected cost of any fulfilling workflow model.

Proof. We start with an observation about the orderings of solutions. Consider a solution of the top element, i.e., a minimal set of production rules that can be used to deliver a value for the top element. If we consider two arbitrary orderings that are used to create two workflow models, both workflow models have the same expected cost. After all, each ordering (Definition 3.14) contains each production rule from the solution exactly once. Because the precedence relations of the product data model are respected within an ordering, each production rule in any ordering has the same probability to succeed and, hence, to create cost.

Suppose now that we could create a workflow model for each individual new case. Assume then – without loss of generality – that for each production rule it is determined a priori whether it will be successful. Then, there may be zero or more solutions of the top element that will yield a value for the top element. If there are no such solutions, then each fulfilling workflow model that sequentially orders all the production rules will yield the same result. The depth-first workflow model is such a model, so the claim holds for the case that there are no successful solutions.

If there is at least one such solution, then it is wise to use the one with the lowest cost. Obviously, for a specific case we do *not* know a priori which production rules will be successful. To decrease the expected cost, we should use for an arbitrary case with unknown success probabilities for the production rules the solution with the lowest *expected* cost first. If it will not succeed, the second least costly solution should be used, next the third lest costly etc. The algorithm *create_df* generates all possible permutations of the same (but arbitrary) orderings of the solutions. As we observed in the start of this proof, it is of no importance which particular ordering is used for each solution. We conclude that the workflow model with the lowest expected cost from all sets generated indeed has the lowest expected cost of all fulfilling workflow models. □

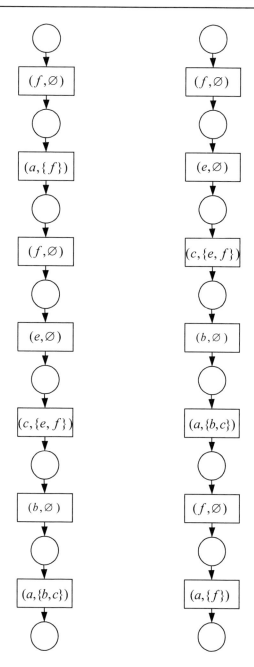

Fig. 3.16. Example set of depth-first workflow models

Discussion

A few remarks can be made about Lemma 3.2. It may seem rather expensive to generate all permutations of (ordered) solutions for the top element. Why not compute the expected cost of each solution and subsequently order them in a sequence of decreasing expected cost? This is the approach as described for ordering tasks with independent execution cost by Van der Aalst (2000b). Although this approach is certainly more efficient, it will not in general yield the best result. Consider, for example, the three solutions for a top element with respect to production rules $p1$, $p2$, ..., $p8$ as depicted in Figure 3.17 as ovals. Assume that the rules $p1$, $p4$, and $p8$ have no cost and that they can deliver a value for the top element with a probability of $1 - q$, i.e., they are knock-outs. These are represented in bold. All other rules are always successful and have a cost of 1 unit.

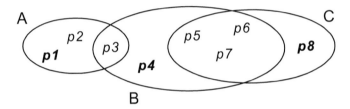

Fig. 3.17. Three overlapping solutions

If we purely consider solutions A and B for making a depth-first workflow, then doing A before B has a lower average cost ($= 2 + 3q$) than doing B before A ($= 4 + q$) with $q < 1$. Note that the cost of executing $p3$ has to be made only once in each scenario. If C is, however, the first solution to be pursued, it is on average cheaper (with $q < 1$) continuing with B and then A ($= 3 + q + q^2$), than continuing with A and then B ($= 3 + 2q$). This is explained by the fact that in doing C first, it takes a small additional cost to do B because of the large overlap between B and C.

In general, the overlap of solutions may be rather large, so that it is more profitable to order in succession of a solution another solution with a large overlap. If the first solution does not yield a value for the top element, the second solution may do this after all, without much additional cost. In a probabilistic sense, the expected cost of a solution as part of a sequential workflow model is *dependent* upon the preceding executed solutions. This observation may help to design a workflow model in a heuristic sense if the number of different solutions is large. Without considering such an approach in detail, a sense of *similarity* between solutions may be used to reduce from the set of workflow models to be considered those ones that do not subsequently order very similar models.

We would like to illustrate another point of interest using again the example product data model of Figure 3.9. We established that this product data model has the following solutions:

1. $\{ (x, \{a, b\}), (a, \varnothing), (b, \{a\}) \}$.
2. $\{ (x, \{a, b\}), (a, \varnothing), (b, \{c\}), (c, \varnothing) \}$.
3. $\{ (x, \{d\}), (d, \varnothing) \}$.

Suppose that for some cost and probability functions of the extended product data model the depth-first workflow model WF orders solutions 1 and 2 directly in succession. Suppose further that for some execution of WF production rules $(a, \varnothing)$ and $(b, \{a\})$ of the first solution will succeed, but that $(x, \{a, b\})$ fails. Execution will continue with an ordering of the second solution. This means that production rule $(c, \varnothing)$ will certainly be applied (note that the production of a leaf is always successful on the basis of Definition 3.2). However, this cost can be seen as *superfluous*. After all, $(x, \{a, b\})$ has already failed and will not be applied a second time. This undesirable effect is the direct result of our notion of fulfillment (see Definition 3.12). This requires the inclusion of each production rule in each firing sequence of a fulfilling workflow model. In other words, there is no possibility to skip a production rule once its application becomes superfluous. The presented heuristic approach does not take into account this type of dependencies. (Note that a similar argument could be formulated for a breadth-first workflow model.)

From a technical viewpoint it is possible to adapt the algorithm that creates the depth-first set of workflow models to incorporate the dependencies as described in selecting the optimal depth-first workflow model. Prior to each transition in a workflow model that is delivered by the procedure *create_df*, a selection transition should be added that determines whether it is useful to proceed with the solution that this transition is part of. Note that this can be decided at any point during the execution of a workflow model if we add to such a workflow model an administration of production rules that were *unsuccessful*. In determining the depth-first workflow model out of the set of such models, this added functionality should obviously be incorporated to determine the expected cost. It is clear that this will blow up the number of interpreted firing sequences of these types of models considerably. A brute-force approach as we have described will proportionally become less attractive. Incorporating heuristics such as described by Orman (1998) or Van der Aalst (2000b) to order the production rules will then be more attractive.

We will not further describe such approaches as described. This is a matter of balance between the complexity of the computations/models on the one hand and the gains they may offer on the other hand. For product data models (a) that are relatively small, (b) where the solutions have a large overlap, (c) where the common production rules are close to the top element, and (d) where the cost of lower production rules is high, the extension of the described approach may be considered. In the opposite case, the described approach may already deliver satisfactory results. Especially because product data models can become quite large, e.g., with 500 information elements, more fine-grained approaches may become infeasible. The expected cost of a depth-first workflow model or even that of the cost optimal plan also may already be acceptable for the organization that hosts the process. In other words, the performance target may be already met. In these cases, the effort for additional optimization is probably not justified or infeasible.

We end the discussion of designing optimal workflows for the common case with the remark that the design of a workflow on the basis of a product data model must be driven by the *optimization criteria that are relevant for the BPR initiative*. These criteria should also drive the analysis phase to gather useful logical and empirical data for the design. Although the criteria of cost, speed, and quality we used are important and much applied in practice, a different list or prioritization may be encountered for specific BPR initiatives. For example, Sharp and McDermott (2001) mention as alternative goals for a new process: flexibility in meeting needs of individual clients, easier to adopt for an entry-level workforce, fewer client interactions, absolute auditability, easier to maintain at international locations, and more suitable for support by commercial off-the-shelf (COTS) software. It is not possible to discuss a design strategy for each of these various cases. In the following section we will nonetheless discuss an approach aimed at delivering a flexible process for each individual client.

The important principle in designing a workflow with PBWD is to find an exploration of the product data model in such a way that its expected performance implements the set targets. At occasions where the product data model is relatively small, it may be feasible to generate all or a large number of different models for the sake of comparison. By this, we mean an even larger number than the described brute-force approach offers. This effort would be greatly simplified by an automated support of tools. It is always good practice to deliver more than just one process design for the evaluation phase. Process designs may be comparable in terms of the primary BPR goals, but may be different from additional relevant viewing points. We will discuss the topic in more detail in the description of the evaluation phase.

Specific Case

Instead of specifying the optimal route through the product data model a priori on the basis of the common characteristics of a case, a more flexible, ad hoc approach is also feasible. This may lead to a process execution where for each case and at any state during the process execution for this case, it may be decided what the exploration of the (rest of the) product data model looks like. More specific, this means that at any time a decision may be made which following production rule(s) should be executed, as long as this execution conforms to the product data model.

There may be different degrees in this type of flexibility. For example, as long as a certain time limit is not exceeded a depth-first strategy is chosen for each case to minimize cost. If for an individual case the time limit approaches, the exploration policy is switched to a breadth-first policy to speed up the work. This is a level of flexibility that implies the same policy for all cases. A stronger form of flexibility is that depending on the client's own preferences a different exploration route is chosen. A client who is interested in a high quality of the delivered service may be willing to pay for more costly production rules. For another client who has fundamental objections to the participation of specific parties in the process some production rules may be excluded.

This flexibility is different from designing a workflow that just incorporates a very large number of alternative routes. Although the latter approach may also lead to a flexible process execution, it is different in the sense that the flexibility is thought out at *build time* instead of at *run time*. Another way of looking at it, is to favor a *pull* mechanism – where an office worker decides on the process exception - over a *push* mechanism – where a system implementing a design prescribes every action. Only when the degree of variability to explore the product data model is really small, a workflow that incorporates a very large number of alternative routes may render the same level of operational flexibility. The combinatorial explosion of different combinations of production rule executions is in practice such that they cannot be incorporated in a build time design. The complexity and maintainability of such a design would be very questionable.

With regard to the question for a high level of operational flexibility the answer should not be found in the design of the workflow, but in the support of office technology that supports the execution of the process. The desirable system must be able to manage the product data model and control for each case whether the execution of production rules conforms to it. At any reachable state during the processing of a case, this system also must be aware of all the available information. Given this information and the product data model, it should present to the relevant end-users which of the production rules can be potentially executed. It is up to these end-users which of the production rules are selected for subsequent execution. Considerations that may be relevant to this choice are: the client's individual whishes or characteristics, the company's operational guidelines, external conditions, or the individual preference of the end-user. Van der Aalst and Berens (2001) describe a system that may be usable for such an approach.

Although the operational flexibility of a system as described is high, we make some critical notes as follows:

- The individual processing of cases may become so diverse that it is impossible to compare them; such a comparison may be valuable for improving the performance of the overall process execution or migrating onto new product data models.
- Operational flexibility may intervene with other goals such as cost reduction and speed enhancement; a well-chosen balance is required.
- Office workers must be able to handle the higher level of responsibility and desired control of the workflow execution; acquiring these skills by training or employment may be required.

We end this part of our description of the design phase by stating that the development of alternative workflow designs is primarily the goal of a design for a population of cases. After all, the described support for flexibly handling arbitrary cases supposes the same product data model for each case.

The design for a specific case, together with the important notions in this phase, is once more given in Figure 3.18. The obvious deliverables of this phase are one or more workflow models, which will be examined in the evaluation phase.

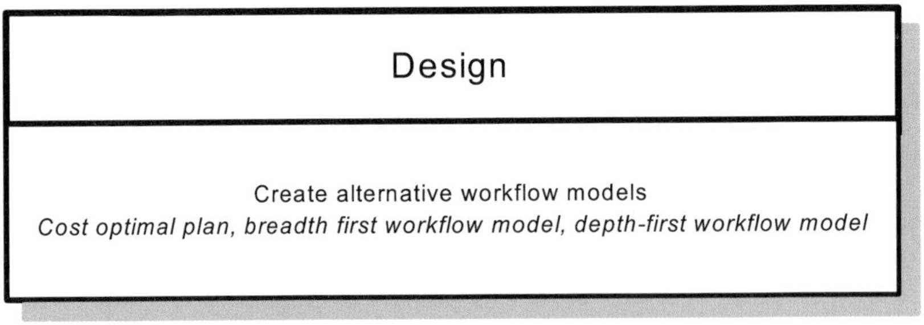

Fig. 3.18. The design phase

3.4.4 Evaluation

By now we have discussed the scoping, analysis, and design phases. The final phase of the PBWD methodology is the evaluation phase. The evaluation phase takes as input the alternative workflow designs derived in the design phase. There are four important steps that should be taken, which are as follows:

1. The correctness of the workflow models should be *verified*.
2. The workflows should be *validated* with experts.
3. The *performance* of the workflows should be established.
4. The results of the previous steps should be *presented* to management.

We will discuss these respective steps in this section.

Verification

Verification involves the checking of the *syntactical* correctness of a workflow model. In contrast to the context of programming languages where *syntax* only refers to the language, we incorporate in our notion of syntactical correctness both the structure and the *behavior* of the workflow model. Although workflow models that have been derived in the way as described in this section already implement some notions of syntactical correctness, models may be extended or changed by human intervention before they are considered complete. Typically, human errors in designing the workflow on the basis of the product data model may cause dead tasks, deadlocks, livelocks, etc. Especially when a workflow model becomes large, i.e., when it incorporates hundreds of tasks, it is difficult for human designers to oversee the complete model. We will not extensively treat the subject of workflow verification here. A discussion is given by Van der Aalst and Ter Hofstede (2000). The tool Woflan, which supports the verification of workflows, is described by Verbeek and Van der Aalst (2000) and Verbeek et al. (2001).

Validation

Perhaps the most important step in the evaluation phase is the validation of the derived workflow designs by experts. Validation involves the *semantic* correctness of the model: are the right things being done? Although the product specification is the proper source for deriving what should be done, misinterpretations or improper use of may be the cause of a faulty workflow design. Note that semantic correctness supposes a syntactic correctness of the workflow involved, as checked in the verification step.

From a system development point of view, it is important to validate a process design prior to the implementation of the workflow and the automation of processing steps. It is well known that design errors that are found late in the project are very costly to correct. Martin (1991) estimated that in software development finding a design error during the programming, testing, and maintenance phases is respectively 3, 10 and 100 times more costly than finding it during the design. From a change management perspective, it is also valuable to confront end-users with a design before further development takes place. This approach involves users in the design and it enables them to give feedback. It is also desirable that end-users realize that although the new process design may be structurally different from the process they are used to, it can be used for delivering the same type of products as before.

For all named validation purposes, there are different means available. Sommerville and Sawyer (1997) name formal inspections, developing draft manuals, paraphrasing, validation checklists, and prototyping. Casimir (1995) also names the *gaming* concept as a means for system design validation.

The particular approach we would like to devote some attention to is the use of a *prototype* as a basis for validation. The idea is then to confront end-users with a system that shows them both the ordering logic of production rules and their content. Usually, implementing a workflow design is a large effort due to the required integration with working transaction systems and the development of new software to implement the production rules. Instead of awaiting these actions, end-users may already develop a good conception of the new workflow by experiencing the handling of partly pre-defined cases. As much as possible, end-users should be enabled to make autonomous decisions in handling these case and accordingly enter information in the system. This is possible as long as this involves relatively simple production logic, which may be either automated within the prototype or done by the end-user himself. Also, pre-defined information can be shown to the end-users if it affects computations that cannot be performed by the prototype. Consistent pre-defined information can be determined off-line on the basis of the product data model and established production rules. A high degree of realism of the workflow to be implemented is nonetheless obtained, because all the tasks and involved information are presented.

Aside from the validation aspect of prototyping it has as additional advantage that it allows end-users to generate meaningful feedback on the design. From a change perspective, it is important that people feel they can influence the end-result of the design project.

In Chapter 7 we will extensively describe a case in which a prototype is used within the context of validating a workflow model rendered with PBWD.

Performance

The design of the workflow with PBWD is driven by design criteria that are specific for the design effort supported. As accurately as possible, relevant performance figures should be estimated as input for the design. Some of these figures may in practice be dependent on many factors that cannot all be taken into account during the design. For example, the throughput time of a workflow is dependent on the response speed of external parties, the actual availability of resources, the types of cases encountered, etc. It is wise to analyze in more depth the performance of the verified and validated workflow design to obtain more reliable information on their performance. We will not in detail treat the performance analysis of workflow models at this place. Simulation may be used for this purpose. An analytical approach for establishing the expected performance of a workflow model that incorporates stochastic delays instead of fixed delays (such as is the case in the extended product data model, see Definition 3.2) is the subject of Chapter 4.

To support the decision process that should take place in the following presentation activity, it is appropriate to compare the performance results of the new design with those of the current process. Especially when the design objectives have been formulated in relative terms to the current performance, this is a necessity.

Presentation

The last step within the evaluation phase - and with it the last step within the PBWD method - is to present the verified and validated workflows to the commissioning management of the design effort. Supporting information from the performance analysis can be used to argue the probability that the design effort will lead to the set goals of the scoping phase. The commissioning party is responsible for selecting and accepting one or none of the presented models to be used for the implementation of the redesign. Typically system development and integration, training of end-users, the development of instruction and procedure manuals, etc. are the follow-up of a process design. In Chapter 7 we will describe a case on how application development may take place on the basis of the deliverables of PBWD.

The evaluation phase is summarized in Figure 3.19. The deliverable of the evaluation phase is a verified and validated workflow model, which is expected to meet the set performance targets and which can be used as a framework to implement the workflow.

3.4 Review

In this section we will critically review the PBWD methodology. We will use the results of the BPR survey of Section 3.1 as a basis for comparison, as well as our practical experience with PBWD in designing workflows (see Sections 7.2 and 7.3).

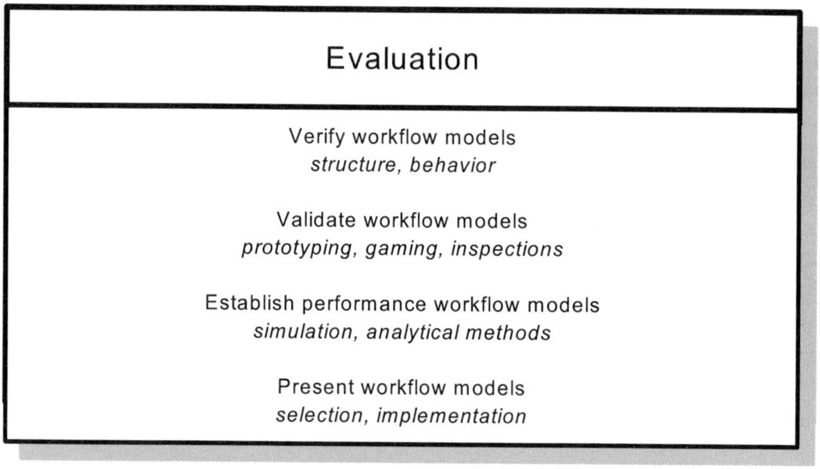

Evaluation

Verify workflow models
structure, behavior

Validate workflow models
prototyping, gaming, inspections

Establish performance workflow models
simulation, analytical methods

Present workflow models
selection, implementation

Fig. 3.19. The evaluation phase

3.4.1 Advantages

The specific features of PBWD concerning its specific clean sheet and analytical nature (see Section 3.2) have three major advantages, which are the following:

1. *Radicalism*: the clean sheet approach allows for maximal space to establish performance improvements.
2. *Objectivity*: the analytical nature is the next best thing to a guarantee for an objective materialization of the workflow design.
3. *System integration*: the analytical approach renders detailed deliverables suitable to use for systems development purposes.

We will elaborate on each of these advantages. Approaches that use the existing process will to some extent copy constructions from the current process that do not support the BPR objectives. This is justified by its mere existence within the current process, which is a questionable basis. Typically, all kinds of constructions such as checks, validations, etc. are added to a workflow to prevent a historical incident from happening again. The loss of performance that these measures cause, however, is never considered again. Applying redesign heuristics to cut out these kinds of inefficiencies may partly elevate the "copy bug". However, applying heuristics will never question the main course of the process. Workflows designed with PBWD may take on *any* form that conforms to the product specification driven by the redesign objectives.

The second major advantage of PBWD is its objectivity. In the first place, because the product specification is taken as the basis for the design of the new workflow, each recognized information element and each production rule can be justified and verified with this specification. As a consequence, there are no unnecessary tasks in the resulting workflow. Secondly, the ordering of (tasks with) production rules themselves is completely driven by the performance targets of the design effort. PBWD is aimed at generating the favorable workflows and discarding the unfavorable ones by means of analytical assessment. We demonstrated how performance notions may be formalized and assessed in Section 3.3.

These two points are in sharp contrast with the results of participative approaches. Then, workshop participants are responsible for summing up all relevant information and logic. The probability that a piece of information is missed or that irrelevant information is included is much greater in this way. The decisions on ordering tasks within a workflow also must be taken on the basis of common sense. It requires workflow participants to estimate and evaluate large amounts of information to asses all the performance consequences of each issue. Very few people may be capable of doing so. Their decision making will rather be driven by "gut feeling" than rationality. Obviously, the selection of necessary information elements and the formulation of involved production rules may involve some sort of subjectivity as well. However, on a level of scale the objectivity of the PBWD approach exceeds that of participative approaches.

The third and last advantage, the integration with a systems development effort, is not extensively discussed in this chapter. However, it can easily be imagined that on the basis of the PBWD deliverables it is possible to develop functional models of the information systems to be developed for (or integrated with) the new workflow design. Production rules can then be seen as functional specifications for services an application should offer. Information elements can be seen as attributes of entities that have to be modeled in a data model. Even then, not the mere speed up of the development process is the beneficial factor, but rather that the workflow model and the systems design is tightly integrated. The PBWD deliverables render information that is a direct translation of business needs on a detail level that is hardly ever encountered by system developers in practice. In participative approaches, which are much, more common, participants of various backgrounds take part in workshops to design a workflow. The great variety in the background of the participants improves the probability that all relevant factors are addressed in the workflow design. At the same time, it prevents that much time can be spend on detailing the workflow, because of the risk of loosing the interest of one or more participants. Also, because the forming of consensus is a major issue in workshop settings, it is tempting to mask the specifics of a workflow design and with it, the related disputes. As a result, workflow designs resulting from participative approaches typically carry too little information for system developers to be useful. A methodology that prescribes how component-based application development can take place on the basis of the deliverables of PBWD is described by Reijers and Van der Toorn (2002). In the cases of PBWD applications in Chapter 7, we will devote some attention to the development of information systems on the basis of PBWD deliverables.

3.4.2 Critique

Because of the controversy over clean sheet approaches it is at this point perhaps fair to evaluate to which extent the commonly formulated claims against them apply to PBWD. Our survey yielded the following (see Section 3.1):

1. There is the danger of designing another inefficient system.
2. The clean sheet approach fails to build on knowledge and experience which has been built up over time and risks mistakes of the past.
3. Workers may be unable to relate to the new process as it bears little resemblance to the work that is being done.
4. By designing a process completely from scratch the scope of the redesign problem is not appreciated.

We will address each of these points. The danger of designing an inefficient system is always present. However, taking an inefficient existing process as a starting point does not appear to be a remedy. By incorporating sufficient competence and experience in a project team that designs the workflow with PBWD, the danger of designing another inefficient system may be constrained. The evaluation phase also should point out whether the new design can indeed live up to its expectations.

Concerning the second point of critique, it would be very serious indeed if relevant knowledge were omitted from the design effort. We believe, however, that it is more applicable to participative approaches than to PBWD. It may very well be that the popularity of taking the existing process as a starting point is a weak alternative for securing that product characteristics are not violated in the new process. Especially when workshop participants have to come up with all important workflow ingredients, chances are that relevant information is forgotten.

Let us consider the third point of critique. That workers will find it hard to relate to a new process design is inherent to radical change. Because PBWD allows for radical change, it is especially applicable to this method. We believe that there should always be a balance between the expected gain of a new workflow design and the likelihood that the design is workable and agreeable. There are two additional remarks that should be made. Firstly, a radically new workflow layout may be *inevitable* to achieve a radical performance improvement. The question, then, is whether the design should be implemented. However, this is not an issue that concerns PBWD. Secondly, even though a workflow is radically different, people may still be willing to work in this way if they see the benefits and recognize that the essence of the process is maintained – generating a specific product. Using prototypes as a means of showing these aspects has proven to be very effective in our experience (see De Crom and Reijers, 2001). Other effective measures include simulation, training and involving people in the implementation phase, etc.

The last point we have to address is the risk of using the wrong scope. Using the existing process, it may be easier to encounter all dependencies with other processes and stakeholders because these are – in the best case – already present in the current process. In any case, the fourth drawback to a clean sheet approach can be partly elevated by deeply considering beforehand the exact scope of the redesign. This is in fact the first phase of PBWD. However, what may take place with PBWD is that historic services delivered by the current process are not recognized as supporting the generation of its corresponding product, for example delivering information to third parties. The question is: are these services really required for delivering the product? We think that applying PBWD is a perfect way of eliminating beforehand all these dependencies if they are not explicitly included within the scope of the product. Really important dependencies will be found anyway and may then be rationally considered for inclusion in the final design.

3.4.3 Drawbacks

From the above discussion it may become clear that traditional disadvantages to clean sheet approaches only partially apply to PBWD. This is not to say that there are no drawbacks at all. During the various projects we have conducted, we identified the following issues:

1. The application of PBWD *presupposes a clear concept of the product* to be delivered. After all, if there is no product specification the basis for PBWD is missing.
2. The application of PBWD is an *intensive effort*. A thorough analysis is required of the product specification, followed by a formal design approach and an extensive evaluation of the workflow delivered. A PBWD project may require an organization awaiting the new design to stand on hold for some time.
3. PBWD *breaks with the leading role of the Technology discipline*. In many organizations, the Information Technology department initiates and carries BPR efforts. But instead of starting with technology-oriented analyses and approaches, a business-oriented analysis starts the PBWD project. This changes the role of people and departments historically connected with BPR.
4. For internal experts that become involved with the PBWD effort, it is *hard to "forget" the existing process*. Not everyone – even after some habituation – is suitable to make this mental leap.

From the first issue it becomes clear that the application of PBWD is restricted to fields where a clear concept of the products to be delivered exists. This means that PBWD is more likely to be applied in legislative settings or within companies that already have some tradition on administrative records, such as banks and insurance companies. It also means that a company should know first *what* to do, before it can consider *how* to do it best.

The second issue is an important factor in the selection of the proper methodology at the dawn of a BPR effort. The benefits in terms of improvement outcomes should be balanced against the duration of the project. If only gradual gains are desired from a redesign project, PBWD may not be the right methodology to carry it out.

The third issue requires that a clear understanding with the Information Technology department is established about the responsibilities of the various stakeholders. In particular, it should be stressed that prior to any information system development effort at least a product data model should be derived. This establishing of responsibilities is also a change management issue, although it does not center on the population that is commonly concentrated on, the end-users.

The fourth and final issue has as a consequence that considerable time should be invested in training and explaining the PBWD concepts to internal experts. Even so, it should be reckoned with that not each professional end-user is able to make a valuable contribution to the PBWD effort. This may limit the use of PBWD to areas of business professionals with a higher educational or technical background.

3.4.4 Points of Interest

By now, we have discussed the major advantages and drawbacks of PBWD. At the conclusion of our treatment of PBWD we would like to point out some other interesting aspects of PBWD. Two more or less neutral differences between PBWD and other design approaches are as follows:

1. PBWD works *backward*: the end product is taken as starting point and unraveled into the required processing steps to produce the end product; other design approaches may work *forward*, starting with the first necessary steps in the process and deduce all the necessary steps to the end.
2. PBWD is *data-centered*: first the relevant data is determined, after which processing steps are defined on the basis of the data manipulations; other design approaches are more *process-centered* as they may typically start with defining abstract processing steps, which are detailed in a later phase of the redesign.

Another interesting issue that we have seen in practice is that as a side effect to the analysis of the product specifications, involved analysts become semi-experts in the field. As a consequence, they are able to discuss and counter criticism on their work from skeptical parties involved. Moreover, because of the detailed fraction analysis (see Section 3.3), analysts get a grip on the impact and plausibility of exceptions that may occur. The emphasis on exceptions that undermines a preliminary workflow design is in our opinion the most common critique on any new workflow design that end-users have. A rational treatment of this critique is greatly assisted with objective figures.

PBWD directly links the content of the final workflow design with the product specification that is used to derive it. End-users that are responsible for carrying out specific tasks can always check on the original source for their justification and explanation. Should the product specification change, it becomes clear from the documentation of the workflow which parts of it are affected by this change. (Note that this requires the non-formal part of the product data model). Changing product specifications are far from hypothetical. In fact, the Unemployment Law, which was the basis for one of the workflow designs we have made, is updated monthly. Minor changes in production rules can be easily incorporated in the existing workflow design. End-users can be informed about the changes each time they are about to execute a task with a new specification. Major changes that deeply affect the dependencies within the product data model may lead to the derivation and evaluation of completely new workflow design. From all of this, it becomes clear that the deliverables of a PBWD are of value even after the resulting workflow has been implemented. Their relation with the product specification should be maintained allowing for flexibility and adaptability of the workflow in effect.

The final aspect of discussion is related to one of the critical points we detected about the application of PBWD: a clear product specification should be present. Although it is limiting the application of PBWD, this rigorous need for a product specification can be an advantage as well. In settings where one is used to administrative records on products, the application of PBWD can be used to identify breaches in the existing product specifications. In the regulations that were used for the design of an unemployment workflow, we found circular references and pointers to out-of-date regulations. At the large Dutch Bank for which we applied PBWD, we found out that the approval procedures within a credit loan process - although effectuated for decades by specialists - were not documented at all. This raised the possibility to reflect on this procedure and to develop a company policy on this point. In general, a close inspection of the product specification may bring to light flaws of it. This gives the organization the opportunity to reflect and even correct them.

4 Performance Evaluation of Workflows

In this chapter two analytical methods are presented for the performance evaluation of workflows. Typically, these methods can be applied to assess whether a
workflow design meets a performance target with respect to its throughput time.
These methods are meant as a support for the designer of workflows, particularly
within the setting of a BPR initiative. In particular, if a workflow is designed using
the product-based method as described in Chapter 3, the presented algorithms are
of use during the evaluation phase when a performance evaluation is due (see Section 3.3). For the specification of a workflow design, we will once again use the
Stochastic Workflow net (SWN) as defined in Chapter 2, as well as the notion of
throughput defined there. The analysis in this chapter focuses on the routing component of a workflow model (see Section 2.2).

Both presented methods assume an infinite amount of resources, i.e., a lack of
available resources does not cause queuing. This assumption typically reflects the
first stage of designing a workflow. Only when the intrinsic quality of the routing
component is sufficient, the allocation component is put into place (see the introduction of Chapter 3).

The focus of this chapter is depicted as the thickly lined box in the center of
Figure 4.1. The overall model describes the relevant entities in a workflow; it has
been introduced in Section 1.4.

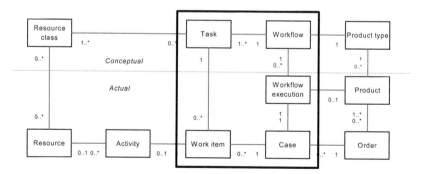

Fig. 4.1. Focus of chapter

The structure of this chapter is as follows. We first consider in Section 4.1 the
field of formal analysis techniques. We will reflect also in this section upon the
importance of the throughput time as performance target. In Section 4.2, we discuss available analysis techniques of other timed, formal models, in particular sto-

H.A. Reijers: Design and Control of Workflow Processes, LNCS 2617, pp. 127-176, 2003.
© Springer-Verlag Berlin Heidelberg 2003

chastic Petri nets. This discussion builds upon the overview of timed Petri net models in Section 2.4. In Section 4.3, we will describe an analysis approach that renders exact analysis results for the throughput time behavior of a business process model that fits within our framework. A special construction method is presented that guarantees that such results can be obtained. In Section 4.4 we will describe an alternative method that, instead of exact results, yields bounds for the throughput time behavior of an SWN. The application area of the approximation method can be expressed in terms of standard properties on Petri nets. Finally, in Section 4.5 we will describe a hybrid approach combining some attractive properties of both approaches.

4.1 Context

4.1.1 Formal Analysis

In general, there are two different categories of formal analysis techniques that can be used in the context of redesigning business processes in general and workflows in particular: qualitative and quantitative techniques. Qualitative techniques focus on the question whether a process design meets a specific property. Quantitative techniques are used to calculate or approximate the size or level of a specific property. For example, a qualitative question may be whether a process design meets the demand that a bank employee can never validate a cash transfer that he has initiated himself. To determine how long clients have to wait before their telephone call is responded to by the call-center typically a quantitative analysis is required.

Quantitative techniques can be categorized further into simulation and analytical techniques. During a simulation of a workflow, at specified intervals cases (e.g., new orders) are generated for the model in execution. In response, each of the components within the model will behave in accordance with its pre-defined specification. For instance, on receipt of a new order the computer will simulate an employee inspecting the order on completeness. The actions performed by the model in execution copy the real-life actions. However, they may be not exactly the same or may not take place at exactly the same moment as in real life. During execution, information is gathered on items that result from the interaction of the modeled components. For example, the frequency of message exchanges between two specific components is measured or the accumulation of work in front of an overloaded resource. For the simulation of business processes, see e.g., Desel and Erwin (2000) or Van der Aalst et al. (2000a).

An analytical technique, on the other hand, is based on an algorithm that yields an exact result on the basis of both the formal model and some well-understood relationships between the specified components. For example, a business process can be modeled as a network of nodes connected to each other by arcs, expressing precedence relations. On the basis of such a network model, the shortest path leading from a new order to fulfillment can be calculated. Popular formalisms and mathematical theories to model and analyze business processes in this analytical way are, for example, Petri nets, Markov chains, queuing networks theory, CPM, PERT and GERT.

Often, an analytical approach is preferred over simulation. However, the complexity of a specific workflow model can be such that a simulation approach is the only feasible means of analysis. Given a specific process model, there are several aspects that determine whether an analytical approach is feasible at all and – if so – preferable over simulation. For example, if both the synchronization structures within a process (e.g., parallelism) and the behavior of resources is too complex, no known general analytical techniques are available to determine the throughput times of cases. Simulation is then the only possible alternative to obtain quantitative results. Although simulation is a very flexible technique suited to investigate almost any type of business process, a common disadvantage is that, in non-trivial situations, numerous and lengthy simulation runs have to be carried out to obtain reliable results. This is particularly troublesome when a large number of different alternative workflow models has to be investigated.

For both qualitative and quantitative types of analysis holds that a formal model of the business process underlies the analysis. Depending on the set of properties that is taken into consideration in the redesign effort, elements of the real business process are incorporated in the model. If, for example, the redesign effort is primarily concerned with the optimization of the logistics of the process, elements typically found in a process model are buffers, resources, routings of cases, service times, and order arrivals. If, for example, the accent is on cost reduction, elements such as labor time, material costs, and depreciation factors will be part of the model.

4.1.2 Throughput Time

One of the most important performance indicators in industry is the throughput time. The throughput time of a specific case is the total amount of time spent from the moment that the case is initiated until the moment it is completed (see Section 2.4). The throughput time of a case is in general a combination of service, queue, and wait times. Service time involves the time that is spend on actually handling the case by executing tasks. Queue times arise because of the unavailability of sufficient resources to work on a case, i.e., a case has to queue. Wait time is all other time a case spends waiting, for example because synchronization must take place with another process.

The wide-spread use of the throughput time as a performance target can be explained from the fact that it is concerned with the "flowing" of work through the business process, rather than with the exact manipulations that take place. [Similarly, workflow management is concerned with the management of the "flow of work" and not with the execution of individual tasks.] Very often, a low or stable throughput time is a desirable or even necessary characteristic of a business process. Imagine, for instance, a government agency that handles tax forms and decides whether they are valid. National regulations may be violated when the processing of a case takes over one year.

The throughput time of a workflow – in contrast to that of a specific case – can be expressed in several ways. After all, cases that are handled by the same workflow often do not share the same throughput time. In other words, there is throughput variance. An ordinary cause for this phenomenon is that resources do not deliver constant productivity. Another cause may be fluctuations in market demand that possibly flood the system, leading to long queues. Finally, cases carry different characteristics causing different routes through the process or tasks being skipped. A very common approach is to express the throughput time of a process as the average throughput time of the cases it handles. Although this may be fine as an approximation, this average is not always a good reflector of the performance of the process. For example, if minimal and maximal throughput times of cases are far apart, the average throughput time is hardly suitable to give clients guarantees about delivery times. An alternative sometimes used, is to define the throughput time of a process by means of a fraction percentage and a cut-off value. For example, 90 % of the cases going through a specific business process are finished within 6 weeks. If the throughput of cases varies, the most detailed expression of the throughput time is as a histogram or a probability distribution of the case throughput times.

Regardless of the exact definition used, the computation of the throughput time for an operational workflow is straightforward. Actual figures on cases can be used. A problem arises when the throughput time is to be determined of a newly designed process. By depending solely on historic information the designer is in an awkward position. He cannot design a process with desirable throughput characteristics without putting the process to work first. Especially when redesign alternatives are to be compared this is not very practical.

In the Sections 4.3, 4.4, and 4.5 we will describe several approaches to characterize the throughput time of a newly designed workflow. Workflow designs are modeled as SWN's, allowing for arbitrary service times and complex routing patterns. No resources are incorporated in the models, reflecting the typical first stage of designing a workflow. Only when the intrinsic quality of the routing component is sufficient, the allocation component is put in place (see Chapter 3). In the next section, we will give an overview of other approaches for performance evaluation such as networking techniques. The focus in this overview is on timed Petri nets in particular.

4.2 Analysis of Timed Petri Nets

As described in Chapter 2, there are many ways to introduce time in Petri nets. In Section 2.4 we gave an overview of existing timed Petri net models. In this section, we will focus on their analysis.

All timed Petri net models are executable. That is to say, it is possible to construct a trace of the modeled system. Therefore, simulation can be used to analyze the model. If all non-determinism is replaced by stochastic measures (i.e., delays and conflict resolution), then simulation can be used to obtain confidence intervals for performance measures such as the utilization and throughput. We already discussed some of the drawbacks of simulation in Section 4.1. In the remainder of this chapter, we will focus on analytical analysis techniques to overcome the limitations of simulation approaches. Since analysis techniques are typically restricted by the type of delay, we first consider timed Petri nets with deterministic timing, then timed Petri nets with non-deterministic timing, and finally timed Petri nets with stochastic timing.

4.2.1 Deterministic Timing

There are several methods to calculate upper and lower bounds for the cycle time of a timed Petri net with deterministic delays, for example: Sifakis (1980), Ramamoorthy and Ho (1980), Ramchandani (1984), and Murata (1992). The cycle time is a criterion for the performance of the system. For the so-called Timed Event Graphs, the exact cycle time can be computed quite efficiently, see Ramamoorthy and Ho (1980) or Chretienne (1983). Other researchers such as Zuberek (1980) analyze deterministic timed Petri nets by building the reachability graph. Although this requires a lot of computing effort, such a graph can be used to answer a variety of questions. The analysis of PERT type of networks (marked graphs) with deterministic timing is straightforward.

4.2.2 Non-deterministic Timing

Most timed Petri net models using non-deterministic delays, such as described by Merlin (1974), Merlin and Faber (1976), Berthomieu and Diaz (1991), Berthomieu and Menasche (1993), Van der Aalst (1993, 1994), and Van der Aalst and Odijk (1995), use intervals to describe lower bounds and upper bounds for the duration of activities. The method presented by Berthomieu, Diaz and Menasche (1983, 1991) uses Merlin's (1974) timed Petri net model. The method generates a reachability graph where nodes represent state classes instead of states. Sets of linear equations are solved to calculate these state classes. The method allows for a reduction of the number of states by using a relative time scale. Another method using interval timed colored Petri nets was presented by Van der Aalst (1993). This method uses an absolute time scale and allows for colored tokens. The method also generates a reachability graph where nodes represent state classes. The number of states is reduced by exploiting "timed" specialization and generalization properties. Van der Aalst and Odijk (1995) describe an application of this method and Van der Aalst (1992) gives two additional analysis methods based on interval timing.

4.2.3 Stochastic Timing

The majority of stochastic Petri net models uses a continuous time domain. In these models, each delay is characterized by a probability density function. For arbitrary probability density functions, usually only simulation and approximation are feasible analysis techniques. Therefore, many stochastic Petri net models impose restrictions on the type of delay distribution that can be used. In the Stochastic Petri Net (SPN) model as described by Molloy (1981) and Florin and Natkin (1982) only exponential delays are allowed. Molloy (1981) and Florin and Natkin (1982) show that due to the memoryless property of the exponential distribution and the race semantics, SPN's are isomorphic to continuous time Markov chains. The number of states of the Markov chain corresponds to the number of reachable markings of the SPN.

The Generalized Stochastic Petri Net (GSPN) model extends the SPN model with immediate transitions. Immediate transitions fire without any enabling time and have priority over timed transitions (i.e., transitions with exponential enabling times under the race semantics). A marking is vanishing if an immediate transition is enabled. A marking is tangible if only timed transitions are enabled. The GSPN model distinguishes between these two types of markings, only transitions from tangible markings consume time. In other words, the average sojourn time of vanishing states is zero and the average sojourn time of tangible states is positive. The dynamics of a GSPN corresponds to a semi-Markov process: the embedded Markov chain which ignores the sojourn time in each state is a discrete time Markov chain. By using the embedded Markov chain, it is fairly straightforward to calculate various performance measures. Because only the tangible states consume time, the vanishing markings are not relevant for most performance measures. Therefore, as shown by Balbo and Silva (1984) and Marsan et al. (1985, 1995), it is possible to reduce the number of states by eliminating the vanishing markings in the embedded Markov chain.

The GSPN model has been extended in various directions. First of all, the GSPN model has been extended with marking dependent transition probabilities and enabling delays. It is easy to see that such an extension can be handled by using an embedded Markov chain as long as immediate and timed transitions do not interfere. Second, the GSPN model has been extended to allow for other, non-exponential types of delay distributions. Basically, there are two ways to incorporate non-exponential delays. First of all, it is possible to introduce transitions with arbitrary delay distributions, as long as none of these transitions can be enabled concurrently. The work of Marsan and Chiola (1987) on the DSPN model is an example of this approach, which allows for timed transitions with either fixed (i.e., deterministic) or exponential enabling times. The DSPN model can be analyzed as a semi-Markov process as long as only one deterministic transition is enabled at the same time and the enabling memory policy is assumed (see Section 2.4). Several variations and refinements of the DSPN have been proposed in literature (pointers are given by Balbo and Silva, 1998). Another approach to incorporate non-exponential delays is to allow for delay distributions which can be represented by a continuous time Markov chain. Examples of such delays are the Erlang, the hyperexponential, and the phase-type distribution. The possibility to in-corporate such delays was already mentioned by Molloy (1981) and Florin and Natkin (1982). The relation between the various memory policies and phase-type distributed transitions is discussed by Balbo and Silva (1984) and Marsan et al. (1995). Using non-exponential delays which are expanded to multiple phases in the corresponding Markov chain typically results in Markov chains which are dif-ficult to analyze. In the worst case, the size of the Markov chain grows exponen-tially in the number of phases.

The most advanced networking techniques, GERT, allows for arbitrary distri-butions and a wide variety of network topologies. Assuming an infinite server se-mantics, the conditional moment generating function (MFG) of the elapsed time required to traverse between any two nodes in the network is determined. Combin-ing these functions with the probabilities for each node that it is being executed and a network topology equation, an overall MFG characterizations of a closed network can be derived. From such a characterization an overall time distribution function can be obtained using inversion integrals, Pearson curves, or Gram-Charlier series. Depending on the chosen time distributions and the topology of the network, obtaining the overall distribution function may be inefficient. Less complex performance criteria, such as the sensitivity of the found solution in a given parameter, may be easier to derive for specific cases.

4.3 Exact SWN Analysis

In this section an exact analytical method is presented to compute the throughput time density or distribution of an SWN. This section is based on earlier papers of Van Hee and Reijers (1999) and Van der Aalst et al. (2000c). The method pre-sented supposes that the designer of the workflow composes the SWN to be ana-lyzed by extending a simple workflow net in an iterative fashion with the elements of a set of building blocks. Because the behavior of these individual building blocks is known and it is ensured that this construction yields a correct model, it is possible to compute a characterization of the throughput time in an efficient way.

Somewhat similar approaches are by Pritsker and Happ (1966), Pritsker and Whitehouse (1966), Neuman and Steinhardt (1979), and Guo et al. (1992), who have been using moment-generating functions to handle this type of problem. However, such an approach complicates the application of peculiar distribution functions, as differentiation is required to obtain results. Moreover, with the de-scribed approach in this section it is possible to characterize a complete through-put distribution function instead of just the expected throughput time mean and variance.

We will first describe the construction method and introduce three basic build-ing blocks. We will illustrate the approach with an example. In the sections fol-lowing, we will introduce additional, sophisticated building blocks.

4.3.1 Basic Method

We will construct SWN's by applying a synthesis method as introduced by Valette (1979) and applied by e.g., Van der Aalst (2000a) and Voorhoeve (2000) in the composition of workflow nets. The construction of an SWN takes place by first constructing a workflow net and then assigning a proper delay and weight function to transform it into an SWN. As the starting point of each SWN construction we will use a so-called simple net. A simple net is structurally equivalent to the net as depicted in Figure 4.2.

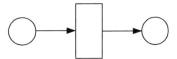

Fig. 4.2. A simple net

A simple net consists of one transition, a source place, a sink place, and relations between them. It is trivial that each simple net is a workflow net and that a simple net with marking   is safe. The construction method is based on replacing a transition in a workflow net by an entire workflow net. Such a replacement is called a synthesis step (see Definition 2.15.). Net synthesis can informally be defined as follows:

1. Obtain a net by defining a simple net.
2. If the obtained net is satisfactory, then end the net synthesis.
3. Otherwise, apply a synthesis step – which replaces a transition with a workflow net – and return to step 2.

In our construction of SWN's, we will initially allow three basic forms of workflow nets that can be used to replace transitions during net synthesis. In other words, a workflow net used in a synthesis step to replace a transition should have a specific net structure. The three net structures of workflow nets that we will allow are depicted in Figure 4.3.

The basic workflow structure that implements parallelism is achieved by sequencing a so-called AND-SPLIT with an AND-JOIN (see Figure 4.3). Likewise, the basic workflow structure that implements a choice is achieved by sequencing an OR-SPLIT and OR-JOIN control (see Figure 4.3). The choice for the basic workflow structures therefore seems to be consistent with the identification of the sequence, OR-SPLIT, OR-JOIN, AND-SPLIT, and AND-JOINS as primary controls in workflow management systems to manage business processes, for example by Van Hee and Reijers (1999) and Kiepuszewski et al. (2001).

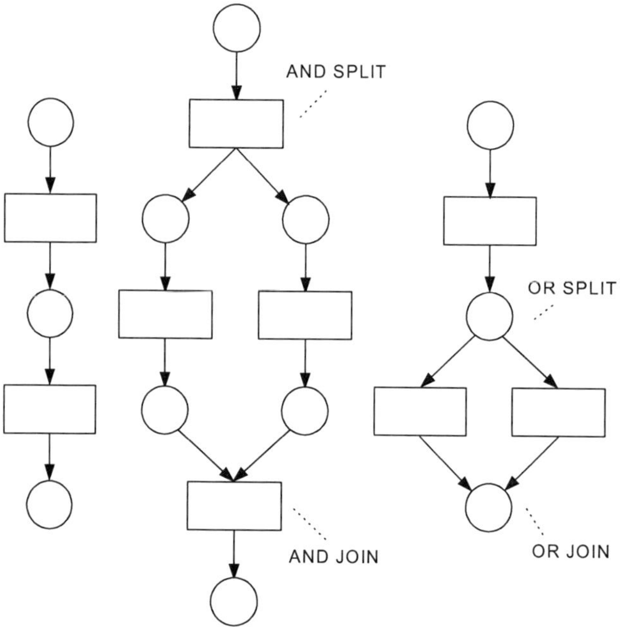

Fig. 4.3. Basic structures: sequence (a), parallelism (b), and choice (c)

Note that the workflow management coalition, the most important standardization organization in the field of workflow management, also identifies another basic control: the iteration construct (see Lawrence, 1997). Similarly, Knolmayer et al. (2000) state that "with respect to modeling the control flow [of a workflow], the following situations have to be covered: sequence of actions, parallel actions, alternate actions, and iterations of actions". These views reinforce the importance of the sequence, parallelism, and choice structures we already identified. The different possibilities to extend our SWN construction method with the iteration construct is the subject of Section 4.3.

For each workflow net that has a net structure of one of the basic forms, a so-called *initial transition* can be distinguished.

Definition 4.1   (Initial transition). For a workflow net (P, T, R) with $i\bullet = \{t\}$ for some $t \in T$, transition t is called its *initial transition*.

As we will see, the initial transition will play an important role in computing the throughput time distribution of a constructed SWN.

It is not hard to verify that for each workflow net WN with a sequence, parallelism, or choice net structure holds that WN is *sound* and (WN, $[\![i]\!]$) is a safe system. From the result of Van der Aalst (2000) about the composition of workflow nets (see Theorem 2.4), it can be derived that a synthesis step which replaces a transition in a sound and safe workflow net by a sound and safe workflow net yields again a sound and safe workflow net. So, safeness and soundness are preserved by recursively applying synthesis steps with workflow nets of the three basic forms on an initial simple net.

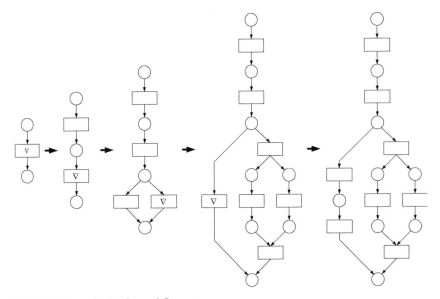

Fig. 4.4. The synthesis of a workflow net

In Figure 4.4 we can see the synthesis of a workflow net in four synthesis steps (see Definition 2.15). Each synthesis step is depicted by a black arrow. Each of the depicted synthesis steps replaces a transition marked with the symbol "∇" with a workflow net with respectively a sequence, choice, parallelism, and sequence structure.

The final step in an SWN construction is to assign both a proper delay and weight function to the workflow net that is synthesized. Recall that the definition of an SWN allows for arbitrary weights and probability distributions (see Definition 2.16). Because the synthesized workflow net is sound, the throughput time distribution is defined for a constructed SWN (see Definition 2.22).

We will now show how the throughput time density (or distribution) of a constructed SWN may be derived on the basis of the throughput time densities (or distributions) of its substituting components. Consider an SWN $WN^1 = (P^1, T^1, R^1, W^1, f^1)$ that has been constructed by assigning a weight function W^1 and delay function f^1 to a workflow net (P^1, T^1, R^1). Assume that this workflow net is the result of net synthesis. Then, the net (P^1, T^1, R^1) is the result of replacing in some workflow net (P^2, T^2, R^2) the transition $t^+ \in T^2$ by some workflow net (P^3, T^3, R^3) with has an initial transition $t^* \in T^3$. Let $WN^3 = (P^3, T^3, R^3, W^3, f^3)$ be the SWN on the basis of (P^3, T^3, R^3), with for each $t \in T^3$, $W^3(t) = W^1(t)$ and $f^3(t) = f^1(t)$. Now suppose that we can compute the throughput time density f_{WN^3} (see Definition 2.24) of the SWN WN^3. Let $WN^2 = (P^2, T^2, R^2, W^2, f^2)$ be the SWN such that for each $t \in T^2$:

- $W^2(t) = \begin{cases} W^2(t) \text{ if } t \neq t^+, \\ W^1(t^*) \text{ if } t = t^+, \end{cases}$

- $f^2(t) = \begin{cases} f^2(t) \text{ if } t \neq t^+, \\ f_{WN^3} \text{ if } t = t^+. \end{cases}$

Then, it is not hard to see that the throughput time density f_{WN^2} equals the throughput time density f_{WN^1}. After all, SWN WN^2 is almost identical to the SWN WN^1 except that transition t^+ takes the place of the subnet SWN WN^3. Transition t^+ has the same weight as the initial transition of (P^3, T^3, R^3) in SWN^1. So, t^+ is selected with the same probability in WN^2 as the subnet WN^3 is selected in WN^1. Moreover, the probability that t^+ imposes some delay d in WN^2 equals the probability that the throughput time of WN^3 equals this delay. So, the throughput time behavior of WN^2 is the same as that of WN^1.

The process of simplifying a constructed SWN WN into an SWN WN' where the time behavior of one of the transitions of WN' equals that of an entire subnet of WN can be followed back along the synthesis steps that have been taken. This process ends when an SWN has been derived that has the net structure of a simple net. The value of the delay function of the sole remaining transition of this SWN is exactly the throughput time density of WN.

The applicability of the described derivation depends on the computability of the throughput time densities of all SWN's with a net structure of one of the basic forms. We will now show how these can be computed. For each of the basic forms we will either describe how the throughput time density or distribution can be calculated. It is a trivial exercise to transform one characterization into the other.

Sequence

Consider an SWN B with a sequence network structure as depicted in Figure 4.5, two timed transitions t and u with delay probability distributions f_t and f_u and general initial timed state M_0 (see Definition 2.18).

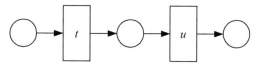

Fig. 4.5. Sequential SWN

SWN B induces the stochastic process SP = { $(X_n, Y_n, Z_n) \mid n = 0, 1, 2, \dots$ } (see Definition 2.19). Note that each transition fires at most once. For each transition $v \in \{t, u\}$, we define random variable $\underline{v}$ which is the delay that transition v

imposes if it fires. Formally, $\underline{v} = e \Leftrightarrow \exists n \in \mathbb{N} : Y_n = v \wedge Z_n = e$. We consider the throughput time density f_B.

Let $y \in \mathbb{N}$, $\displaystyle f_B(y) = \sum_{i=0}^{y} \mathbb{P}(\underline{t} = i \wedge \underline{u} = y - i) = \sum_{i=0}^{y} \mathbb{P}(\underline{t} = i)\mathbb{P}(\underline{u} = y - i) = $

$f_t \otimes f_u(y)$.

To constrain the computation effort, the convolution $f_t \otimes f_u$ can be computed with the Fast Fourier Transform and its inverse (see Appendix A). As a result, we can compute a vector representation of $f_t \otimes f_u$ in $O(n \log n)$ time, with n the smallest power of two that is at least twice as large as the maximal delay for which either $f_t(n)$ or $f_u(n)$ is unequal to zero. Note that a straightforward computation would have required n^2 steps.

Parallelism

Consider an SWN B with the a parallelism network structure as depicted in Figure 4.6. Assume that B has initial timed state M_0. For the moment, also assume that the initial transition s of the underlying workflow net, as well as the transition v with $\{v\} = \bullet o$ are both immediate. The remaining transitions t and u are timed with delay probability distributions F_t and F_u. SWN B induces the stochastic process SP $= \{ (X_n, Y_n, Z_n) \mid n = 0, 1, 2, \ldots \}$ (see Definition 2.19). Given the net structure and the general initial time state, each transition fires at most once. For each transition $w \in \{s, t, u, v\}$, we define random variable $\underline{w}$ which is the delay that transition w imposes if it fires. Formally, $\underline{v} = e \Leftrightarrow \exists n \in \mathbb{N} : Y_n = v \wedge Z_n = e$. We consider the throughput time distribution F_B.

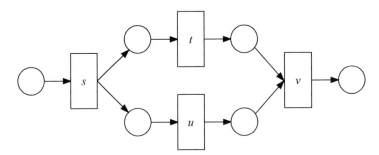

Fig. 4.6. Parallel SWN

Let $y \in \mathbb{N}$, $F_B(y) = \mathbb{P}(\underline{t} \leq y \wedge \underline{u} \leq y) = F_t(y) \cdot F_u(y)$.

The computation of the distribution function F_B can be performed in n steps, with n the minimal delay for which both $F_t(n)$ and $F_u(n)$ are equal to 1.

For the general case where transitions s and v are timed, let $f^*(y)$ be the throughput time density in y that can be derived from the throughput time distribution $F_s(y) \cdot F_u(y)$. On the basis of the throughput time density expression for a workflow net with a sequence structure, we may derive that if s and v *are* timed and we use f_B as the throughput time density of the entire SWN B, then:

$$\text{for } y \in \mathbb{N}, \ f_B(y) = f_s \otimes f^* \otimes f_v(y).$$

This convolution can be computed in $O(n \log(n \log n))$ time, with n the smallest power of two that is at least twice as large as the maximal delay for which $f_s(n)$, $f^*(n)$ or $f_v(n)$ is unequal to zero. Note that a straightforward computation would have required m^3 steps, with $m \in \mathbb{N}$ the maximal time unit for which either $f_s(m)$, $f^*(m)$ or $f_v(m)$ is unequal to zero.

Choice

The final block to consider is the choice block. Let B be an SWN initially marked at initial timed state M_0 with a choice network structure (see Figure 4.3).

Assume that the initial transition s of the underlying workflow net is immediate. The other two transitions t and u are timed with delay probability densities f_t and f_u and weights w_t and w_u. Let SWN B induce the stochastic process SP = { $(X_n, Y_n, Z_n) \mid n = 0, 1, 2, \dots$ } (see Definition 2.19).

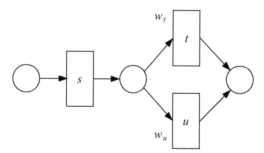

Fig. 4.7. SWN with choice structure

Given the net structure and the general initial timed state, each transition fires at most once. For each transition $v \in \{s, t, u\}$, we define random variable $\underline{v}$ which is the delay that transition v imposes if it fires. Formally, $\underline{v} = e \Leftrightarrow \exists n \in \mathbb{N} : Y_n = v \wedge Z_n = e$. We consider the throughput time density f_B.

$$\text{Let } y \in \mathbb{N}, f_B(y) = \mathbb{P}(\underline{t} = y \vee \underline{u} = y) = \frac{w_t \cdot f_t(y)}{w_t + w_u} + \frac{w_u \cdot f_u(y)}{w_t + w_u}.$$

From this expression follows that we can compute f_B in $O(n)$ time, with n equal to the maximal delay for which either $f_t(n)$ or $f_u(n)$ is unequal to zero.

For the general case where s is timed, we denote with $f^*(y)$ the throughput time density $\dfrac{w_t \cdot f_t(y)}{w_t + w_u} + \dfrac{w_u \cdot f_u(y)}{w_t + w_u}$. On the basis of throughput time density expression for a workflow net with a sequence structure, we may derive that if s is timed and we use f_B as the throughput time density of the entire SWN B, then:

for $y \in \mathbb{N}$, $f_B(y) = f_s \otimes f^*(y)$.

This computation has a similar complexity as the computation required for an SWN with a sequence structure.

We will illustrate here the approach to compute the throughput time density of a constructed SWN. We use as basis for this construction the rightmost workflow net as synthesized in Figure 4.4. The SWN that has been constructed is depicted at the left-hand side of Figure 4.8. Recall that ordinary transitions in an SWN are timed and are depicted as transparent blocks labeled with their identity; immediate transitions are depicted as black bars and are usually not labeled (see also Figure 2.3).

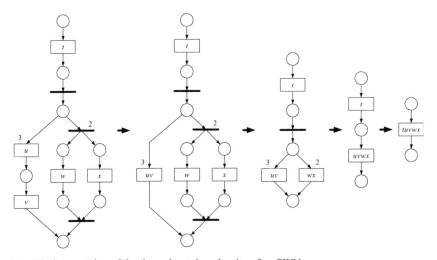

Fig. 4.8. Computation of the throughput time density of an SWN

Only two transitions of the leftmost SWN in Figure 4.8 have been assigned weights that are unequal to 1. Three transitions have been assigned delay functions such that their time behavior is immediate; these transitions are not labeled. The other transitions t, u, v, w, and x are probability density functions as depicted in Figure 4.9.

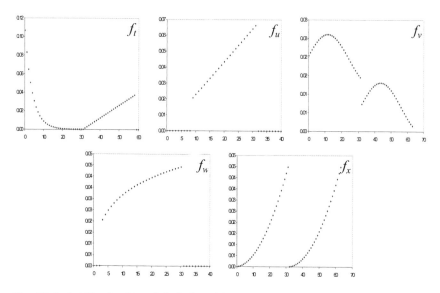

Fig. 4.9. Probability densities f_t, f_u, f_v, f_w, and f_x

The first step in computing a throughput time density of the entire SWN is to replace the sequence subnet of transitions t and u with a transition tu. (Recall that the last step in the synthesis of the underlying workflow net inserted this sequence structure.) The probability density function of tu is computed using the previously found relation. This step is depicted in Figure 4.8 as the leftmost arrow. Next, the parallelism subnet of w and x is replaced by transition wx. This replacement as well as the computation of the probability density function of wx is depicted as the second arrow from the left in Figure 4.8. The choice subnet of transitions tu and wx is subsequently replaced by transition $uvwx$. Finally, the sequence subnet of transitions t and $uvwx$ is replaced by a transition $tuvwx$. The probability density function f_{tuvwx} is exactly the throughput density function of the SWN. This and the other, intermediate probability density functions are depicted in Figure 4.10.

It is straightforward to extend the presented basic structures of sequence, parallelism, and choice to structures with n transitions in sequence, n transitions in parallel or n alternative transitions. The expressions for the associated throughput density (distribution) functions can be found as generalizations of the presented expressions for the basic structures. This extension adds no additional expressive power in the construction of an SWN, but it reduces the number of intermediate probability distributions in the computation of the throughput density (distribution) function of the constructed SWN.

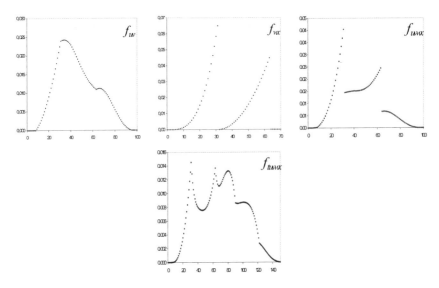

Fig. 4.10. Probability densities f_{uv}, f_{wx}, f_{uvwx}, and f_{tuvwx}

4.3.2 The Iteration Structure

As mentioned in the previous section, the iteration structure can be considered as another basic structure with which a workflow net can be synthesized. With an iteration it can be represented that some work that already has been done for a specific case must be redone and possibly some additional work too. In workflows, the reason for an iteration is commonly that a party does not agree with the quality of the earlier delivered work. For example, a junior clerk may determine the conditions under which a loan is granted to a client; on checking these conditions, his superior may decide that the junior clerk should constrict these conditions.

Note that if the basic set of network structures introduced in this section is augmented with the iteration structure, the same expressive power is attained as the process algebra ACP, as described by Bergstra and Klop (1984). Process-algebraic expressions with ACP can be constructed using the merge ($\|$), choice ($+$), sequential ($\cdot$), and star ($*$) operators which correspond with the parallelism, choice, sequence, and iteration structure.

A common way of modeling an iteration with Petri nets is presented in Figure 4.11. It is easy to check that a Petri net PN with an iteration structure is a workflow net, that it is sound, and that the system (PN, $[\![i]\!]$) is safe. For reasons we described in the previous section, the use of a net with a structure like this in the synthesis of a workflow net yields a safe and sound workflow net again.

It is worthwhile to consider the semantics of the iteration construct in more detail. The stochastic process that is imposed by an SWN with an iteration part may not end. Once the part of the SWN with the iteration construct is initiated it is not guaranteed that the iterations will stop. Because all weights of the transitions are positive, there is always a probability that another iteration is initiated.

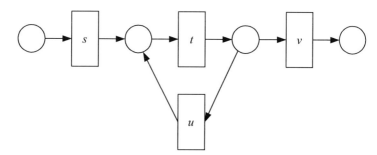

Fig. 4.11. The iteration construct

In our model, the issue whether a new iteration is started is independent of the number of previous iterations. This may in fact be a realistic way of modeling when, for example, the probability to re-iterate is relatively low, the time that is involved with rework is relatively low, or the iteration decisions are relatively independent. In an actual workflow this may not be the case. For example, a decision to re-iterate may be highly dependent on the number of iterations already encountered. It can be expected in a realistic workflow that after a fixed number of iterations (the *cut-off* number) a new iteration may be excluded or the process may be completely aborted. These options respectively represent the operational decision to lower the quality criteria or the conclusion that an acceptable quality level will never be obtained for this part of the work.

We will study in this section the time behavior of a conventional iteration construct as depicted, and a special version with a cut-off number. As we will see, the conventional iteration, which we will simply refer to as *iteration*, requires a specific approach to obtain a throughput time characterization with a finite domain. The other type of iteration, which we will call the *n-iteration*, requires an extension of the stochastic behavior that can be induced by an SWN. Both structures are recognized by Kiepuszewski et al. (2001) as possible ways to model an iteration.

Iteration

Consider an SWN $B = (P, T, R, W, f)$ with $T = \{s, t, u, v\}$ and an iteration network structure, such as depicted in Figure 4.11. Assume that B has the general initial timed state M_0. For the moment, also assume that the initial transition s of the underlying workflow net, as well as the transition v with $\{v\} = \bullet o$ are both immediate. Let t and u be the transitions such that $s\bullet = \bullet t$ and $s\bullet = u\bullet$. Let their delay probability densities be given by f_t and f_u. Given the net structure and the general initial timed state, transitions s and v fire one time, transition t fires one or more times and transition u fires one time less than t. SWN B induces the stochastic process SP = { $(X_n, Y_n, Z_n) \mid n = 0, 1, 2, \dots$ } with throughput time Γ (see Definition 4.19 and Definition 2.22). For each transition $w \in \{s, t, u, v\}$, we define random variable $\underline{w}_i$ ($i \in \mathbb{N}\backslash\{0\}$) which is the delay that transition w imposes if it fires for an ith time. We consider the throughput time density f_B.

Let $y \in \mathbb{N}$, then

$$f_B(y) = \sum_{n=0}^{\infty} \frac{w_v}{w_u + w_v} \left(\frac{w_u}{w_u + w_v} \right)^n \mathbb{P}\left(\sum_{j=1}^{n+1} t_j + \sum_{j=1}^{n} u_j = y \right) =$$

$$\sum_{n=0}^{\infty} \frac{w_v w_u^n}{(w_u + w_v)^{n+1}} \left(\bigotimes_{j=1}^{n+1} f_t \otimes \bigotimes_{j=1}^{n} f_u(y) \right),$$

with notation $\displaystyle\bigotimes_{j=1}^{n} a_j = a_1 \otimes a_2 \dots \otimes a_n$.

In general, this exact representation does not allow for a convenient computation of $f_B(y)$ although this depends on the properties of f_t and f_u.

At this point, we will discuss a generally applicable method to efficiently determine a finite representation of $f_B(y)$. We will use the Discrete Fourier Transform for this purpose, which is explained in some detail in Appendix B. When the vector $\vec{y}$ is the Discrete Fourier Transform of vector $\vec{a}$ with length n we write $\vec{y} = DFT_n(\vec{a})$. We will consider $\vec{B}$, the vector representation of f_B. If we define α

$= \dfrac{w_u}{w_u + w_v}$, then its Discrete Fourier Transform is:

$$DFT_l(\vec{B}) = DFT_l\left(\sum_{n=0}^{\infty} (1-\alpha)\alpha^n \left(\bigotimes_{j=1}^{n+1} \vec{t} \otimes \bigotimes_{j=1}^{n} \vec{u} \right) \right) =$$

$$\sum_{n=0}^{\infty} (1-\alpha)\alpha^n DFT_l^{n+1}(\vec{t}) \, DFT_l^n(\vec{u}) = \frac{(1-\alpha)DFT_l(\vec{t})}{1 - \alpha DFT_l(\vec{t})DFT_l(\vec{u})},$$

with $l = \infty$.

We do not know a finite size l of the vectors we have to "feed" the DFT. We cannot expect that there is an upper bound for the delay. Or, in other words, that there is a value $x \in \mathbb{N}$ such that for all $y > x$, $f_B(y) = 0$. After all, t and u can be executed infinitely often as $w_u > 0$. We will show how a relevant length of $\vec{B}$ can be determined before actually computing $\vec{B}$. As a starting point, we would be most pleased to find a value such that it is highly improbable that the throughput time exceeds it. In other words, we are looking for a $q \in \mathbb{N}$ such that for some very small ε holds that $\mathbb{P}(\Gamma \geq q) \leq \varepsilon$. We recall Chebyshev's inequality (see e.g.,

Thomasian, 1969): for any random variable $\underline{x}$ for which exists $E\underline{x}^2$ holds that $\mathbb{P}(|\underline{x} - E\underline{x}| \geq c) \leq \dfrac{\operatorname{var} \underline{x}}{c^2}$. Using this inequality, and the expected throughput time and its variance, it can be determined which part of the probability density falls before and which part falls behind a hypothetical border. We will denote the expected delay of transition $w \in \{t, u\}$ by $E\underline{w}$ and the variance of the firing delay by $\operatorname{var} \underline{w}$. The expected value and variance of the throughput time Γ of B are given by:

$$E\Gamma = \frac{E\underline{t} + \alpha E\underline{u}}{1 - \alpha}$$

$$\operatorname{var} \Gamma = \frac{\operatorname{var} \underline{t} + \alpha \operatorname{var} \underline{u}}{1 - \alpha} + \alpha \left(\frac{E\underline{u} + E\underline{t}}{1 - \alpha} \right)^2 ,$$

so that we can derive using Chebyshev and our desired value ε that:

$$q = E\Gamma + \sqrt{\frac{\operatorname{var} \Gamma}{\varepsilon}} .$$

Given f_t and f_u, we can compute $E\underline{t}$, $E\underline{u}$, $\operatorname{var} \underline{t}$, and $\operatorname{var} \underline{u}$. But then we can also calculate a vector representation of f_B for the iteration block by using the *DFT*:

$$DFT_q(\vec{B}) = \frac{(1 - \alpha)DFT_q(\vec{t})}{1 - \alpha DFT_q(\vec{t})DFT_q(\vec{u})} ,$$

with q the smallest power of two such that $q = E\Gamma + \sqrt{\dfrac{\operatorname{var} \Gamma}{\varepsilon}}$ and $\alpha = \dfrac{w_u}{w_u + w_v}$.

With the *DFT* we can compute a vector representation of f_B in $(q \log q)$ time, with q as specified. To appreciate its efficiency we have to establish the computing time of calculating f_B in a straightforward manner. The complexity of this calculation depends on the maximal number of successive times that transitions t and u can be executed. We know that if both $f_t(0)$ and $f_u(0)$ are equal to zero (their imposed delay is positive), at most q executions of these transitions are of interest. Any more executions of transitions t and u would result in throughput times that we do not take into consideration. As a result, a straightforward approach requires the convolution of q times the function f_t and f_u. This is an operation requiring $O(n^q)$ time, with n the smallest value such that for all $m > n$, $f_t(m) = f_u(m) = 0$. A comparison with the $O(q \log q)$ time required by the earlier found computation method illustrates the efficiency of the latter. Note that our choice for a discrete time domain for the delay functions (see Definition 2.16) has considerably simplified the application of the Fourier Transform.

N-iteration

We will first make the semantics operational of an n-iteration with an example, before we analyze the throughput time characterization of such a net. Consider the Stochastic Petri net B = (P, T, R, W, f) as depicted on the upper side of Figure 4.12. The initial timed state of B is M with $M(p) = [\![0]\!]$, $M(q) = [\![0^3]\!]$ and for all other places **0**. The Stochastic Petri net B induces the stochastic process SP = { $(X_n, Y_n, Z_n) \mid n = 0, 1, 2, \ldots$ } On the basis of the initial timed state it is ensured that transition t fires at most 4 times and transition u fires at most 3 times. Because (P, T, R) is not a workflow net, its throughput time is not defined. Suppose, however, that we are interested in the *unsound throughput time* U: for $n \in \mathbb{N}$, $U = n \Leftrightarrow$ $\exists m \in \mathbb{N}$: $time(X_m) = \infty \wedge X_m(o)(r) = 1$ as a way of making the duration of the process SP operational. The Stochastic Petri net with arbitrary weights and throughput densities implements a 3-iteration of which we are interested in its unsound throughput time.

Note that if our definition of workflow nets (Definition 2.13) would have allowed so-called *weighted* arcs, then the upper model could be translated into an SWN by making q an output place of s with weight 3.

Now consider the SWN B' = (P', T', R', W', f') as depicted on the lower side of Figure 4.12.

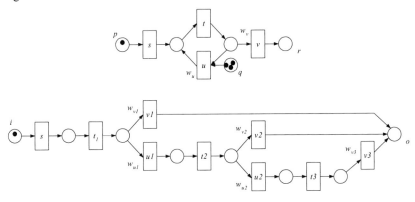

Fig. 4.12. Stochastic Petri net and SWN implementing a 3-iteration

The initial timed state of B is M_0. The SWN B' induces the stochastic process SP' = { $(X'_n, Y'_n, Z'_n) \mid n = 0, 1, 2, \ldots$ }. As (P', T', R') is a sound workflow net, the throughput time T is defined for B'. Furthermore, suppose that:

– $f'(s1) = f(s)$,
– $f'(t1) = f'(t2) = f'(t3) = f(t)$,

- $f'(u1) = f'(u2) = f(u),$
- $f'(v1) = f'(v2) = f'(v3) = f(v),$
- $w'_{u1} = w'_{u2} = w_u,$ and
- $w'_{v1} = w'_{v2} = w'_{v3} = w_v.$

Then, it is not hard to see that although the stochastic processes SP and SP' differ, the unsound throughput time U of B exactly equals the throughput time T of B'. In other words, we can use B' to determine a throughput time characterization of a Stochastic Petri net that implements a 3-iteration. Without formally proving it, we claim that it is always possible to construct an n-iteration with an SWN on the basis of a workflow net, following the lines of the example. Obviously, the assignment of similar weights and throughput densities to the relevant transitions is essential. So, our "construction box" can be extended with the n-iteration.

To characterize the throughput time of an SWN with an *n*-iteration structure, we consider a Stochastic process B with a network structure as the one in the upper half of Figure 4.12. The initial timed state of B is M with $M(p) = [\![0]\!]$, $M(q) = [\![0'']\!]$ and for all other places **0**. For now, we will assume that transitions t and u are timed with delay probability densities f_t and f_u and the other transitions are immediate. Given the net structure and the initial timed state, transitions s and v fire one time, transition t fires one up to $n+1$ times and transition u fires zero up to n times. SWN B induces the stochastic process SP = $\{ (X_n, Y_n, Z_n) \mid n = 0, 1, 2, \dots \}$ with *unsound throughput time* U: for $n \in \mathbb{N}$, $U = n \Leftrightarrow \exists m \in \mathbb{N}: time(X_m) = \infty \wedge X_m(o)(r) = 1$. For each transition $w \in \{s, t, u, v\}$, we define random variable w_i ($i \in \mathbb{N}\backslash\{0\}$) which is the delay that transition w imposes if it fires for an ith time and ∞ otherwise. We consider the unsound throughput time density f_B.

Let $y \in \mathbb{N}$, then $f_B(y) =$

$$\sum_{m=0}^{n} \frac{w_v}{w_u + w_v} \left(\frac{w_u}{w_u + w_v} \right)^m P\left(\sum_{j=1}^{m+1} t_j + \sum_{j=1}^{m} u_j = y \right) =$$

$$\sum_{m=0}^{n} \frac{w_v w_u^m}{(w_u + w_v)^{m+1}} \left(f_t \otimes \bigotimes_{j=1}^{m} f_t \otimes f_u(y) \right),$$

with notation $\bigotimes_{j=1}^{n} a_j = a_1 \otimes a_2 \dots \otimes a_n$.

If we define $f_{tu}^m(y) = f_t \otimes \bigotimes_{j=1}^{m} f_t \otimes f_u(y)$, then it is not hard to see that $f_{tu}^{m+1}(y) = f_t \otimes f_u \otimes f_{tu}^m(y)$. Once the convolution $f_t \otimes f_u(y)$ is determined for all $y \in \mathbb{N}$, the convolution for iteration $m + 1$ can be determined on the basis of the convolution for iteration m. So, for the n-iteration we require the computation of $n + 1$ convolutions. Each convolution requires $O(l \log l)$ steps with l the smallest power of two that is at least twice as large as the maximal delay for the probability densities that are being convoluted.

For the general case where s and v are timed, we denote for $y \in \mathbb{N}$ with $f^*(y)$

the throughput time density $\sum_{m=0}^{n} \frac{w_v w_u^m f_{tu}^m(y)}{(w_u + w_v)^{m+1}}$. On the basis of the network struc-

ture of the Stochastic Petri Net B, we may derive that if s and v are timed and we use f_B as the unsound throughput time density of the entire Stochastic Petri Net B, then:

$$\text{for } y \in \mathbb{N}, \ f_B(y) = f_s \otimes f^* \otimes f_v(y).$$

This computation has a similar complexity as the computation required for an SWN with a parallelism structure. As we have argued before, the unsound throughput time density of a Stochastic Petri net with the structure and marking such as depicted in the upper half of Definition 4.12 equals the throughput time density of an SWN with the structure and marking such as depicted in the lower half of the same figure.

4.3.3 Other Extensions

It is possible to extend the set of structures that can be used to synthesize workflow nets in the construction of SWN's in several directions. The main requirement on such a structure would be that it is a sound workflow net which is safe on the basis of marking $[\![i]\!]$, so that soundness and safeness are preserved during net synthesis. In the section we will discuss two further, simple extensions. We will also illustrate a possible extension of the approach with a rather complex *repeater* structure. As we will see, the latter extension is based on a class of Petri nets that incorporates so-called *inhibitor arcs*. The notion of soundness for such a net will be discussed, so that the repeater structure may be applied in our approach.

The first two structures that we will discuss are the *interleaving* and the *logic choice* structures. Two workflow nets with these respective structures are depicted at the top and bottom side of Figure 4.13.

Both structures are recognized by Kiepuszewski et al. (2001) as control patterns that are applied in models to be used for the execution of Workflow Management Systems. It is not hard to see that a workflow net with either structure is sound and that it is safe on the basis of the initial marking $[\![i]\!]$. The proof could easily be given by a finite reachability graph. As a result, safeness and soundness are preserved in net synthesis on the basis of these net structures. Note that a net with an interleaving structure is, however, not free-choice. We will subsequently discuss the semantics and throughput characterization of both structures.

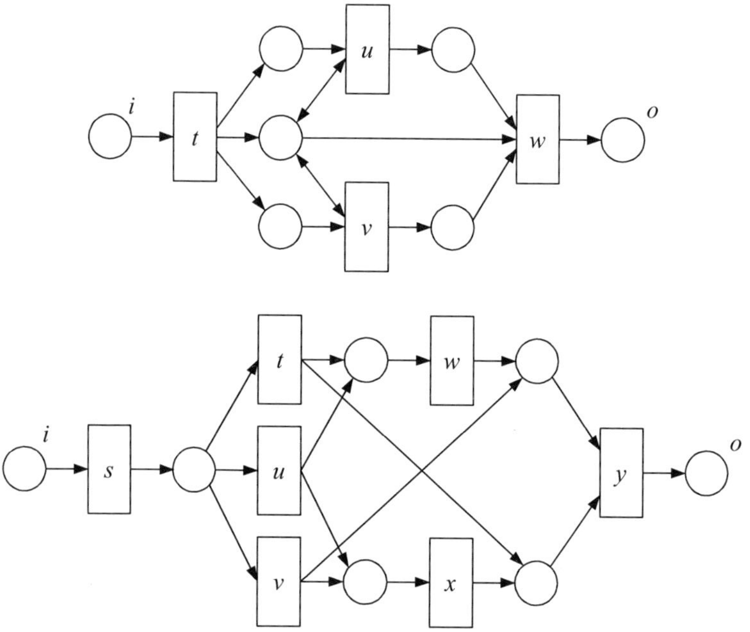

Fig. 4.13. Workflow nets with *interleaving* and *logic choice* structure

Interleaving

The interleaving structure can be used to specify that two tasks are to be executed one after another, although it is not deterministically specified which task should be executed first or second. The tasks are said to be *interleaved*. This kind of structure is typically relevant in situations where resources are to be shared among tasks. When an SWN is constructed on the basis of the workflow net at the top side of Figure 4.13 the tasks that are interleaved are represented by transitions u and v. By assigning (un)equal weights to t and u, the probabilities of the different orderings are (a)symmetric.

Let B be an SWN initially marked at general timed state M_0 on the basis of the workflow net at the top side of Figure 4.13. Assume that transitions t and w are immediate. The other two transitions u and v are timed with delay probability densities f_u and f_v and weights w_t and w_v. Let SWN B induce the stochastic process SP $= \{ (X_n, Y_n, Z_n) \mid n = 0, 1, 2, \ldots \}$. Given the net structure and the initial timed state, each transition fires at most once. For each transition $s \in \{t, u, v, w\}$, we define random variable $\underline{s}$ which is the delay that transition s imposes if it fires. We also define random variable $\underline{x}$, which takes on either the value u or v, depending on which transition fires first. (Note that all transition firings are ordered, see Definition 2.19.) We consider the throughput time density f_B.

Let $y \in \mathbb{N}, f_B(y) -$

$$\sum_{i=0}^{y} \mathbb{P}(\underline{u} = i \wedge \underline{v} = y - i \wedge \underline{x} = u) + \sum_{i=0}^{y} \mathbb{P}(\underline{u} = i \wedge \underline{v} = y - i \wedge \underline{x} = t) =$$

$$\sum_{i=0}^{y} \mathbb{P}(\underline{u} = i \wedge \underline{v} = y - i) = f_u \otimes f_v(y).$$

This computation is identical to that of the sequence construction that we discussed before and it has an identical complexity. The extension of this specific case to the general case where transitions t and w are also timed is straightforward.

Logic Choice

The logic choice structure can be used to specify that, considering two tasks a and b, one of the following events may happen:

- Exactly one of these tasks is executed (either a or b).
- Both tasks are executed.

We may say that $a \vee b$ is executed, hence the name *logic choice*. When an SWN is constructed on the basis of the workflow net at the bottom side of Figure 4.13, a logic choice between two tasks can be modeled using the transitions w and x. By assuming an initial marking $[\![i]\!]$ of the corresponding workflow net, the model has the following semantics:

- Execution of transition t means that transition w is to be executed, but not x.
- Execution of transition u means that both transition w and x are to be executed.
- Execution of transition v means that transition x is to be executed, but not w.

To represent a correct time behavior of this logical construction within an SWN, transitions w and x are assigned proper delay probability densities, while all other transitions are modeled as immediate transitions. Transitions are assigned proper weights to express the probabilities of each of the three possible executions of the net. Let B be such an SWN, with delay probability distributions F_w and F_x and weights w_t, w_u, and w_v. Let SWN B induce the stochastic process SP = { $(X_n, Y_n, Z_n) \mid n = 0, 1, 2, \ldots$ }. Given the net structure and the initial timed state, each transition fires at most once. For each transition $r \in \{s, t, u, v, w, x, y\}$, we define random variable $\underline{r}$ which is the delay that transition r imposes if it fires. We consider the throughput time distribution F_B.

Let $y \in \mathbb{N}, F_B(y) =$

$$\mathbb{P}\big((\underline{w} \le y \wedge \underline{x} = \infty) \vee (\underline{w} = \infty \wedge \underline{x} \le y) \vee (\underline{w} \le y \wedge \underline{x} \le y)\big) =$$

$$\frac{w_t \cdot F_w(y) + w_v \cdot F_x(y) + w_u \cdot F_w(y) \cdot F_x(y)}{(w_t + w_u + w_v)}.$$

The computation of the distribution function F_B can be performed in n steps, with n the minimal delay for which both $F_w(n)$ and $F_x(n)$ are equal to 1. The extension of this specific case to the general case where the other transitions are also timed is straightforward.

Repeater

We end this part by considering the *repeater* network structure. A repeater is another recognized common control in workflow processes (see Kiepuszewski. 2001). It should be possible to execute some task one or more times, without a build-time confinement on the maximal number of executions. Furthermore, the multiple instantiations of this task may be executed in parallel. A Petri net with this structure is depicted in Figure 4.14. The task that can be repeated is modeled by the transition w.

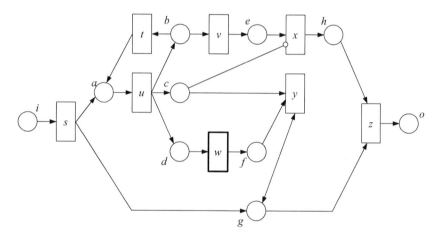

Fig. 4.14. Workflow net with repeater structure

In the depicted Petri net, a new kind of arc - an *inhibitor arc* - is used connecting place c with transition x. It is represented by a line terminating with a small circle at the transition instead of an arrowhead. An inhibitor arc disables the transition when the input place has a token and enables the transition when it has no token and other (normal) input places contain at least one token. No tokens are moved through an inhibitor arc when the transition fires. A class of Petri nets with inhibitor arcs is referred to as *extended Petri nets* (see e.g., Murata, 1989). The extended Petri net may very well be used as the basis for notions such as the *extended workflow net*, the *Stochastic Extended Petri net* (SEPN), and the *Stochastic Extended Workflow net* (SEWN). We will not formally define these notions here, but confine ourselves to an informal discussion of the modifications required.

We suppose that an extended Petri net can be characterized by a tuple (P, T, R, E), where E is an inhibitor relation similar to R, the flow relation. E represents the inhibitor arcs in effect, which may only lead from places to transitions. For each inhibitor arc leading from place p to transition t, place p is said to be an inhibitor place of t. Standard notions such a safeness, liveness, etc. apply to extended Petri nets. Any extended Petri net (P, T, R, E) can be considered to be an extended workflow net iff (P, T, R) is a workflow net. In other words, if by disregarding the inhibitor arcs the remaining net is a workflow net, we consider the original net to be a valid extended workflow net. We will identify the special source place and sink place of such an extended workflow net with the common identifiers i and o. The soundness property for an extended workflow can be formulated in exactly the same terms as for common workflow nets.

An SEPN (P, T, R, E, W, f) is an extended Petri net (P, T, R, E) with weights (W) and a delay function (f) associated with it. The weights and delay function are similarly defined as in the definition of a Stochastic Petri net (see Definition 2.16). The state of an SEPN may be characterized also by the common notion of a timed state. The stochastic behavior that is induced by an SEPN is, however, different from that of a Stochastic Petri net. In particular, the original function *fire* (see Definition 2.19) that is used in the characterization of the induced stochastic process needs some modification. In an SEPN with some timed state s, only those transitions qualify to be part of *fire*(s), if their inhibitor places (if any) are empty. Finally, an SEPN (P, T, R, E, W, f) is a valid SEWN iff (P, T, R, E) is an extended workflow net. Because soundness is defined for extended workflow nets, the throughput time is defined as well.

Now we return our attention to the net in Figure 4.14 which is clearly an extended workflow net. It can be used to construct an SEWN to analyze the time behavior of (a part of) a workflow where a particular task is executed repetitively, without a prior specification of the number of times it is executed. This particular task should be modeled by assigning to transition w the appropriate delay characterization. The weights that are assigned to the transitions t and v in such an SEWN determine the likelihood that w is executed multiple times. If it is to be ensured that the multiple executions of transition w are enabled at exactly the same time, transitions t and v should be immediate. Although it is not strictly necessary for obtaining a throughput characterization of an SEWN on the basis of this repeater structure, we will assume that transitions s, w, x and z are always the only timed transitions.

It is not hard to see that the extended workflow net in Figure 4.14 is not safe if it is initially marked at $[\![i]\!]$. In particular, places c, d, and f are not bounded. The net, however, is sound. We will use a graph of the relations between the reachable markings from $[\![i]\!]$ as depicted in Figure 4.15 to argue the soundness.

In the graph 6 states are recognized, labeled with M_i for $i \in [0..5]$. A soon as transition s fires on the basis of state $[\![i]\!]$ (M_0), state M_1 is reached with $K = 0$ and $L = 0$. So, the first time state M_i is encountered the marking equals $[\![a,g]\!]$. Each time that transition u fires in a state M_1 for some K, $L \in \mathbb{N}$, a state M_2 is reached where both K and L are raised by one. The firing of transition t in state M_2 for some K, $L \in \mathbb{N}$ brings the system back in state M_1 with unchanged K and L.

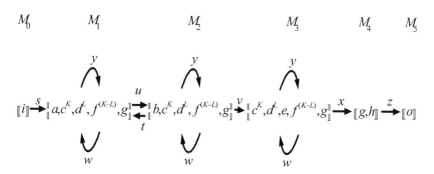

Fig. 4.15. Reachable markings of the repeater net

Analogously, the firing of transition v in state M_2 for some $K, L \in \mathbb{N}$ brings the system to state M_3 with unchanged K and L. In state M_3 holds that if $K = 0$, then transition x may fire bringing the system to state M_4 and, by firing z, in the final state o (M_5). For each of the states M_1, M_2, and M_3 with some K and L holds that if $L > 0$, then transition w may fire. The firing of w lowers the value of L by 1. Similarly, for each of the states M_1, M_2, and M_3 with some K and L holds that if $K > 0$ and $K - L > 0$ then transition y may fire. The firing of y lowers the value of K by 1.

From the graph of reachable states, it may be concluded that for each state M_1, M_2, and M_3 holds that $K \geq L \geq 0$. The probability that v will never fire is equal to zero, because the net is eager and the weight of v positive. Therefore, it is ensured that M_3 is reached eventually. As long as $L > 0$, the only transitions that may fire in this state are y and w. Their firing respectively lower the values of K and L until $L = 0$. Then, only transition x may fire followed by the firing of z. So, there is only one final state, it will always be reached, and this final state is $[\![i]\!]$. Hence, the extended workflow net with a repeater structure is sound. At this point, it is clear that we may consider the throughput time behavior of an SEWN on the basis of a repeater network structure.

Now we turn to the formal analysis of the repeater structure. Let B be an SEWN constructed on the basis of an extended workflow net with a structure such as in Figure 4.14. B has a delay probability distribution F_w and weights w_t and w_u. Assume furthermore that all other transitions are immediate. Let SEWN B induce the stochastic process SP = { $(X_n, Y_n, Z_n) \mid n = 0, 1, 2, \dots$ }. Given the net structure and the initial timed state, transitions t, u, w, and y may fire multiple times. Every other transition fires at most once. For each transition $r \in \{s, t, u, v, w, x, y\}$, we define random variable $\underline{r}_i$ ($i \in \mathbb{N} \backslash \{0\}$) which is the delay that transition r imposes if it fires for an ith time. Note that although the multiple firings of w take place at the same time, there is a firing order that can be distinguished (see Definition 2.19). We also define random variable $\underline{n}$, which is the number of times that w is executed before the final state is reached. We consider the throughput time distribution F_B.

$$\text{Let } z \in \mathbb{N}, F_B(z) = \sum_{i=1}^{\infty} \mathbb{P}(\underline{n} = i \wedge (\max \ j : 1 \le j \le i : \underline{w}_j) \le z) =$$

$$\sum_{i=1}^{\infty} \frac{w_v w_t^{i-1}}{(w_t + w_u)^i} \prod_{j=1}^{i} F_w(z) = \frac{w_v F_w(z)}{w_t + w_u - w_t F_w(z)}.$$

The computation of the distribution function F_B can be performed in m steps, with m the minimal delay for which $F_w(m)$ is equal to 1. The extension of this specific case to the general case where transitions s, v, x, and z are also timed is straightforward.

Note that because an extended workflow net with a repeater structure initially marked at $[\![i]\!]$ is not safe, it is not ensured by applying a synthesis step on an arbitrary transition in such a net that another sound extended workflow net is obtained (see Theorem 2.4). Note also that we have considered one of several ways to model a net with a repeater structure. A similar network may also be constructed by adding priorities to the standard Petri net or by introducing recursion.

The discussion of the repeater network ends this section. In the next section we will discuss an approach that delivers probabilistic *bounds* for the throughput time, instead of exact results.

4.4 Bounded SWN Analysis

In this section we present a computational approach that determines for any place in a sound, free-choice, and acyclic SWN an upper and lower bound for the probability that a token arrives in it at a specific time, assuming the general initial timed state M_0 (see Definition 2.18). In other words, given a specific time value we have bounds for the probability that a token arrives at or before that time. Obviously, for the special sink place o of a workflow net this yields a characterization of the throughput time.

The bounds that we present in this section are based on two ideas. The first idea is that a lower bound for the probability that a token arrives at or before a specific time can be obtained by treating the arrival times of tokens in places as independent events. This is, in general, not the case. Take, for example, two places that are the output places of the same transition (and only of this transition). The arrivals of tokens in these places will always take place at the same time. Assuming this independency will give a *pessimistic* estimation of the firing times of transitions that synchronize these tokens, i.e., to fire later. On an abstract level, this idea can be seen as an application of a theorem by Barlow and Proshan (1975). They proved that if X is a vector of associated random variables, then its independent version is stochastically greater than X.

The other idea exploits that a transition can never fire until tokens for all its input places have arrived. Considering the arrival of tokens in only one of these input places will always give an *optimistic* estimation of the firing time of such a transition, i.e., to fire earlier. To prevent from being overly optimistic, the place is taken that probably has the latest arrival time.

Consider the example SWN WF = (P, T, R, W, f) in Figure 4.16. The SWN WF has a delay function f as given in Table 4.1. All weights equal 1. Note that for each transition s, f_s is a probability density function over $\mathbb{N}$. So for each $f_s(v)$ with $v \in \mathbb{N}$ that is not listed holds that $f_s(v) = 0$.

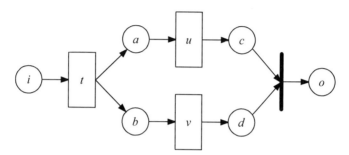

Fig. 4.16. Example SWN for bounds

Table 4.1. Delay densities

transition s	$f_s(0)$	$f_s(1)$	$f_s(2)$	$f_s(3)$	$f_s(4)$
t	0	1/2	0	1/2	0
u	0	1/2	0	1/2	0
v	0	0	1/2	0	1/2

If we define for each transition $s \in T$ the random variable $\underline{s}$ as the delay of its firing and for each place $p \in P$ the random variable $\underline{p}$ as the arrival time of a token, it can be easily determined that Table 4.2 describes the complete time behavior of WF. Each entry of this table links a combination of possible delays of transitions t, u and v to the arrival times of tokens in the places of WF. Each combination of delays is equally probable (= 1/8).

Table 4.2. Time behavior of WF

t	*u*	*v*	*i*	*a*	*b*	*c*	*d*	*o*
1	1	2	0	1	1	2	3	3
1	1	4	0	1	1	2	5	5
1	3	2	0	1	1	4	3	4
1	3	4	0	1	1	4	5	5
3	1	2	0	3	3	4	5	5
3	1	4	0	3	3	4	7	7
3	3	2	0	3	3	6	5	6
3	3	4	0	3	3	6	7	7

On the basis of this time behavior it is possible to compute for places c and d distribution functions F_c and F_d. For example, the probability that a token arrives in c at or before the time of 4 is 6/8, as 6 out of the 8 possible and equally probable events satisfy this property (see Table 4.2). The distribution functions are given in Table 4.3. Note that for each time value below 2 either distribution function yields 0 and for each value above 7 either function yields 1.

Table 4.3. Probability distributions for c and d

x	$F_c(x)$	$F_d(x)$
2	2/8	0
3	2/8	2/8
4	6/8	2/8
5	6/8	6/8
6	1	6/8
7	1	1

The computation of the lower bound treats the arrival times in places such as c and d as independent random variables. If this was true in the case of the example, the value of the throughput time distribution of WF for time value x, $F_{WF}(x)$, could be computed as the product of $F_c(x)$ and $F_d(x)$ (see the parallelism structure in Section 4.3). The upper bound takes for each time value x the minimum of the distribution functions $F_c(x)$ and $F_d(x)$. The outcomes of the approaches are given in Table 4.4, as well as the real distribution function. Note that for each time value below 2 all functions yield 0 and for each value above 7 all functions yield 1.

Table 4.4. Pessimistic, real, and optimistic throughput time distributions for WF

x	$F_c(x) \cdot F_d(x)$	$F_{WF}(x)$	$\min(F_c(x), F_d(x))$
2	0	0	0
3	4/64	1/8	2/8
4	12/64	2/8	2/8
5	36/64	5/8	6/8
6	6/8	6/8	6/8
7	1	1	1

For this example, it can be verified that the pessimistic approach indeed renders a lower bound for the throughput time distribution of WF and that the optimistic approach renders an upper bound. Note that the example SWN has the parallelism structure as discussed in Section 4.3. We already presented an approach to give an exact solution for this case. The bounds that we discuss in this section, however, are applicable to the entire class of SWN's with a sound, free-choice, and acyclic underlying workflow net.

In the remainder of this section we will first formally define the bounds as informally introduced. Before we prove the correctness of these bounds on the basis of the stochastic process an SWN induces, we will present some supporting properties and lemmas. In the last subsection we will illustrate the approach with a more complicated example.

4.4.1 Bounds and Supporting Notions

The bound functions $\underline{F}$ and $\overrightarrow{F}$ that can be used to approximate the throughput time behavior of an SWN are defined as follows.

Definition 4.2   (Lower arrival bound $\underline{F}$). Given a sound, free-choice, and acyclic SWN WF = (P, T, R, W, f) that is marked at general initial timed state M_0, for each place $p \in$ P the lower arrival bound $\underline{F}_p$ is defined as:

– $\underline{F}_p(m) = 1$, for $m \in \mathbb{N}$ and $p = i$,

– $\underline{F}_p(m) = \displaystyle\sum_{n=0}^{m} \sum_{t \in \bullet p} f_t(n) \cdot \dfrac{w(t)}{\displaystyle\sum_{u \in [t] \cap T} w(u)} \cdot \prod_{q \in \bullet t} \underline{F}_q(m-n)$, for $m \in \mathbb{N}$ and $p \neq i$.

If confusion can arise about the SWN context of $\underline{F}$, we use the notation $\underline{F}_{WF}$.

Definition 4.3   (Upper arrival bound $\overrightarrow{F}$). Given a sound, free-choice, and acyclic SWN WF = (P, T, R, W, f) that is marked at general initial timed state M_0, for each place $p \in$ P the upper arrival bound $\overrightarrow{F}_p$ is defined as:

– $\overrightarrow{F}_p(m) = 1$, for $m \in \mathbb{N}$ and $p = i$,

– $\overrightarrow{F}_p(m) = \displaystyle\sum_{n=0}^{m} \sum_{t \in \bullet p} \min_{q \in \bullet t} \left(f_t(n) \cdot \dfrac{w(t)}{\displaystyle\sum_{u \in [t] \cap T} w(u)} \cdot \overrightarrow{F}_q(m-n) \right)$.

If confusion can arise about the SWN context of $\overrightarrow{F}$, we use the notation $\overrightarrow{F}_{WF}$.

We claim for any SWN WF with initial timed state M_0, special sink place o and $m \in \mathbb{N}$ that $\underline{F}_o(m)$ is a lower bound and $\overrightarrow{F}_p(m)$ is an upper bound for the value of the throughput time distribution $F_{WF}(m)$ (see Definition 4.22). We will formalize and prove this claim further in this section. First we focus on the computation of these bound functions $\underline{F}$ and $\overrightarrow{F}$, which can be computed for any sound, free-choice and acyclic SWN by making one pass through the net and inspecting each of its nodes exactly once. We will first informally describe such a computation.

First, an upper bound N $\in \mathbb{N}$ for the total throughput time must be established. A simple upper bound for the maximal throughput time is, for example, |T|·d, with

|T| the number of transitions of the SWN under consideration and d the maximal delay any of these transitions may impose. Obviously, the bound functions for any place may safely be set to 1 for each value that supercedes the maximal through-put time: the probability that a token arrives before this time in any place is 1.

Next, for each place in the net the value of the bound functions for domain values between 0 and N must be established. An efficient way of computing the values for the bound functions is to distinguish an ordered set of layers in the net and compute the bounds of the places per layer. The first layer consists of place i only, the second layer consists of all places that are output places of transitions that have places from the former layer as input places, etc. Distinguishing layers like this is feasible as the SWN's under consideration are acyclic. By this layer-wise inspection, each place is inspected exactly once. When the highest layer – that consists of place o only – is inspected the computation is finished. In Figure 4.17, the SWN that has been constructed in Section 4.3 is once more depicted (see Figure 4.4). Each place is assigned to one of the ordered layers 0 to 6 in the above described fashion.

Before we will prove the correctness of the defined bounds on the basis of the stochastic process an SWN induces, we consider some properties of the underlying workflow nets that will prove to be useful. We start with observations about the number of firings and the number of times that places are marked.

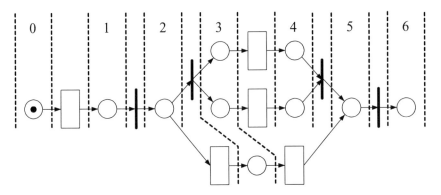

Fig. 4.17. Layers in an acyclic SWN

Lemma 4.1   **(Single firing of transitions.)** Given a safe and acyclic workflow net $W = (P, T, R)$ initially marked at $[\![i]\!]$, it holds that if $M \xrightarrow{t_1} M_1$, $M_1 \xrightarrow{t_2} M_2$, ..., $M_{n-1} \xrightarrow{t_n} M_n$ are transition firings with M reachable from the initial marking $[\![i]\!]$, then each transition will fire at most once:

$(\forall\ i, j: 1 \leq i \leq n \wedge 1 \leq j \leq n: t_i = t_j \Rightarrow i = j)$.

Proof. Consider transition firings $M_{i-1} \xrightarrow{t_i} M_i$ and $M_{j-1} \xrightarrow{t_j} M_j$ and suppose that $t_i = t_j$. Without loss of generality, also assume that $1 \leq i < j \leq n$. Given is that if $\sigma = t_i t_{i+1} t_{i+2}..t_{j-1}t_j$, then $M_{i-1} \xrightarrow{\sigma} M_j$. Define $V = \{\ t_l \mid i \leq l \leq j \wedge path(t_i \rightarrow t_l)\ \}$ and

$U = \{\ t_l \mid i \le l \le j\ \} \setminus V$. Suppose that there are $v \in V$ and $u \in U$ such that $v\bullet \cap \bullet u$ $\ne \varnothing$; then there is a path from v to u and therefore from t_i to u; so $u \in V$ which leads to a contradiction. We conclude that $V\bullet \cap \bullet U = \varnothing$. On the basis of the Exchange Lemma (see Theorem 2.1) we may now deduce $M_{i-1} \xrightarrow{\sigma|_U \sigma|_V} M_j$. Consider the first possible case: $t_j \in V$. Because we assumed that $t_i = t_j$, there must be a path from t_j to t_i on the basis of the definition of V, i.e., there is a cycle. Because the net is acyclic, this leads to a contradiction. Consider the second possible case, $t_j \in U$. Note that the last element of $\sigma|_U$ is t_j and the first element of $\sigma|_V$ is t_i. Let $V' = V\setminus\{\ t_i\ \}$ and $U' = U\setminus\{\ t_j\ \}$. Then $M_{i-1} \xrightarrow{\sigma|_U \sigma|_V} M_j$ can be rewritten as $M_{i-1} \xrightarrow{\sigma|_{U'} t_j t_i \sigma|_{V'}} M_j$. Because there are no causal relations between t_j and t_i (acyclicness) and $t_i = t_j$ this means that there is a marking M' such that $M_{i-1} \xrightarrow{\sigma|_{U'}} M'$ and t_j and t_i both enabled at M'. As $t_i = t_j$ this means that t_i is enabled multiple times. Because the system $(W, [\![i]\!])$ is safe, this leads to a contradiction. As t_j is neither part of U or V, our assumption that $t_i = t_j$ while $i \ne j$ must be invalid. $\square$

Definition 4.4   (Single-marking workflow net). A workflow net $W = (P, T, R)$ is said to be *single-marking* if for any place $p \in P$ and for each sequence of transition firings $M \xrightarrow{t_1} M_1, M_1 \xrightarrow{t_2} M_2, ..., M_{n-1} \xrightarrow{t_n} M_n$ where M marks p and M is reachable from initial marking $[\![i]\!]$ holds that place p will not be marked again after it becomes unmarked:
$$(\forall i : 1 \le i \le n: M(p) > 0 \land M_i(p) = 0) \Rightarrow (\forall j : i < j \le n: M_j(p) = 0).$$

The following lemma gives the relation between the introduced notions.

Lemma 4.2   (Single-firing of place predecessors follows from single-marking). If the workflow net $W = (P, T, R)$ initially marked at $[\![i]\!]$ is single-marking, it holds that if $M \xrightarrow{t_1} M_1, M_1 \xrightarrow{t_2} M_2, ..., M_{n-1} \xrightarrow{t_n} M_n$ are transition firings with M reachable from the initial marking $[\![i]\!]$, then for each place $p \in P$ at most one transition $t \in \bullet p$ will fire:
$$(\forall\ i, j: 1 \le i \le n \land 1 \le j \le n: t_i\bullet \cap t_j\bullet \ne \varnothing \Rightarrow i = j).$$
Proof. Suppose there are transitions t_i and t_j such that $t_i\bullet \cap t_j\bullet \ne \varnothing$ and $i \ne j$. Then there is at least one place $p \in P$, $p \in t_i\bullet \cap t_j\bullet$ that will be marked more than once. This leads to a contradiction. $\square$

Lemma 4.2 states that in a single-marking workflow net each transition can fire at most once. The single-marking property can be derived from other standard properties of workflow nets.

Lemma 4.3   (Single marking lemma.) A sound, free-choice, and acyclic workflow net $W = (P, T, R)$ is single-marking.

Proof. Consider an arbitrary place $p \in P$ and arbitrary transition firings $M \xrightarrow{t_1} M_1, M_1 \xrightarrow{t_2} M_2, ..., M_{n-1} \xrightarrow{t_n} M_n$ where M marks p and M is reachable from initial marking $[\![i]\!]$. For $p = o$ follows that this place will never become empty after it becomes marked (soundness). Now consider the case $p \neq o$. On the basis of the soundness and free-choice property of W, we deduce that (W, i) is safe (see Theorem 2.3). Suppose a marking M_i, $1 \leq i \leq n$, such that $M_i(p) = 0$ and it is the first one too. Also suppose a marking M_j, $i < j \leq n$, such that $M_j(p) = 1$. Then, place p is marked, unmarked and marked again. Define $E = [p] \cap T$ (the set of transitions with p as input place). On the basis of the firing rule, $t_i \in E$. Because the net is sound, there must also be a transition firing $M_{k-1} \xrightarrow{t_k} M_k, j < k \leq n$, which removes the token from the non-sink place p. Obviously, $t_k \in E$. But because the net is free-choice, M_{k-1} enables all transitions in E including t_i. So, a firing sequence $\rho = t_1 t_2 .. t_i .. t_j .. t_i$ can be constructed such that $M \xrightarrow{t_1 t_2 .. t_i .. t_j .. t_i} M'$ is a firing sequence for some marking M' with t_i occurring twice. But we know that each transition can fire at most once in a safe and acyclic net (see Lemma 4.1). So, the existence of markings M_i and M_j must be in error. $\square$

On the basis of this lemma, we can establish for each sound, free-choice, and acyclic SWN that during the stochastic process induced by it, it is ensured that there is at most one, unique time stamp for each of its places for all the timed states encountered.

We end this section by the presentation of a general result which is used in the proof in the following section of the correctness of the bounds as defined with Definition 4.2 and Definition 4.3.

Theorem 4.1   **(Monotonicity inequality).** Let f and g be either monotonic nondecreasing or monotonic nonincreasing, positive functions on $\mathbb{N}$ and let $\underline{x}$ be a random variable. Then for random variables $f(\underline{x})$ and $g(\underline{x})$ holds that:

$\mathbb{E} f(\underline{x}) g(\underline{x}) \geq \mathbb{E} f(\underline{x}) \mathbb{E} g(\underline{x})$.

Proof. See Ross (1996). $\square$

4.4.2 Correctness of Lower and Upper Bounds

We introduce in this section two types of random variables on the stochastic process an SWN induces:

a. A_p is the value (time stamp) of the token if a token ever arrives in place p and it equals ∞ if no token ever reaches place p,

b. B_t is the delay that transition t imposes if it fires and it equals ∞ if the transition will never fire.

Their formal definitions are as below.

Definition 4.5   **(Random variables A, B).** Given an SWN WF = (P, T, R, W, *f*) with general initial timed state M_0 and the stochastic process it induces, SP = { $(X_n, Y_n, Z_n) \mid n = 0, 1, 2, \ldots$ } (see Definitions 2.16 and 2.19), random variables A and B are defined as follows, $k, e \in \mathbb{N}$:

1. for $p = i$, $A_p = 0$,
   for $p \in P\backslash\{\, i\,\}$, $A_p = k$
2. $\Leftrightarrow \exists t \in \bullet p : \exists e, n \in \mathbb{N} : Y_n = t \wedge time(X_n) = k - e \wedge Z_n = e$,
3. for $t \in T$, $B_t = e \Leftrightarrow \exists n \in \mathbb{N} : Y_n = t \wedge Z_n = e$.

With these random variables we can express the goal of the functions $\underline{F}$ and $\overrightarrow{F}$ as: for each place p and for any time value $n \in \mathbb{N}$, $\underline{F}_p(n)\,[\,\overrightarrow{F}_p(n)\,]$ gives a lower bound [upper bound] for the probability that A_p equals or is less than n. These claims will be formalized as Theorems 4.2 and 4.3. The value of random variable A_p for any place p depends on the delay of the transition that marked p and the time stamps of its input places.

Lemma 4.4   **(Arrival time depends on firing).** Given an SWN WF = (P, T, R, W, *f*) with general initial timed state M_0, the stochastic process it induces, SP = { $(X_n, Y_n, Z_n) \mid n = 0, 1, 2, \ldots$ } (see Definitions 2.16 and 2.19), and random variables A and B (Definition 4.5), for each place $p \in P\backslash\{\, i\,\}$ and $k \in \mathbb{N}$ holds that

$$A_p = k \Leftrightarrow \exists t \in \bullet p : \max_{q \in \bullet t} A_q + B_t = k .$$

Proof. First we prove $A_p = k \Rightarrow \left[\exists t \in \bullet p : \max_{q \in \bullet t} A_q + B_t = k \right]$.

(1) Definition 4.5.1 states that
$$A_p = k \Leftrightarrow \left[\exists t \in \bullet p : \exists e, n \in \mathbb{N} : Y_n = t \wedge time(X_n) = k - e \ \wedge Z_n = e \right],$$

(2) From Definition 4.5.2 follows that
$$Y_n = t \wedge Z_n = e \Rightarrow B_t = e,$$

(3) (1) and (2) lead to:
$$A_p = k \Rightarrow \left[\exists t \in \bullet p : \exists e, n \in \mathbb{N} : B_t = e \wedge Y_n = t \wedge time(X_n) = k - e \right],$$

(4) So, $A_p = k \Rightarrow$
$$\left[\exists t \in \bullet p : \exists e \in \mathbb{N} : B_t = e \wedge \exists n \in \mathbb{N} : Y_n = t \wedge time(X_n) = k - e \right].$$

We need the following property:
(5) $\max_{q \in \bullet t} A_q = l \Leftrightarrow \left[\exists n \in \mathbb{N} : time(X_n) = l \wedge Y_n \in [t] \right]$

The proof of this property is as follows:
- because the net WN is free-choice, one of the transitions in cluster $[t]$ will fire if $\max_{q \in \bullet t} A_q = l$ because only transitions in cluster $[t]$ are enabled by $\bullet t$,

– from the definition of g follows that SP is eager. In other words, if a transition t can fire at time l it will fire at time l, unless a conflicting transition u fires, disabling t.

(6) On the basis of (4) and (5):

$$\left[\exists n \in \mathbb{N} : Y_n = t \wedge time(X_n) = k - e\right] \Rightarrow$$
$$\left[\exists n \in \mathbb{N} : time(X_n) = k - e \wedge Y_n \in [t]\right] \Rightarrow \max_{q \bullet t} A_q = k - e,$$

(7) $A_p = k \Rightarrow \left[\exists t \in \bullet p : \exists e \in \mathbb{N} : B_t = e \wedge \max_{q \bullet t} A_q = k - e\right] \Leftrightarrow$

$$\left[\exists t \in \bullet p : \max_{q \bullet t} A_q + B_t = k\right].$$

This is the first part of the proof.

Now we prove that $\left[\exists t \in \bullet p : \max_{q \bullet t} A_q + B_t = k\right] \Rightarrow A_p = k.$

(8) $\left[\exists t \in \bullet p : \max_{q \bullet t} A_q + B_t = k\right] \Leftrightarrow$

$$\left[\exists t \in \bullet p : \exists e \in \mathbb{N} : B_t = e \wedge \max_{q \bullet t} A_q = k - e\right],$$

(9) On the basis of (5) and (8):

$$\left[\exists t \in \bullet p : \max_{q \bullet t} A_q + B_t = k\right] \Rightarrow$$
$$\left[\exists t \in \bullet p : \exists e \in \mathbb{N} : B_t = e \wedge \exists n \in \mathbb{N} : time(X_n) = k - e \wedge Y_n \in [t]\right]$$

(10) Because $B_t = e$, transition t fires and only one transition in $[t]$ can fire,

$$\left[\exists t \in \bullet p : \exists e \in \mathbb{N} : B_t = e \wedge\right.$$
$$\exists n \in \mathbb{N} : time(X_n) = k - e \wedge Y_n \in [t]\right]$$
$$\Rightarrow \left[\exists t \in \bullet p : \exists e \in \mathbb{N} : B_t = e \wedge\right.$$
$$\exists n \in \mathbb{N} : time(X_n) = k - e \wedge Y_n = t\right],$$

(11) From Definition 4.5.2 follows that $B_t = e \Rightarrow \left[\exists m \in \mathbb{N} : Y_m = t \wedge Z_m = e\right]$ and because t fires at most once (results from the single-marking property of WN, Lemma 4.3), it holds that $m = n$, so we can conclude that

$$\left[\exists t \in \bullet p : \exists e \in \mathbb{N} : B_t = e \wedge\right.$$
$$\exists n \in \mathbb{N} : time(X_n) = k - e \wedge Y_n = t\right] \Rightarrow$$
$$\left[\exists t \in \bullet p : \exists e, n \in \mathbb{N} : B_t = e \wedge\right.$$
$$time(X_n) = k - e \wedge Y_n = t \wedge Z_n = e\right].$$

(12) From (9), (10), (11) and Definition 4.5.1 we conclude

$$\left[\exists t \in \bullet p : \max_{q \in \bullet t} A_q + B_t = k\right] \Rightarrow A_p = k.$$

□

At this point, we can express the probability that a place p is marked with time stamp k.

Lemma 4.5   **(Arrival probability).** Given an SWN WF = (P, T, R, W, f) with general initial timed state M_0, its stochastic process SP = { $(X_n, Y_n, Z_n) \mid n = 0, 1, 2, \dots$ } (see Definitions 2.16 and 2.19) and random variables A and B (see Definition 4.5), for each place $p \in P \backslash \{ i \}$ and $k \in \mathbb{N}$ holds that:

$$\mathbb{P}[A_p = k] = \sum_{l=0}^{k} \sum_{t \in \bullet p} f_t(k-l) \frac{w(t)}{\sum_{u \in [t]} w(u)} \ \mathbb{P}\left[\max_{q \in \bullet t} A_q = l\right]$$

Proof.

$\mathbb{P}[A_p = k]$

= { Lemma 4.4 }

$$\mathbb{P}\left[\exists t \in \bullet p : \max_{q \in \bullet t} A_q + B_t = k\right]$$

= { because WN is a single-marking workflow Lemma 4.2 applies: there is at most one transition $t \in \bullet p$ that fires; therefore, probabilities may be summed }

$$\sum_{t \in \bullet p} \mathbb{P}\left[\max_{q \in \bullet t} A_q + B_t = k\right]$$

= { calculus }

$$\sum_{l=0}^{k} \sum_{t \in \bullet p} \mathbb{P}\left[B_t = k - l \wedge \max_{q \in \bullet t} A_q = l\right]$$

= { apply auxiliary lemma (5) used in the proof of Lemma 4.4 }

$$\sum_{l=0}^{k} \sum_{t \in \bullet p} \mathbb{P}[B_t = k - l \wedge \exists n \in \mathbb{N} : time(X_n) = l \wedge Y_n \in [t]]$$

   = { Definition 4.5.2 }

$$\sum_{l=0}^{k} \sum_{t \in \bullet p} \mathbb{P}[\exists n \in \mathbb{N} : Y_n = t \wedge Z_n = k - l \wedge time(X_n) = l \wedge Y_n \in [t]]$$

= { because WN is a single-marking workflow Lemma 4.2 applies: there is just one n such that $Y_n = t$; so, probabilities may be summed }

$$\sum_{l=0}^{k} \sum_{t \in \bullet p} \sum_{n \in \mathbb{N}} \mathbb{P}[Y_n = t \wedge Z_n = k - l \wedge time(X_n) = l \wedge Y_n \in [t]]$$

= { probability calculus }

$$\sum_{l=0}^{k}\sum_{t\in\bullet p}\sum_{n\in\mathbb{N}}\mathbb{P}\big[Z_n = k-l \mid Y_n = t \wedge time(X_n) = l \wedge Y_n \in [t]\big] \cdot$$

$$\mathbb{P}\big[Y_n = t \mid Y_n \in [t] \wedge time(X_n) = l\big] \cdot$$

$$\mathbb{P}\big[Y_n \in [t] \wedge time(X_n) = l\big]$$

= { definition of Z_n and Y_n, see Definition 2.19; conditional independence of Z_n; $Y_n \in [t]$, so fire$(X_n) \supseteq [t]$ }

$$\sum_{l=0}^{k}\sum_{t\in\bullet p}\sum_{n\in\mathbb{N}} f_t(k-l)\cdot\frac{w(t)}{\sum_{u\in[t]}w(u)}\cdot\mathbb{P}\big[Y_n \in [t] \wedge time(X_n) = l\big]$$

= { calculus }

$$\sum_{l=0}^{k}\sum_{t\in\bullet p} f_t(k-l)\cdot\frac{w(t)}{\sum_{u\in[t]}w(u)}\cdot\mathbb{P}\big[\exists n \in \mathbb{N}: Y_n \in [t] \wedge time(X_n) = l\big]$$

= { again apply auxiliary lemma (5) used in proving Lemma 4.4 }

$$\sum_{l=0}^{k}\sum_{t\in\bullet p} f_t(k-l)\cdot\frac{w(t)}{\sum_{u\in[t]}w(u)}\cdot\mathbb{P}\Big[\max_{q\in\bullet t} A_q = l\Big]$$

□

On the basis of Lemma 4.5, we can define the probability that a place p is marked at or before time k.

Lemma 4.6   **(Accumulated arrival probability).** Let WF = (P, T, R, W, f) be an SWN with general initial timed state M_0, that induces the stochastic process SP = { $(X_n, Y_n, Z_n) \mid n = 0, 1, 2, \dots$ } (see Definitions 2.16 and 2.19) with random variables A and B (see Definition 4.5). For each place $p \in P\backslash\{ i \}$ and $m \in \mathbb{N}$:

$$\mathbb{P}[A_p \le m] = \sum_{n=0}^{m}\sum_{t\in\bullet p} f_t(n)\cdot\frac{w(t)}{\sum_{u\in[t]}w(u)}\cdot\mathbb{P}\Big[\max_{q\in\bullet t} A_q \le m-n\Big].$$

Proof.

$\mathbb{P}[A_p \le m]$

= { probability calculus }

$$\sum_{k=0}^{m}\mathbb{P}[A_p = k]$$

= { apply Lemma 4.5 }

$$\sum_{k=0}^{m}\sum_{l=0}^{k}\sum_{t\in\bullet p} f_t(k-l)\cdot\frac{w(t)}{\sum_{u\in[t]}w(u)}\cdot\mathbb{P}\Big[\max_{q\in\bullet t} A_q = l\Big]$$

= { introduce variable $n = k - l$, so $l = k - n$; change order of summation k and n: $n = 0\dots m$, $k = n\dots m$ }

$$\sum_{n=0}^{m}\sum_{t\in\bullet p} f_t(k-l)\cdot\frac{w(t)}{\sum_{u\in[t]}w(u)}\cdot\sum_{k=n}^{m}\mathbb{P}\!\left[\max_{q\in\bullet t} A_q = k-n\right]$$

= { calculus }

$$\sum_{n=0}^{m}\sum_{t\in\bullet p} f_t(k-l)\cdot\frac{w(t)}{\sum_{u\in[t]}w(u)}\cdot\mathbb{P}\!\left[\max_{q\in\bullet t} A_q \le m-n\right]$$

□

Random variable A_p depends on the delays of transitions that have led to the specific time stamp encountered. Together with Theorem 4.1, this lemma will be used to prove that $\underline{F}_p(m)$ is a correct lower bound (Theorem 4.2).

Lemma 4.7   **(Dependency of arrival on delays).** Given an SWN WF = (P, T, R, W, f) with general initial timed state M_0, its stochastic process SP = { (X_n, Y_n, Z_n) | n = 0, 1, 2, ... } (see Definitions 2.16 and 2.19) and random variables A and B (see Definition 4.5), the time stamp of place p can be expressed as a *monotonic, nondecreasing* function of the delays imposed by a set of transitions, each of which is on a path from the initial place to place p. Formally,

$$\forall p \in \text{P}: A_p = h_p\left(B_{t_1}, B_{t_2}, ..., B_{t_n}\right),$$

for some h_p: $\mathbb{N}^n \to \mathbb{N}$, $n \in \mathbb{N}$ and $\{t_1, t_2, ..., t_n\} \subseteq \{t \in \text{T} \mid (i, t) \in \text{R}^* \wedge (t, p) \in \text{R}^*\}$.

Proof. A_p is defined for each $p \in \text{P}$. We apply induction on the order of the places of the net. For each node $n \in \text{P} \cup \text{T}_i \cup \text{T}_t$:
- or(n) = 0, if n = i,
- or(n) = (max m: $m \in \bullet n$: or(m) + 1), if $n \ne i$.

Base. For place i, A_p = 0 (Definition 4.5), so the claim holds.

Step. Suppose that for each place $q \in \text{P}$ with or(q) $\le j$, or(i) $\le j$ < or(o), holds that:
- $A_q = h_q\left(B_{t_{q,1}}, B_{t_{q,2}}, ..., B_{t_{q,n(q)}}\right)$ with $\{t_{q,1}, t_{q,2}, ..., t_{q,n(q)}\} \subseteq \{t \in \text{T} \mid (i, t) \in \text{R}^* \wedge (t, q) \in \text{R}^*\}$, $n(q) \in \mathbb{N}$, and
- h_q is monotonic nondecreasing in each of its parameters.

Now consider place $p \in \text{P}$ with or(p) = j + 1. Then $A_p = \max_{q\in\bullet t} A_q + B_t$ for some t

$\in$ T (Lemma 4.4). As or(q) < or(p), $A_p = \max_{q\in\bullet t} h_q\left(B_{t_{q,1}}, B_{t_{q,2}}, ..., B_{t_{q,n(q)}}\right) + B_t$. Because

for each $q \in \bullet t$, h_q is monotonic and nondecreasing, this expression for A_p is monotonic and nondecreasing in the parameters B_t and $B_{t_{q,1}}, B_{t_{q,2}}, ..., B_{t_{q,nq}}$ for each

$q \in \bullet t$. Also, $\bigcup_{q\in\bullet t} \{t_{q,1}, t_{q,2}, ..., t_{q,n(q)}\} \cup \{t\} \subseteq \{t \in \text{T} \mid (i, t) \in \text{R}^* \wedge (t, p) \in \text{R}^*\}$:

all referred transitions in the expression for A_p are on a path from i to p. □

We now formally express our claim that $\underline{F}$ and $\vec{F}$ are correct lower and upper bounds for the arrival times of tokens in sound, free-choice, and acyclic workflow nets. At this point, we can also give the proof.

Theorem 4.2   (**Lower bound for arrival probability**). Let WF = (P, T, R, W, f) with general initial timed state M_0 be an SWN that induces the stochastic process SP = { $(X_n, Y_n, Z_n) \mid n = 0, 1, 2, \dots$ } (see Definitions 2.16 and 2.19) with random variables A and B (see Definition 4.5). If (P, T, R) is a sound, free-choice, and acyclic workflow net, then for each place $p \in$ P and for each $m \in \mathbb{N}$ holds that:

$$\mathbb{P}[A_p \leq m] \geq \underline{F}_p(m) \cdot$$

Proof. A_p is defined for each $p \in$ P. We apply induction on the order of the places of the net.

Base. For place i, $A_p = 0$ (Definition 4.5), $\mathbb{P}[A_p \leq m] = 1$ for any $m \in \mathbb{N}$. So the claim holds.

Step. Suppose that for each place $q \in$ P with or$(q) \leq j$, or$(i) \leq j <$ or(o), holds that $\mathbb{P}[A_q \leq m] \geq \underline{F}_q(m)$ for any $m \in \mathbb{N}$. Let $p \in$ P with or$(p) = j + 1$ and $m \in \mathbb{N}$. Then,

$$\mathbb{P}[A_p \leq m] = \sum_{n=0}^{m} \sum_{t \in \bullet p} f_t(n) \cdot \frac{w(t)}{\sum\limits_{u \in [t]} w(u)} \cdot \mathbb{P}\left[\max_{q \in \bullet t} A_q \leq m - n\right] \text{ on the basis of Lemma}$$

4.6 [equality (i)]. We focus on the last part of equality (i) and substitute l for $m - n$:

$$\mathbb{P}\left[\max_{q \in \bullet t} A_q \leq l\right]$$

= { calculus }

$$\mathbb{P}\left[\forall q \in \bullet t : A_q \leq l\right]$$

= { order the set $\bullet t$ as $\{q_1, q_2, \dots, q_c\}$; suppose on the basis of Lemma 4.7 for each q_i, $1 \leq i \leq c$, a function h_{q_i} such that $A_{q_i} = c$ and h_{q_i} monotonic nondecreasing in its parameters }

$$\mathbb{P}\left[\max_{1 \leq i \leq c} h_{q_i}\left(B_{t_{i,1}}, B_{t_{i,2}}, \dots, B_{t_{i,n(i)}}\right) \leq l\right]$$

= { consider q_1 and let B = { $B_{t_1}, B_{t_2}, \dots, B_{t_b}$ } be the delays used as parameters of h_{q_1} such that each delay B_{t_j}, $1 \leq j \leq b$, is *also* used as a parameter for a function h_{q_i}, $2 \leq i \leq c$. Define $\tilde{h}_{q_1}\left(B_{t_1}, \dots, B_{t_b}, B_{t_{b+1}}, \dots, B_{t_{n(1)}}\right) = h_{q_1}\left(B_{t_{1,1}}, B_{t_{1,2}}, \dots, B_{t_{1,n(i)}}\right)$ (reordering and renaming of delays) }

$$\mathbb{P}\left[\tilde{h}_{q_1}\left(B_{t_1}, \dots, B_{t_b}, B_{t_{b+1}}, \dots, B_{t_{n(1)}}\right) \underline{\max} \max_{2 \leq i \leq c} h_{q_i}\left(B_{t_{i,1}}, B_{t_{i,2}}, \dots, B_{t_{i,n(i)}}\right) \leq l\right]$$

= { Define H$\left(B_{t_1}, \dots, B_{t_b}, B_{t_{n(1)+1}}, B_{t_{n(1)+2}}, \dots, B_{t_{n(1)+n(h)}}\right) =$

$\max_{2 \leq i \leq c} h_{q_i}\left(B_{t_{i,1}}, B_{t_{i,2}}, ..., B_{t_{i,n(i)}}\right)$ for a suitable $n(h) \in \mathbb{N}$ (reordering and renaming of delays) }

$\mathbb{P}\left[\tilde{h}_{q_1}\left(B_{t_1}, ..., B_{t_b}, B_{t_{b+1}}, ..., B_{t_{n(1)}}\right) \underline{\max}\right.$

$\left. H\left(B_{t_1}, ..., B_{t_b}, B_{t_{n(1)+1}}, B_{t_{n(1)+2}}, ..., B_{t_{n(1)+n(h)}}\right) \leq l\right]$

= { probability calculus }

$\sum_{b_1, b_2, ..., b_b \in \mathbb{N}} \mathbb{P}\left[\tilde{h}_{q_1}\left(b_1, ..., b_b, B_{t_{b+1}}, ..., B_{t_{n(1)}}\right) \leq l \wedge\right.$

$\left. H\left(b_1, ..., b_b, B_{t_{n(1)+1}}, B_{t_{n(1)+2}}, ..., B_{t_{n(1)+n(h)}}\right) \leq l\right] \cdot$

$\mathbb{P}\left[B_{t_1} = b_1, B_{t_2} = b_2, ..., B_{t_b} = b_b\right]$

= { on the basis of B and H: independence of $B_{t_{b+1}}, ..., B_{t_{n(1)}}$ and

$B_{t_{n(1)+1}}, B_{t_{n(1)+2}}, ..., B_{t_{n(1)+n(h)}}$ }

$\sum_{b_1, b_2, ..., b_b \in \mathbb{N}} \mathbb{P}\left[\tilde{h}_{q_1}\left(b_1, ..., b_b, B_{t_{b+1}}, ..., B_{t_{n(1)}}\right) \leq l\right] \cdot$

$\mathbb{P}\left[H\left(b_1, ..., b_b, B_{t_{n(1)+1}}, B_{t_{n(1)+2}}, ..., B_{t_{n(1)+n(h)}}\right) \leq l\right] \cdot$

$\mathbb{P}\left[B_{t_1} = b_1, B_{t_2} = b_2, ..., B_{t_b} = b_b\right]$

$\geq$ { on the basis of Lemma 4.7 it can be verified that $\tilde{h}_{q_1}$ and H are monotonic nondecreasing functions in their parameters; apply Theorem 4.1 }

$\mathbb{P}\left[\tilde{h}_{q_1}\left(b_1, ..., b_b, B_{t_{b+1}}, ..., B_{t_{n(1)}}\right) \leq l\right] \cdot$

$\mathbb{P}\left[H\left(b_1, ..., b_b, B_{t_{n(1)+1}}, B_{t_{n(1)+2}}, ..., B_{t_{n(1)+n(h)}}\right) \leq l\right]$

=   { definitions $\tilde{h}_{q_1}$ and H }

$\mathbb{P}\left[\max_{2 \leq i \leq c} h_{q_i}\left(B_{t_{i,1}}, B_{t_{i,2}}, ..., B_{t_{i,n(i)}}\right) \leq l\right]$

$\geq$ { successively consider the delays of $q_2, q_3, ..., q_c$ in a similar fashion as for q_1}

$\prod_{1 \leq i \leq c} \mathbb{P}\left[h_{q_i}\left(B_{i,1}, B_{i,2}, ..., B_{i,c_i}\right) \leq l\right]$

= { definition h_{q_i} }

$\prod_{q \in \bullet t} \mathbb{P}\left[A_q \leq l\right]$

$\geq$ { induction hypothesis }

$\prod_{q \in \bullet t} F_q(l)$

We will refer to this derivation as inequality (ii).

We consider now again equality (i): $\mathbb{P}[A_p \le m] =$

$$\sum_{n=0}^{m}\sum_{t\in\bullet p} f_t(n) \cdot \frac{w(t)}{\sum_{u\in[t]} w(u)} \cdot \mathbb{P}\left[\max_{q\in\bullet t} A_q \le m-n\right]$$

$\ge \{$ apply inequality (ii) with $m - n = l \}$

$$\sum_{n=0}^{m}\sum_{t\in\bullet p} f_t(n) \cdot \frac{w(t)}{\sum_{u\in[t]} w(u)} \cdot \prod_{q\in\bullet t} \underleftarrow{F}_q(m-n)$$

$= \{$ Definition 4.2 $\}$

$\underleftarrow{F}_p(m)$

$\square$

Theorem 4.3   **(Upper bound for arrival probability).** Let WF = (P, T, R, W, f) with general initial timed state M_0 be an SWN that induces the stochastic process SP = $\{ (X_n, Y_n, Z_n) \mid n = 0, 1, 2, \ldots \}$ (see Definitions 2.16 and 2.19) with random variables A and B (see Definition 4.5). If (P, T, R) is a sound, free-choice, and acyclic workflow net, then for each place $p \in$ P and for each $m \in \mathbb{N}$:

$\mathbb{P}[A_p \le m] \le \overrightarrow{F}_p(m)$.

Proof. Again we apply induction on the order of the places.
Base. For place i, $A_p = 0$ (Definition 4.5), $\mathbb{P}[A_p \le m] = 1$ for any $m \in \mathbb{N}$. So the claim holds.
Step. Suppose that for each place $q \in$ P with or(q) $\le j$, or(i) $\le j <$ or(o), holds that $\mathbb{P}[A_q \le m] \le \overrightarrow{F}_p(m)$ for any $m \in \mathbb{N}$. Let $p \in$ P with or(p) $= j + 1$ and $m \in \mathbb{N}$. Then,

$\mathbb{P}[A_p \le m]$
$= \{$ Lemma 4.6 $\}$

$$\sum_{n=0}^{m}\sum_{t\in\bullet p} f_t(n) \cdot \frac{w(t)}{\sum_{u\in[t]} w(u)} \cdot \mathbb{P}\left[\max_{q\in\bullet t} A_q \le m-n\right]$$

$\le \{$ probability calculus, $\forall r : r \in \bullet t : \mathbb{P}\left[\max_{q\in\bullet t} A_q \le m-n\right] \le \mathbb{P}[A_r \le m-n] \}$

$$\sum_{n=0}^{m}\sum_{t\in\bullet p} \min_{q\in\bullet t}\left(f_t(n) \cdot \frac{w(t)}{\sum_{u\in[t]} w(u)} \cdot \mathbb{P}[A_q \le m-n] \right)$$

$\le \{$ induction hypothesis $\}$

$$\sum_{n=0}^{m}\sum_{t\in\bullet p} \min_{q\in\bullet t}\left(f_t(n) \cdot \frac{w(t)}{\sum_{u\in[t]} w(u)} \cdot \overrightarrow{F}_q(m-n) \right)$$

= { Definition 4.3 }

$\overrightarrow{F}_p(m)$

□

4.4.3 Efficiency

To illustrate the approach as presented in the previous sections, we use the SWN WF (P, T, R, W, f) as depicted in Figure 4.18.

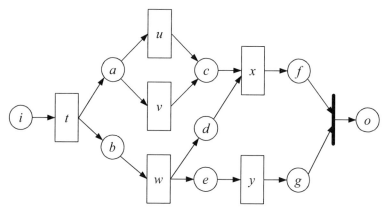

Fig. 4.18. SWN WF for computation of bounds

Note that in contrast to the example we used in the introduction of Section 4.4 the workflow net structure of WF could not have been synthesized on the basis of the basic structures as discussed in Section 4.3. The reason for this is that the net cannot be completely partitioned in parts that can be analyzed locally. For example, the behavior of the upper part of the net (transitions u, v, x; places a, c, f) cannot be isolated from the lower part of the net (transitions w, y; places b, e, g), because of place d that connects both parts.

The SWN WF has a delay function f and a weight function W as given in Table 4.5. Note that for each transition s, f_s is a probability density function over $\mathbb{N}$. So for each $f_s(v)$ with $v \in \mathbb{N}$ that is not listed holds that $f_s(v) = 0$.

If we apply the algorithm on WF, we obtain the upper and lower bounds as depicted in Figure 4.19. The exact distribution function is obtained by calculating all possible executions of the net. Note that the latter is only feasible for this example because of the small size of the net and the small number of different delays that are feasible.

Table 4.5. Time and weight function for WF

	$f_{task}(0)$	$f_{task}(1)$	$f_{task}(2)$	$f_{task}(3)$	$f_{task}(4)$	$f_{task}(5)$	$f_{task}(6)$	W_{task}
t	0	¼	1/8	5/8	0	0	0	1
u	0	¼	¾	0	0	0	0	1
v	0	0	0	¾	¼	0	0	2
w	½	¼	¼	0	0	0	0	1
x	0	0	¼	3/8	3/8	0	0	1
y	0	½	0	0	0	0	½	1

On the basis of this example, we cannot say anything decisive about the quality of the bounds. This quality is highly influenced by the chosen delay functions, the chosen weights, and the network structure. In a net without parallelism, the bounds exactly match the exact data distribution. In a net with parallel branches that are highly balanced, i.e., for each execution the branches take almost as much time to complete, the bounds become very loose.

This larger example does give us the opportunity to reflect on the efficiency of calculating the exact probability distribution in comparison with calculating the bounds. The exact distribution can be computed on the basis of all different delay combinations of the transitions. If we denote the largest used delay with d and the number of transitions with $|T|$, then the number of delay combinations equals $d^{|T|}$. The number of required multiplications is therefore $O(|T| \cdot d^{|T|})$. For this small example alone, this means that a brute force approach requires over $5 \cdot 10^6$ multiplications.

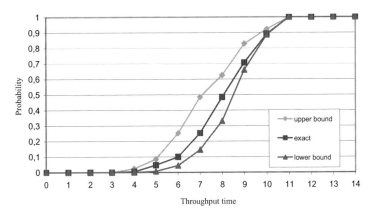

Fig. 19. Lower/upper bounds for, and exact probability distribution function F_W

To compute either an upper or lower bound, we have to perform for each place a number of calculations that equals the number of discrete delays between zero and the maximal throughput time. After all, for each of these values a token arrival may be possible. If we use as bound for the maximal throughput time the figure $|T| \cdot d$ (see Section 4.4) and if we assume further that the number of input places is of the order of the total number of place $|P|$, then the number of multiplications is $O(|P|^2 \cdot |T| \cdot d)$. For the used example, this figure is less than $5 \cdot 10^3$. Further comparison is possible if we realize that in practical situations often $|P| \approx |T|$ and that this figure usually ranges from a couple of dozens to one or two hundreds.

This example illustrates that the presented approximation method can give approximations for nets for which no exact results can be computed with the exact approach of Section 4.3. Clearly, the application of both methods also overlap for some part. In the following section we will discuss a hybrid approach.

4.5 Hybrid Approach

In Sections 4.3 and 4.4 we presented respectively an exact and approximated analytical approach to determine the throughput time behavior of SWN's. In this section we will discuss how to combine the accuracy of the former approach with the application area of the latter. We will refer to this combination as the *hybrid approach*. The basis for the hybrid approach is similar to that of the exact approach, which is as follows:

1. A workflow net is synthesized.
2. An SWN is constructed on the basis of this workflow net.
3. A throughput characterization for this SWN is determined on the basis of the followed synthesis order and the throughput characterization of the smaller parts of the SWN.

In the hybrid approach both the constructions as used in the exact and approximated approaches can be used. In determining a throughput time characterization of the SWN, both the exact computation as the computation of bounds can be used. We will discuss each of these aspects.

4.5.1 Constructing a Hybrid Net

For the hybrid approach, both the net synthesis and the notion of a synthesis step are equivalent to the definitions in Section 4.3. A transition in the workflow net under synthesis may be replaced (cf. Definition 2.15) by one of two following types of workflow nets:

a. A workflow net with of one of the structures as discussed in Section 4.3 (choice, sequence, parallelism, logic choice, etc).
b. An arbitrary sound, free-choice and acyclic workflow net with an initial transition.

This in contrast to the exact approach of Section 4.3 where only the first option is taken into account. The soundness of the synthesized net is guaranteed under the conditions of the Compositionality Theorem (see Theorem 2.4).

After a satisfactory, hybrid workflow net is synthesized, a corresponding SWN is constructed by adding an appropriate weight function W and delay function f to it.

4.5.2 Analyzing a Hybrid Net

We will now show how approximations of the throughput time density (or distribution) of a constructed SWN may be derived on the basis of exact or approximated characterizations of the throughput time densities (or distributions) of its substituting components. Obviously, if only the known blocks of the exact analysis approach are used, then an exact throughput time characterization can be computed. In the more general case where at least one synthesis step takes place of type (b) (see the previous section), the analysis of a hybrid net yields an upper and lower bound for the throughput time density (or distribution) of the complete, constructed net.

We consider the situation as shown in Figure 4.20. We suppose that net A is the net in which we are interested in. It could be either that it is the original, constructed hybrid net or that it is an intermediate net of which the throughput behavior gives an adequate bound for this original net. This is not of any importance for the analysis. We suppose that net A is constructed on the basis of net B, where net C – without its source and sink place – has replaced transition t^+.

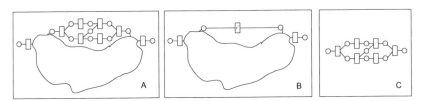

Fig. 4.20. Relations between net in the analysis of a hybrid net

In general – not considering the specific structure of net C in the example – there are now two possibilities as follows:

1. Either an exact throughput time density can be computed of net C (see Section 4.3), or
2. Lower and upper bound probability density functions can be computed for the throughput time density of C (see Section 4.4).

Possibilities 1. and 2. respectively coincide with a synthesis step where either a type (a) or (b) workflow net has been used (see the previous section).

In the first case, net B has *exactly* the same throughput time behavior of net A when for transition t^+ a delay function is taken that equals the throughput time density of C. This has been argued in Section 4.3. Note that it is essential that t^+ also assumes the weight of the initial transition of net C.

In the second case – which is the new element of the hybrid approach – we claim that the (exact) throughput time distribution of the net B that uses as a delay function for t^+ the *lower* bound throughput time density of net C is a *lower* bound throughput time distribution for net A. Similarly, using the *upper* bound throughput time density of net C for the delay function of transition t^+ in net B, we obtain an *upper* bound throughput time distribution for net A. We will formalize and prove this claim with the following lemma.

Lemma 4.8   **(Bounds for a hybrid net).** Consider an SWN $WN^1 = (P^1, T^1, R^1, W^1, f^1)$ that has been constructed by assigning a weight function W^1 and delay function f^1 to a workflow net (P^1, T^1, R^1). Let this workflow net be the result of net synthesis (see Definition 2.15), where (P^1, T^1, R^1) is the result of replacing in some workflow net (P^2, T^2, R^2) the transition $t^+ \in T^2$ by some workflow net (P^3, T^3, R^3) with has an initial transition $t^* \in T^3$. Let $WN^3 = (P^3, T^3, R^3, W^3, f^3)$ be the SWN on the basis of (P^3, T^3, R^3), with for each $t \in T^3$, $W^3(t) = W^1(t)$ and $f^3(t) = f^1(t)$. Let $WN^2_{low} = (P^2, T^2, R^2, W^2, f^2_{low})$ and $WN^2_{up} = (P^2, T^2, R^2, W^2, f^2_{up})$ be SWN's such that for each $t \in T^2$:

$$- \quad W^2(t) = \begin{cases} W^3(t) \text{ if } t \neq t^+, \\ W^1(t^*) \text{ if } t = t^+, \end{cases}$$

$$- \quad f^2_{low}(t) = \begin{cases} f^2(t) \text{ if } t \neq t^+, \\ \underrightarrow{f}_{WN^3} \text{ if } t = t^+, \end{cases}$$

$$- \quad f^2_{up}(t) = \begin{cases} f^2(t) \text{ if } t \neq t^+, \\ \overrightarrow{f}_{WN^3} \text{ if } t = t^+, \end{cases}$$

with $\underrightarrow{f}$ and $\overrightarrow{f}$ the density functions that correspond respectively with the bounding distribution functions $\overrightarrow{F}$ and $\underrightarrow{F}$ as defined in Definition 4.2 and Definition 4.3. Then:

$F_{WN^2_{low}}(k) \leq F_{WN^1}(k) \leq F_{WN^2_{up}}(k)$ for $k \in \mathbb{N}$.

Proof. First we prove that $F_{WN^2_{low}}(k) \leq F_{WN^1}(k)$. Let $SP^i = \{ (X^i_n, Y^i_n, Z^i_n) \mid n = 0, 1, 2, \ldots \}$ be the stochastic process induced by WN^i for $i \in \{1, 2, 3\}$ as defined above and let $SP^4 = \{ (X^4_n, Y^4_n, Z^4_n) \mid n = 0, 1, 2, \ldots \}$ be the stochastic process induced by WN^2_{low}. For each stochastic process SP^i, $i \in \{1, 2, 3, 4\}$, the random variable A^i_p is defined for each place $p \in P^i$ as in Definition 4.5. Let $T^2 = \{ t_1, t_2, \ldots, t_q \}$, $t^+ = t_q$, and $T^3 = \{ t_{q+1}, t_{q+2}, \ldots, t_{q+r} \}$. So, $T^1 = \{ t_1, t_2, \ldots, t_{q-1}, t_{q+1}, \ldots, t_{q+r} \}$.

For each stochastic process SP^i the random variable B_t^i is defined for each transition $t \in T^i$ as in Definition 4.5.

Let us consider for $k \in \mathbb{N}$,

$\quad F_{WN^1}(k)$

$=$ { Definition 2.22, on the basis of Lemma 4.7 with $T_{WN^2} = A_o^2$ and $T_{WN^3} = A_o^3$, there are monotonic nondecreasing functions $g: \mathbb{N}^q \to \mathbb{N}$ and $h: \mathbb{N}^r \to \mathbb{N}$ such that $T_{WN^2} = g(B_{t_1}^2, B_{t_2}^2, ..., B_{t_q}^2)$ and $T_{WN^3} = h(B_{t_{q+1}}^3, B_{t_{q+2}}^3, ..., B_{t_{q+r}}^3)$; as $t^+ = t_q$ and $W^2(t^+) = W^1(t^*)$, we know on the basis of the construction of WN^1 by replacing t^+ in WN^2 by WN^3 with initial transition t^* that $T_{WN^1} = A_o^1 = g(B_{t_1}^2, B_{t_2}^2, ..., B_{t_{q-1}}^2, T_{WN^3})$ }

$\quad \mathbb{P}(g(B_{t_1}^2, B_{t_2}^2, ..., B_{t_{q-1}}^2, T_{WN^3}) \le k)$

$=$ { probability calculus }

$\quad \displaystyle\sum_{b_1, b_2, ..., b_{q-1} \in \mathbb{N}} \mathbb{P}(g(b_1, b_2, ..., b_{q-1}, T_{WN^3}) \le k) \cdot \mathbb{P}(B_{t_1}^2 = b_1, B_{t_2}^2 = b_2, ..., B_{t_{q-1}}^2 = b_{q-1})$

$=$ { g is continuous and monotonic nondecreasing in T_{WN^1}; for each continuous, monotonic decreasing function $g: \mathbb{N} \to \mathbb{N}$ holds that there is a function $l: \mathbb{N} \to \mathbb{N}$ such that $g(x) \le k \Leftrightarrow x \le l(k)$; assume such a function l }

$\quad \displaystyle\sum_{b_1, b_2, ..., b_b \in \mathbb{N}} \mathbb{P}(T_{WN^3} < l(k, b_1, b_2, ..., b_{q-1})) \cdot \mathbb{P}(B_{t_1}^2 = b_1, B_{t_2}^2 = b_2, ..., B_{t_{q-1}}^2 = b_{q-1})$

$\ge$ { definition of F_{WN^3}; because WN^3 is of type (b), it is possible to compute a lower bound function $\underline{F}_{WN^3}$ such that for all $n \in \mathbb{N}$, $\underline{F}_{WN^3}(n) \le F_{WN^3}(n)$ }

$\quad \displaystyle\sum_{b_1, b_2, ..., b_b \in \mathbb{N}} \underline{F}_{WN^3}(l(k, b_1, b_2, ..., b_{q-1})) \cdot \mathbb{P}(B_{t_1}^2 = b_1, B_{t_2}^2 = b_2, ..., B_{t_{q-1}}^2 = b_{q-1})$

$=$ { requirement $f_{low}^2(t_q) = \underline{f}_{WN^3}$; SP^4 is the stochastic process induced by WN_{low}^2 }

$\quad \displaystyle\sum_{b_1, b_2, ..., b_b \in \mathbb{N}} \mathbb{P}(B_q^4 < l(k, b_1, b_2, ..., b_{q-1})) \cdot \mathbb{P}(B_{t_1}^2 = b_1, B_{t_2}^2 = b_2, ..., B_{t_{q-1}}^2 = b_{q-1})$,

$=$ { WN^2 and WN_{low}^2 only differ in the time behavior of transition t_q, random variables B are mutually independent, so $\mathbb{P}(B_{t_1}^2 = b_1, B_{t_2}^2 = b_2, ..., B_{t_{q-1}}^2 = b_{q-1}) = \mathbb{P}(B_{t_1}^4 = b_1, B_{t_2}^4 = b_2, ..., B_{t_{q-1}}^4 = b_{q-1})$; use assumed relation between functions g and l }

$\quad \mathbb{P}(g(B_{t_1}^4, B_{t_2}^4, ..., B_{t_{q-1}}^4, B_{t_q}^4) \le k)$

$=$ { $T_{WN^2} = g(B_{t_1}^2, B_{t_2}^2, ..., B_{t_q}^2) \Leftrightarrow T_{WN_{low}^2} = g(B_{t_1}^4, B_{t_2}^4, ..., B_{t_q}^4)$ }

$\quad F_{WN_{low}^2}(k)$.

Analogously we can prove that $F_{WN^1}(k) \leq F_{WN^2_{up}}(k)$. So,

$$F_{WN^2_{low}}(k) \leq F_{WN^1}(k) \leq F_{WN^2_{up}}(k) \text{ for } k \in \mathbb{N}.$$

$\square$

The proof of the lemma that treats the replacement of type (b) may cause the reader to suppose that the number of SWN's that is necessary to estimate the throughput time behavior of the original SWN can grow exponentially in the number of synthesis steps: each time that a synthesis step of type (b) has been applied this requires the analysis of two other SWN's. This is, however, not the case. If at a certain point two SWN's have been distinguished to approximate the throughput behavior of the original net SWN WF, one of these SWN's – say WF$_{low}$ – is used to compute a lower bound, the other – say WF$_{up}$ – for an upper bound of F_{WF}. If during the analysis of, for example, WF$_{low}$ another synthesis step of type (b) is encountered, two more SWN's may be constructed. One of these SWN's – say WF$_{low-low}$ – is used to compute a lower bound, the other – say WF$_{low-up}$ – for an upper bound of $F_{WF_{low}}$. It is guaranteed for each $n \in \mathbb{N}$ that because $F_{WF_{low}}(n) \leq F_{WF}(n)$ and $F_{WF_{low-low}}(n) \leq F_{WF_{low}}(n)$ that $F_{WF_{low-low}}(n) \leq F_{WF}(n)$. But on the basis of $F_{WF_{low}}(n) \leq F_{WF}(n)$ and $F_{WF_{low-up}}(n) \geq F_{WF_{low}}(n)$ for $n \in \mathbb{N}$ nothing conclusive may be said about the relation between $F_{WF}(n)$ and $F_{WF_{low-up}}(n)$. So, only the SWN WF$_{low-low}$ is of interest to compute a lower bound for F_{WF}. Analogously, during the analysis of WF$_{up}$ at most one SWN will be used to utterly determine the upper bound for F_{WF}.

By following the opposite route of the net synthesis it is always possible to obtain two nets – one if the exact approach is totally applicable – with the structure of the simple net (see Figure 4.2). One of these nets has a delay function which is a lower bound for the throughput time density of the hybrid SWN; the other gives the upper bound.

By now, we have shown how the throughput behavior of an SWN can be analyzed that has been constructed with a hybrid approach. The approach synthesizes a workflow net out of both basic blocks and arbitrary sound, free-choice and acyclic workflow subnets. The synthesis rules are similar to those of the basic approach sketched in Section 4.3. The bounding functions that are obtained are comparable with the approach described in Section 4.4. The resulting, hybrid approach exploits the synthesis capabilities of the former method, while the application area is extended with that of the latter.

4.6 Review

In Section 4.3 we discussed a variety of network structures of workflow nets that may be used to synthesize another workflow net, ultimately leading to the construction of an SWN. In Section 4.4 we described an approach for computing throughput time bounds for a general class of workflow nets. All workflow nets as discussed in the previous sections share an important characteristic: their soundness. This property guarantees a meaningful interpretation of the throughput time of the process induced by the constructed SWN. We have seen that many of the structures discussed in the exact approach were safe and free-choice, but these are not necessary characteristics to be applied in the synthesis of a workflow net (e.g., check the logic choice or repeater). Obviously, many more structures may be added.

As a final note, all presented approaches assume an infinite server capacity. We claim that this assumption is more or less natural during the first stages in designing a workflow. If a new design without resource constraints (i.e., no queuing can take place) does not satisfy the desired performance requirements, a workflow with resource constraints (i.e., queuing takes place if all resources are occupied) will utterly fail these requirements. The design should then be improved. However, for estimating the performance of a workflow in a practical setting, conditions such as the availability and responsiveness of people, information systems, and computer networks play a very important role. The presented algorithms can be of limited use only in such a case, for example by hard-coding estimated queue and wait times in the model as delays. Such an approach obviously offers very small explanatory power or accuracy. Other evaluation methods such as simulation or prototyping will prove to be much more helpful.

The behavior of resources is also indispensable for actually controlling a workflow. The control topic of assigning resources in a workflow with respect to minimizing the throughput time in an operational workflow is the subject of the following chapter.

5 Resource Allocation in Workflows

The subject of this chapter is the allocation of resources in a workflow. In Section 1.1 the resource dimension of a business process has already been introduced. A resource is a generic term for all means that are required to produce a product within the setting of a business process. With respect to the model as introduced in Section 1.4, the focus of the chapter is depicted as a thickly lined box at the left side of Figure 5.1.

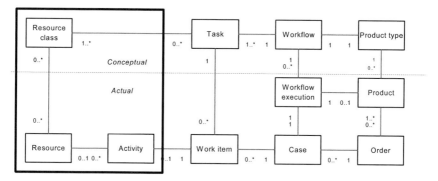

Fig. 5.1. Focus of Chapter 5

A proper resource allocation ensures that each activity is performed by a suitable resource. As expressed in Figure 5.1, an activity is an actual manifestation of a task that is performed for a specific case by a specific resource. In other words, the resource allocation takes care of handing out so-called work items to resources, which – within the setting of a workflow – are often people (see Section 1.4). The rules that implement the preferred allocation of resources are known as allocation principles (Van der Aalst and Van Hee, 2002). The model of Figure 5.1 assumes that allocation principles are specified on the level of resource classes, instead of individual resources. A resource class is a group of resources with similar characteristics. For each task, the allocation principles in use determine one or more resource classes of which their members – the individual resources – have the qualifications and the authorization to perform it. In practice, all kinds of criteria may be taken into account by allocation principles. For example, if there is a call for urgent medical assistance, the geographic location of the emergency may be used to find the nearest general practitioner's practice.

H.A. Reijers: Design and Control of Workflow Processes, LNCS 2617, pp. 177-206, 2003.
© Springer-Verlag Berlin Heidelberg 2003

Allocating resources in a workflow can be seen as both a build-time and a run time issue in BPM decision making (see Section 1.2). It is a build-time issue when a workflow is still in its design phase. If one has a design of the routing structure of a workflow, for example derived with the PBWD methodology (see Chapter 3), it needs to be decided who will carry out the distinguished tasks before the design can be put to work. Allocating resources is a run-time issue when we consider a workflow during execution, e.g., when an extra resource becomes available that has to be assigned to a resource class. Either way, the allocation of resources is clearly to be settled by the allocation component of a workflow model (see Section 2.2). Note that we have argued in the introduction of Chapter 3 the particular design order of specifying the routing structure first and the allocation component second.

When the allocation component is to be given its initial form, i.e., at build-time, several issues have to be settled. In the first place, the required qualifications of the resources have to be determined. These qualifications should be matched to those of the available workforce to decide whether it can do the job or that additional resources have to be hired. This subject is treated by Aldowaisan and Gaafar (1999). From a systems perspective, these qualifications may also be used as functional requirements on existing or future information systems. Other important issues in creating the allocation component are the proper distinction of resource classes and the allocation principles that will be used to allocate work items to member of a resource class. Another issue is how individual resources themselves decide upon the order in which they process work items assigned to them. We will not discuss either of these issues, but refer the interested reader to Van der Aalst and Van Hee (2002) for a more detailed description.

In this chapter, we focus on determining the proper number of resources within each resource class. This decision should balance the performance targets on the one hand and the cost involved in hiring (for human resources) or buying/building (for non-human resources) on the other. Clearly, determining resource numbers presupposes the existence of a workflow's routing structure, identified resource classes, and allocation principles. We will assume these issues to be settled for the specific cases we describe.

In this chapter we will present an algorithm to determine the right allocation of resources with the aim to minimize the average throughput time of the workflow. The algorithm was introduced in this context by Van Hee et al. (2001). It can be used to support both build-time and run-time decision making. The presented algorithm is a marginal allocation strategy, which means that a proper allocation of resources is determined by assigning them one by one. To make the analysis of such an algorithm feasible, we adhere to a very simple allocation situation. Its basic characteristics are given in Table 5.1, where they are compared to more realistic circumstances.

Table 5.1. Comparison of the used model with reality

	Used allocation model	*Reality*
Number of resource classes a single resource is part of	1	any number
Number of resource classes allocated to a single task	1	any number
Number of tasks for a single resource class	1 or 2	any number
Selection policy for work items by resources	First-Come-First-Served	various
Availability resource within the same workflow	100 %	any percentage
Willingness resources to start work when free	eager	less than eager
Allocation principles during workflow execution	fixed	variable

Obviously, the throughput time that is to be minimized by the presented algorithm is yet one of the many interesting performance indicators, although it is indeed a very important one (see Section 4.1). We will show that the presented algorithm in this chapter is optimal for a class of workflows that have, among other characteristics, a state machine net structure, i.e., that exclude concurrent behavior. We will also give an idea of the effectiveness of the algorithm by applying it on a number of workflow models that do not fall within this class. Simulation will be used for this purpose. The set of models considered include some notoriously difficult constructions, as well as some models derived from practice.

The structure of this chapter is as follows. First we will informally present an extension of the Stochastic Workflow Net as presented in Section 2.4, that can be used to realistically model the effect of a limited number of resources in a workflow. Next, we will discuss in Section 5.2 an allocation strategy as described by Goldratt and Cox (1984). This strategy has served as an inspiration for developing our algorithm as presented in Section 5.3. The latter section also includes a discussion of the optimality of the algorithm. In Section 5.4, we will present a workbench of workflow models to which the presented allocation strategy has been applied.

5.1 The Resource-Extended SWN

The SWN model (see Definition 2.20) does not incorporate a notion of resources. It was useful in this form in Chapters 3 and 4, where a situation of an infinite number of available resources was assumed. Also, up till this point we have considered SWN's as reflecting the life-cycle of a *single case* (see Section 2.4). However, when resources will work on multiple cases, the handling of cases will affect each other's throughput time. So, to realistically model this effect we have to allow for more cases within the context of the same workflow model.

For these reasons, the SWN model used so far needs an extension, which we will now informally discuss. We will assume that the workflow model is modeled as an SWN first, with appropriate weights and delay distributions. Given a transition in such an SWN that is used to model a task, that same task is modeled in the resource-extended SWN by a start transition, an end transition, a busy place, and an idle place as follows:

- The *start transition* indicates that the task becomes an activity; it takes on the weight and delay characteristics of the original transition.
- The *end transition* indicates that the activity is completed; it has an arbitrary weight but it is immediate (i.e., consumes no time).
- The *busy place* holds a combination of a case and a busy resource and indicates that the task is an activity.
- The *idle place* holds the idle resources.

The net in Figure 5.2 is a task that was modeled in an SWN by a single timed transition with two input places and two output places. Because there is a token in the busy place, this task is an activity for the case associated with that token.

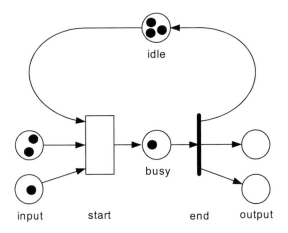

Fig. 5.2. The task model in a resource-extended SWN

Note that cases are associated with tokens and that the start transition needs to be able to distinguish tokens from different cases: it should be enabled only if each input place contains a token associated with the same case. For this reason, we assume some color to exist in the resource-extended SWN: each case has a unique identity, tokens associated with a case have the color of that case, and transitions are only allowed to use case tokens (resource tokens have no identity) with the same identity during one execution. With respect to the example of Figure 5.2, if one of the tokens in the upper input place of the start transition has the same identity as the token in the other input place, the task is a work item for the case associated with both tokens. Otherwise, the task is not a work item for any case. Note also that the depicted task contains four available resources: three idle and one busy. If resources can work on more than a single task, the idle places of the respective tasks should be joined. This is, for example, required for the analysis of the big nets in Section 5.4.2.

For ease of use, we will use boxes to visualize tasks quite similar to the model of an SWN, but we will suppose an internal behavior as discussed. Immediate transitions will still be depicted as black bars (see Section 2.4.5).

To analyze a workflow's throughput time, we will need an arrival pattern of new cases. Note that this was not required when we looked at single cases in isolation. We will allow for arbitrary arrival patterns to be in effect. Each new case arrives at the source place of the workflow.

In summary, the resource-extended SWN is characterized as follows:

- Tasks are modeled as boxes, each of which has an internal behavior with a start transition, end transition, busy, and idle place.
- Each initial transition has an arbitrary service time distribution that is independently sampled each time it is executed; other transitions are immediate.
- All tokens are colored except for the uncolored resource token, i.e., each token has a value denoting the identity of the corresponding case.
- The firing rule of an SWN is extended with the requirement that tokens in input places must have the same color, except for the uncolored resource tokens.
- For each task, there is positive number of available resources, which are initially idle (i.e., reside in the initial places).
- Each initial transition of a task has a weight: if a choice is to be made between two (or more) enabled initial transitions then these weights are taken into account to determine which one is executed first conform the firing rule of an SWN.
- The process has an arbitrary arrival time distribution, which specifies the arrival pattern of new cases; each new case is assumed to arrive at the source place of the workflow.

The performance indicator that we will consider in this chapter can now be defined as the average time it takes the resource-extended SWN net to move a case from the source place to the sink place. Note that the soundness of the net and the positive number of resources for each task do not themselves ensure a meaningful interpretation of this figure. The system may get clogged when the in-flow of cases is larger than its out-flow, so that the number of tokens in input places of tasks grow infinitely large. We will in this chapter only consider resource-extended SWN's that have a steady state. The throughput time of a *case* through an SWN is then the sum of the following:

- *Service time*: the time that somewhere within the SWN the case is being processed, i.e., there is at least one token with the case's identity that resides in some task's "busy" place.
- *Queue time*: the time during which no work item that belongs to this case is being processed within the SWN, i.e., not one of the case tokens resides in some task's "busy" place.

Note that "queue time" derives its name from the cause of the absence of any processing: somewhere queuing takes places. Aggregated service and queue times of cases are often used as a quality criterion for the complete workflow.

It often is interesting to consider the service and queue times from a *task* perspective, instead of from the case perspective. For a *task* the following holds:

- Its *service time* is the time that it takes to process a work item, i.e., the time that a token stays in the "busy" place".
- Its *queue time* is the time that a work item must wait for this task before it can be executed because of a lack of resources for this task, i.e., the time between the last arrival of a case token in the task's input places until the time the case arrives in the "busy" place.
- Its *wait time* is the time it takes for a work item to become complete, i.e., the time between the first arrival of a case token in an input place until the arrival of the last one.

Service, queue, and wait times of individual tasks are relevant to identify "traffic jams" within a workflow. The "bottleneck" concept which is discussed in Section 5.2 is an example on this note.

We illustrate the introduced time notions with Figure 5.3. On the left-hand side of the figure, a simple resource-extended SWN is shown. On the right-hand side of the figure, the execution of this workflow for one particular case is schematically depicted, both from the case and the task perspective.

With respect to the task perspective, one can see the following in the upper part of the right-hand side of the figure. For each of the tasks A, B, C, and D its relative start and end time are given in Figure 5.3 by horizontal lines. Parts of these lines are labeled with identifiers "q", "w", and "s", denoting respectively queue, wait and service times of each task in its execution for this particular case. At time x_1 the case arrives within the process. It queues until a resource become available to execute task A, which happens at time x_2. Task A is being executed until time x_3. Following the completion of A, for both tasks B and C, the case has to queue. At time x_4, a resource becomes available for the execution of C. At time x_5, this happens for task D, which is completed at time x_6. At time x_7, task C is also completed. From x_7 until x_8 the case queues because of a lack of resources for task D. From x_8 until x_9, task D is executed, which ends the processing of the case. Note that from x_6 until x_7, there is wait time for task D: not all its inputs are already available. During this time, task C is still being executed.

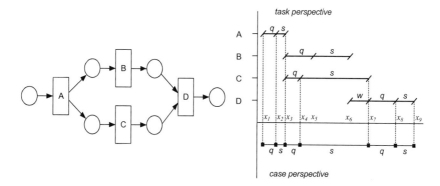

Fig. 5.3. Service, queue, wait, and throughput times

With respect to the case perspective, the throughput time is given as a horizontal line in the lower part of the right-hand side of the figure. The throughput time of this particular case is the time that elapses between x_1 and x_9. This throughput time is the sum of smaller parts of queue time ("q") and service time ("s"). A part of the throughput time is considered as service time from the case perspective when *at least* one of the tasks is being executed for this particular case. Queue time is the remaining part of the throughput time.

According to the introduced notions, it is clear that the throughput time of a case in general does not equal the sum of the service times of the tasks that were executed for it. In a workflow where parallel executions of tasks can take place, the summed service times of tasks may exceed that of individual cases.

Also note that wait times can only occur at synchronizing transitions, i.e., transitions with multiple input places (task D in Figure 5.3). The practical relevance of distinguishing between *queue* and *wait* time from a task perspective will become clear in Section 5.3.

5.2 Goldratt's Conjecture

In 1984, Goldratt published "The Goal", a textbook in the form of a novel (Goldratt and Cox, 1984). This bestseller quickly gained popularity with manufacturing and logistic industries. "The Goal" describes various techniques to improve the performance of business processes. Because the nature of the descriptions is informal, the semantics of these techniques is – to some extent – up to the reader. Goldratt's view on the logistic structures of business processes is very much like the workflows that can be build using the elementary sequential, choice and parallelism structures as described in Section 4.3.1. An interesting, explicitly stated claim to improve the rate at which cases are being completed is to add resources at so-called *bottlenecks*. We will refer to it as the *Goldratt algorithm*, although it is not described as such by Goldratt and Cox.

5.2.1 The Goldratt Algorithm

The Goldratt algorithm starts to identify a bottleneck within the process among the so-called *work centers*. A work center is any group of which its members are capable of executing the same operations. Note that this "work group" concept is very similar to our notion of a "resource class" (see Section 1.1.6). The bottleneck is principally defined by Goldratt as the work group that has a utilization that exceeds 1. Obviously, in this situation there is no steady state for the process (queues grow infinitely large) and the mean throughput time is meaningless. For these reasons, we turn this definition aside and focus on the secondary definition Goldratt provides: "work centers that have the largest amount of work-in-process sitting in front of it are the bottlenecks". This is obviously a rather ambiguous specification. We do not think that Goldratt suggests the physical size of a queue or even the number of cases in a queue as accurate indicators of the pressure on a work group, as they are clearly not. We will distinguish two interpretations of this bottleneck definition, as follows:

1. *Mean queue time*:
   the bottleneck is the resource class that is assigned to the task where the mean queue time is maximal.
2. *Utilization*:
   the bottleneck is the resource class with the highest mean utilization.

The Goldratt algorithm ends by stating that if an extra resource is available it should be placed at the bottleneck to increase the overall performance of the process measured in the throughput rate. Clearly, the latter figure is the inverse of our throughput time notion.

5.2.2 Limits

The intuition behind the Goldratt algorithm is apparent: increase the number of resources that are pressured the hardest to improve the throughput rate. However, consider the following example. A telephonist of a service organization handles incoming complaints. The telephonist can handle 90% of all incoming complaints. On average, this takes him two and a half minutes. For the remaining 10%, one of the ten service men has to visit the complainant. On average, a visit takes three hours and 50 minutes (230 minutes). So, the mean service time of an arbitrary complaint is 25,25 minutes. The service times of tasks T ("Telephonist") and S

("Service men") have a negative exponential distribution. The arrivals of complaints is Poisson-distributed. On average, every two and a half minutes a new complaint arrives ($\lambda = 1/2,5$). This workflow is depicted as a resource-extended SWN in Figure 5.4.

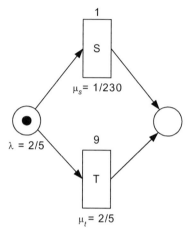

Fig. 5.4. Example of a service organization

The number of service men and telephonists will be denoted with n_S and n_T respectively. The intensity of the arrival is denoted with λ; the intensities of the service times of handling the call by phone (T) or by visit (S) are respectively given by μ_t and μ_s.

As all probabilities in the depicted resource-extended SWN are independent, the performance of this workflow can be analytically determined by splitting it up into two well-known queuing systems: an M/M/10 and an M/M/1 queuing system, with respective Poisson arrival rates of 1/25 and 9/25. The respective mean service time of each separate system is 230 minutes and of the system

The mean queue time for task S, W_S, is approximately 209,7 minutes and the mean queue time for task T, W_T, equals 22,50 minutes. Combined with the mean service time of 25,25 minutes, the mean throughput time is therefore about 41,22 minutes. We will first consider the first interpretation of the bottleneck in applying Goldratt's algorithm. Then, the bottleneck turns out to be task S, as its mean queue time exceeds that of task T.

Now suppose that the service company's management is not content with the current throughput time and that there are sufficient funds to hire another resource. Also suppose that hiring a telephonist or service men is just as expensive. Hiring an eleventh service man yields a mean queue time W_S of 60,75 minutes. This is a local gain of almost 150 minutes. While the processing in the other part of the system does not change, this results in a mean queue time of approximately 26,33 minutes. Given the mean service time of handling a complaint of 25,25 minutes this leads to a mean throughput time of 51,58 minutes.

However, if the management had hired a second telephonist instead of an eleventh service man, then the mean queue time W_T would be 0,635 minutes. This is a local gain of more than 20 minutes, resulting in a mean queue time of 21,54 minutes and a mean throughput time of 46,79 minutes. These are lower figures than the former scenario, making the hire of a second telephonist more attractive.

The results from this example are summarized in Table 5.2.

Table 5.2. Results service organization

n_S	n_T	W_S	W_T	mean queue time	mean throughput time
10	1	209,7	22,50	41,22	66,47
10	2	209,7	0,635	21,54	46,79
11	1	60,75	22,50	26,33	51,58

It is clear from the table that Goldratt's algorithm is not optimal for the first interpretation of the bottleneck. It is possible to gain more time at other places in the process than at the bottleneck. The effect is obtained by the following:

1. The higher marginal effect of one extra telephonist, where there is just one telephonist working, compared to the benefit of adding a service man to the ten service men already working.
2. The higher execution frequency of the telephonist task.

Note that if we had used the utilization rate as criterion to identify the bottleneck, task S would still have been the bottleneck: the utilization rate of the service men initially equals 92%, where the utilization rate of the telephonist equals 90%.

5.3 The Method of Marginal Allocation

As an alternative to the Goldratt algorithm, we propose a method of marginal allocation. We consider a resource-extended SWN that consists of N tasks. The service times of the tasks $t_1, t_2,...,t_N$ are arbitrarily distributed, characterized by $\Lambda = [\mu_1, \mu_2,... \mu_N]$ with μ_i for $1 \leq i \leq N$ containing all parameters to characterize the service time distribution of task t_i. The arrival process of new cases is arbitrarily distributed with characterization λ. We suppose that initially a sufficiently large number of resources is allocated to each task to ensure that the mean queue time is finite for every queue in the system. This is a number that in general can be easily determined by using the frequency of each task execution and its mean service time. M additional resources are available to be freely allocated amongst the tasks ($M \in \mathbb{N}\setminus 0$). Each resource can be allocated to any of the tasks. However, after its allocation, a resource can only work on work items that are to be executed for the task it has been allocated to. Let n_i for $1 \leq i \leq N$ be the number of resources that is dedicated to task i after M additional resources have been allocated to the process. We denote $\Gamma = [n_1, n_2,\dots n_N]$. The mean throughput time of the process after adding M extra servers can then be expressed as a function $f(\lambda, \Lambda, \Gamma)$. Suppose that after marginally allocating M-1 resources the number of resources at task i is m_i. We denote for $1 \leq k \leq N$ with ϑ_k the allocation $[n_1, n_2,\dots,n_N]$ where $n_k = m_k + 1$ and $n_j = m_j$ for $j \neq k$ and $1 \leq j \leq N$. The method of marginal allocation is to allocate the Mth resource to a task l such that

$$f(\lambda, \Lambda, \vartheta_l) = \left(\underline{\min}\ k : 1 \leq k \leq N : f\left(\lambda, \Lambda, \vartheta_k\right)\right) \tag{i}$$

In some cases the quantity $f(\lambda, \Lambda, \vartheta_k)$ can be calculated from an explicit formula; in other cases it can be estimated by simulation. If M additional servers are to be applied, the marginal allocation requires $N \cdot M$ evaluations of the throughput time. If, instead of marginal allocation all possible allocations were to be tried, $\binom{M + N - 1}{N - 1}$ evaluations are required.

5.3.1 Application of Marginal Allocation

We use the setting of the service organization again (see Figure 5.4) to demonstrate the method of marginal allocation. Table 5.2 shows the mean throughput times of three possible resource allocations: $[n_T, n_S] = [1, 10]$ and both possible successors of this allocation. From this table, we deduce that an additional telephonist should be hired, because an extra telephonist reduces the mean throughput time most. Suppose the service organization's management can hire six additional employees. Table 5.3 shows the mean throughput times of the workflow for allocations up to 17 employees in total.

Table 5.3. Mean throughput times service organization

| | | \multicolumn{7}{c}{n_S} | | | | | | |
		10	11	12	13	14	15	16
	1	41,22	26,33	22,70	21,33	20,74	20,47	20,35
	2	21,54	6,65	3,02	1,66	1,07	0,80	
	3	21,04	6,15	2,52	1,06	0,57		
n_T	4	20,98	6,09	2,46	1,09			
	5	20,97	6,08	2,45				
	6	20,97	6,08					
	7	20,97						

From this table, we deduce that the first employee to hire would be a telephonist (because $21,54 < 26,33$), the second would be a service man ($21,04 > 6,65$), the third a service man ($6,15 > 3,02$), etc. In the end, three telephonists and fourteen service men are employed. Note that this is the optimal solution with regard to the throughput time for seventeen employees. The allocation decisions are graphically depicted as a path that has been accentuated with gray.

Using Goldratt's algorithm, we first hire three service men, then a telephonist, and then two more service men, resulting in a non-optimal situation. This final allocation is shown as a box with curved lines. If we use the utilization as a criterion for the bottleneck, we first hire a service man, then a telephonist, and then four service men, resulting in the same, non-optimal, situation.

5.3.2 Optimality

In this section we prove that the marginal allocation strategy is optimal for two subclasses of resource-extended SWN's. Both classes of SWN's have a state machine net structure.

Definition 5.1   (State machine). A Petri net (P, T, R) is a state machine iff for each transition $t \in T$ holds that $|{\bullet}t| = |t{\bullet}| = 1$.

Theorem 5.1   (Optimality of marginal allocation for SWN's with only source and sink places). Let WF be a resource-extended SWN with net structure (P, T, R), $T = t_1, t_2, ..., t_N$, and $P = (i, o)$. Let the service times of the tasks $t_1, t_2, ..., t_N$ be arbitrarily distributed, characterized by $\Lambda = [\mu_1, \mu_2, ... \mu_N]$. The arrival process of new cases is arbitrarily distributed with characterization λ. Suppose that the initial resource allocation $\Gamma = [n_1, n_2, ... n_N]$ of K resources ensures that the mean queue time is finite for every queue in the system. Then, the marginal allocation strategy leads to an allocation $\Gamma' = [n'_1, n'_2, ... n'_N]$ that minimizes the expected throughput time for WF for each $M > K$ such that $M = n'_1 + n'_2 ... + n'_N$ and $n'_1 \geq n_1, n'_2 \geq n_2 ... n'_N \geq n_N$.

Proof. Because $P = (i, o)$, (P, T, R) is a state machine. So, the wait time for each task is zero. As a result, the mean throughput time equals the sum of the mean total service time and the mean total queue time. This implies that minimizing the mean queue time for WF suffices to minimize its mean throughput time. After all, the mean service time is constant. Because there is only one input and one output place, immediately after a case arrives at the source place i, it is routed to one of the N tasks after which processing ends. So, WF can be divided into N independent G/GI/m queuing systems. Using the notation as introduced in Section 5.3 and denoting the expected queue time at task t after allocating M servers to the total system by $W_t(\lambda_t, \mu_t, n_t)$ with λ_t the expected arrival rate of cases at task t, the allocation problem can then be formulated as:

$$\min_{n_1, n_2, \dots n_N} \left\{ \sum_{t=1}^{N} W_t \left(\lambda_t, \mu_t, n_t \right) \right\} \text{ with } M = \sum_{i=1}^{N} n_i . \tag{ii}$$

Fox (1966) showed that for this kind of problem a marginal allocation algorithm is optimal if the function $W_t \left(\lambda_t, \mu_t, n_t \right)$ is non-increasing and convex in n_t. In other words, for any task t:

$$W_t \left(\lambda_t, \mu_t, n_t \right) - W_t \left(\lambda_t, \mu_t, n_t + 1 \right) \geq$$
$$W_t \left(\lambda_t, \mu_t, n_t + 1 \right) - W_t \left(\lambda_t, \mu_t, n_t + 2 \right) \geq 0 \tag{iii}$$

This condition expresses that the marginal effect of adding another resources decreases. This ensures that it is never necessary to remove already placed resources.

Weber (1980) proved that a G/GI/m queue is convex and non-increasing in the number of servers m. So, in combination with Fox' result, we can determine that marginal allocation is optimal for WF. □

The resource-extended SWN in Figure 5.4 is an example of a resource-extended SWN that falls within the scope of Theorem 5.1. The class of nets covered by Theorem 5.1 is rather small, because of its limited structure. However, note that the arrival pattern, the weights, and delay characterizations may be of *arbitrary* form. In comparison, the class of resource-extended SWN's that we will discuss next has a more restricted type of arrival pattern and delay characterizations, but allows for more complex network structures.

Theorem 5.2   (Optimality of marginal allocation for state machine SWN's with a product-form). Let WF be a resource-extended SWN with net structure (P, T, R), such that (P, T, R) is a state machine and T = $t_1, t_2, \dots, t_N$. The service times of the tasks $t_1, t_2, \dots, t_N$ have a negative exponential distribution, characterized by $\Lambda = [\mu_1, \mu_2, \dots \mu_N]$. The arrival process of new cases is Poisson with intensity λ. Suppose that the initial resource allocation $\Gamma = [n_1, n_2, \dots n_N]$ of K resources ensures that the mean queue time is finite for every queue in the system. Then, the marginal allocation strategy leads to an allocation $\Gamma' = [n'_1, n'_2, \dots n'_N]$ that minimizes the expected throughput time for WF for each $M > K$ such that $M = n'_1 + n'_2 \dots + n'_N$ and $n'_1 \geq n_1, n'_2 \geq n_2 \dots n'_N \geq n_N$.

Proof. First, we consider the well-known open Jackson queuing network. Such a network consists of M nodes, each of which has an infinite storage capacity and operates according to a first-come-first-served queuing discipline. Node $j, j = 1, \dots, M$, consists of m_j servers, each with exponentially distributed service time with parameter μ_j. External customers may arrive at node j from the outside world according to a Poisson process with rate r_j. In addition, internal customers may arrive from other servers in the network. Upon completing service at node j, a customer is routed to node k with probability p_{jk}. The outside world is often indexed by 0, so that the fraction of customers leaving the network after service at j is denoted by p_{j0}.

It is straightforward to see that WF can be mapped onto a (single class) open Jackson queuing network. For Jackson networks it is a well-known result that the equilibrium distribution can be determined analytically (Jackson, 1957; Jackson, 1963). In steady state, each node in a Jackson network behaves as if it were in isolation and subject to Poisson arrivals, although the arrivals may in fact not be Poisson. Using the Jackson equilibrium formula and Little's law, it is possible to express the mean queue time at each task t as a function of the arrival rate of cases for this particular task (λ_t), its service rate (μ_t), and the number of resources working on that task (n_t) (see e.g., Chao et al., 1999):

$$\frac{(1/n_t\mu_t)(\lambda_t/\mu_t)^{n_t}}{n_t!(1-\lambda_t/n_t\mu_t)^2}\left[\sum_{j=0}^{n_t-1}\frac{(\lambda_t/\mu_t)^j}{j!}+\frac{(\lambda_t/\mu_t)^{n_t}}{n_t!(1-\lambda_t/n_t\mu_t)}\right]^{-1}. \qquad (iv)$$

This is the standard expression for the expected queue time of an M/M/n_t queue. In steady state, λ_t can be determined on the basis of the arrival rate of new cases and the weights applied; μ_t and n_t are given. Note that these parameters are independent of the other queues in the network. Dyer and Proll (1977) proved that the expected queue time for an M/M/m queue (formula iv) is a non-increasing and convex function of m. But then, the proof follows from the proof of Theorem 5.1.

□

For both classes of resource-extended SWN's we exploited the property that arrival and queuing processes for each task within a net of each class may be treated as if it were independent of arrivals and queues at other tasks. This is not generally the case in resource-extended SWN's. In the first place, the arrival and queuing processes among the tasks in such a net are in general not independent. The structure of the net, as well as the service time distributions of the tasks may influence the arrival and queuing processes at other tasks. In the second place, minimal queue times a tasks do not guarantee a minimal throughput time, which will be illustrated by the example in Section 5.3.

5.3.3 Limits

From the following example it becomes clear that the marginal allocation strategy is in general not optimal if concurrency is allowed in the process. Figure 5.5 shows a resource-extended SWN. Note that to prevent this system from getting clogged, we need initially at least three resources at each task.

Because of the synchronization following tasks P1 and P2, we cannot compute results for this example analytically using queuing theory. Note that because cases can overtake each other, it is essential to take the color of the tokens into account when synchronizing. We used simulation with the software package ExSpect (Van Hee et al., 1989; Van der Aalst et al., 2001a) to get approximated results.

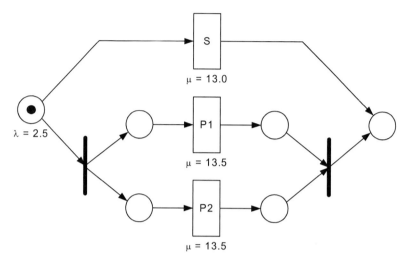

Fig. 5.5. Counter example for both strategies

To clearly show the characteristics of the example we used as service time distribution for each transition a beta distribution with modus (and, because the distribution is symmetric, mean) μ, minimum $9\mu/10$, maximum $11\mu/10$, and variance $\mu/900$. The beta distribution is often very well suited to express the variance in time behavior for tasks that are executed by humans. (Similar results for this example could have been obtained with e.g., negative exponential service times, but then the confidence intervals would have been wider.)

Using ExSpect as the simulation tool, we simulated for several resource allocations 52 subruns of length 40.000 time units each. Only the latter 50 subruns were taken into account for the simulation results, i.e., the first two were seen as start-up phase.

We obtained the results as shown in Figure 5.6, which covers five different resource allocations. For the tasks S, P1, and P2 the queue times are expressed (see Section 5.1). For the synchronizing transition following P1 and P2, its wait time is shown (see Section 5.1). Finally, for each allocation the mean throughput time is given.

Note that these results clearly show that allocation [4,3,3] performs better than allocation [3,4,4]. The simulation results indicate that the optimal allocations for 9, 10 or 11 resources are [3,3,3], [4,3,3] and [3,4,4]. So, if we have one additional resource available, then the optimal allocation would be [4,3,3]. If we would have two extra resources, then it would be [3,4,4]. Apparently, for an optimal allocation strategy we need to be able to *reallocate* resources. Both the Goldratt algorithm and the marginal allocation strategies lack this possibility and are hence not optimal in this case.

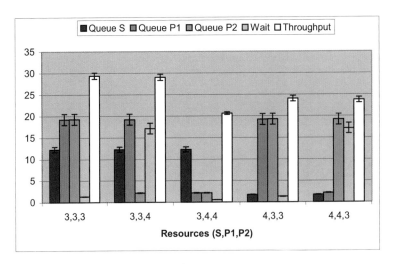

Fig. 5.6. Simulation results counter example

Note that the distinction of wait time clearly helps to explain why the throughput time of scenario [3,3,4] is hardly less than that of the initial situation [3,3,3]. Although the queue time at task P2 sharply decreases, the wait time at the synchronization task increases with almost the same amount.

5.4 Workbench

In Section 5.3 we demarcated a class of resource-extended SWN's for which the marginal allocation algorithm is optimal and we gave an example of a net for which the algorithm did not work. In this section we explore the applicability of the algorithm further by applying it to a set of resource-extended SWN's. This so-called *workbench* consists of three categories of nets:

1. *pathological nets*: these are artificial, small nets that incorporate a special feature which causes expectations to be that marginal allocation is troublesome,
2. *big nets*: these are artificial nets with a simpler structure than the pathological nets, but with a larger number of tasks,
3. *practical nets*: these nets are derived from actual workflows used in practice.

Application of the marginal allocation on the workbench is not expected to extend our knowledge about the applicability of the algorithm in a mathematical sense. Contrary to a solid proof, the approach is inductive rather than deductive, i.e., experiments are used to gain insight. Nonetheless, using a workbench may help to develop the intuition to distinguish more and less attractive area's of practical application of the algorithm.

Most of the nets of the workbench do not allow for an analysis with known analytical techniques, e.g., because of the structure and/of the net or the stochastic characterizations of the delays. Therefore, we use simulation to determine the formula $f(\lambda, \Lambda, \Gamma)$ of Section 5.3, i.e., the mean throughput time of the net in question with a specific allocation of resources. With the package ExSpect, Petri net models are specified that implement the properties of the resource-extended SWN as described in Section 5.1. The simulation of each model with a specific allocation was split up into 50 subruns with a length of 20.000 time units, including 10 start runs. (If minutes are used as time unit, a start run amounts to more than eight working weeks of 40 hours). A more detailed description of the technical side of the use of ExSpect to support the experimentation in this chapter is given in Appendix C.

Using simulation to obtain our results implies that we have no *exact* knowledge about the optimal solution. This imposes a methodological problem: it is in general not possible to decide on the basis of a simulation which allocation is optimal. The computation of confidence intervals on the simulation results – supported by ExSpect – does allow for statements with a certain statistic confidence. However, confidence intervals of different scenario's may be overlapping, so that no ordering of scenario's is possible. If this situation occurs, we adopt a practical strategy. Of all simulations scenario's, the optimal scenario is the one with the lowest (simulated) mean throughput time. This is the approach which reflects a strategy that can be generally used in practice. A list of historical occurrences of new cases may then be used to simulate the new allocation scenario. The scenario which leads to the lowest expected mean throughput time over this fixed number of cases is then seen as the optimal one. This seems to be acceptable if the list of historical occurrences is representative for the future workflow's work load. Note that another practical procedure could be to compare each subrun among the candidates and select the one with the largest number of subruns with the lowest average throughput time ("wins"). Yet another procedure would be to treat allocations similar when their confidence intervals on the mean throughput time overlap. (A transitive notion of equality could be used to define proper equivalence classes.) This would allow for more than one optimal solution.

In the following subsections we will introduce the nets of the different categories, discuss their structure, and the simulation results. We will assess the quality of the strategies based on both of the two interpretations of the Goldratt algorithm and on the marginal allocation strategy. For each net, the situation is considered of a steady-state resource-extended SWN for which two (or more) extra resources are available to be freely allocated. A situation is considered to be a steady state if for each resource class the utilization rate is less than 1. Note that we again assume that resources are equally expensive to hire; it is not difficult to extend the strategy with weights to reflect asymmetric resource costs.

5.4.1 Pathological Nets

The Tandem Net

The first of the pathological nets is the tandem net as depicted in Figure 5.7. It consists of three tasks and an equal number of disjunctive resource classes. The particular characterizations of the stochastic delays in effect are given alongside each task, just as the number of resources (servers) that are initially available. Each task has the internal structure as explained in Section 5.1. Recall that weights equal to 1 are omitted (see Section 2.4).

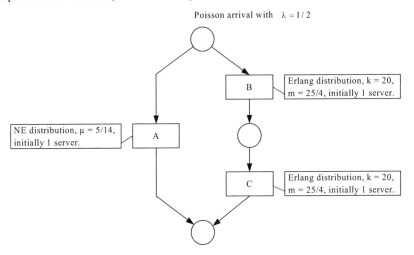

Fig. 5.7. The tandem net

The tandem net leads cases with equal probability to the execution of either task A or both task B and C, the latter of which are executed in tandem. As each resource class is allocated to exactly one task and vice versa, we will refer to the resource classes as A, B, and C.

The *structure* of the tandem net is similar to that of the class of workflow nets for which the optimality of the marginal allocation strategy is proven (see Section 5.3). However, the used *delays* do not have a negative exponential distribution, so that optimality is not ensured.

Initially, the utilization of the resource (server) in B is 0,8 (= $1/4 \cdot 20 \cdot 4/25$); similar for the server working on C. The utilization for the server of A is 0,7 (= $1/4 \cdot 14/5$). Because of these utilization rates, the net is in steady state.

In Figure 5.8, resource allocations are represented as follows: for $a, b, c \in \mathbb{N}$, $[a, b, c]$ denotes a resource *allocation* of a resources in class A, b in B, and c in C. For a given allocation $[a, b, c]$, the allocation $[a', b', c']$ is considered to be a (potential) *successor* if $a'+b'+c' = a+b+c+1$ where there is a $d \in \{a, b, c\}$ such that $d' = d+1$ and for all $e \in \{a, b, c\}\backslash d$ holds that $e' = e$.

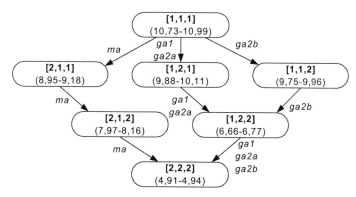

Fig. 5.8. Allocation decisions for tandem net

Three allocation strategies are considered: *ma* indicates the path of allocations decisions taken when the marginal allocation strategy is applied (see Section 5.3), *ga1* the path for the Goldratt algorithm with the first interpretation of the bottleneck, and *ga2* the path for Goldratt algorithm with the second interpretation of the bottleneck (see Section 5.2). An arrow always leads from an allocation to a successor. An arrow is labeled with one or more allocation strategy identifiers, indicating which resource class would be extended with another resource according to this strategy.

Under each resource allocation, the lower and upper bound of the 90 % confidence interval on its mean throughput time are given between parentheses. A strategy identifier is followed by another index, when this strategy is at some place ambiguous for deciding on the next allocation decision. For example, in Figure 5.8 strategy identifiers *ga2a* and *ga2b* occur because at the initial allocation [1, 1, 1] both resource classes B and C have an equal utilization. Note that the exact utilization of a resource class can always be determined. For the marginal allocation strategy and the first interpretation of the Goldratt algorithm, an allocation decision is considered ambiguous if for two or more successors of an allocation the 90 % confidence intervals on respectively the mean throughput time or the mean queue time overlap.

Recall that we use the mean throughput time as optimality algorithm. All allocations of one, two, or three extra resources have been considered to decide upon this optimality, although for the sake of clarity not all of them have been depicted in Figure 5.8. The number of different allocations of one, two, or three resources to three classes equals respectively 3, 6, and 10.

Analysis of the tandem net shows that for one additional resource the marginal allocation decision is optimal, for two additional resources the Goldratt algorithm (with either interpretation), and for three additional resources all strategies lead to the optimal allocation. The marginal allocation strategy for the tandem net "misses" the dependency between tasks B and C. The strategy will initially not propose to add an additional resource to resource classes B or C, as it will not decrease the overall throughput time. But by deciding for class A, it cannot find the optimal allocation of *two* additional resources. After all, [1, 2, 2] is not a successor of [2, 1, 1]. The marginal allocation strategy by definition lacks the ability to re-place an already placed server. Because of the slight stochastic variation in the service times of working on task B and C, it eventually does lead to the right allo-cation. This would have been different if tasks B and C were characterized by similar but deterministic service times or if there had been a deterministic arrival pattern. Note that the use of negative exponential distributions would have put this net in the class of nets for which optimality of the marginal allocation is proven.

The N-construction

The net in Figure 5.9 incorporates a so-called "N" structure, which derives its name from the resemblance of the middle part of the net with the respective up-percase letter. It can be proved that partially ordered multisets composed with se-quential, choice, and concurrency primitives cannot include this construction (Basten, 1997). Because of the semi-concurrency of the tasks A and C on the one hand and tasks B and D on the other, one may expect that the discussed allocation strategies for this net will perform badly.

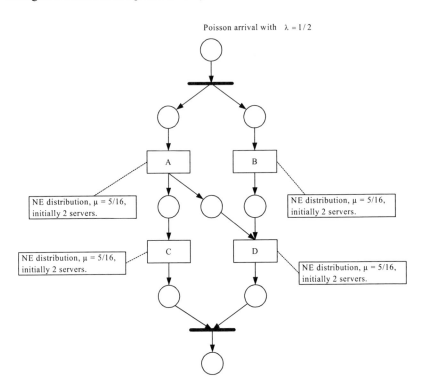

Fig. 5.9. The N-construction

As each resource class is allocated to exactly one task and vice versa, we will refer in this section to the resource classes as A, B, C, and D.

In Figure 5.10, only decision paths through allocations are depicted for the marginal allocation algorithm and the *first* interpretation of the Goldratt algorithm.

The use of the utilization rate as a criterion to identify the bottleneck leads to 24 different allocations of three resources over four resource classes, as the utilization rates of all classes are initially equal. These paths are not depicted. Similar to the tandem net we already discussed, all allocations of 1, 2, and 3 additional resources have been considered in the analysis.

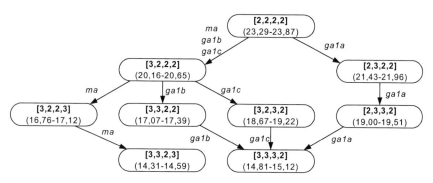

Fig. 5.10. Allocation decisions for N-construction

From the analysis of the N-construction net it follows that the marginal allocation strategy leads to the optimal allocation of the three extra resources for this case. The first interpretation of the Goldratt algorithm leads to an inferior allocation, even though it has several decision paths. For example, the next resource allocation at allocation [3, 2, 2, 2] is ambiguous, as the 90 % confidence intervals on the mean queue times at task B and C overlap. Also note that taking the decision path labeled with *ga1b* from the initial allocation leads to a resource allocation of *two* extra resources that is somewhat comparable with [3, 2, 2, 3], as the confidence intervals on the throughput times overlap slightly.

The second Goldratt interpretation – which is not depicted – may by chance lead to the optimal allocation, as [3, 3, 2, 3] belongs to the 20 possibilities that the application of this algorithm allows for. If arbitrary choices are made in ambiguous situations, then the likelihood of finding the optimal allocation is rather small.

Contrary to our expectations the marginal allocation algorithm performs quite well in this net with concurrency. The marginal allocation algorithm seems to appreciate that initially task A is crucial in the overall performance of the net, as both tasks C and D rely on the speed of its processing. After a first allocation of an extra resource to this task, task D becomes the bottleneck because of its dependencies on both task A and B. Both other algorithms are rather blind for these dependencies.

5.4.2 Big Nets

Parallel Sequential

To investigate the effects of the allocation strategies on rather large nets, the net in Figure 5.11 was designed.

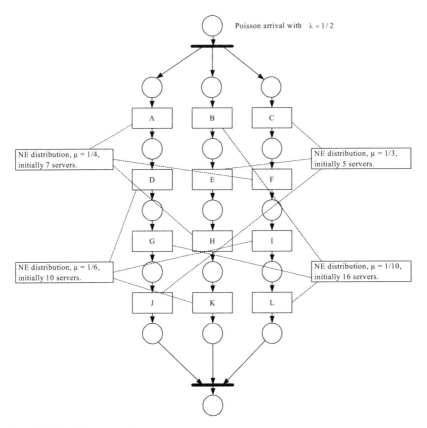

Fig. 5.11. Parallel sequential net

The figure contains three parallel sequences of tasks and four resource classes. The size of this somewhat artificial net was chosen such that accurate simulation results could be obtained within reasonable time. Therefore, the number of resource classes is chosen smaller than the number of tasks. After all, the number of different allocation scenario's grows exponentially in the number of resource classes. The number of tasks is still small in comparison with some actual workflows found in banking and insurance companies, but not uncommon. On the other hand, the number of resources, the number of resource classes, and the multiple tasks assigned to each resource class are quite realistic.

As each resource class works on several tasks, we will refer to the three classes as AFH, BGL, CIJ, and DIK (in this particular order) with obvious semantics. In Figure 5.12, the subsequent resource allocations have been depicted that result from applying the various allocation strategies. For the sake of readability, not all four possible allocations of one additional resource and not all 10 possible allocations of two additional resources to the four resource classes have been depicted.. The analysis of this net did, however, include each of these, to decide upon the overall optimality of the outcomes of the considered allocation strategies.

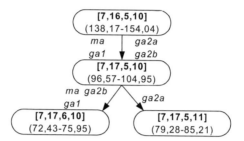

Fig. 5.12. Allocation decisions for parallel-sequential net

From the analysis it followed that both the marginal allocation and the first interpretation of the Goldratt algorithm lead to the optimal allocation of two additional resources. The second interpretation of the Goldratt algorithm leads to two outcomes, one of which the optimal one. At allocation [7, 17, 5, 10], the utilization rate for resource classes CEJ and DIK is equal (= 0,9). Placing an extra resource in class CEJ leads to the same optimal allocation as the other strategies; placing one in class DIK leads to an inferior allocation. So, for this particular net the different allocation strategies seem to act almost similarly.

Alternative Sequential

Another "big" net is the one as depicted in Figure 5.13. Its structure resembles that of Figure 5.11, save for the fact that the three sequences of tasks are *alternatives* for each case. On the basis of the optimality result for the marginal allocation as discussed in Section 5.3, a good performance of the marginal allocation algorithm was expected because of the lack of concurrency within this net. The net does not obviously fall in the category of nets for which optimality is proven, because of the multiple tasks that resource classes work on. There are four separate resource classes, to which we will refer for obvious reasons as AFH, BGL, CEJ, and DIK.

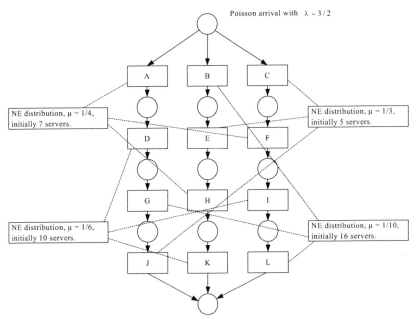

Fig. 5.13. Alternative sequential net

The outcome of the different allocation strategies is depicted in Figure 5.14. The number of resources is between straight brackets using the order AFH, BGL, CEJ, and DIK. As before, not all resource allocations have been depicted, although they are all included in the analysis.

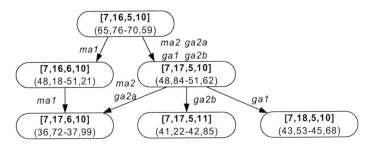

Fig. 5.14. Allocation decisions for alternative-sequential net

The analysis of the different allocations showed that the marginal allocation strategy leads to the optimal allocation. This in spite of the ambiguous alternatives initially, where the mean throughput times of [7, 16, 6, 10] and [7, 17, 5, 10] are similar. The application of the Goldratt algorithm using the mean queue time as the bottleneck selection criterion (*ga1*) quite definitely leads to an inferior allocation, namely [7, 18, 5, 10]. Using the utilization rate for the bottleneck identification, the Goldratt algorithm leads to two alternative allocations of which one is the optimal one (*ga2*) and the other an inferior one (*ga1*).

In accordance to our expectations the marginal allocation algorithm performs well for this net. The other allocation strategies lead to an overall disappointing result.

5.4.3 Practical Nets

Handling Appeals

The workflow that is in use with the Gemeenschappelijk Administratie-Kantoor (GAK) to handle appeals against one type of its decisions is depicted in Figure 5.15. The main task of the GAK is to decide upon claims for allowances with respect to unemployment or labor disability. Tasks A, B, C, and E are in use for the registration of an appeal against such a decision and to ensure a formal completeness of the appeal. Task D is used to decide whether an intermediary hearing is due or that a formal decision can be taken immediately. The outcome of a hearing may be that the appeal is withdrawn or that a formal decision can be made; a hearing may be adjourned several times (tasks F, G, H, I, J).

The displayed resource-extended SWN is a simplification of the actual workflow, as in reality a more complex allocation is used with e.g., overlapping resource classes. We will distinguish for each task a separate resource class. Note that some tasks are part of the net that consume time, but do not require a resource. Task C, for example, signifies a time-out when additional information of the plaintiff is not returned in time. We will refer to the resource classes with the identifiers of the tasks that require a resource, respectively A, D, E, F, I, J, and K. All depicted time-units are in minutes.

The allocation decisions taken by following either interpretation of the Goldratt algorithm are depicted in Figure 5.16. The initial resource allocation [7, 4, 1, 3, 1, 1, 5] gives the initial number of resources in the respective classes A, D, E, F, I, J, and K. The application of the marginal allocation strategy is not depicted, as it is rather troublesome. All 7 resource allocations of 1 additional resource have an overlapping 90 % confidence interval on the throughput time. This also holds for all 28 allocations of two resources and all 84 allocations of three additional resources. In other words, the differences between the resource allocations are too small to make a proper decision on the basis of the marginal allocation algorithm.

Both Goldratt applications lead to the optimal allocation of three resources to seven resource classes. Recall that we consider as optimal allocation the one with the lowest absolute mean throughput time, regardless of its confidence interval. It is noteworthy to consider the same absoluteness in selecting a successor according to the marginal allocation strategy, i.e., taking the successor with the absolute lowest mean throughput time regardless of its confidence interval. This strategy would have led to the same optimal allocation [8, 5, 1, 3, 1, 1, 6]. It is, however, improbable ($p = 1/84$) that making random choices between similar successors, i.e., with overlapping mean throughput time confidence intervals, would have the same result.

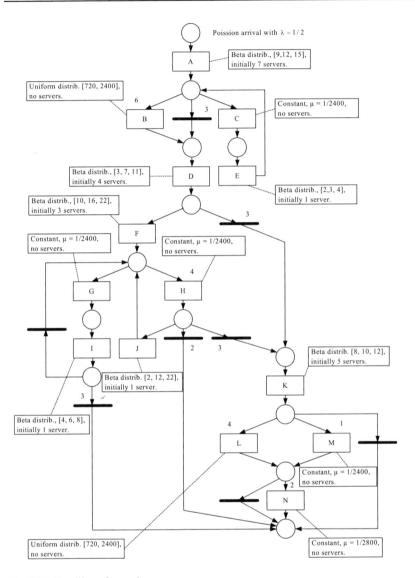

Fig. 5.15. Handling of appeals

The results of the marginal allocation algorithm are disappointing. The cause for this is the large portion of the total throughput time that consists of time that is not dependent upon the number of resources, see e.g., task B. If an infinite number of resources within each class is assumed, the mean throughput time is 4482,03 time units. With respect to this net, the figures of mean queue time and resource utilization did allow for their unambiguous interpretation.

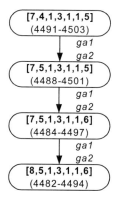

Fig. 5.16. Allocation decisions for appeals handling

Money Transfers

In Figure 5.17, a resource-extended SWN is depicted that is in use to process complex money transfers at the Postbank, a Dutch bank. The workflow involves several checks that have to be satisfied (A and B), before a preliminary money transfer can be made (task C). Task E attempts to finalize the transfer, but this may fail if several financial requirements are not met. If it fails, the final transfer may be retried the next working day (task D) or it may be rejected. In case of rejection, task H corrects the preliminary booking. If the transfer is successful, some after-processing is required (tasks F and G).

Just as is the case for the workflow depicted in Figure 5.15, some tasks do not require a resource but do consume time. For example, task D represents a time period of 1 working day (8 hours) that has to pass before a transfer is again attempted to be executed when it has failed before because of a deficit. As each resource class is allocated to exactly one task and vice versa, we will refer in this section to the resource classes with the identifiers tasks. Only resource classes exist for tasks that require a resource, respectively A, B, E, F, and H.

The decision paths through the subsequent allocations taken by all considered allocation strategies are depicted in Figure 5.18. The initial resource allocation [6, 4, 5, 2, 1] denotes the initial availability of 6 resources in class A, 4 in class B, 5 in class E, 2 in class F and 1 in class H. Not all resource allocations have been depicted, although they were all included in the analysis.

The analysis of the different resource allocations showed that two of the three paths that are consistent with the marginal allocation strategy lead to the optimal solution of [6, 6, 5, 3, 1]. The three paths are labeled with *ma1*, *ma2*, and *ma3*. Note that there are three of these paths, because the 90 % mean throughput time confidence intervals of allocations [6, 5, 5, 3, 1] and [6, 6, 5, 2, 1] are overlapping, as well as those of the allocations [6, 5, 6, 3, 1] and [6, 6, 5, 3, 1]. Neither of the routes that implements a Goldratt strategy leads to the optimal scenario. Note the two alternatives for applying the Goldratt algorithm with the recourse utilization as selection criterion (*ga2a* and *ga2b*).

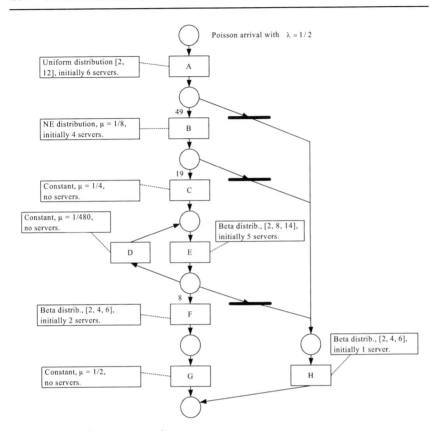

Fig. 5.17. Complex money transfers

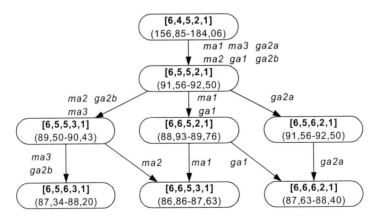

Fig. 5.18. Allocation decisions for complex money transfers

For this practical net, the marginal allocation performs rather well. According to the marginal allocation algorithm, resource class E is not so important to extend with an extra resource. This in contrast with the applications of the Goldratt algorithm. The effectiveness of the marginal allocation algorithm is not impaired by large influences on the throughput time by tasks without resources, like it was the case for the previous practical net ("handling of appeals"). Do note that the confidence intervals on the allocations [6, 5, 6, 3, 1], [6, 6, 5, 3, 1] and [6, 6, 6, 2, 1] either overlap or are very close. Only the absoluteness of our optimality criterion allows for a proper selection.

5.4.4 Evaluation

The most important conclusion that can be drawn from the workbench experimentation is that the application of the marginal allocation is limited when throughput times depend only slightly on queue times (see the "handling of appeals" net in Section 5.4). For practical situations, this will very often be the case. In many practical situations a large part of the throughput time depends on communications with external parties, fixed schedules for carrying out some part of the work, etc. The "intake workflow" that is yet to be introduced in the following chapter (see Section 6.2) is another illustration of these characteristics in practice.

For a relative overall comparison of the marginal allocation algorithm with the Goldratt algorithm, the following procedure is applied. For each of the treated nets in the workbench, the probability is determined for each allocation strategy that it leads to the optimal allocation of one, two, or three additional resources. (For the big nets, only the probabilities for one or two additional resources have been computed.) Once again recall that we have applied the lowest absolute mean throughput time as optimality criterion. Because the strategies are sometimes ambiguous in the selection of an allocation successor, we assume an equal probability for selecting one out of more alternatives. For example, there is an 0,5 probability that resource allocation [6, 6, 5, 2, 1] is chosen as successor for the allocation [6, 5, 5, 2, 1] when following the marginal allocation strategy in the "money transfer" net of Section 5.4. The probability figures for each net are depicted in Table 5.4.

The results of this table give a mixed view. For the N-construction, the parallel sequential net, and the alternative sequential net the marginal allocation delivers the best results. For the tandem net and the money transfers there is no obvious best strategy. For the handling of appeals net, the marginal allocation makes the worst score. An optimistic conclusion may be that the marginal allocation delivers comparable or better results than the Goldratt strategies, except when queue time makes only a small portion of the throughput time (e.g., in the case of the handling of appeals). Obviously, such a conclusion assumes equal importance of all scenario's.

Table 5.4. Probabilities of finding the optimal allocation for different numbers of additional servers. MA = Marginal Allocation; GR1 = Goldratt 1 (queue time); GR2 = Goldratt 2 (utilization).

	tandem net			N-construc-tion			paral. seq.		altern. seq.		handling appeals			money transfers		
Extra serv.	*1*	*2*	*3*	*1*	*2*	*3*	*1*	*2*	*1*	*2*	*1*	*2*	*3*	*1*	*2*	*3*
MA	1	0	1	1	1	1	1	1	$\frac{1}{2}$	1	$\frac{1}{7}$	$\frac{1}{28}$	$\frac{1}{84}$	1	$\frac{1}{3}$	$\frac{2}{3}$
GR1	0	1	1	$\frac{2}{3}$	0	0	1	1	0	0	1	1	1	1	1	0
GR2	0	1	1	$\frac{1}{4}$	$\frac{1}{10}$	$\frac{1}{20}$	1	$\frac{1}{2}$	0	$\frac{1}{2}$	1	1	1	1	0	0

5.5 Conclusion

As we have remarked in the introduction of this chapter, the allocation of the right number of resources to resource classes is just one element in the overall field of resource allocation in the design and control of workflow. It is nonetheless an important one, where guidance in practice is much in demand. This demand is also the justification for allowing the very simple model of the way that resources are allocated in a workflow (see Table 5.1). Clearly, the evaluation of the type of algorithms as presented is much more complicated for models which are less simple.

Other important issues within the field of resource allocation are the selection of resource classes and the specification of allocation principles such that the requirements on the execution of a workflow can be met. These subjects are not treated here. In the following chapter, some heuristics are proposed that may help to make this type of decisions. A framework is also introduced to assess the impact of a (resource allocation) decision, which takes a wider viewpoint than considering the throughput time only.

6 Heuristic Workflow Redesign

In this chapter we will give an overview of heuristics that can be used to improve a workflow. The character of the chapter is rather informal. We will not try to prove or quantify in general terms the superiority of the design measures we discuss. Instead, we will illustrate a heuristic redesign of workflows by presenting a realistic example workflow to which we will apply these measures. A heuristic redesign of a workflow contrasts rather sharply with the product-based workflow design approach that we have discussed in Chapter 3. We characterized the latter as an analytic and clean sheet approach. The approach of this chapter takes an existing workflow as starting point. The heuristics that we apply are also typically on a check-list of a team that redesigns a workflow in a participative way.

The scope of this chapter is very broad. Almost all relevant concepts in a workflow context (see Chapter 1) are touched by one or more of the heuristics presented. We have visualized the scope of the chapter with the thickly outlined shape in Figure 6.1. The original, underlying model was introduced in Section 1.4.

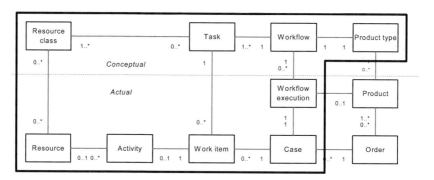

Fig. 6.1. Focus of Chapter 6

The purpose of this chapter is twofold. In the first place, it is an attempt to bring together known workflow redesign rules. In the second place, the presentation and application of the heuristics on the example may serve as an inspiration for a better quantification and rationalization of the redesign measures in future research.

H.A. Reijers: Design and Control of Workflow Processes, LNCS 2617, pp. 207-243, 2003.
© Springer-Verlag Berlin Heidelberg 2003

6.1 Redesign Heuristics

In this section we will present about thirty workflow redesign heuristics and discuss their supposed effects. The main part of the heuristics we present have been derived from literature (Hammer and Champy, 1993; Rupp and Russell, 1994; Klein, 1995; Peppard and Rowland, 1995; Poyssick and Hannaford, 1996; Berg and Pottjewijd, 1997; Seidmann and Sundararajan, 1997; Van der Wal, 1997; Van der Aalst, 2000b; Zapf and Heinzl, 2000; Van der Aalst and Van Hee, 2002). A smaller part is based on our own experiences, which has been partly described in earlier work (e.g., Reijers and Goverde 1998; Reijers and Goverde, 1999a) or in this monograph (see Chapter 7).

Not each heuristic which we have encountered in our literature survey is incorporated in this overview. Some of them focused more on the strategic level, e.g., on the selection of products to be offered, or were too much concerned with manufacturing processes. We also thought some heuristics to be of very limited general application.

Before we discuss the various heuristics, we will describe a model that serves as a frame of reference in their assessment. The other parts of this section contain the descriptions of the heuristics, using a breakdown as follows:

- *Task rules*, which focus on optimizing single tasks within a workflow.
- *Routing rules*, which try to improve upon the routing structure of the workflow.
- *Allocation rules*, which involve a particular allocation of resources.
- *Resource rules*, which focus on the types and number of resources.
- *Rules for external parties*, which try to improve upon the collaboration and communication with the client and third parties.
- *Integral workflow rules*, that apply to the workflow as a whole.

Note that this distinction is not mutually exclusive. In other words, it is to some degree arbitrary to which category a heuristic is assigned.

6.1.1 The Devil's Quadrangle

Brand and Van der Kolk (1995) distinguish four main dimensions in the effects of redesign measures: time, cost, quality, and flexibility. Ideally, a redesign of a workflow decreases the time required to handle the case, it decreases the required cost of executing the workflow, it improves the quality of the service delivered, and it improves the ability of the workflow to react to variation. The appealing property of their model is that, in general, improving upon one dimension may have a weakening effect on another. For example, reconciliation tasks may be added in a workflow to improve on the quality of the delivered service, but this may have a drawback on the timeliness of the service delivery. To signify the difficult trade-offs that sometimes have to be made they refer to their model as the devil's quadrangle. It is depicted in Figure 6.2.

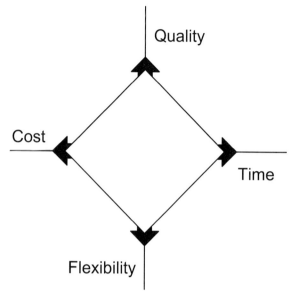

Fig. 6.2. The devil's quadrangle

Awareness of the trade-off that underlies a redesign measure is very important in a heuristic redesign of a workflow. Sometimes, the effect of a redesign measure may be that the result from some point of view is worse than the existing workflow. The application of several redesign rules may also result in the partly deactivation of the desired effects of each of the single measures.

Each of the four dimensions of the devil's quadrangle may be made operational in different ways. For example, there are several types of cost and even so many directions to focus on when attempting to decrease cost. The translation of the general concepts time, cost, quality, and flexibility to a more precise meaning is context sensitive. The key performance indicators of an organization or – more directly – the performance targets formulated for a redesign effort should ideally be formulated as much more precise applications of the four named dimensions.

In our discussion of the effects of redesign measures we will not try to assess their effectiveness in every thinkable aspect of each of the four dimensions. We will focus on some particular issues of interest.

Time

An important performance concept of a workflow is the throughput time, which we have discussed before at several points during this monograph. It is the time that it takes to handle a case from start to end. Although it is usually the aim of a redesign effort to reduce the throughput time, there are many different ways of further specifying this aim. For example, one can aim at a reduction of the average throughput time or the maximal throughput time. Both of these entities are absolute measures. It is also possible to focus on the ability to meet throughput times that are agreed upon with a client at run time. This is a more relative interpretation of the throughput time dimension. Yet another way of looking at the throughput time is to focus on its variation (see Buzacott, 1996; Seidmann and Sundararajan, 1997).

Other aspects of the time dimension come into view when we consider the constituents of throughput time as we have described them in Section 2.4, which are as follows:

- *Service* times: the time that resources spend on actually handling the case.
- *Queue* times: the time that a case spends waiting in queue because there are no resources available to handle the case.
- *Wait* times: all other time a case spends waiting, for example because synchronization must take place with another process.

In general, there are different ways of measuring each of these constituents. An elegant way of coping with these notions is given in Section 5.1 (see also Figure 5.3).

Cost

The most common performance targets for redesign projects are of a financial nature. Brand and Van der Kolk (1995) have chosen to distinguish the cost dimension, but it would also have been possible to put the emphasis on turnover, yield, or revenue. Obviously, an increase of yield may have the same effect on an organization's profit as a decrease of cost. However, redesign is more often associated with reducing cost and not so much with increasing the yield. (We will mention in our overview one redesign measure which is more involved with yield than cost.)

There are different perspectives on cost. In the first place, it is possible to distinguish between fixed and variable cost. Fixed costs are overhead costs which are (nearly) not affected by the intensity of processing. Typical fixed costs follow from the use of infrastructure and the maintenance of information systems. Variable cost is positively correlated with some variable quantity, such as the level of sales, the number of purchased goods, the number of new hires, etc.

A cost notion which is closely related to productivity is operational cost. Operational costs can be directly related to the outputs of a workflow. A substantial part of operational cost is usually labor cost, the cost related to human resources in producing a good or delivering a service. Within BPR efforts, it is very common to focus on reducing operation cost, particularly labor cost. The automation of tasks is often seen as an alternative for labor. Obviously, although automation may reduce labor cost it may cause incidental cost involved with developing the respective application and fixed maintenance cost for the life time of the application.

Quality

The quality of a workflow can be viewed from at least two different angles: from the client's side and from the worker's side. This is also known as the distinction between external quality and internal quality.

The external quality can be measured as the client's satisfaction with either the product or the process. Satisfaction with the product can be expressed as the extent to which a client feels that his specifications or expectations are met by the delivered product. A client's satisfaction with the workflow concerns the way how it is executed. A typical issue is the amount and quality of the information that a client receives during execution on the progress being made.

The internal quality of a workflow involves the condition of working in the workflow. Typical issues are: the level that a worker feels he or she is in control of the work performed, the level of variation experienced, and whether working in the particular workflow is felt as challenging.

It is interesting to note that there are various direct relations between the quality and other dimensions. For example, the external process quality is often measured in terms of time, e.g., the throughput time.

Flexibility

The least noted criterion to measure the effect of a redesign measure is the workflow's flexibility. Flexibility can be defined as the ability to react to changes. These changes may concern various parts of the workflow as follows:

- The ability of resources to execute different (numbers of) tasks.
- The ability of a workflow as a whole to handle various cases and changing workloads.
- The ability of the workflow's management to change the used structure and allocation rules.
- The organization's ability to change the structure and responsiveness of the workflow to wishes of the market and business partners.

Another way of approaching the flexibility issue is to distinguish between run time and build time flexibility (see Section 1.2). Run time flexibility concerns the possibilities to handle changes and variations while executing a specific workflow. Build time flexibility concerns the possibility to change the workflow structure.

It is important to distinguish the flexibility of a workflow from the other dimensions, as will be clear from the discussion of the various heuristics in the next sections.

We will present in the following subsections the rules. Each of the sections concerns one category of heuristic rules as distinguished at the begin of Section 6.1. For each heuristic, we will present an acronym (in capitals, between brackets), its general formulation, its desirable effects and possible drawbacks. For each of the rules – except for the integral workflow rules – a symbolic depiction of its essence is given. We will also indicate similarities in heuristics and provide references to their origin.

6.1.2 Task Rules

Task Elimination (ELIM)

The heuristic of *task elimination* runs as follows: eliminate unnecessary tasks from a workflow (see Figure 6.3).

Fig. 6.3. Task elimination

A common way of regarding a task as unnecessary is when it adds no value from a client's point of view. Typically, control tasks in a workflow do not do this; they are incorporated in the model to fix problems created or not elevated in earlier steps. Control tasks can often be found back as iterations and reconciliation tasks. The aims of this heuristic are to increase the speed of processing and to reduce the cost of handling a case. An important drawback may be that the quality of the service deteriorates.

The heuristic is widespread in literature, for example see Peppard and Rowland (1995), Berg and Pottjewijd (1997), and Van der Aalst and Van Hee (2002). Buzacott (1996) illustrates the quantitative effects of eliminating iterations with a simple model.

Task Addition (ADD)

The *task addition* heuristic is: check the completeness and correctness of incoming materials and check the output before it is send to clients (see Figure 6.4).

Fig. 6.4. Task addition

This heuristic promotes the addition of controls to a workflow. It may lead to a higher quality of the workflow execution and, as a result, to less required rework. Obviously, an additional control will require time and will absorb resources. Note the contrast of the intent of this heuristic with that of the task elimination heuristic.

The heuristic is mentioned by Poyssick and Hannaford (1996).

Task Composition (COMPOS)

The content of the *task composition* heuristic is: combine small tasks into composite tasks and divide large tasks into workable smaller tasks (see Figure 6.5).

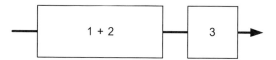

Fig. 6.5. Task composition

Combining tasks should result in the reduction of setup times, i.e., the time that is spent by a resource to become familiar with the specifics of a case. By executing a large task which used to consist of several smaller ones, some positive effect may also be expected on the quality of the delivered work. Making tasks too large may result in (a) smaller run-time flexibility and (b) lower quality as tasks may become unworkable. Both effects are exactly countered by dividing tasks into smaller ones. Obviously, smaller tasks may result in longer set-up times.

This is probably the most cited heuristic rule, mentioned by Hammer and Champy (1993), Rupp and Russell (1994), Peppard and Rowland (1995), Berg and Pottjewijd (1997), Seidmann and Sundararajan (1997), Reijers and Goverde (1999a), Van der Aalst (2000b), and Van der Aalst and Van Hee (2002). Some of these authors only consider one part of the heuristic, e.g., combining smaller tasks into one. Buzacott (1996), Seidmann and Sundararajan (1997) and Van der Aalst (2000b) provide quantitative support for the optimality of this heuristic for simple models.

Task Automation (AUTO)

The *task automation* heuristic is: consider automating tasks (see Figure 6.6).

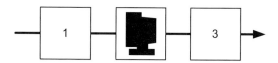

Fig. 6.6. Task automation

The positive result of automating tasks in particular may be that tasks can be executed faster, with less cost, and with a better result. An obvious disadvantage is that the development of a system that performs a task may be costly. Generally speaking, a system performing a task is also less flexible in handling variations than a human resource. Instead of fully automating a task, an automated *support* of the resource executing the task may also be considered. This heuristic is a specific application of the technology heuristic, which we have yet to discuss.

The heuristic is specifically mentioned as a redesign measure by Peppard and Rowland (1995) and Berg and Pottjewijd (1997).

6.1.3 Routing Rules

Resequencing (RESEQ)

The content of the *resequencing* heuristic is: move tasks to more appropriate places (see Figure 6.7).

Fig. 6.7. Resequencing

In existing workflows, actual tasks orderings do not give full information on the logical restrictions that have to be maintained between tasks. Therefore, it is sometimes better to postpone a task if it is not required for immediately following tasks, so that perhaps its execution may prove to become superfluous. This saves cost. A task may be moved into the proximity of a similar task also, in this way diminishing set-up times. Specific applications of the resequencing heuristics are the knock-out heuristic, control relocation and the parallelism heuristic which we will subsequently discuss.

The resequencing heuristic is mentioned as such by Klein (1995).

Knock-Out (KO)

The *knock-out* heuristic is: order knock-outs in a decreasing order of effort and in an increasing order of termination probability (see Figure 6.8).

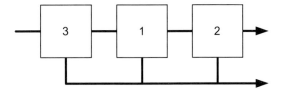

Fig. 6.8. Knock-out

A typical part of a workflow is the checking of various conditions that must be satisfied to deliver a positive end result. Any condition that is not met may lead to a termination of that part of the workflow, the knock-out. If there is freedom in choosing the order in which the various conditions are checked, the condition that has the most favorable ratio of expected knock-out probability versus the expected effort to check the condition should be pursued. Next, the second best condition, etc. This way of ordering checks yields on average the least costly workflow execution. There is no obvious drawback on this heuristic, although it may not always be possible to freely order these kinds of checks. Implementing the heuristic also may result in a (part of a) workflow that takes a longer throughput time than a full parallel checking of all conditions.

Reijers and Goverde (1999a) and Van der Aalst (2000b) mention this heuristic. Van der Aalst (2000b) also gives quantitative support for its optimality.

Control Relocation (RELOC)

The *control relocation* heuristic means: move controls towards the client (see Figure 6.9).

Fig. 6.9. Control relocation

Different checks and reconciliations that are part of a workflow may be moved towards the client. Klein (1995) gives the example of Pacific Bell that moved its billing controls towards its clients eliminating in this way the bulk of its billing errors. It also improved client satisfaction. A disadvantage of moving a control towards a client is higher probability of fraud, resulting in fewer yields.

The heuristic is named by Klein (1995).

Parallelism (PAR)

The *parallelism* heuristic runs as follows: consider whether tasks may be executed in parallel (see Figure 6.10).

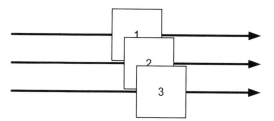

Fig. 6.10. Parallelism

The obvious effect of applying this heuristic is that the throughput time may be considerably reduced. The applicability of the heuristic in workflow redesign is large. In practical experiences we have had with analyzing existing workflows, tasks were mostly ordered sequentially without the existence of hard logical restrictions prescribing such an order. We already discussed the causes for this in Section 3.2. The advantage of parallel workflows in terms of throughput time is the basis for the breadth-first workflows that are designed with PBWD (see Section 3.3.)

A drawback of introducing more parallelism in a workflow that incorporates possibilities of knock-outs is that the cost of workflow execution may increase. The management of workflows with concurrent behavior can become more complex also, which may introduce errors (quality) or restrict run-time adaptations (flexibility).

The heuristic is mentioned by Rupp and Russell (1994), Berg and Pottjewijd (1997), and Van der Aalst and Van Hee (2002). Van der Aalst (2000b) provides quantitative support for this heuristic.

Triage (TRI)

The main interpretation of the *triage* heuristic is: consider the division of a general task into two or more alternative tasks (see Figure 6.11). Its opposite (and less popular) formulation is: consider the integration of two or more alternative tasks into one general task.

When applying the heuristic in its main form, it is possible to design tasks that are better aligned with the capabilities of resources and the characteristics of the case. Both of these improve the quality of the workflow. Distinguishing alternative tasks also facilitates a better utilization of resources, with obvious cost and time advantages. On the other hand, too much specialization can make processes become less flexible, less efficient, and cause monotonous work with repercussions for quality. This is lifted by the alternative interpretation of the triage heuristic.

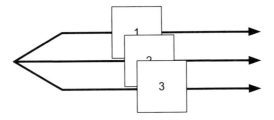

Fig. 6.11. Triage

A special form of the triage heuristic is to divide a task into *similar* instead of alternative tasks for different subcategories of the case type. For example, a special cash desk may be set up for clients with an expected low processing time.

The triage heuristic is related to the task composition heuristic in the sense that it is concerned with the division and combination of tasks. Note that the heuristic differs from it in the sense that alternative tasks are considered.

The triage concept is mentioned by Klein (1995), Berg and Pottjewijd (1997), and Van der Aalst and Van Hee (2002). Zapf and Heinzl (2000) show the positive effects of triage within the setting of a call center.

6.1.4 Allocation Rules

Case Manager (MAN)

The *case manager* heuristic runs as follows: appoint one person as responsible for the handling of each case, the *case manager* (see Figure 6.12).

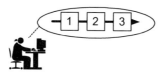

Fig. 6.12. Case manager

The case manager is responsible for the case, but he or she is not necessarily the (only) resource that will work on work items for this case. The most important aim of this heuristic is to improve upon the external quality of a workflow. The workflow will become more transparent from the viewpoint of a client as the case manager provides a single point of contact. This positively affects client satisfaction. It may also have a positive effect on the internal quality of the workflow, as someone is accountable for correcting mistakes. Obviously, the assignment of a case manager has financial consequences as capacity must be devoted to this job.

The heuristic is mentioned by Hammer and Champy (1993) and Van der Aalst and Van Hee (2002). Buzacott (1996) has provided some quantitative support for a specific interpretation of this heuristic.

Case Assignment (ASSIGN)

The *case assignment* heuristic is: let workers perform as many steps as possible for single cases (see Figure 6.13).

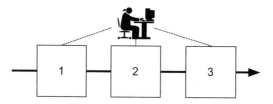

Fig. 6.13. Case assignment

This heuristic is different from the case manager heuristic we mentioned before. Although a case manager will be responsible for a case, he or she does not have to be involved in executing the workflow. By using case assignment in the most extreme form, for each work item the resource is selected from the ones capable of performing it that has worked on the case before – if any. Rather confusingly, this person is sometimes also referred to as case manager. The obvious advantage of the rule is that this person will get acquainted with the case and will need less set-up time. An additional benefit may be that the quality of service is increased. On the negative side, the flexibility of resource allocation is seriously reduced. A case may experience substantial queue time when its "case manager" is not available.

The case assignment heuristic is described by Rupp and Russell (1994), Reijers and Goverde (1998), and Van der Aalst and Van Hee (2002).

Customer Teams (TEAM)

The *customer team* heuristic is: consider assigning teams out of different departmental workers that will take care of the complete handling of specific sorts of cases (see Figure 6.14).

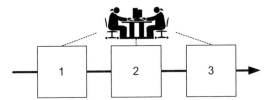

Fig. 6.14. Customer teams

This heuristic is a variation of the case assignment heuristic. Depending on its exact desired form, the customer team heuristic may be implemented by the case assignment heuristic. A customer team may involve more workers with the same qualifications also, in this way relaxing the strict requirements of the case assignment rule.

Advantages and disadvantages are similar to those of the case assignment heuristics. In addition, work as a team may improve the attractiveness of the work and a better understanding, which are both quality aspects.

The heuristic is mentioned by Peppard and Rowland (1995) and Berg and Pottjewijd (1997).

Flexible Assignment (FLEX)

The *flexible assignment* heuristic runs as follows: assign resources in such a way that maximal flexibility is preserved for the near future (see Figure 6.15). For example, if a work item can be executed by either of two available resources, assign it to the most specialized resource. In this way, the possibilities to take on the next work item by the free, more general resource are maximal.

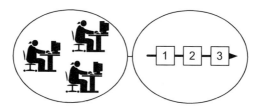

Fig. 6.15. Flexible assignment

The advantage of this heuristic is that the overall queue time is reduced: it is less probable that a case has to await the availability of a specific resource. Another advantage is that the workers with the highest specialization can be expected to take on most of the work, which may result in a higher quality. The disadvantages of the rule can be diverse. For example, work load may become unbalanced resulting in less job satisfaction. Possibilities for specialists to evolve into generalists are reduced also.

This heuristic is mentioned by Van der Aalst and Van Hee (2002).

Resource Centralization (CENTR)

The *resource centralization* heuristic is: treat geographically dispersed resources as if they are centralized (see Figure 6.16).

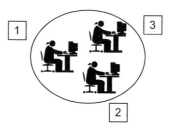

Fig. 6.16. Resource centralization

This heuristic is explicitly aimed at exploiting the benefits of WfMS's. After all, when a WfMS takes care of handing out work items to resources it has become less relevant where these resources are located geographically. In this sense, the heuristic is a special form of the technology heuristic. Moreover, it can also be seen as the opposite of customer teams heuristic. The specific advantage of this measure is that resources can be committed more flexibly, which gives a better utilization and possibly a better throughput time. The disadvantages are similar to that of the technology heuristic.

This heuristic is mentioned by Van der Aalst and Van Hee (2002).

Split Responsibilities (SPLIT)

The *split responsibilities* heuristic is: avoid assignment of task responsibilities to people from different functional units (see Figure 6.17).

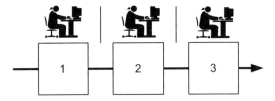

Fig. 6.17. Split responsibilities

The idea behind this heuristic is that tasks for which different departments share responsibility are more likely to be a source of neglect and conflict. Reducing the overlap in responsibilities should lead to a better quality of task execution. A higher responsiveness to available work items may be developed also, so that clients are served quicker. On the other hand, reducing the effective number of resources that is available for a work item may have a negative effect on its throughput time, as more queuing may occur.

This specific heuristic is mentioned by Rupp and Russell (1994) and Berg and Pottjewijd (1997).

6.1.5 Resource Rules

Numerical Involvement (NUM)

The *numerical involvement* heuristic runs: minimize the number of departments, groups and persons involved in a workflow (see Figure 6.18).

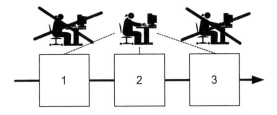

Fig. 6.18. Numerical involvement

Applying this heuristic should lead to less coordination problems. Less time spent of coordination makes more time available for the processing of cases. Reducing the number of departments may lead to less shared responsibilities, with similar pros and cons as the *split responsibilities* heuristic. In addition, smaller numbers of specialized units may prohibit the build of expertise (a quality issue) and routine (a cost issue).

The heuristic is described by Hammer and Champy (1993), Rupp and Russell (1994), and Berg and Pottjewijd (1997).

Extra Resources (XRES)

The *extra resources* heuristic is: if capacity is not sufficient, consider increasing the number of resources in a certain resource class (see Figure 6.19).

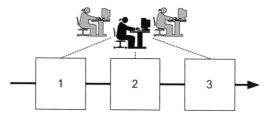

Fig. 6.19. Extra resources

This straightforward heuristic speaks for itself. Note that the subject of Chapter 5 of this monograph is concerned with the optimal allocation of additional resources. The obvious effect of extra resources is that there is more capacity for handling cases, in this way reducing queue time. It may also help to implement a more flexible assignment policy. Of course, hiring or buying extra resources has its cost. Note the contrast of this heuristic with the numerical involvement heuristic.

The heuristic is mentioned by Berg and Pottjewijd (1997).

Specialist-Generalist (SPEC)

The *specialist-generalist* heuristic is: consider making resources more specialistic or more generalistic (see Figure 6.20).

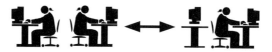

Fig. 6.20. Specialist-generalist

Resources may be turned from specialists into generalists or the other way round. A specialist resource can be trained for other qualifications; a generalist may be assigned to the same type of work for a longer period of time, so that his other qualifications become obsolete. When the redesign of a new workflow is considered, application of the heuristic comes down to considering the specialist-generalist ratio of new hires.

A specialist builds up routine more quickly and may have a more profound knowledge than a generalist. As a result he or she works quicker and delivers higher quality. On the other hand, the availability of generalists adds more flexibility to the workflow and can lead to a better utilization of resources. Depending on the degree of specialism or generalism, either type of resource may be more costly.

Note that this heuristic differs from the triage concept in the sense that the focus is not on the division of tasks.

Poyssick and Hannaford (1996) and Berg and Pottjewijd (1997) stress the advantages of generalists. Rupp and Russell (1994), Seidmann and Sundararajan (1997), and Reijers and Goverde (1998) mention both specialists and generalists. Van der Wal (1997) provides some insight into the use of generalists ("butterflies"). For the example he uses, it follows that a small number of generalists may indeed improve the performance of a system, but increasing this number does not yield additional benefits.

Empower (EMP)

The *empower* heuristic is: give workers most of the decision-making authority and reduce middle management (see Figure 6.21).

Fig. 6.21. Empower

In traditional workflows, substantial time may be spent on authorizing work that has been done by others. When workers are empowered to take decisions independently, it may result in smoother operations with lower throughput times. The reduction of middle management from the workflow also reduces the labor cost spent on the processing of cases. A drawback may be that the quality of the decisions is lower and that obvious errors are no longer found. If bad decisions or errors result in rework, the cost of handling a case may actually increase compared to the original situation.

The heuristic is named by Hammer and Champy (1993), Rupp and Russell (1994), and Poyssick and Hannaford (1996). Buzacott (1996) shows with a simple quantitative model that this heuristic may indeed increase performance.

6.1.6 Rules for External Parties

Integration (INTG)

The *integration* heuristic is as follows: consider the integration with a workflow of the client or a supplier (see Figure 6.22). This heuristic can be seen as exploiting the *supply chain* concept known in production. In practice, the application of this heuristic may take on different forms. For example, when two parties have to agree upon a product they commonly produce it may be more efficient to perform several intermediate reviews than performing one large review when both parties have completed their part.

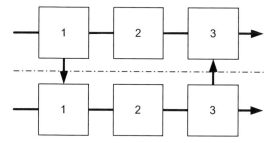

Fig. 6.22. Integration

In general, integrated workflows should render a more efficient execution, both from a time and cost perspective. The drawback of integration is that dependence grows and therefore, flexibility may decrease

Both Klein (1995) and Peppard and Rowland (1995) mention this heuristic.

Outsourcing (OUT)

The *outsourcing* heuristic is: consider outsourcing a workflow in whole or parts of it (see Figure 6.23).

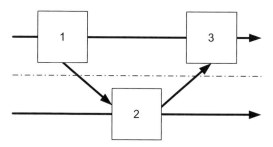

Fig. 6.23. Outsourcing

Another party may be more efficient in performing the same work, so they might as well perform it. The outsourcing heuristic is similar to the workflow integration heuristic in the sense that it reflects on workflows of other parties.

The obvious aim of outsourcing work is that it will generate less cost. A drawback may be that quality decreases. Outsourcing also requires more coordination efforts and will make the workflow more complex.

The heuristic is mentioned by Klein (1995) and Poyssick and Hannaford (1996).

Interfacing (INTF)

The *interfacing* heuristic is: consider a standardized interface with clients and partners (see Figure 6.24).

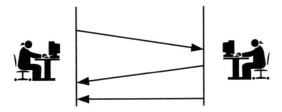

Fig. 6.24. Interfacing

The idea behind this heuristic is that a standardized interface will diminish the probability of mistakes, incomplete applications, unintelligible communications, etc. A standardized interface may result in fewer errors (quality), faster processing (time), and less rework (cost). The interfacing heuristic can be seen a specific interpretation of the integration heuristic.

This principle is mentioned by Hammer and Champy (1993) and Poyssick and Hannaford (1996).

Contact Reduction (REDUC)

The *contact reduction* heuristic is: reduce the number of contacts with clients and third parties (see Figure 6.25). The exchange of information with a client or third party is always time-consuming. Especially when information exchanges take place by regular mail, substantial wait times may be involved. Each contact also introduces the possibility of intruding an error. Hammer and Champy (1993) describes a case where the multitude of bills, invoices, and receipts creates a heavy reconciliation burden. Reducing the number of contacts may therefore decrease throughput time and boost quality. Note that it is not always necessary to skip certain information exchanges, but that it is possible to *combine* them with limited extra cost. A disadvantage of a smaller number of contacts might be the loss of essential information, which is a quality issue. Combining contacts may result in the delivery or receipt of too much data, which involves cost.

Fig. 6.25. Contact reduction

Note that this heuristic is related to the interfacing heuristic in the sense that they both try to improve on the collaboration with other parties.

The heuristic is mentioned Hammer by and Champy (1993) and Reijers and Goverde (1999a). The heuristic is used in the redesign case in Chapter 7. Buzacott (1996) has investigated this heuristic quantitatively.

Buffering (BUF)

The *buffering* heuristic runs as follows: instead of requesting information from an external source, buffer it by subscribing to updates (see Figure 6.26).

Fig. 6.26. Buffering

Obtaining information from other parties is a major, time consuming part in many workflows. By having information directly available when it is required, throughput times may be substantially reduced. This heuristic can be compared to the *caching* principle microprocessors apply. Of course, the subscription fee for information updates may be rather costly. This is especially so when we consider the situation that an information source may contain far more information than is ever used. Substantial cost may also be involved with storing all the information.

Note that this heuristic is a weak form of the integration heuristic. Instead of direct access to the original source of information – the integration alternative – a copy is maintained.

This heuristic is mentioned by Reijers and Goverde (1999a).

Trusted Party (TRUST)

The *trusted party* heuristic is as follows: instead of determining information one-self, use results of a trusted party (see Figure 6.27).

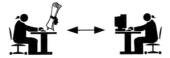

Fig. 6.27. Trusted party

Some decisions or assessments that are made within workflows are not specific for the workflow they are part of. Other parties may have determined the same information in another context, which – if it were known – could replace the decision or assessment part of the workflow. An example is the creditworthiness of a client that bank A wants to establish. If a client can present a recent creditworthiness certificate of bank B, then bank A will accept it. Obviously, the trusted party heuristic reduces cost and may even cut back throughput time. On the other hand, the quality of the workflow becomes dependent upon the quality of some other party's work. Some coordination effort with trusted parties is also likely to be required.

Note that this heuristic differs from the outsourcing heuristic. When outsourcing, a work item is executed at *run time* by another party. The trusted party heuristic allows for the use of a result in the recent *past*. It is different from the buffering heuristic, because the workflow owner is not the one obtaining the information.

This heuristic rule results from our own reengineering experience.

6.1.7 Integral Workflow Rules

Case Types (TYP)

The *case types* heuristic can be formulated as: determine whether tasks are related to the same type of case and, if necessary, distinguish new workflows and product types.

Especially Berg and Pottjewijd (1997) convincingly warn for subflows that are not specifically intended to handle the case type of their umbrella workflow (the superflow). Ignoring this phenomenon may result in a less effective management of this subflow and a lower efficiency. Applying the heuristic may yield faster processing times and less cost. Distinguishing common subflows of many different flows may yield efficiency gains also. Yet, it may also result in more coordination problems between the workflow (quality) and less possibilities for rearranging the workflow as a whole (flexibility).

Note that this heuristic is in some sense similar to the triage concept. The main interpretation of the triage concept can be seen as a translation of the case type heuristic on a task level.

This heuristics has been mentioned in one form or another by Hammer and Champy (1993), Rupp and Russell (1994), Peppard and Rowland (1995), and Berg and Pottjewijd (1997).

Technology (TECH)

The *technology* heuristic is as follows: try to elevate physical constraints in a workflow by applying new technology.

In general, new technology can offer all kinds of positive effects. For example, the application of a WfMS may result in less time that is spent on logistical tasks. A Document Management System will open up the information available on cases to all participants, which may result in a better quality of service. New technology can also change the traditional way of doing business by giving participants complete new possibilities.

The purchase, development, implementation, training, and maintenance efforts related to technology are obviously costly. In addition, new technology may arouse fear with workers or may result in other subjective effects; this may deteriorate the quality of the workflow.

The heuristic is mentioned by Klein (1995), Peppard and Rowland (1995), Berg and Pottjewijd (1997), and Van der Aalst and Van Hee (2002).

Exception (EXCEP)

The *exception* heuristic is: design workflows for typical cases and isolate exceptional cases from normal flow.

Exceptions may seriously disturb normal operations. An exception will require workers to get acquainted with a case although they may not be able to handle it. Setup times are then wasted. Isolating exceptions, for example by a triage, will make the handling of normal cases more efficient. Isolating exceptions may possibly increase the overall performance as specific expertise can be build up by workers working on the exceptions. By filtering out all exceptions, it may be possible to offer Straight-Through-Processing (MacSweeney, 2001). The price paid in isolating exceptions is that the workflow will become more complex, possibly decreasing its flexibility. Also, if no special knowledge is developed to handle the exceptions (which is costly) no major improvements are likely to occur.

The heuristic is mentioned by Poyssick and Hannaford (1996).

Case-Based Work (CASEB)

The *case-based work* heuristic is: consider removing batch-processing and periodic activities from a workflow.

Although workflows are essentially case-based and make-to-order (see Section 1.4), several features may be present in practical workflows that are on bad-terms with these concepts. The most notable examples are (a) the piling up of work items in batches and (b) periodic activities, depending on computer systems which are only available for processing at specific times. Getting rid of these constraints may significantly speed up the handling of cases. On the other hand, efficiencies of scale can be reached by batch processing. The cost of making information systems permanently available may be costly also.

This heuristic rule results from our own reengineering experience.

6.2 The Intake Workflow

In this section we will illustrate the redesign of an existing workflow, using the heuristics as described in Section 6.1. We introduce a workflow which is used at a mental health care institute to process new requests for non-urgent treatment. It will be referred to as the *intake workflow*. The intake workflow is a slightly adapted version of an actual workflow as described by Reijers (1994). Before we will give a description of the original workflow and possible redesign measures, we will describe how we represent the workflow.

6.2.1 Workflow Notations

For a convenient description and manipulation of the intake workflow, we will use the process modeling tool Protos (Pallas Athena, 1997). A Protos model extends the graphical notation of workflow nets as introduced in Section 2.4 with triggering symbols and conditions on outgoing arcs. The description of both triggers and preconditions we will now give is informal, which fits the illustrative character of this section.

Triggers

The trigger concept has been introduced in Section 1.1. A trigger is an event which is additionally required for the execution of a task. For a transition in a stochastic workflow net, a trigger symbol in its immediate proximity specifies that the occurrence of the trigger is required in addition to the other conditions of the firing rule as described in Section 2.4. We distinguish two types of triggers, which are as follows:

1. The *time trigger*, for example the start of a new working day, the termination of the regular maintenance interval, or the expiration of a deadline.
2. The *external trigger*, for example an electronic document that is delivered by e-mail, a filled out form that arrives by regular post, or a client that arrives at a counter.

Examples of both types of triggers have been respectively modeled at the left-hand side and the right-hand side of Figure 6.28. At the left-hand side, a transition is modeled that expresses the task of assigning intakers to a specific patient. The assignment can only take place at the staff meeting which is scheduled every

Wednesday morning. This latter condition is modeled with a time trigger "Wednesday morning".

Fig. 6.28. Triggers

At the right-hand side of Figure 6.28, a transition is modeled that represents the task of updating a patient file with the medical information received by a doctor. This task can only be performed when the medical file has been actually received. This is modeled using an external trigger of the name "Medical file".

We will use the convention that a transition with no triggers is supposed not to require an external or time event in addition to its normal enabling conditions. In a description that accompanies a workflow net, the meaning of each depicted trigger is clarified.

Conditional Arcs

A conditional arc leading from a transition to a place in a workflow net can be seen as a specification when the firing of this transition will indeed mark this place. Normally, all output places of a transition are marked when it fires. So, a condition on an arc limits the normal behavior of a workflow net. The precondition is expressed textually along the arc. Note that the use of conditional arcs supposes some color to exist within the Petri net. We will only use conditions that refer to characteristics of the case; not to the specific marking of the net. The description of a condition should speak for itself, but will always be explained in the accompanying text of the workflow net. Arcs that lead from a transition to one of its output places without conditions will be supposed to indicate places that will always be marked when a transition fires. An example of the use of conditions is given in the workflow net of Figure 6.29.

The transition "Store and print notice" has two outgoing arcs leading to output places, both of which are labeled with a condition. The model represents the situation that only for new clients the creation of a new patient file is required. For known clients, the existing file can be used to which a print of the notice is added. Note that the conditions "Patient is known" and "Patient is unknown" are mutually exclusive, so exactly one of the output places of the transition "Store and print notice" will be marked when it fires. This exclusiveness is, however, not required for the use of conditions.

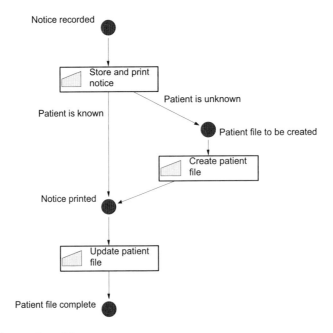

Fig. 6.29. The use of conditions

6.2.2 Initial Situation

In this section we will describe the intake workflow, starting with a verbal account of the followed procedure.

Procedure

The intake workflow starts with a notice by telephone at the secretarial office of the mental health care institute. This notice is done by the family doctor of somebody who is in need of mental treatment. The secretarial worker inquires after the name and residence of the patient. On the basis of this information, the doctor is put through to the nursing officer responsible for the part of the region that the patient lives in.

The nursing officer makes a full inquiry into the mental, health, and social state of the patient in question. This information is recorded on a registration form. At the end of the conversation, this form is handed in at the secretarial office of the institute. Here, the information on the form is stored in the information system and subsequently printed. For new patients, a patient file is created. The registration form as well as the print from the information system are stored in the patient file. Patient files are kept at the secretarial office and may not leave the building. At the secretarial office, two registration cards are produced for respectively the future first and second intaker of the patient. The registration card contains a set of basic patient data. The new patient is added on the list of new notices.

Halfway the week, at Wednesday, a staff meeting of the entire medical team takes place. The medical team consists of social-medical workers, physicians, and a psychiatrist. At this meeting, the team-leader assigns all new patients on the list of new notices to members of the team. Each patient will be assigned to a social-medical worker, who will act as the first intaker of the patient. One of the physicians will act as the second intaker. In assigning intakers, the team-leader takes into account their expertise, the region they are responsible for, earlier contacts they might have had with the patient, and their case load. The assignments are recorded on an assignment list which is handed to the secretarial office. For each new assignment, it is also determined whether the medical file of the patient is required. This information is added to the assignment list.

The secretarial office stores the assignment of each patient of the assignment list in the information system. It passes the produced registration cards to the first and second intaker of each newly assigned patient. An intaker keeps this registration with him at times when visiting the patient and in his close proximity when he is at the office. For each patient for which the medical file is required, the secretarial office prepares and sends a letter to the family doctor of the patient, requesting for a copy of the medical file. As soon as this copy is received, the secretarial office will inform the second intaker and add the copy to the patient file.

The first intaker plans a meeting with the patient as soon as this is possible. During the first meeting, the patient is examined using a standard checklist which is filled out. Additional observations are registered in a personal notebook. After a visit, the first intaker puts a copy of these notes in the file of a patient. The standard checklist is also added to the patient's file.

The second intaker plans the first meeting only after the medical information of the physician – if required – has been received. Physicians use dictaphones to record their observations made during meetings with patients. The secretarial office types out these tapes, after which the information is added to the patient file.

As soon as the meetings of the first and second intaker with the patient have taken place, the secretarial office puts the patient on the list of patients that reach this status. For the staff meeting on Wednesday, they provide the team-leader with a list of these patients. For each of these patients, the first and second intaker together with the team-leader and the attending psychiatrist formulate a treatment plan. This treatment plan formally ends the intake procedure.

Workflow Components

In Chapter 2 we have described the different components that constitute a workflow model. We will identify and model each of these components for the intake procedure as described in some more detail before we proceed with redesigning the workflow.

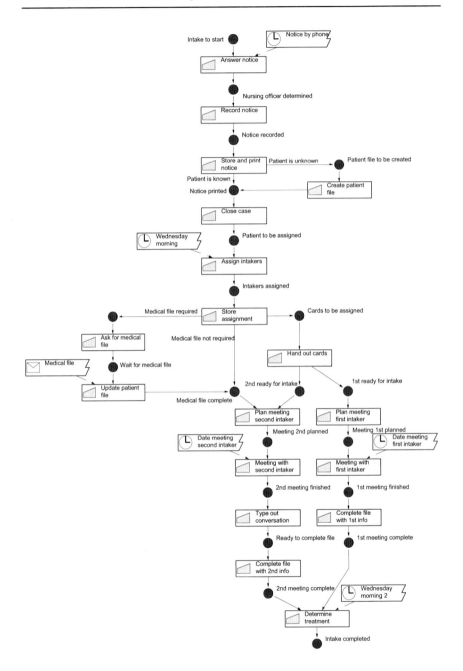

Fig. 6.30. The intake workflow

With respect to the case component of this workflow, we can determine that this workflow is in use to handle all non-urgent notices for mental health-care to people who reside in the region that this institute is responsible for. In a real workflow model that is used for the enactment of the described procedure, at the beginning of the workflow a selection should take place that ensures that only these types of cases are admitted to be handled. We leave this selection implicit.

The routing component of the described procedure is depicted as a workflow net in Figure 6.30. Note the use of the triggers "Wednesday morning" and "Wednesday morning 2". They refer to the same event and indicate that the respective tasks "Assign intakers" and "Determine treatment" have to await the first staff meeting, which takes place every Wednesday.

With respect to the allocation component (see Section 2.2), we can distinguish the following roles:

− Secretarial worker.
− Nurse officer.
− Medical team member.
− Social-medical worker.
− Physician.
− Psychiatrist.
− Team-leader.
− First intaker.
− Second intaker.

These roles and their inter-dependencies are depicted in Figure 6.31. Each role is depicted as a *cap* with its corresponding name. An arrow that leads from one cap to another signifies that each person that fulfills the former role also fulfills the latter role.

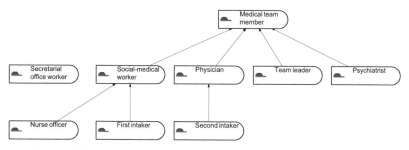

Fig. 6.31. Roles within the intake workflow

Note that roles are not the only important characteristic to classify the resources in this workflow. Next to the different roles, there is also an organizational characteristic which is used to distinguish resource classes. After all, the nurse officer that will have the first contact with the family doctor is associated with the region that the client lives in. Also, the treatment plan of a patient is determined by a *team* of persons with different roles. We will refer to it as the *treatment team*, which consists of the first intaker, the second intaker, the (medical) team-leader, and the psychiatrist.

The allocation principles – which form an essential part of the allocation component – are outlined in Figure 6.32 (see also the introduction of Chapter 5). Each black dot at the intersection of a role and a task signifies that work items corresponding to the latter will be allocated to the former. Arrows between dots show the precedence relations that are in effect according to the routing component. Note that for the special task of determining the treatment plan, work items are assigned to the whole treatment team. This is signified by a dotted line behind this task, which encompasses all roles that are part of the treatment team.

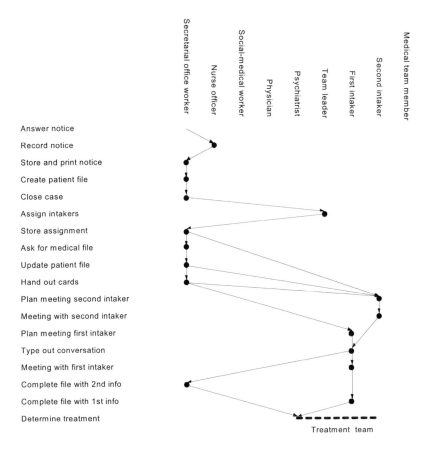

Fig. 6.32. Allocation principles

The depicted assignment logic does not give all the information on the assignment logic in use. After all, work items for the *same* case should be handled by the *same* first intaker and the *same* second intaker. The treatment team that will determine a treatment plan for a patient has to contain the first and second intakers that have talked with the patient also. There are no such requirements for other resources.

For the execution component we will simply assume that a First come – First served discipline is maintained by all resources.

Performance

Within the setting of this workflow, the medical team consists of 16 people: eight social medical workers, four physicians, two team-leaders, and two psychiatrists. Each member of the medical team works full-time and spends about 50 % of his time on the intake of new cases, except for the psychiatrists who spend 10 % of their time on the intake of new cases. (Most of the resources' remaining time is spent on the treatment of patients). The secretarial office consists of eight workers, who work full time. About 50 % of their time is spent on the intake of new cases.

The current performance of the workflow is measured in two ways. As a way of making the external quality of the workflow operational, the average throughput time is taken. For the internal efficiency, the average total service time per case is taken.

The average throughput time is slightly more than 10 working days. On each case, the following time is spent on average:

- By the secretarial office: 46 minutes.
- By the social-medical workers: 65 minutes.
- By the physicians: 37 minutes.
- By the team-leaders: 15 minutes.
- By the psychiatrists: 10 minutes.

Therefore, the total time spent on a new case averages two hours and 52 minutes. This means that the total service time makes up slightly less than 4 % of the total throughput time. Each day, slightly less than 20 cases arrive. By using Little's law, we can deduce that at any time there are on average some 200 new, non-urgent requests for treatment in process.

This concludes the description of the initial situation. Note that we did not give full information on the durations of tasks, the variation of their durations, and the routing fractions of the cases. Instead of merely summing these up, we will present these figures when discussing the effects of the investigated redesign measures. (Some of these figures will turn out to be surprising on closer inspection.) Each unmentioned figure is used *ceteris paribus* for each situation described. Each figure that is expected to change due to a redesign measure is explicitly stated when describing a redesign scenario.

6.2.3 Redesign

We will discuss in this section several scenarios. Each of these is an alternative to the intake workflow. The effect of each scenario with respect to the total average service time follows directly from the described changes or from exact analysis of the workflow model. Changes in throughput times follow from simulation experiments with the alternative workflow design. The reliability of these results is reported upon at the end of this section.

Post

A considerable part of the throughput time in the intake workflow is taken by the wait time for the medical file to arrive by post. On the basis of the *integration* (INTG) and *technology* (TECH) heuristics we consider the alternative that medical files become on-line available to the mental health care institute. (In practice, this should presumably be restricted to read-only access for patients that are indeed reported to the mental health-care institute.) Note that this alternative supposes a considerable application degree of technology: doctors should store their patient information electronically and communication facilities should be present.

By the direct availability of the medical file, the task "Ask for medical file" in Figure 6.30 is replaced by a task "Access medical file" which is performed by the secretarial office. The same time they used to spend on preparing and sending a request letter is now assumed to be required for accessing and printing the patient file. The task "Update client file" stays in place, but it loses the external trigger "Medical file".

The wait time for the medical file is completely reduced, which leads to an average throughput time of approximately 8,5 days. This is a reduction of 16 %. The total service time spent on a case is not reduced.

Periodic Meetings

In the intake workflow the staff meeting is planned at regular weekly intervals on the Wednesday. During a staff meeting two important things take place, which are as follows:

1. For new cases, the first and second intakers are assigned.
2. For cases for which both intake interviews have taken place, treatment plans are determined.

From a workflow perspective, periodic restrictions on activities are rather odd. Additional analysis of the intake workflow points out that the first activity does not really require a meeting context, provided that the team-leader has sufficient information on the criteria used for new assignments. On the other hand, the second activity is indeed best performed in the context of a meeting. This is because of the limited availability of the psychiatrists which prohibits more flexible measures.

On the basis of the *case-based work* heuristic (CASEB) we consider as an alternative for the current workflow that the team-leader will carry out new case assignments as soon as they are due; the weekly meeting is strictly used for determining treatment plans. The workflow structure as depicted in Figure 6.30 then changes in the sense that the time trigger is removed from the task "Assign intakers". Because the information is available to the team-leader to base his assignment decision on, we expect that the original duration of the task also decreases from 5 to 2 minutes on average. This time includes the report of the assignment to the secretarial office. Both the social-medical worker and the physician will no longer spend this time on the case.

The throughput time of an average case will drop by about 2,5 working days, as this is the expected time a new case has to wait before it is assigned (half a working week). This is a reduction of 25 %. The reduction of the total service time is 13 minutes, an 8 % reduction.

Note that a similar result could be achieved by doubling the frequency of the staff meetings (assuming this is possible). For each meeting, the expected wait time of 2,5 workdays drops to 1,25 days, which leads to an overall reduction of the throughput time of 2,5 working days.

Social-Medical Worker

We consider on the basis of the *extra resources* heuristic (XRES), the hire of an additional resource within the setting of the intake workflow. Because the social-medical worker spends on average the most time on each new case, the choice for hiring an extra social-medical worker is made. He or she will exclusively work on the intake of new cases.

The average time spent on a case does not change on the basis of this measure. Also, the throughput time does not notably decrease either. This is due to the fact that most of the throughput time in the intake workflow is determined by wait time – not by queuing.

Medical File

For each new case it is decided whether his or her medical file will be asked for. This information is then requested from the family doctor. The family doctor is also the one who notifies the new case at the start of the workflow. This raises the question whether the *contact reduction* heuristic (REDUC) may be applicable. Closer inspection of the routing of individual cases shows that in 95 % of all new cases the medical file is requested for. This extremely high figure justifies consideration of the *exception* heuristic (EXCEP). After all, not requiring the medical information seems to be the exception.

A combined application of the *contact reduction* heuristic, the *exception* heuristic and the *resequencing* heuristic (RESEQ) leads to an alternative workflow design where the secretarial office directly asks for the medical file after the family doctor makes contact with the mental health care institute. The routine to determine for each case at a staff meeting whether medical information is required is dropped, which in itself does not lead to a reduction of service time. The workflow structure of this alternative is depicted in Figure 6.33.

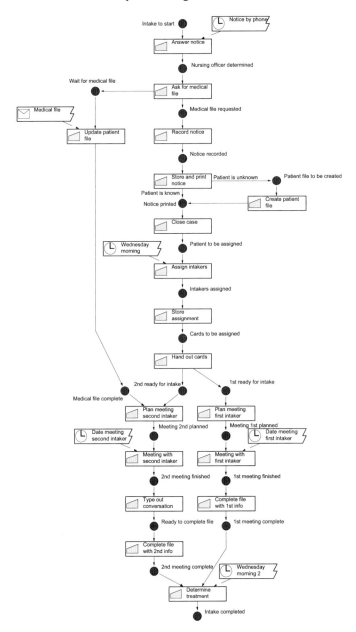

Fig. 6.33. Direct request for medical file

Note that in this case, the exception heuristic coincides with the secondary interpretation of the *triage* heuristic (TRI). The once alternative task of asking for medical information has become a general part of the workflow.

The average total service time increases by one extra minute, as the secretarial office will have to request for *each* case – and not for 95 % only – the medical information. This is an increase of 1 %. The average throughput time is reduced by 1,4 working days, which is a reduction of 13 %.

Notice Recording

Within the intake workflow, the nurse officer records the notice by the family doctor on a conventional form. This information is subsequently entered in the information system of the institute. On the basis of the *task automation* heuristic (AUTO) we investigate the following alternative. An electronic version of the registration form is designed that is used by the nursing officer to record the new case. The information from a completed electronic form will be automatically transferred into the information system of the institute. It will also be automatically printed at the secretarial office and the new application checks whether the patient is already known.

Compared to the original structure of the workflow as depicted in Figure 6.30, the complete task "Save and print file" can be omitted. We can interpret this as an application of the *task elimination* heuristic (ELIM). This elimination reduces the work effort of the secretarial office on storing and printing, which on average took 10 minutes. The task "Record notice" is now assumed to be supported in the way as described. We do not expect significant changes in the service time of this task spent by the nursing officer.

The average throughput time is not notably influenced by this measure. The total service time is reduced by ten minutes, which is a reduction of 6 %.

Registration Cards

The secretarial office in the intake workflow produces the registration cards for the future first and second intaker of the new case, completes the patient file with the registration form, and adds the patient on the list of new notices. These three actions are combined in the "Close case" task. On the basis of the *task composition* heuristic (COMPOS) we question the composition of this task. If we consider the registration cards for a case, it is clear that they are only required *after* the intakers are assigned. Only the addition of the patient on the list is required for assigning a new case. We assume that the completion of the file will be required just before the cards are handed out.

Dividing the "Close case" into its separate parts allows us to put the production of the registration cards and the completion of the patient file in parallel to the assignment subflow of the workflow. This is an application of the *parallelism* heuristic (PAR). We assume that the original average service time of the "Close case" task of 4,5 minutes is equally divided over the three new tasks, but we expect an additional set-up time for each of these tasks of 1 minute. The resulting workflow structure is depicted in Figure 6.34. Note that for routing reasons a transition labeled "Skip" is added; it represents no real task.

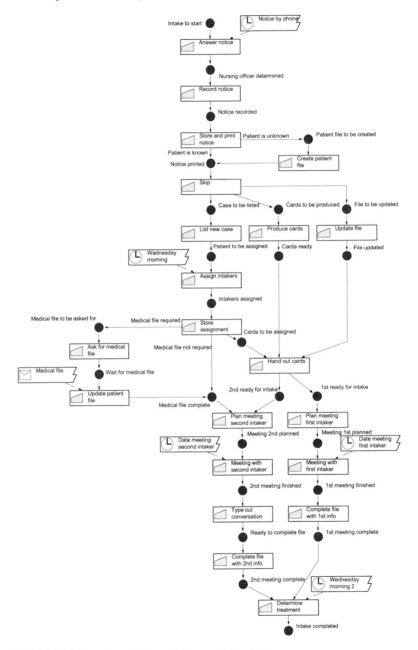

Fig. 6.34. Division and parallelism of the completion task

In spite of the parallelism, the throughput time in this scenario is not reduced. This can be explained from the fact that the effect of parallel executions of the new tasks "List case", "Produce cards", and "Update file" do not speed up the average wait time of 2,5 days for the staff meeting. The service time does increase with 3 minutes, which is a 2 % change for the worse.

Treatment Plan

In the original workflow, the treatment plan is determined by a team of the first intaker, the second intaker, the psychiatrist, and the team-leader. Closer inspection on how a treatment actually comes about in the intake is that the first and second intaker propose a treatment plan, which is usually approved of by the psychiatrist and team-leader. On the basis of the *empower* heuristic (EMP), we consider as a design alternative the situation that the intakers themselves determine the treatment plan. Note that in reality, this kind of measure may not conform to accepted medical protocols. However, it can be envisioned that the treatment plan is only checked by the team-leader and psychiatrist afterwards.

As a result of this measure, the intakers have to meet with each other to determine a treatment plan. It is reasonable to expect that this meeting takes approximately as long as the discussion during the staff meeting, on average 10 minutes. It is expected also that because of planning reasons this meeting is maximally delayed with one day after the last intake interview has taken place. The wait time of 2,5 working days on average for the staff meeting is on the other hand eliminated. As a result, the total throughput time is reduced by 2 days, which is a reduction of 20 %. The total service time is reduced by 20 minutes, because the team-leader and the psychiatrist are ejected from the decision making process. This is a 12 % reduction.

Results

The results of the various redesign scenarios we considered in this section are summarized in Table 6.1.

For the reduction of the throughput time, the "Periodic meetings" scenario is the most favorable one. This scenario was based on application of the *case-based work* heuristic. A cut of service time is best accomplished by the "Treatment plan" scenario, based on the *empower* heuristic. Both scenarios eliminate traditional workflow structures, respectively non-case based work and hierarchy.

The application of the *extra resources* heuristic in the form of the "Social-medical worker" scenario is rather disappointing. It does not speed up the workflow. The automation of a task in the "Notice recording" scenario also has no effect on the throughput time. The important thing that can be learned from these results is that throughput times may consist for only a small part of queue time and for an even smaller part of service time.

Table 6.1. Summary redesign alternatives results

Redesign scenario	Gain avg. throughput time (days)	Gain avg. throughput time (%)	Gain avg. total service time (min.)	Gain avg. total service time (%)
Post INTG & TECH	1,6	16	0	0
Periodic meetings CASEB	2,5	25	13	8
Social-medical worker XRES	0	0	0	0
Medical file REDUC, EXCEP, RESEQ & TRI	1,4	13	-1	-1
Notice recording AUTO & ELIM	0	0	10	6
Registration cards COMPOS & PAR	0	0	-3	-2
Treatment plan EMP	2	20	20	12

The most unsatisfactory scenario is the "Registration cards" scenario. Although it exploits one of the most powerful heuristics available – the *parallelism* heuristic – it renders no result. Yet, the scale of parallelism in this case was small. Actual benefits from this heuristic can be rather expected in settings where substantial parts of the workflow are put in parallel.

We end this chapter with a justification of the throughput time results of the various scenarios. These results have been obtained by simulation using the package ExSpect (Van Hee et al., 1989; Van der Aalst et al., 2000a). Each simulation of a scenario has been split up into 2 start runs and 10 subruns of 20 working days each.

Presented in Table 6.2 are the 99 % confidence intervals of the measured average throughput time for each simulation. For other measurements, this type of information is not given. From this table it follows that the confidence intervals of the original situation, the "Social-medical worker" scenario, the "Notice recording" scenario, and the "Registration cards" scenario overlap. In other words, the named scenarios are no improvements of the throughput time of the intake workflow.

6.3 Conclusion

The former section illustrates the application of some heuristic rules and their possible effects. However, the results were very specific for the case presented. Furthermore, their selection was rather intuitive. It seem that there is a clear practical use for more quantitative and explicit guidance in the selection of the type of heuristics and their expected gain.

Table 6.2. Simulation analysis throughput times

Simulations	Left bound 99 % confidence interval of avg. throughput time (days)	Avg. throughput time (days)	Right bound 99 % confidence interval of avg. throughput time (days)
Original situation	10,13	10,20	10,27
Post	8,45	8,59	8,73
Periodic meetings	7,59	7,66	7,73
Social-medical worker	10,11	10,16	10,21
Medical file	8,80	8,91	9,02
Notice recording	10,04	10,14	10,19
Registration cards	10,05	10,18	10,30
Treatment plan	8,09	8,18	8,26

7 Systems and Practical Experience

We present in this chapter three cases that illustrate the practical application of the workflow modeling, design, analysis, and control concepts that were presented in the previous chapters. The emphasis in this chapter is on the application of PBWD for the redesign of a workflow (see Chapter 3).

In Section 7.1, a case description is given of an innovative application of modeling, simulation, and workflow management tools for the sake of operational control. This application is labeled with the term "short-term simulation". In particular, it is shown how a simulation model can be built on the basis of information from a process definition tool and operational workflow management data. The workflow components as introduced in Section 2.2 are used to discuss the various aspects of the model. The first description of a workflow redesign is discussed in Section 7.2. The actual project was carried out for the GAK agency. The presentation of the case focuses on the technical derivation of a workflow structure from a product specification. This case clearly illustrates how the technical analysis and design theory of Chapter 3 can be put into practice.

The case description of the workflow redesign for the ING Bank in Section 7.3 gives a broader treatment of the application of PBWD than the previous case, highlighting each of its phases (see Section 3.3). This description gives an idea of the various organizational, technical, and project management issues that are typically related to business process redesign.

All case descriptions are derived from actual projects that were carried out on behalf of Deloitte & Touche management consultants during the years 1998-2001. The author was involved in all three projects. Some experiences on the application of PBWD to which the author was only indirectly involved are given in the last part of Section 7.3.

7.1 Short-Term Simulation for the GAK Agency

Before we present the actual case description, the concept of short-term simulation is explained. Traditionally, simulation of business processes in general and of workflows in particular is used to support strategic decision making. Simulation is then used as a tool to analyze long-term effects of certain decisions (see e.g., Shannon, 1975; Szymankiewicz et al., 1988). Simulation is hardly used for operational control, because building a simulation model takes too much time to evaluate short-term effects. However, an increasing number of workflows is executed

H.A. Reijers: Design and Control of Workflow Processes, LNCS 2617, pp. 245-282, 2003.
© Springer-Verlag Berlin Heidelberg 2003

under the control of a WfMS (see Section 1.4). These systems have an up-to-date description of the structure of the workflow and its current state. This raises the opportunity to generate a simulation model that can be used to evaluate the short-term effects of a decision, without building such a model from scratch.

In this section, a case description is presented that illustrates the use and applicability of *short-term simulation*, as introduced by Reijers and Van der Aalst (1999). One can think of short-term simulation as a quick look in the near future, i.e., a kind of "fast forward" button. By pushing this button, it is possible to see what happens if the current situation is extrapolated some time in the future, typically hours or days. It is also possible to see the effect of certain decisions (e.g., hiring additional employees or renounce new orders) in the near future. This way short-term simulation becomes a powerful tool for operational control. In particular, imbalances between work supply and resource capacities can be spotted and the effects of counter measures can be investigated.

Imagine, for example, a company that carries out repairs on television sets. It guarantees its clients that repairs will be carried out within 24 hours. A short-term simulation may indicate that given the actual amount of work, new repairs are impossible to complete within three days. The manager of this company may decide not to take on new orders for a while, to hire extra resources, or to let his engineers work over time. Another option would be to organize the repair workflow somewhat differently to buy time. For example, clients may be asked to pick up their repaired TV-set themselves instead of having it delivered to their houses. Again, the effects of each of these alternatives can be examined using a short-term simulation.

There are several differences between short-term simulation and the more traditional long-term simulation. First of all, a short-term simulation is concerned with the effects of a decision in the near future. Second, the impact of the decisions that are evaluated is limited. Third, the simulation does not start in an artificial initial state but in the actual current state of a process. Fourth, simulation is not used to analyze the steady-state behavior of the workflow execution: there is no steady state because of the length of the simulation period and the dependency on the initial state. In case of short-term simulation, we are particularly interested in the transient phase. Figure 7.1 illustrates the difference between short-term and long-term simulation.

For short-term simulation, the initial state is vital. Because of the short simulation period, the results highly depend on the initial state. The longer the simulation period, the smaller the effect of the initial state.

Before we present the actual case description, we reflect upon the content of the workflow model used for the short-term simulation, in particular on the notion of the current state. We will refer to this workflow model throughout this section as the *simulation model*. Finally, the case description follows which includes the developed architecture that facilitates short-term simulation, as well as aspects of an actual model.

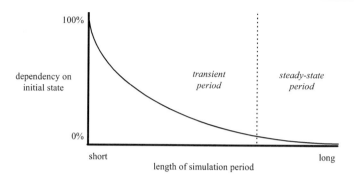

Fig. 7.1. Impact of initial state on simulation results

7.1.1 Current State

Important for a short-term simulation is the notion of the *current state*. It is this current state that forms part of the initial state of the short-term simulation. Obviously, the current state of a workflow execution has a great impact on the dynamics of the workflow during the period immediately following that point of time. There are two parts of a current state that we distinguish: (i) the *actual work distribution* and (ii) the *case characteristics*.

The actual work distribution specifies for each case under processing what the exact work status is. Recall that for a workflow we use a breakdown of tasks to express the work that has to be carried out for each case (see Section 2.2). Furthermore, we have identified work items as tasks for specific cases and activities as work items in execution (see Section 1.1). At any given point, we can identify different phases for the different manifestations of tasks. When we "freeze" the workflow execution, we may distinguish one or more tasks that have already been *routed*, which means that it has been decided that these tasks are to be performed for the case in question. For some of these tasks, it has already been decided to whom the task is *allocated*. In other words, they have become work items. A yet smaller subset of these work items has already been *selected* by either the WfMS or a specific resource to be performed. In other words, they have become activities. Once again, a finer distinction can be made. Some of these activities are already *started*, while an even smaller part of them has *ended* too. In the latter case, a new routing decision may be required. We have depicted the different phases in Figure 7.2.

The second aspect of the current state consists of the characteristics of the cases in processing. Just as a WfMS has to know the characteristics of a new case to determine the initial route it has to follow, the system will need to know the characteristics of the cases already being processed to determine the rest of the route. An actual record of these characteristics is required, as the workflow may have changed the initial characteristics during execution so far.

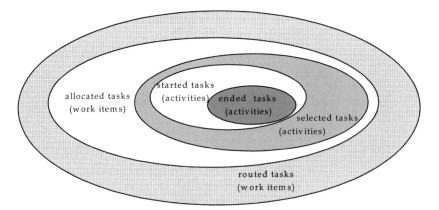

Fig. 7.2. Status of tasks in progress

Information about the current state of the WfMS is most of the time available in the run-time part of the database that supports the system. Usually, there is no direct export facility for this kind of information. Many WfMS's are supported by relational databases for the storage of data. So, database specific query tools can be used to extract the required state data. It has to be noted, however, that not every WfMS presents a clear external notion of its state at any given moment, so extraction may be somewhat complex.

7.1.2 Architecture

In this section we will present a system architecture that integrates operational control and simulation facilities. Our starting point is the reference model as developed by the Workflow Management Coalition (WfMC) (Lawrence, 1997). The reference model of the WfMC distinguishes the enactment service as a central component with several interfaces to five specific other components of a workflow system. These components are: (1) the process definition tools, (2) the workflow client applications, (3) the invoked applications, (4) other workflow engines, and (5) the administration and monitoring tools. These components are depicted in the lower, right part of Figure 7.3. Also depicted at the top-left of the figure is the simulation engine, of which the functionality is comparable to the workflow engine: it enacts the simulation model for the purpose of simulation. The rest of the figure consists of extensions of the model that we will subsequently discuss.

With the process definition tools of a WfMS, workflow definitions, resource classes, allocation rules, etc. are defined. In the depicted extended reference model, there is a link from this type of information to the simulation engine (I). This signifies the use of this information for simulation purposes. Additional information with an exclusive simulation purpose may also be recorded in this store. Usually, the proprietary WfMS definition or configuration file must be converted into a format that is understandable by the simulation tool. This is a relatively simple exercise. We have practical experience with translations of both ERP (e.g., BAAN) and WFM (e.g., COSA) system definition files into simulation models.

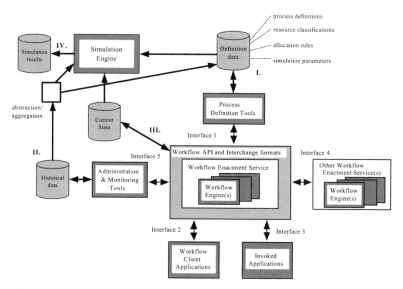

Fig. 7.3. Short-term simulation embedded in the reference model of the WfMC

To obtain historical information for the purpose of a simulation, a link is available from the administration tools – that can be used to access the administration of the WfMS – to the simulation engine (II). Not every WFM system is equally well equipped to extract this kind of data using its standard tools. Usually, a direct extraction from the enterprise system database is possible. Depending on the desired level of re-use of historical information, the data may be aggregated or abstracted from. The results may be directly used during simulation, or they can be used to adapt the simulation model as translated from the definition data. The latter is typically applicable when we use historical information to derive simulation parameters, e.g., for routing probabilities.

When we want to perform a short-term simulation we have to tap into the current information a WfMS uses (III). This kind of tap is not explicitly foreseen by the WfMC, although it can be compared with the exchange of operational information with other workflow systems (Interface 4). Any WfMS will maintain this kind of information, as it is required for proper operation. However, it may be rather tricky to obtain this information by lack of documentation or openness of the particular system. Furthermore, a proper translation of the system's notion of a current state to that of the simulation system must be made.

Finally, to enable the analysis of the simulation results, the results of the simulation may be stored in a separate component (IV).

7.1.3 GAK Case

In this section, the actual application of short-term simulation is described for the *Gemeenschappelijk Administratie-Kantoor* (Social Security Administration Office) or *GAK* for short in 1998-1999. The GAK is one of the agencies that implements the social security legislation in the Netherlands. It handles on a daily basis large amounts of requests for unemployment benefits and occupational disability allowances. Social security laws as well as contracts with employer organizations impose restrictions on the way these requests are handled. Within the workflows of the GAK, many different tasks can be distinguished. These include administrative checks, registration acts, interviews with applicants, granting allowances, etc. Various kinds of resources are involved in these workflows also, such as paralegals, clerks, back-office workers, jurists, etc.

At the end of 1997 the GAK initiated the 'ESPRIT' project with the intent to design a framework to improve the management, control, and support of their workflows. One of the outcomes of the project was an architecture to integrate the following:

1. Workflow modeling capabilities.
2. Workflow management capabilities.
3. Simulation capabilities.

During the first part of 1998 a number of tools was selected to fulfill the capabilities distinguished in this architecture. The architecture, as well as the chosen tools are schematically depicted in Figure 7.4. Several pilot workflows were selected to put this architecture to the test, among which the workflow in Figure 7.5.

With respect to the architecture, the tool Protos (Pallas, 1997) was selected for covering the workflow modeling capabilities. The WfMS COSA (Cosa, 1996) was selected for carrying out the workflow management tasks in the pilot projects. For the workflow simulation, the tool ExSpect (Van Hee et al., 1989; Van der Aalst et al., 2000a) was chosen.

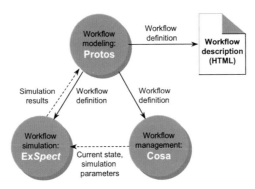

Fig. 7.4. Workflow framework and tools for GAK

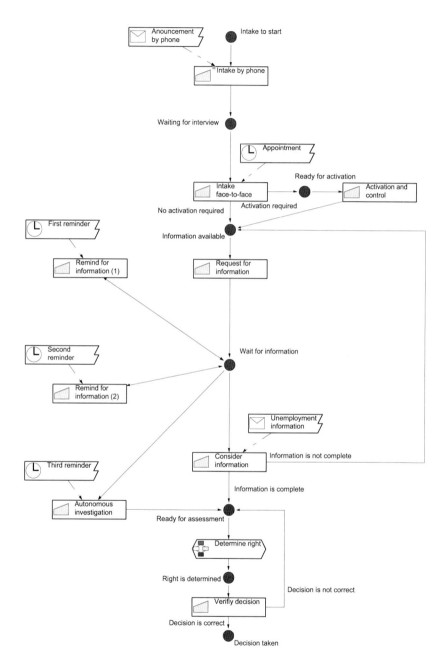

Fig. 7.5. GAK workflow for unemployment benefits

Principal to the architecture of Figure 7.4 is the central management of workflow definitions with Protos. Workflow definition files that are native for the workflow management and the simulation tools can be automatically generated on the basis of a central Protos file, thus creating consistency between them. The 'ESPRIT' project designated simulation as the main instrument to carry out forecasting and capacity planning on the operational and tactical level. The underlying idea is to accurately copy the current state of a workflow, including operational data, to a simulation model. With simulation runs it can be examined how this state evolves in the near future, possibly under the assumption of different capacity scenarios. Results from the simulation runs may in their turn be used to adapt the original workflow definition. Apart from their proprietary form, Protos workflow definitions could also be exported for reporting purposes in an HTML format.

A subproject within the 'ESPRIT' project was initiated to test the technical feasibility of this concept on the basis of the selected tools. At the start of this subproject, the Protos tool already incorporated some basic export facilities to COSA and ExSpect. During the subproject, these export facilities were extended and the other integrating links were built. The integration among the tools was simplified because of a conceptual link between them: Protos models could be mapped onto high-level Petri nets (see Section 2.4), which also forms the basis of both the COSA WfMS and the ExSpect simulation tool.

To illustrate the application of this architecture in practice, we will consider one of the GAK workflows under study of the 'ESPRIT' project. This workflow, as depicted in Figure 7.5, is concerned with handling initial requests for unemployment benefits.

On the basis of a telephonic request, the GAK invites the person in question for an interview. During that interview a preliminary assessment is made on the circumstances of the request. Next, all relevant persons and organizations are asked to submit additional information on this case. When all information is available - possibly after several reminders - the right for an unemployment benefit is determined. [Note that the task "Determine right" has a special notation in this figure. It represents a subworkflow within the overall unemployment benefits workflow. Its is this subworkflow that is being redesigned with PBWD, as described in Section 7.2.]

We will present the content of the various components of the workflow model (see Section 2.2) to show the information that is required for a short-term simulation model of this workflow.

Case

The generation of cases, i.e., unemployment benefit requests, was filled in the ExSpect simulation model by the content of the Protos definition file. Protos allows the end-user to use one of many available probability distributions to realistically grasp the occurrence pattern of new requests. By using the automatic export facility of Protos, an ExSpect model is generated which is parameterized by this information. Although the historical occurrence pattern as stored by the WfMS could have been used to create this occurrence listing, no direct system coupling was used. However, historical occurrences of requests logged by the WfMS were used to validate the estimated parameters of the simulation model.

For actual simulation, an almost complete abstraction from case characteristics was pertained. Although case characteristics have a significant effect on the way actual requests are processed, at each possible moment where these characteristics could have played a role a probabilistic estimation was applied. For example, whether or not activation was required after execution of the "Intake" task is determined this way. As a consequence, the case generator in ExSpect was not required to generate realistic case characteristics.

Routing

The existing automatic Protos export was capable of generating an ExSpect model that incorporates the actual tasks and the order between those tasks. The export of triggers was not yet supported. Although a Protos model can also incorporate the true business logic used to determine e.g., the choice of alternative routings, for the purpose of simulation a probabilistic binomial function was specified for each conditional task. For example, it was specified that in 30 % of all cases a repeated call for additional information was to take place. For this type of approximation, historical information was used that encompassed about a year of workflow executions. The particular information was extracted during the project from several traditional information systems in use at the GAK.

The modeling and automatic export of triggers was tackled by developing specific Petri net patterns that reflect these dynamics. The export facility maps the distinguished event and trigger types onto small workflows that simulate the receipt of external triggers and sending of triggers to the outer world. Such an event takes place on probabilistic grounds in relation to the case under processing. For example, when an organization asked to supply additional information it can be specified in ExSpect that an answer is returned in 85 % of the cases, taking eight days on average from the moment the request is sent out. This type of dynamic behavior was also estimated using the historical records mentioned earlier. No data accompanying the triggers was simulated, because the routing and allocation were based on probability functions during the simulation.

Allocation

The workflow definition in Protos can incorporate a great deal of information on the resources. An automatically generated ExSpect model on the basis of such a workflow definition can contain the distinct resource classes as well as the actual allocation rules in effect. In the workflow under consideration (see Figure 7.5), two resource classes were distinguished. Both the classes and the allocation rules as specified in the Protos model were actually used by the WfMS to allocate work. As the allocation rules and the relationships between the resource classes in the workflow under consideration were relatively simple, the export facility supported their translation into the simulation model too. More sophisticated allocation rules and/or relationships would have required a manual extension of the generated Ex-Spect simulation model.

For the availability of resources within each class, a fixed number was specified in the model for each resource class. This information was included in the automatic export. The information used was based on physical records of the respective departments on the presence of the employees. Prior to an actual simulation of the generated model, the ExSpect user interface supported the specification of an alternative availability scenario. This option is used to carry out *what-if*-scenarios. In other words, with the simulation model it could be investigated what would happen in the short term if the availability of resources changed.

Execution

The resource behavior was, for the greater part, specified within the ExSpect model. For this particular project, a "greedy" behavior of the resources was modeled. This means that a resource takes on work as soon as it becomes available. Furthermore, a First-In-First-Out policy was implemented reflecting the actual policy used within the workflow. (The richness of ExSpect environment would also allow for other policy types.)

To capture realistic service times for each task, specific SQL queries were constructed to obtain historical service time averages and variances from the COSA WfMS database. These figures were used for modeling the service times in the simulation model as normally distributed random variables. A converter written in the AWK language combines an ExSpect model as generated by Protos with these figures obtained from the WfMS history. This in accordance with the architecture as depicted in Figure 7.3. As an alternative to the end user, the default estimations of these service times within the Protos model were also available. This allowed for additional what-if analysis possibilities. Note that Protos offers a wide range of mathematical functions to accurately model these service times.

Current State

Finally, the actual work distribution, the current state, was required to perform a short-term simulation. As the workflow models of the various tools could be mapped onto Petri nets, it was possible to capture and transfer the current state of work very accurately.

For each case under processing we distinguished a subset of relevant tasks. In the first place, this subset contained each task that was already being executed; secondly, it contained each tasks that was already routed. In the terminology of Section 1.1, these are respectively the work items and activities for each case. For the purpose of the experiment, a more fine-grained distinction between the status of work conform Figure 7.2 was not required. We developed one single SQL query that extracts the fore-mentioned list from the database used by COSA for its internal administration. For each activity, this query also yields its start time. On the basis of the query result, a converter written in the AWK processing language then creates an initial state file. It is this file that can be used as a starting point for an actual simulation run. The ExSpect model uses this file as a so-called initial state. For activities, the simulation takes their start times into account for determining realistic remaining service times. For the work items, all information is available within the simulation model to make the proper allocation and execution decisions.

To give an idea of the output that is generated with the type of simulations performed in the GAK setting, we present Figure 7.6.

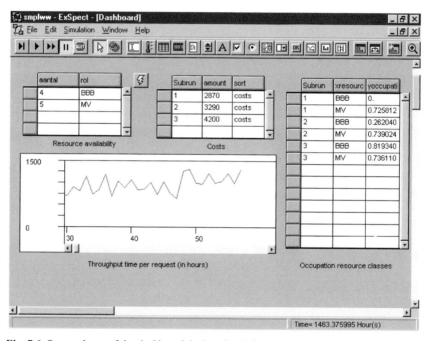

Fig. 7.6. Screen dump of the dashboard during simulation

The table in the top-left corner of Figure 7.6 indicates the number of resources available to each of the two resource classes within the simulated workflow, BBB and MV. It is this number which can be set at the start of each simulation. The table in the middle and at the right side of the screen provide information on respectively the cost per subrun and the resource occupation per subrun. Note that a simulation with ExSpect is split up into subruns to determine confidence intervals for the determined figures. The graph at the bottom of the screen indicates the throughput time for each processed request. For an actual application of short-term simulation, the manager's preferences for performance indicators are the starting point for developing a dashboard as the one depicted.

The subproject supported the view that short-term simulation is technically feasible in a practical environment. In a laboratory setting at the GAK, short-term simulations were used for determining the effects of different capacity planning schedules for several workflows including the workflow of Figure 7.5. Current states and simulation parameters could be automatically extracted from an operational WfMS. This information was automatically incorporated in simulation models, of which the process structure, resource classes, and allocation rules were generated by the workflow definition tool. Field experts have used and evaluated the prototypes delivered by the project. In these experiments, they could at runtime assess the effects of rearranging the workforce.

On the level of the 'ESPRIT' project, the workflow framework was accepted as an architecture for workflow modeling, enactment, and simulation within the GAK. Due to a drastic reorganization of the social security field within the Netherlands, the GAK postponed at the end of 2000 all innovative application of information technology. This with the exception of implementing WfMS's for the operational support of some major workflows. When the several separate Dutch social security agencies have merged during 2002, it is expected that budgets for innovative office work technologies will be re-opened. Short-term simulation may be one of the projects that will be prolonged into actual application.

7.2 Product-Based Workflow Design for the GAK Agency

The method of Product-Based Workflow Design (PBWD) was applied for the first time in 1999 within the setting of the GAK agency (see the previous section). The informational product under consideration during this project was the decision if an claimant is entitled to unemployment benefits when he or she claims to have become unemployed. The GAK has 20 regional offices handling this type of claims. The sizes of these offices vary. The reference office for this project was a medium-sized office of 10 FTE's working on this decision, on average handling a little less than 10.000 claims a year. The procedure to make this decision is a subworkflow of the overall unemployment benefits workflow in effect (see Figure 7.5). The subworkflow was treated as autonomous within the setting of the overall workflow. In particular, the retrieval of information required for the decision making was considered to be the responsibility of the subworkflow itself.

Regulations regarding the unemployment benefits decision are mainly laid down in the Dutch Unemployment Law. The GAK also maintains operational interpretations of it in handbooks. The GAK furthermore maintains a detailed administration of causes for denying unemployment benefits to individual cases, as well as other statistical figures on its operations.

In a period of three months, a new workflow design has been derived for the described product. The main driver for the final design was the GAK's wish to decrease the expected average effort in terms of human labor hours. Opportunities to automate processing steps within the decision making process were explicitly targeted. An additional requirement to the design was that the workflow should be optimized for the application of the case assignment heuristic: the same resource executes each step within the workflow for each particular case (see Section 6.1). The third and last design directive was that the number of contacts with clients should be minimized (compare this with the contact reduction heuristic of Section 6.1).

In this section we will describe workflow design case using PBWD, illustrating how the theory of Chapter 2 is applied in practice. We will focus on the heart of the PBWD methodology, the analysis and design phases of the PBWD. The treatment of the redesign in this section is precise, but not very formal. The emphasis is rather on illustrating the approach without too much attention for formula manipulation. The figures provided and the verbal derivation are nonetheless such that it is easy to verify the correctness and optimality of the design.

7.2.1 Analysis

The analysis phase yielded an initial number of 51 information elements, which were numbered as i1, i2, ..., i51. The earlier named law and handbooks were used as the source for these information elements. Closer inspection of these elements led to the elimination on logical grounds of six of these elements from the product data model (i12, i19, i20, i22, i26, i46). These did not add value to the ultimate decision making. The relations between the remaining information elements are given in Figure 7.7.

Each information element is depicted in this figure as a box, labeled with its identity, e.g., i11. Each incoming arrow of an information element represents a production rule for this information element. An arrow may have multiple starts, signifying all the information elements that are required to apply it. These are the so-called *inputs* of the production rule in question. In the figure, multiple starts of an arrow are joined into one by small black dots. For example, the outgoing arrows of information elements i29, i40 and i48 are joined into one single arrow pointing to information element i31. It represents a production rule for i31 with information elements i29, i40 and i48 as inputs.

Crossings of arrows that are not covered by a black dot have no semantics. For example, information element i25 is not in use as an input for the (single) production rule for i3, although an arrow leading from i25 crosses an arrow leading to i3.

Most information elements are represented precisely once in the figure. There are two exceptions: information elements i25 and i36. These are both depicted *twice* to prevent too much entanglement of arrows. Their double occurrences are indicated by the bold and italic form of their identifiers.

Six production rules are depicted like dashed lines. These six are production rules for the information i11, i16, i34, i40, i42, and i43. We return to their special characteristics in the detailed discussion of the production rules. We will then also explain the technical reasons why the information elements i38, i50 and i51 are not depicted.

From the figure, it follows that from a total of 42 depicted information elements 18 information elements are leafs and 24 information elements are nodes. Furthermore, 32 production rules are depicted. Note that the production rules for obtaining values of the 18 leafs are not represented. It can also be derived from the figure that for some information elements more than one production rules

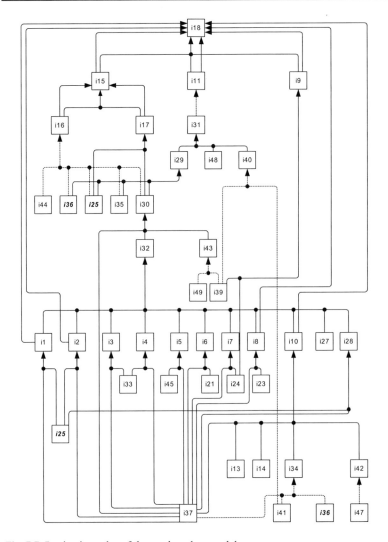

Fig. 7.7. Production rules of the product data model

exist. For example, for information elements i15 three production rules exist, represented by the similar number of incoming arrows. Analogously, the number of production rules in which an information elements play a role as an input can be deduced from the total number of its outgoing arrows. For example, information element i37 is used in 11 production rules.

The top element in this figure is i18, which represents the decision whether someone is entitled for (pay-related) unemployment benefits. There are 8 knock-out production rules: their execution may lead to the determination of a value for the top element after which the processing can end. We will informally discuss these knock-outs here to illustrate the model. A straightforward way of decision making is to check whether the claimant is insured against becoming unemployed (i9), whether the claimant satisfies a so-called "refer requirement" (i11), *and* whether the claimant satisfies a so-called "labor history requirement" (i15). If all these conditions apply, the claimant will receive his or her periodical unemployment benefits. Either unsatisfactory outcome of one of these three conditions will disqualify the claim. The latter 3 production rules are represented by the single arrows leading from respectively i9, i11, and i15 to i18. There are 4 more conditions which may also stop the processing if their outcome is unsatisfactory. These three conditions directly depend on the values of respectively i1, i2, i8 and i10. For example, if the claimant is unemployed while he or she is on a holiday the claim will not be rewarded. This can be deduced from the value of information element i8.

Finally, its should be noted that 7 production rules are omitted from the figure. These are all direct knockouts on the basis of respectively i3, i4, i5, i6, i7, i27 and i28. Although the logical relations exist, an occurrence analysis on the basis of the historical cases showed that it was applied in less than 1 out of 10.000 cases.

The informal description of the meaning of each of the information elements is given in Table 7.1. We will not discuss the meaning of these elements in detail

Table 7.1. Meaning of the information elements

Inf. element	Description
i1	period in which claimant receives illness benefits
i2	period in which claimant receives combined social benefits
i3	period claimant lives/resides outside the Netherlands
i4	period in which claimant does not rightfully live in the Netherlands
i5	period in which claimant is detained/imprisoned
i6	period in which the claimant is 65 years or older
i7	period in which the claimant has legal scruples against insurance
i8	period in which claimant enjoys holiday
i9	period in which claimant is an employee
i10	period in which claimant is unemployed
i11	claimant satisfies refer requirement
i13	date from which claimant lost the right for payment
i14	data from which the claimant is available to accept labor
i15	claimant satisfies labor history requirement
i16	claimant satisfies 4-out-of-5-years requirement
i17	claim is directly following labor disablement benefits
i18	claimant is entitled to (pay-related) unemployment benefits
i21	birth date of the claimant
i23	claimant's holiday administration
i24	registration of unemployment insurance
i25	registration of social benefits
i27	claimant's unemployment is caused by strike/ work stoppage
i28	period in which applicant receives re-integration benefits
i29	refer period for claimant
i30	first day of unemployment of claimant

i31	number of weeks claimant worked in refer period
i32	first week of unemployment of claimant
i33	registration of housing
i34	average number of labor hours per week of claimant
i35	first day of labor history for applicant
i36	day status survey of claimant's labor history
i37	loss pattern of labor hours of claimant
i38	care data on claimant
i39	employment function of which the claimant has become unemployed
i40	employment functions that have been followed up by the employ- ment function of which the claimant has become unemployed
i41	earlier employment functions of the claimant
i42	approved labor courses for unemployed
i43	common first labor day for claimant
i44	list of claimant's yearly worked days
i45	register of convictions
I47	claimant's courses that precede or follow on the loss of labor hours
I48	weeks in refer period already taken into account
I49	labor pattern of claimant
I50	register of special classes of employment functions
I51	claimant has taken care of under–age children

A further analysis of the product data model focused on the following questions:

1. Could its content be specified in the form of an algorithm?
2. Under which conditions is it applicable?
3. With which probability does it render a result?
4. What is the involved cost of its execution?

We will discuss the issues involving these questions briefly before we present the specific outcomes for each of the production rules.

Algorithms

Considering question 1, a far-reaching automation of production rules was very welcome for the GAK because of the expected gain in efficiency. The application of information systems in the prior setting of the decision making process only concerned storage and retrieval. It was expected that a large part of the processing would be suitable for automation. As it turned out, most of the 32 depicted production rules proved to be of an algorithmic nature. In fact, 26 production rules of these were algorithms and only 6 production rules could not be (completely) specified in the form of an algorithm. The latter are the earlier stated production rules for the information elements i11, i16, i34, i40, i42, and i43. However, even the logic of these production rules could be specified in the form of a formal algorithm if the values of their inputs agree to specific values. For example, the computation of i34 (average number of labor hours) can be formalized when the claimant had a constant number of labor hours for each job he or she holds when becoming unemployed. Otherwise, a non-algorithmic production rule is involved which relies for a large part on human judgment. Then, a GAK clerk should decide on the number of labor hours which may be incorporated in the computation of the average number of labor hours. Therefore, for each of the six special production rules, a combined production rule was derived, existing of a formal and a non-formal part. The three information elements which are omitted from the figure (i38, i50 and i51) all concern the decision whether a production rule can be specified formally. In this case, they are not treated.

As far as the production rules were concerned that obtain values for the 18 leaf nodes (not depicted in Figure 7.7), an analysis has taken place of the various suppliers of this information. This selection process involved issues of quality, reliability and cost. As it turned out, 10 of the leaf information elements are directly and permanently available to the GAK itself (i21, i24, i25, i33, i35, i41, i44, i45, i48, i49). This either because the GAK maintains the data itself or because it has access to data of third parties. For example, for each insured employee his or her date of birth is known (i21). No production rules are required for these information elements and no cost for obtaining it is applied. For each of the other 8 leaf information elements, exactly one production rule was specified which is used throughout the project. the source of the information is in all cases the claimant self. The characteristics of the final production rules for each of the leafs are included in the presentation of all the production rules (see Table 7.1).

Applicability of the Production Rules

The analysis of the conditions under which the production rules are applicable (question 2) proved to be straightforward. The law and handbooks were the source for this information. Where interpretation issues arose, experts of the GAK as well as precedents were studied.

Probabilities

Thanks to the aggregated administration of historical cases the GAK maintained, a quantitative survey could be easily executed after the probabilities under which the production results produce the desired result (question 3). Although these probabilities are actually not independent of each other, there were no records of the dependencies among them.

Cost

As far as the cost of the production rules was concerned (question 4), it was decided to express it in terms of the average time in minutes a GAK clerk has to spend on it. For the execution of production rules that could be specified in the form of an algorithm, no cost figures were imposed. Although the actual development of information systems that support these rules is obviously a costly affair, the redesign issue was to minimize the operational labor cost. Evidently, a decision on the implementation of the ultimate workflow design should balance the improved operational labor cost against other issues, such as the IT development effort, training cost, etc. These issues are not treated here.

For the part of the production rules that incorporates a manual part – the 6 "special" production rules and a further 8 of all the production rules obtaining leaf values – actual and standard figures of the GAK were available which were extended with experimental figures. For the six special production rules, the total average cost was determined on the basis of the weighted cost for manual and automated cost. For example, the production rule for information element i11 must be executed manually in 15 % of the cases; in 85 % of the cases there is no labor cost. As the average cost for manual execution of this production rule is 4 labor minutes, the weighted average is $0{,}15 * 4 = 0{,}6$ minutes.

The outcomes of the latter part of the analysis are represented in Table 7.2. Each production rule is listed. The column "automatic?" indicates for a production rule for a *node* element whether it can be specified in the form of an algorithm. For a production rule for a *leaf* element it indicates whether it is available and accessible. For both types of rules, a positive answer to this question implies that it can be automatically made available to the workflow. Hence, no labor cost is involved. For information rules for node elements, it may be the case that it is not completely algorithmically specifiable. Partly handwork is still required. It is indicated by the value "partly" in the "automatic?" column. The other columns are directly derived from the formal product data model.

Table 7.2. Production rules

production rule	automatic?	constraint	cost	probability
(i1, {i25, i37})	yes	true	0	1,0
(i2, {i25, i37})	yes	true	0	1,0
(i3, {i33, i37})	yes	true	0	1,0
(i4, {i33, i37})	yes	true	0	1,0
(i5, {i37, i45})	yes	true	0	1,0
(i6, {i21, i37})	yes	true	0	1,0
(i7, {i24, i37})	yes	true	0	1,0
(i8, {i23, i37})	yes	true	0	1,0
(i9, {i24, i39})	yes	true	0	1,0
(i10,{i13,i14, i34, i37, i42})	yes	true	0	1,0
(i11, i31)	partly	true	0,6	1,0
(i13, ∅)	no	true	0,08	1,0
(i14, ∅)	no	true	0,08	1,0
(i15, {i16})	yes	i16 = true	0	0,997
(i15, {i17})	yes	i17 = true	0	0,003
(i15, {i16, i17})	yes	true	0	1,0
(i16,{i25,i30,i35,i36,i44})	partly	true	5,61	1,0
(i17, {i25, i30})	yes	true	0	1,0
(i18, {i1})	yes	i37 in i1	0	0,009

(i18, {i2})	yes	i37 in i2	0	0,013
(i18, {i8})	yes	i37 in i8	0	0,016
(i18, {i9})	yes	i9 = false	0	0,002
(i18, {i10})	yes	i10 not defined	0	0,068
(i18, {i11})	yes	i11 = false	0	0,079
(i18, {i15})	yes	i15 = false	0	0,21
(i18, {i9, i11, i15})	yes	true	0	1,0
(i21, ∅)	yes	true	0	1,0
(i23, ∅)	no	true	0,67	1,0
(i24, ∅)	yes	true	0	1,0
(i25, ∅)	yes	true	0	1,0
(i27, ∅)	no	true	0,08	1,0
(i28, {i25, i37})	yes	true	0	1,0
(i29, {i25, i30, i35, i36})	yes	true	0	1,0
(i30, {i32, i37, i43})	yes	true	0	1,0
(i31, {i29, i40, i48})	yes	true	0	1,0
(i32, {i1, i2, i3, i4, i5, i6, i7, i8, i10, i27, i28})	yes	true	0	1,0
(i33, ∅)	yes	true	0	1,0
(i34, {i36, i37, i41})	partly	true	4,2	1,0
(i35, ∅)	yes	true	0	1,0
(i36, ∅)	no	true	1,0	1,0
(i37, ∅)	no	true	1,67	1,0
(i39, ∅)	no	true	0,17	1,0
(i40, {i39, i41})	partly	true	0,3	1,0
(i41, ∅)	yes	true	0	1,0
(i42, {i47})	partly	true	0,3	1,0
(i43, {i39, i49})	partly	true	0,6	1,0
(i44, ∅)	yes	true	0	1,0
(i45, ∅)	yes	true	0	1,0
(i47, ∅)	no	true	0,33	1,0
(i48, ∅)	yes	true	0	1,0
(i49, ∅)	yes	true	0	1,0

The exact specifications of the production rules are not presented here, concerning its sheer size (30 pages). They are described in the design report produced for the GAK (Reijers and Goverde, 1999a).

7.2.2 Design

The design of the workflow focused on the average case. Aside from the product data model, the design was driven by the earlier stated design objectives, summarized as follows:

- A minimization of cost.
- A maximal automation of production rules.
- Usage of the case assignment heuristic (see Section 6.1).
- A minimum number of contacts with the claimant.

We will discuss the results of these objectives for our design approach. The objective to minimize the cost puts a high-level depth-first strategy in favor for exploring the product data model (see Section 3.3). The maximal automation of production rules objective works out for the design as follows: all production rules that can be automatically executed are supposed to be available as functionality of yet-to-be-build information systems. As a result, production rules which are automatically executable and which can be performed simultaneously will be put in parallel. This does not affect the cost of the design and it speeds up the processing. Note that this mixed high-level depth-first, low-level breadth-first strategy nicely goes along with the case assignment heuristic, which in its ultimate form requires (human) tasks to be performed sequentially. The objective to minimize the number of contacts with the claimant is made operational by the decision to gather *all* information elements that must be supplied by the claimant as soon as *one* information element is required.

We approached the design by considering one imaginary case. This is valid as all cases will be treated equally. Even if the claimant has not issued the claim already, we will assume a notion of it to make reasoning about it simpler. We will refer to production rules that have a positive labor cost as "manual production rules" and to all others as "automatic production rules". As a start situation, the GAK always holds the information i21, i24, i25, i33, i35, i41, i44, i45, i48, i49. The available information elements are depicted as hatched boxes in Figure 7.8.

No automatic production rules can be performed on the basis of this information. After all, at least one piece of information from the claimant should be available. For example, if i37 would be available then production rule (i5, {i37, i45}) can be applied. Recall that all leafs that are not readily available to the GAK have to be provided by the claimant. So, we may deduce that in the first step of the workflow, all other 8 leaf production rules are executed. Having done that, the workflow execution up to that point has an average cost of 4,08 minutes (= 0,08+0,08+0,67+0,08+1+1,67+0,17+0,33) and the following information is available: i13, i14, i21, i23, i24, i25, i27, i33, i35, i36, i37, i39, i41, i44, i45, i47, i48, i49. The available information elements at this point are depicted as hatched boxes in Figure 7.9.

On the basis of this information, the following (automatic) production rules may be applied without any cost:

1. (i1, {i25, i37})
2. (i2, {i25, i37})
3. (i3, {i33, i37})
4. (i4, {i33, i37})
5. (i5, {i37, i45})

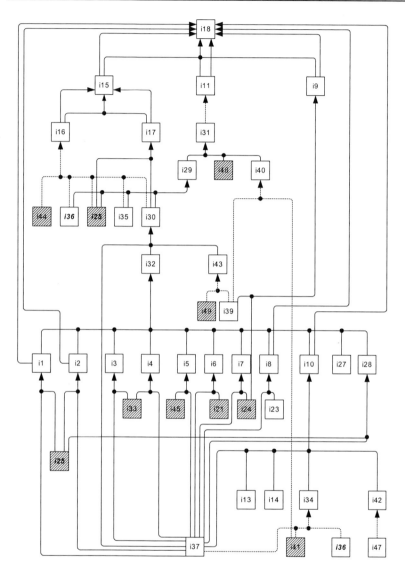

Fig. 7.8. Initially available information

6. (i6, {i21, i37})
7. (i7, {i24, i37})
8. (i8, {i23, i37})
9. (i9, {i24, i39})
10. (i28, {i25, i37})

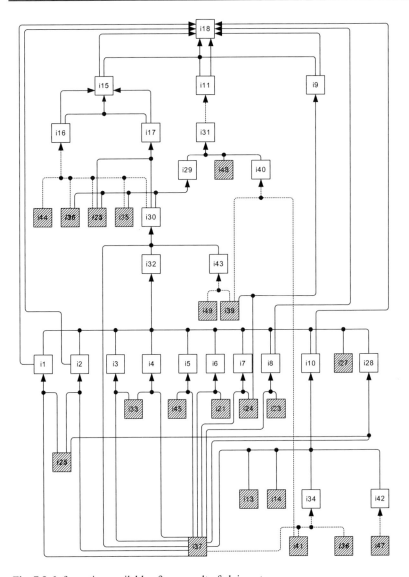

Fig. 7.9. Information available after consult of claimant

The total available information is now: i1, i2, i3, i4, i5, i6, i7, i8, i9, i13, i14, i21, i23, i24, i25, i27, i28, i33, i35, i36, i37, i39, i41, i44, i45, i47, i48, i49. The available information elements at this point are depicted as hatched boxes in Figure 7.10.

Already, we now have a probability of 0,04 (= 0,009+0,013+0,016+0,002) that the processing may end by an additional execution of one of the knock-outs (i18, {i1}), (i18, {i2}), (i18, {i8}) or (i18, {i9}) in case either i1, i2, i8 or i9 not satisfied. So, for 4 % of the cases an average cost of only 4,08 minutes may be expected.

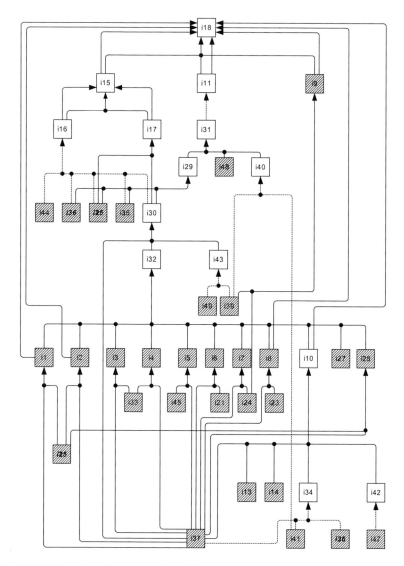

Fig. 7.10. Information after automatic production rules

In case there is no knock-out, processing must proceed. By now, there is no other option than to execute a (partly) manual production rule. We recall that these are as follows:

1. (i11, {i31})
2. (i16, {i25, i30, i35, i36, i44})
3. (i34, {i36, i37, i41})
4. (i40, {i39, i41})
5. (i42, {i47})
6. (i43, {i39, i49})

Would these production rules be totally independent of each other, 6! different orderings should be considered for the rest of the workflow design. However, we can limit the number of alternatives by inspecting the dependencies of the product data model. The optimal choice for a production rule is the one that increases the probability of a knock-out at the lowest possible cost (compare the knock-out heuristic, Section 6.1). On the basis of the product data model it can be concluded that there are two manual production rules which are always required for any of the remaining knock-out possibilities: (i34, {i36, i37, i41}) and (i42, {i47}).

If the execution of (i34, {i36, i37, i41}), (i42, {i47}) and (i10, {i13, i14, i34, i37, i42}) did not facilitate a knock-out, the automatic production rule (i32, {i1, i2, i3, i4, i5, i6, i7, i8, i10, i27, i28}) may be executed. This makes the following information available: i1, i2, i3, i4, i5, i6, i7, i8, i9, i10, i13, i14, i21, i23, i24, i25, i27, i28, i32, i33, i34, i35, i36, i37, i39, i41, i44, i45, i47, i48, i49. The available information elements at this point are depicted as hatched boxes in Figure 7.11.

Again, a choice has to be made which manual production rule must be applied. All remaining knock-outs rely on the result of (i43, {i39, i49}), so this is our obvious next choice. It will facilitate the automatic execution of (i30, {i32, i37, i43}) followed by the parallel execution of automatic production rules (i17, {i25, i30}) and (i29, {i25, i30, i35, i36}). On the basis of the information on i17, there is a slight probability of 0,003 that i15 can be determined on the basis of (i15, {i17}). If so, the probability for a knock-out is also there using (i18, {i15}).

At this point we have to make an important remark. Until now, we completely abstracted from the content of the production rules and its constraints. However, by using this information it becomes clear that the former execution is impossible. If (i15, {i17}) can be applied, i17 will evaluate to true due to the specific content of the production rule. The constraint for using (i18, {i15}) is, however, that i17 evaluates to false. [Note that this is a derivation of the theoretical requirements on the constraint as posed in Section 3.3.] So, the scenario does not exist. Although we could have ignored it, it would not lead to a better workflow. Instead, we are satisfied with the observation that if (i15, {i17}) can be applied, the execution of production rule (i16, {i25, i30, i35, i36, i44}) is superfluous. The obvious sequel in this case would be to execute (i40, {i39, i41}), (i31, {i29, i40, i48}), (i11, {i31}), and (i18, {i9, i11, i15}). This will be incorporated in the final design. Note that the production rule (i18, {i11}) is not interesting, because (i18, {i9, i11, i15}) has a wider applicability at no cost.

Assuming the general case – (i17, {i25, i30}), (i29, {i25, i30, i35, i36}), (i30, {i32, i37, i43}), (i43, {i39, i49}) are executed and (i15, {i17}) cannot – we have the following information available: i1, i2, i3, i4, i5, i6, i7, i8, i9, i10, i13, i14, i17,

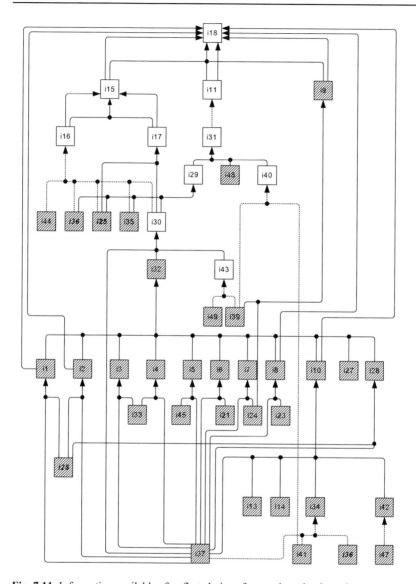

Fig. 7.11. Information available after first choice of manual production rules

i21, i23, i24, i25, i27, i28, i29, i32, i33, i34, i35, i36, i37, i39, i41, i43, i44, i45, i47, i48, i49. The available information elements at this point are depicted as hatched boxes in Figure 7.12.

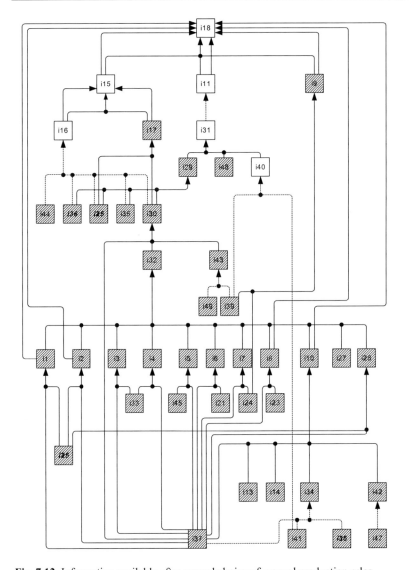

Fig. 7.12. Information available after second choice of manual production rules

Another manual production rule must now be executed. We recall that the only remaining manual production rules are as follows:

1. (i11, {i31}),
2. (i16, {i25, i30, i35, i36, i44}),
3. (i40, {i39, i41}).

Inspecting their dependencies, it is obvious that (i40, {i39, i41}) must precede (i11, {i31}). What is more, the scenario of subsequent executions of (i40, {i39, i41}), (i16, {i25, i30, i35, i36, i44}), and (i11, {i31}) is not a smart one. After all, if (i16, {i25, i30, i35, i36, i44}) is executed, a knock-out may follow making the prior effort to execute (i40, {i39, i41}) superfluous. The only sensible scenario's to order the remaining manual production rules are as follows:

1. (i40, {i39, i41}), (i11, {i31}), (i11, {i31}), (i16, {i25, i30, i35, i36, i44}).
2. (i16, {i25, i30, i35, i36, i44}), (i40, {i39, i41}), (i11, {i31}), (i11, {i31}).

Note that the actual execution of these scenarios would obviously also require the execution of some automatic production rules. We will consider the merits of both scenarios.

Scenario 1. This scenario will start with the subsequent execution of (i40, {i39, i41}), (i31, {i29, i40, i48}) and (i11, {i31}). With a probability of 0,079, the knock-out (i18, {i11}) can take place. With a probability of 1-0,079, subsequent execution of (i16, {i25, i30, i35, i36, i44}), (i15, {i16, i17}) and (i18, {i9, i11, i15}) is still required. Note that the knock-out (i18, {i15}) is of no relevance in this scenario, as the production rule (i18, {i9, i11, i15}) always yields a value for i18 without any cost. The total average cost of this (partial) scenario is 6,07 minutes (= 0,3+0,6+(1-0,079)*5,61).

Scenario 2. This scenario will start with the execution of (i16, {i25, i30, i35, i36, i44}), followed by the automatic production rule (i15, {i16, i17}). With a probability of 0,21, the knock-out (i18, {i15}) can take place. With a probability of 1-0,21, subsequent execution of (i40, {i39, i41}), (i31, {i29, i40, i48}), (i11, {i31}) and (i18, {i9, i11, i15}) is still required. Note that the knock-out (i18, {i11}) is of no relevance in this scenario, as the production rule (i18, {i9, i11, i15}) always yields a value for i18 without any cost. The total average cost of this (partial) scenario is 6,32 minutes (=5,61+(1-0,21)*(0,6+0,3)).

As can be seen, the cost of these scenario's are not very different from each other. The most preferable alternative is scenario 1. After its execution, all information including the top element is available for all cases.

This concludes the design of the GAK workflow. The complete model is depicted as a workflow net in Figure 7.13. The notation of the figure is similar to that of Figure 6.4 with the notations as explained in Section 6.2. Alongside or inside each task, an ordered enumeration of production rules is listed. The production rules are executed in this order when the corresponding task is executed. In italics, the condition is expressed for the corresponding routing of each alternative path. These conditions are derived from the constraints in Table 7.2.

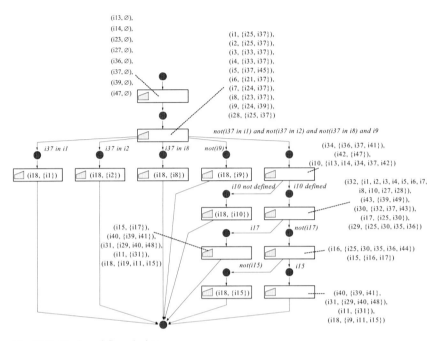

Fig. 7.13. Final workflow design

7.2.3 Evaluation

For the sake of validation, a simulation model of the newly designed workflow
was developed using the ExSpect tool. The workflow design was transformed into
a prototype in the form of an interactive simulation model. Furthermore, the algorithms were specified with the ExSpect specification language. To the end-user of
the prototype four different, predefined cases were presented that referred to real
cases and included real data. When using the prototype to enact the handling of
such a case, automatic tasks were executed by ExSpect itself; manual tasks were
to be performed by the end-user of the prototype using the dashboard facility of
ExSpect and graphical user interfaces build with Visual Basic.

GAK professionals of the Venlo office have used this prototype in workshops
held during the last weeks of 1999. Aside from some minor remarks, the prototype
was accepted as reflecting a way of working that was sufficient and acceptable to
determine the right for an unemployment allowance. In Section 7.3, which describes the application of PBWD for the ING Bank Nederland, we will describe
the use of a prototype like this in more detail.

Analytical evaluation of the validated workflow design pointed out that all design objectives were met by it. In particular, cost was drastically minimized. The
average execution cost of the new workflow design for a single case turned out to

be 14,58 minutes. This is a 73 % reduction of the original average throughput time
of 53,8 minutes of the real workflow. This reduction was mainly due to the high
level of automation within the design. In comparison with the existing workflow
in operation, about 75 % of its operations was automated. To a lesser degree, the
specific ordering of knock-outs contributed to this decrease. As a side-effect it was
observed that for 10 % of all cases no human intervention at all would be required
to determine the right for a claim. In this situation, we can speak of Straight-
Through-Processing or Unattended Workflow (see Section 1.4).

Additional performance evaluation of the model with simulations indicated an
expected reduction of the throughput time in between 32 % and 97 %, depending
on the specific resource scenario. In other words, this part of the overall workflow
which lasted on average 6,2 working days would be reduced to a period of 0,2 and
4,2 working days using the new design. The respective resource scenario's were
designed by the GAK professionals themselves and included various capacity
numbers and levels of responsiveness. Reduction of the throughput time was primarily contributed to by the design objective of combining the points of external
contacts. Note that the reduction of the throughput time was not a primary design
objective.

On a higher level, the PBWD methodology was positively evaluated by the project team as follows:

- The evaluation of the workflow design was positive.
- The methodology proved to be useful to identify tasks that could be automated.
- Intermediate deliverables of the methodology (product data model, algorithms
  in pseudo code, etc.) proved to be effective communication means with business professionals.
- Clarification of the purpose of all operations was attained by linking them to either regulations or business objectives.

On the other hand, the methodology proved to be rather labor intensive. Not
only did this apply to the analysis of the regulations in effect, but especially to obtaining the information for realistically estimating probabilities, durations, etc.

The methodology has been recommended to the GAK agency by Deloitte &
Touche as its workflow design methodology.

7.3 Product-Based Workflow Design for the ING Bank

The second application of PBWD was a large-scale workflow redesign for the
ING Bank Nederland (IBN). The IBN is part of the ING Group, which is a global
financial institution of Dutch origin, active in the field of banking, insurance, and
asset management in 65 countries with more than 100.000 employees. The project
in which we participated took place during the years 2000 and 2001. Its primary
aim was to redesign the IBN's workflow for handling credit applications of commercial parties. The workflow that was to be redesigned is executed at all the 350

Dutch offices the IBN. With this type of workflow, some 25.000 applications for loans and credit facilities are handled on a yearly basis. The project also involved the development of new applications, systems integration with existing applications, and the introduction of a WfMS to support the process execution. Overall, the size of the project team consisted of some 40 full-time equivalents. The project is still underway in 2002, rolling out the redesigned processes and new applications throughout the Dutch offices. Because of the sheer size of the project, it is only possible to highlight some of our experiences with the application of PBWD. We will use the phases of the PBWD methodology as introduced in Section 3.3 as a structure for the case description.

7.3.1 Scoping

The credit application workflow was selected for reengineering because of the IBN's top management suspicions that considerable cost reduction could be achieved within this workflow; earlier projects indicated large inefficiencies in current working practice.

The initial boundaries of the redesign project were subsequently determined by selecting two products out of a range of six similar credit products: the current account credit (RCK) and the loan with fixed interest (RVL). At the time of selection, the two products generated 70 % of the total credit facility turnover of the IBN. After the initial workflow design would be completed for these two products, the redesign of the other products would follow during the project.

Initially, considerable effort had to be paid to further specify the scope of the redesign project. Illustrative for the involved issues is the following further specification of the redesign scope:

– Increases of credit limits on existing RCK and RVL contracts were included in the redesign scope.
– Within the redesign project the workflows would be considered for handling applications for RCK and RVL products *until the moment* that the first parcel of the credit would be available to the client; processes to support the use of the credit facility were excluded.
– The client segments within the redesign scope were all commercial parties, excluding the top multinational accounts and the private banking accounts.
– The primary channel to be considered for the application of credit were those that stream in through the standing offices; all other channels (e.g., Internet) were initially excluded from the scope of the project.

Considering this scope, the redesign objective for the project was formulated as follows:

Realize a substantial efficiency increase of the processes within the offices and operations for handling applications of RVL and RCK credit and shorten the throughput time of those processes by redesigning them from client to client using automation, outplacement, or rendering superfluous.

The "substantial efficiency increase" was not formally made operational, but among the project members and project management a figure of 30 % was considered as a minimal requirement. With respect to the throughput time, an average of 2 working days was thought to be a fine result.

A short feasibility study was performed to assess the applicability of the PBWD methodology. This study focused on two issues, which are as follows:

1. The adequateness of the material to base the PBWD analysis upon.
2. The adequateness of the expected gains of applying PBWD in this particular project.

With respect to the first issue the information specified in the form of formal procedures, circulars, commercial objectives, etc. seemed in general adequate to describe most of the involved product specifics. One notable exception pertained to the authorization part of the workflow: under what conditions would an account manager's tender for a credit loan be authorized for disclosure to a client? As it turned out, this part of the workflow was rather governed by custom than by formal procedure. A special workgroup was established to formulate the company's policy in this area.

The second issue was addressed with the outcomes of a previous project, ZORRO, which identified as a primary source of inefficiency that similar information was entered multiple times during the workflow execution. It was expected that a workflow design based upon a non-redundant product data model would elevate this inefficiency for the greatest part. ZORRO also indicated that considerable time and effort was spent on writing an explanatory memorandum that accompanied the credit proposal. From a preliminary study of the product specification, the need for the memorandum did not become clear.

Finally, a considerable number of information systems were identified that were not allowed to be subject to system development efforts. In other words, these systems should be left unchanged (see the "black boxes" of Section 3.3). The primary reason for these systems being treated as black boxes was that most of these systems were either in use to support workflows delivering other products, that they did not belong to the IBN, or that their content was used by other systems. The most prominent examples were the RR system, which was used for storing client information, and the FINAN system, which includes most of the financial information on clients, for example used by the IBN's general ledger system.

7.3.2 Analysis

The major part of the product specification analysis of the RCL and RVL products was carried out in three months by a mixed team of seven consultants and banking professionals. Considerable effort was required and spent on training all team members with the PBWD way of information analysis and reporting. It proved to be hard for people familiar with the existing workflow to release the existing conceptions on the ordering and content of work. Moreover, business people tended to find the information-driven analysis not always that appealing. Some attention also had to be paid in maintaining a comparable level of detail in the description of information elements delivered by different members. Finally, periodic meetings and inspections were required to ensure that information elements were specified only once.

The initial, complete product data model comprised 580 information elements. Somewhat over 120 information elements were linked to the initial application for credit and the characteristics of the client. Almost half of all the information elements were associated with the tender sent to a client in response to a credit application, which specified the conditions under which the loan could be granted. Other information elements were the result of e.g., checks, intermediate credit calculations, and internal communications.

Initially, a spreadsheet was maintained for the administration of information elements and their specific attributes. When the number of information elements grew, updates of earlier established information had to take place, and project team members were increasingly distributed over several locations, the need for a more sophisticated storage and retrieval means grew. The application Zakinthos was developed in response to this need, build with the Microsoft Access tool. Zakinthos offered general facilities to store different versions of information elements, their descriptions, and the specification of production rules. Also, it included the possibility to group information elements on virtual windows to facilitate the logical design of user interfaces, but this functionality was not much used. The general functionality of Zakinthos was exploited when it was re-used in another PBWD project for the IBN.

After the initial analysis and design phase, the decision was taken to determine the overlap of information element structures of the RCK and RVL products on the one hand, and the remaining credit loan products on the other. This was to determine whether the workflow design on the basis of the initial product data model could be used for handling other credit products. Large similarities were found, which resulted in so-called *generic* product data models. In a generic product data model, information elements are depicted that may be used by a single product or by more products. In the depiction of such a model, an information element is tagged by a label that indicates its application. Note that this way of making generic product data models is not generally applicable. It supposes a large overlap in the structure of the production rules.

A specific part of the analysis phase concentrated on the information exchange with the black box systems. As we explained in the previous section, these systems were to be left unchanged. However, these systems provided relevant information for credit loans, e.g., current credit rates, creditworthiness scores, etc. So, in order to obtain this information to handle actual loan applications it was vital to obtain the information that was required to operate these systems first.

When the analysis phase was concluded, a comparison was made between the information found elements and the information being processed in the existing workflow. It showed that almost 30 % of the originally obtained pieces of information was superfluous, i.e., they could not be justified on the basis of the credit product specification. Likely reasons for this part of information were system migrations, temporary (marketing) needs, etc.

7.3.3 Design

The design of the first workflow version took place during the next two months of the project. On the basis of the product data model, an initial workflow design was derived.

First, a set of workable tasks was determined that each incorporated one or more production rules. At the highest level, the design pursued a depth-first strategy, ordering the existing knock-out tasks in a sequential and optimal way. A certain knock-out within the process was, for example, the applicant's appearance on a black list.

In between the knock-out tasks of the workflow, tasks that were not causally related were structured sequentially when there were strong ergonomic reasons for this and put in parallel otherwise. For example, the respective tasks of entering general proposal data and entering data for the proposal on the specific credit products were sequentially ordered, because account managers thought this be a natural order. However, on the basis of the product-data model there were no reasons to order them. An example of tasks that were put in parallel are the issuing of the order for the credit availability, the actual release, and the reporting to the Dutch National Bank (DNB).

So, at a low level, a breadth-first strategy was pursued with the design when this did not interfere with logical wishes of the workflow executors. A simplified version of the designed workflow is depicted in Figure 7.14. For the sake of readability, production rules and place labels are omitted.

An interesting side-effect of the commercial intent of the IBN, was that there were almost no absolute knock-outs. Rather, when a particular application becomes less attractive from the bank's viewpoint, conditions are tightened on the loan from the applicant's viewpoint. It is left to the applicant to decide whether the loan proposal is still attractive enough to accept it.

One important additional measure was made that had an impact on the design. This decision involved the authorization procedure and the memorandum we mentioned earlier. Empirical study showed that the memorandum was in many cases not used by people authorizing credit proposals. Only for the really difficult 30 % of credit applications, the memorandum was seen by the people authorizing the proposals as adding value. As a result, the formal policy proposed by the special workgroup included a triage for simple and difficult applications. Difficult applications would require an accompanying memorandum, where simple ones would not. This distinction resulted in a similar distinction within the workflow design with a so-called *Fast Track* for simple applications and a *Regular track* for complex ones (see the task "Determine track" in Figure 7.14).

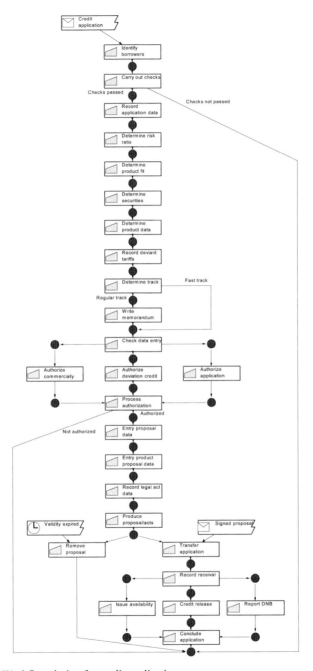

Fig. 7.14. Workflow design for credit applications

The development of the new application, KRETA, actually simplified the enforcement of this new policy, as account managers writing the proposals did not get the opportunity to specify this kind of information anymore: the user-interface of KRETA simply did not include space for it when it was determined that the credit application was simple.

The next stage of the design phase of the project involved the extension of the derived workflow model with the other credit products.

7.3.4 Evaluation

The evaluation of the workflow design took place on several levels. In the first place, the workflow model was checked with the tool Woflan (Verbeek and Van der Aalst, 2000) to detect logical errors. Manual inspections on the ordering of the production rules were performed to check their consistency with the product-data model. The latter activity was rather laborious, which gave rise to the need for automated support.

With respect to the validation of the derived workflow model, the first validation step took place within the project group. Halfway the project, the project group was extended with business professionals from office branches that worked on handling credit applications and had deep knowledge of the existing process and common work practice. On the basis of their comments, stricter orderings were made within the workflow to enhance its usability. A second validation step took place by designing Graphical User Interfaces (GUI) windows of the yet to be designed KRETA system. For each task of the workflow, one or more GUI windows were designed. A GUI window displayed all the information elements that were available for carrying out the corresponding task and also displayed the information elements of which the values should be determined within this task. Although the windows were "dumb", i.e., no production logic was involved, this way of validation indicated a number of information elements (+/- 20) that were not completely well defined, and a smaller number of missing information elements. The design was corrected in response to these findings.

A thorough performance evaluation of the designed workflow with respect to the work capacity took place with the tool ExSpect. The simulation study indicated an expected decrease of labor hours of 40 %. Alternative workflow designs with e.g., different orderings of tasks were also studied, but did not yield significantly higher expected savings. The single entry of each piece of information, the identification of the "Fast Track" and the automated, integrated support to the workforces by the new KRETA system were identified as the major sources of efficiency gains.

On a minor scale, a more focused definition of tasks contributed to the efficiency gains. A simultaneous independent evaluation of the Human Resources task group of the BPR project group on the basis of the new task descriptions rendered almost the same expected gain.

The final step in the evaluation phase was a pilot project for the Dordrecht and Zeeland Districts during the last months of 2000. This project was conducted when the KRETA system was being developed, so the new procedure – including the single recording of information and the different tracks – was used in handling some 140 new applications. The pilot evaluation indicated an efficiency increase of 15 % and a reduction of the throughput time to an average of less than 1 working day. On a more qualitative level, the workflow design was evaluated by the business professionals as workable and agreeable. The throughput time and the qualitative evaluation were highly satisfactory given the project goals, but the efficiency increase was slightly disappointing – despite the lack of automated support of the new workflow. Closer inspection indicated that the ratio of simple and complex applications during the pilot project was 41:59 instead of the 70:30 assumed during the design and performance evaluation. Not only was there a coincidental increase of difficult applications, it was also found that people were rather reluctant to decide that a application was simple, even when the formal definition was satisfied. A considerable learning effect had taken place also. This could be established on the basis of the number of calls to the support desk, which steeply declined when the pilot project continued. Overall, the results of the pilot project were thought to be convincing enough to decide on a roll-out of the new workflow design throughout the Dutch IBN branches and further development of the new KRETA application. These activities have continued throughout 2001 and 2002.

7.3.5 Other Applications of PBWD within ING Bank Nederland

Aside from the major redesign project of the loans and credit facilities, two other applications of PBWD took place within the IBN. We were not actively involved in carrying out these projects, so their treatment will be brief.

Bank Bonds

For the *bank bond* product of the IBN, the PBWD method was applied in 2000. Bank bonds are continuously offered by banks in the form of obligations with a yearly interest payment. Bank bonds have a varying issuing course and are transferable through the stock exchange. The purpose of applying PBWD was to determine whether an already derived workflow redesign by the IBN itself was correct and complete. The project that resulted in the existing design had already started before PBWD was introduced within the IBN. Because of PBWD's successful application in other areas, the question arose whether the existing efforts had become superfluous. Instead of starting from scratch, it was proposed to use the information analysis of PBWD to check whether the existing design was complete and correct. The project was performed by a single consultant of Deloitte & Touche Bakkenist in a time period of four weeks.

All relevant information for the bank bond product was systematically derived from existing product specifications, such as procedures and product descriptions. The partial application of PBWD rendered in an information element structure of almost 200 information elements. A comparison with the existing workflow design indicated that 5 % of these were not distinguished. Moreover, 10 % of the derived information elements proved to be incorrectly specified in the checked workflow design. The workflow design was updated with this information and the project implemented the updated design within the IBN.

This application shows a peculiar application of PDWD. Rather than a cost-effective tool for the evaluation of the outcomes of other approaches, we think that the political circumstances gave rise to this occasion. While some viewed other process design methods with some suspicion during the project as described, others were wavering to disband already reached results. Understandably, we would favor the direct application for workflow design over its use as a validation method when the circumstances allow for it.

Payments and Savings

In 2001 a new design was derived for the workflow that is used by the IBN to handle applications for standard payment and savings facilities, such as private accounts, check guarantee cards, credit cards, and interactive banking facilities. The goal of the project was to realize a workflow that would efficiently integrate the use of several information systems that play a role within this workflow: all kinds of conditions are to be checked when a client applies for a payment and savings facility and, in case of acceptance, these facilities have to be specified and arranged for. The duration of the project was 3 months; the product-data model contained some 300 information elements.

Peculiar for this project in comparison with a pure application of PBWD was that instead of the existing product specifications of the payment and savings facilities being the starting point of the project, rather the information "needs" of the existing systems and the information "supplied" by the forms in use were driving the design. As a consequence, no reflection on the optimality and efficiency of the processing and storage of these systems could take place. On the other hand, this approach enabled quick results as the information elements could be easily identified from system manuals and paper forms. Despite the straightforward determination of the information elements, it was possible to derive a much more efficient flow along the several information systems. Evaluation of the design indicated savings of labor hours in the order of 100 Full Time Equivalents per year, which is a 15 % reduction in comparison to prior practice.

Another interesting aspect was the thorough validation that has taken place of the derived workflow design using prototyping, as reported on by De Crom and Reijers (2001). To validate the design, a total of 5 prototype sessions with account managers and their assistants was held in 2001 at local IBN offices. In each session, an average number of 10 of this type of personnel participated. The workshop attendees had no problem at all in understanding the created prototype. A small introductory talk proved to be sufficient. On the question if they would like to work with the proposed application, one of the attendees responded with: "Yes. This is exactly what we are looking for!". The strength of the PBWD prototype is that is very much looks and reacts like a real application, that it is fed with real data, and that it leads the participant through all the process steps in the new business process (De Crom and Reijers, 2001).

After the prototype sessions the optimal process was modified on a considerable number of points. From the removal of unneeded information elements, the addition of information elements that were forgotten, to the rearranging of steps, groups and fields on the user-interface of the prototype. In general, the lay-out of the derived workflow was kept untouched, but the specific content of some individual tasks was improved.

The current status of the project is that the new workflow design is to be implemented during 2002 at all branches that process applications for payment and savings facilities.

7.4 Conclusion

This chapter has shown the application of Business Process Management in practice from different angles. Both design and control issues were presented. In particular, this chapter contained two case descriptions where the PBWD method has been applied. Both cases indicate that substantial actual gains may be accomplished by workflow designs derived by it. Different ways of extending the approach will be discussed in the following chapter.

8 Conclusion

This final chapter is split into two parts. The first part is a short reflection on the presented research, with a special emphasis on its application area and the style of the thesis. The second part presents the encountered open questions and possible directions for future research.

8.1 Reflection

8.1.1 Area of Application

Although the context of the research is the business processes found within large administrative organizations, some of the techniques and results are applicable within other areas. A good example is the construction of software, for which Component-based Development (CBD) is currently a popular paradigm (Szyperski, 1998). Instead of programming software programs from scratch, components with a well-defined functionality are interconnected. Petri nets and, more specifically, workflow nets – the subject of chapter 2 – can also be used to represent the dynamic behavior of those components (see e.g., Van der Aalst et al., 2002). More importantly, typical logistic constructions found in business processes can be useful for specifying the interaction between components. The algorithms of chapter 4 may, therefore, be applicable to the performance evaluation of software assembled from components. In fact, the assumption of infinite resources (i.e., no queuing) of these algorithms may be less restrictive within this area. On the other hand, time scales in software development are very different to those in business process management, but this should be no real restriction.

It is also conceivable that the concept of PBWD, as explained in chapter 3, is applicable to component-based software development. The desired post-condition of handling a transaction by a 'componentized' software system may then be used as a starting point. This specification can be used to select the appropriate components and to derive a favorable method for them to interact.

Another obvious area in which the concepts of this thesis may be applied is project planning. A project plan that consists of interrelated activities may also incorporate typical elements of the workflow net that we considered.

Finally, resource planning within manufacturing may use the insights that are were gained from chapter 5. The algorithms that were presented to allocate re-

H.A. Reijers: Design and Control of Workflow Processes, LNCS 2617, pp. 283-288, 2003.
© Springer-Verlag Berlin Heidelberg 2003

sources in a workflow can also be used to decide how to dedicate discrete resources in a manufacturing setting.

8.1.2 Style

In this thesis, business process management issues have been handled from a typical engineering perspective. What is characteristic here is that it is not the business
process itself that has been subjected to analysis and manipulation, but a formal
process model. A model is by definition an abstraction of reality. For something as
complex as a business process – which involves clients, procedures, workers, information technology, documents etc. – this means that some parts receive more
attention than others, while some other parts are omitted altogether.

An important aspect that has only been touched upon is the human factor. In
chapter 1 we discussed the sociocultural effects of changing a business process.
We mentioned the intrinsic variability of people's work speed in discussing the
stochastic workflow model in chapter 2. In chapter 6 we spoke about quality issues of a business process from a worker's perspective. However, the human factor
is at the background of this thesis. This in no way qualifies the human factor as
being unimportant in business process management. In fact, the complexity of
human behavior, in general, and in a business context, in particular, is such that
we either do not fully understand it or are incapable of capturing it in a formal
model.

The dangers of oversimplifying the human factor in BPM are evident, as treated
by Sierhuis (2001) for example. In this thesis, the choice has been made to deviate
from unknown or overly complex human factors in favor of a comprehensive view
on the business process. For example, in chapter 6 a simple machine metaphor
was used to model human performance within the setting of a business process.
People carry out tasks that are assigned to them and they perform these tasks
whenever they are available (although their working speed varies). Of course, an
important issue in the mind of some managers is how to make people *work at all*.
So, in a sense, we have treated the human aspect from an overly optimistic, engi-
neer's perspective.

Does the exclusion or simplified modeling of human behavior nullify the contributions of the work in this thesis? In our opinion it does not. Knowledge often
arises from simple models with simple approaches that are gradually refined and
extended, or that lead to insights for totally different approaches. Each step results
in a better fit of theory to reality. For example, the stochastic workflow model of
chapter 2 is a much better vehicle for timing specification in workflows than the
General Stochastic Petri net (Marsan et al., 1984). If we consider the opposite approach to ours – starting by describing reality as precisely as possible – this seems
much less fruitful. For example, by using a completely realistic model of resource
behavior in chapter 5, an analytical evaluation of the marginal allocation algorithms would have been impossible. We would not have gained much insight by
using such an approach. We have always looked for techniques, algorithms, guide-

lines and methodologies that make a practical contribution to the field, although we are aware of their limits.

A last point that we feel is worth mentioning is the computing science influence on this work. This is best noted in chapter 3, which discusses a design methodology for workflows. Finding values for pieces of related information is the cornerstone of this methodology. Obviously, the metaphor of a workflow process as an information processor is used. We realize that this is just one of the metaphors available to look at a business process or organizations (see e.g., Morgan, 1986). However, there is considerable merit in this focus. On the basis of our industrial experience, we have the impression that workflow design is often an intuitive activity. In practice workflow design aims rather at *outlining* than *specifying* the new design. We may conjecture that many BPR projects fail because they lack (i) rational support for changes in a workflow and (ii) precision in prescribing the intended changes. The essence of computing science precisely is to develop algorithms in a formal and well-founded manner. Even though the PBWD method of chapter 3 has its own drawbacks, computing science offers a valuable perspective on many BPM issues.

Finally, this thesis tips to the side of breadth, rather than depth. Instead of selecting one BPM issue and exploring it to its fullest extent, gentle headway has been made with a number of problems. In the next section we will explain that some of these problems are not solved and that many more issues await further research.

8.2 Future Work

8.2.1 Workflow Design

In this thesis, we have basically concentrated on two ways of workflow design and redesign. The PBWD method is a completely new approach to design a workflow from scratch, as described in chapter 2. A list of redesign heuristics is also presented in chapter 6, which mainly originates from existing literature and partly from our own reengineering experience. These heuristics can be used to incrementally redesign an already existing workflow. We will discuss the directions for further work in both fields separately.

With respect to PBWD, the most obvious need for extension is a practical one: the development of supporting software tools. As the analysis of information elements may result in a large administrative burden, ways of systematically filing the various versions of these elements and their relations is highly desirable. Implementations of the algorithms to find cost-optimal plans, as well as depth-first and breadth-first designs, would also be helpful in practical situations. Finally, a tool to check the conformance of a manually edited workflow with the underlying product data model would be valuable, especially when the workflow model grows large. A totally different way of extending the PBWD method is to integrate it with system development methodologies. Software development and systems integration are major ingredients for almost any actual redesign effort in practice. Obviously, the characteristics of the PBWD method can form a solid basis for these activities, due to the central role of data and data processing.

From a research perspective on PBWD, an interesting direction would be to improve the search for favorable depth-first workflows. A rather brute force algorithm is given in section 3.3.3. A more efficient yet heuristic way of finding such a design might be to exploit the level of overlap between the various solutions. In that sense, solutions would be pursued to be carried out closely after one another if the overlap of information is great. Experimentation and simulation may be useful for finding an appropriate heuristic.

As far as the heuristic redesign is concerned, much work still needs to be done. To start with, most of the presented rules in chapter 6 lack quantitative support for their effectiveness. An interesting research direction is to establish the conditions under which each rule is applicable, the exact implementation of the rule, and the expected effects. An empirical assessment of the popularity of these rules could be useful to prioritize research into these rules. On a more abstract level, given some redesign targets, it would be interesting to establish which rules are needed and in which order they should be applied. This step could be the start of an overall redesign methodology for changing existing workflows.

8.2.2 Performance

Part of the presented work focuses on the computation of either the exact or approximated performance of models of workflow processes, as measured in throughput time (see chapter 4). It should once again be noted that the throughput time is merely one of the many performance indicators of interest in the area of BPM. Another important restriction of the presented models is that they do no take the effect of scarce resources into account, i.e., there is no queuing. As stated earlier, this type of algorithm is valuable in the early stage of developing a new workflow. From an algorithmic point of view, the absence of resources can be seen as a trade-off of the permitted very general structures of the underlying model, as well as the arbitrary timing information that can be defined. It does not seem likely that both exact and efficient algorithms can be developed for similar underlying models *with* resource restrictions. The *de facto* limits in queuing network analysis in the form of BCMP networks (Baskett et al., 1975) seem to support this observation. Efforts should actually be aimed at finding useful analytical approximations of the performance of such workflow models.

We also have some specific remarks about the performance algorithms of chapter 4. The first of them was based on using building blocks to construct a workflow model (see section 4.3). An open question is how to determine whether a given workflow model can be composed using a set of well-defined building blocks and – if it can – what subsequent synthesis steps are needed. The answer to this question would be of considerable practical value. It may result in a set of analyzable workflow nets that are not constructed by iteratively applying the building blocks. The addition of other building blocks to the ones already presented is another obvious extension. The workflow patterns as presented by Kiepuszewski et al. (2001) may be a source of inspiration for such new building blocks. Furthermore, in the presented iteration building block, the use of Chebyshev's inequality may be replaced by a sharper criterion. Finally, the use of discrete time enabled the use of the efficient Fast Fourier Transform (Appendix B). If continuous time is applied to specify the delays within the workflow nets, it will be no straightforward matter to find an efficient alternative. One way of dealing with this issue may be to exploit the properties of Phase-Type distributions, similar to the efforts of Cumani (1985).

The most obvious extension of the analysis of performance bounds (see section 4.4), is to determine the precision of the computed bounds. We have already indicated some of the factors that influence this precision in section 4.4.3.

8.2.3 Resources

In the introduction of chapter 5, we described the various aspects of the allocation component of a workflow model. We addressed only a single aspect in the remainder of that chapter, the proper allocation of resources to minimize the throughput time of the workflow. There are two important directions for further research. The first is to search for algorithms that may be helpful in facing this separate issue with a *wider* applicability than the algorithms presented in sections 5.2 and 5.3. One idea would be to exploit the maximal level of concurrency in a workflow to decide on the number of resources that are allocated simultaneously. This would be much less efficient than the marginal allocation algorithm, but it would circumvent the problem of the counter example of section 5.3.3. In this example, the effect of adding an extra resource to only one of the two concurrent parts of the workflow did not speed up the entire process. From the experimentation with the workbench, we also learned the relative effect of the marginal allocation algorithm. When queuing time accounts for only a small part of the overall throughput time (e.g., because of lengthy communications with the outer world) another approach is required. The effectiveness of the presented allocation algorithms under more realistic conditions is also of interest. For example, important restrictions in effect in chapter 5 are that each task is carried out by at most one class of resources and that a resource is part of at most one resource class. In reality, people work on more than one task in a workflow, and even in multiple workflow processes.

The second direction for further research is given by the other aspects of the allocation component. An open question is how organizations should define the boundaries between resource classes, and how they should choose the right allocation principles. In the practice of workflow management, the facilities of WfMS's in this area are hardly exploited. Some WfMS's incorporate ample facilities for sophisticated allocation principles. We may conjecture that the neglect of this functionality is caused by the limited insight into their effects. Similarly, the discipline that resources may use to order the work that is allocated to them is not investigated well in the area of workflows (e.g., First-In-First-Out, Earliest-Due-

Date, etc.). Much inspiration can be derived from existing manufacturing knowledge, for both the allocation principles and ordering disciplines.

8.2.4 Other Workflow Issues

Even if we only consider workflows, BPM is broader than the areas that have been dealt with in the previous chapters. Without claiming completeness, we will briefly consider some other interesting issues at the end of this thesis. A large portion of research efforts in the field of workflow management is currently directed at handling the dynamics of a workflow execution. In particular, different compromises are pursued between supporting a standardized way of working, on the one hand, and deviating from this standard in the case of exceptions, on the other hand. Both formal and practical ways of dealing with this *flexibility* issue are emerging (e.g., Agostini and De Michelis, 2000; Van der Aalst and Berens, 2001).

In addition to flexibility, verification of workflows is another hot topic. This area of research focuses on answering the question of whether a given workflow model agrees with some formal notion of correctness, such as the soundness criterion (Definition 2.14). A very obvious gap in the functionality of existing WfMS's is the absence of such checks, with obvious practical consequences. Research in the area of verification and correction has been carried out by e.g., Verbeek et al. (2001) and Dehnert (2002).

In the past few years, attention has also been moving away from workflows within a single organization towards inter-organizational workflows (e.g., Grefen et al., 2001; Lazcano et al., 2001). It is apparent that business processes do not exist in isolation. For example, a large part of the throughput time of workflows in practice consists of wait time for external events. An important issue is how to ensure that workflows cooperating across different organizations yield correct and efficient results. Future research could be aimed at predicting and improving the performance of inter-organizational workflows, e.g., by restructuring workflows in such a way that wait times for external events can be reduced.

Yet another direction that is receiving more attention is empirical research in the area of workflow management. A joint effort by the Technische Universiteit Eindhoven and Deloitte & Touche Bakkenist is currently investigating the effects of workflow management technology in practice (Molenaar, 2002). Logistic parameters such as throughput time, resource utilization, and service time are measured within approximately ten Dutch service organizations, both before and after workflow implementations. From an analysis and comparison of these outcomes, we hope to deduce the effectiveness of the workflow technology itself. Aside from the scientific light this may shed on the (presumed) advantages of workflow technology, this type of research may also help to unleash the true power of workflow technology in business.

A The Bottom-Level Workflow Model

The workflow model as introduced in Definition 3.3 in Section 3.3 specifies on an abstract level what a workflow design looks like. It is an outline of the ordering pattern of production rules. Its attractivity lies in its compact form and explanatory power to end-users. This appendix describes the bottom-level workflow model.

A bottom-level workflow model may be derived from a workflow model and the product-data model it conforms to (Definition 3.4). Its primary purpose is the specification of the exact semantics of the workflow model. In other words, the bottom-level workflow model makes the workflow model operational. Its secondary use is that it allows for automated support for execution and evaluation purposes. An intermediate workflow model – the so-called stretched workflow model – is presented to partition the transformation of a model into a bottom-level model in two manageable parts. The different models are depicted in Figure A.1.

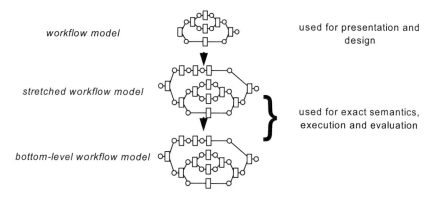

workflow model — used for presentation and design

stretched workflow model

bottom-level workflow model — used for exact semantics, execution and evaluation

Fig. A.1. Workflow models in design

We recall the semantics of the workflow model, as informally described in Section 3.3. If a transition in a workflow model to which a production rule (p, cs) is associated fires, this firing should be interpreted as an application of the production rule if at the time of firing the following is true:

1. The constraint for (p, cs) holds.
2. The values for each of the information elements in cs are known.
3. No value for p is already known.

H.A. Reijers: Design and Control of Workflow Processes, LNCS 2617, pp. 289-302, 2003.
© Springer-Verlag Berlin Heidelberg 2003

4. No value for the information element <u>top</u> is already known.

5. No task to which the production rule (p, cs) is associated has already fired.

In all other cases, the production rule (p, cs) is *not* applied. In other words, although the transition fires, the production rule is skipped.

Furthermore, when a production rule is applied there is a probability of *prob(p, cs)* that it is successful, and a probability of 1- *prob(p, cs)* that it is not. If the production rule (p, cs) rule is successfully applied, a value for p becomes known. Initially, no values of information elements are known at all.

The bottom-level workflow model enforces this behavior by modeling the separate states and dependencies in a classical Petri net way. It would also have been possible to use a High-level Petri net formalism to model a bottom-level model. The availability of information elements, for example, would then be modeled as the color of the tokens in the net. We prefer, however, the Stochastic Workflow net which we have defined in Section 2.4. The use of the Stochastic Workflow net enables us to use the already defined stochastic and timing mechanisms of this net. Also, standard classical Petri net analysis methods are available to evaluate the underlying workflow net of the Stochastic Workflow net which is a classical Petri net. Lastly, the semantic of the bottom-level workflow model is almost totally defined by its graphical presentation. The disadvantage of our choice is that a bottom-level workflow model may become rather large.

We allow for one particular High-level Petri net construct in the bottom-level workflow model, the *precondition*. The incorporation of preconditions enables a meaningful structural analysis of the bottom-level workflow model. In non-trivial practical cases, it will be hard to model all different values of the preconditions used in a product-data model as classical Petri net places. Even if this would be possible, structural analysis becomes awkward because of the resulting complexity.

Note that if a transition becomes enabled in a Stochastic Workflow net, the probability that it will fire is determined by its weight relative to that of other transitions that are enabled at the same time state (see Definition 2.19). By the extension with preconditions, the firing probability condition of a transition is strengthened by requiring also that its precondition should evaluate to true. Although it is possible to give a formal definition of such a Petri net, we believe that at this place it would take the attention too far away from the subject of designing a workflow. We will return to the specific consequences of adding preconditions when we want to determine classical Petri net properties of the bottom-level workflow model.

The formal derivation of a bottom-level workflow model from a workflow model takes place in two steps. Firstly, a so-called stretched workflow model is derived that reveals the behavior of the workflow model without any timing or probabilities. Secondly, the stochastic properties are added to this model, which completes the translation.

For the stretched workflow model we will start with its formal definition. Next, we will explain the various part of this definition. Finally, we will illustrate the notion of a stretched workflow model with an example.

Definition A.1   (Stretched workflow model). If PM = (P, T, R, *prod*) is a workflow model that conforms to the extended product data model (*D, C, pre, F, constr, cst, flow, prob*) then the stretched workflow model PM' = (P', T', R', *prod*) is defined as follows, using the following abbreviations:

- $T^* = \{\, t \in T \mid prod(t) \in F \,\}$ (transitions with a production rule not equal to *skip*}

- $F^* = \bigcup_{t \in T^*} \{prod(t)\}$ (all production rules in use)

- $D^* = \{ d \in D \mid \exists (p,cs) \in F^* : (d = p \vee d \in cs) \}$ (all used information elements)

- $C^* = \left(\bigcup_{t \in T^*} \{constr(t)\} \right)$ (all used constraints)

The set P' of places of PM is defined by:

- $P_1 = \{\, q_{(p,cs)} \mid (p,\,cs) \in F^* \,\}$ (positive places of production rules)

- $P_2 = \{\, \overline{q}_{(p,cs)} \mid (p,\,cs) \in F^* \,\}$ (negative places of production rules)

- $P_3 = \{\, q_d \mid d \in D^* \,\}$ (positive places of information elements)

- $P_4 = \{\, \overline{q}_d \mid d \in D^* \,\}$ (negative places of information elements)

- $P_5 = \{\, q_t^{app} \mid t \in T^* \,\}$ (to indicate that the rule associated with *t* can be applied)

- $P_6 = \{\, q_t^{suc} \mid t \in T^* \,\}$ (to indicate that the rule associated with *t* is successfully applied)

- $P_7 = \{\, q_t^{fin} \mid t \in T^* \,\}$ (to indicate that the rule associated with *t* is finished)

- $P' = \{i^{init}\} \cup P \cup \bigcup_{n=1}^{7} P_n$

The set of transitions T' is defined by:

- $T_1 = \{\, \overline{u}_{t,\overline{q}_d} \mid t \in T^* \wedge d \in D^* \wedge$

   $\exists (p,cs) \in F^* : prod(t) = (p,cs) \wedge d \in cs \,\}$ (transitions for each missing input elements)

- $T_2 = \{\, \overline{u}_{t,(p,cs)} \mid t \in T^* \wedge (p,cs) \in F^* \wedge prod(t) = (p,cs) \,\}$ (transitions for already applied production rules)

- $T_3 = \{\, \overline{u}_{t,q_p} \mid t$

   $\in T^* \wedge p \in D^* \wedge \exists (d,cs) \in F^* : prod(t) = (d,cs) \wedge d = p \,\}$ (transitions for known output elements)

- $T_4 = \{\, \overline{u}_{t,q_{top}} \mid t \in T^* \wedge \exists (p,cs) \in F^* : prod(t) = (p,cs) \wedge p \neq \underline{top} \,\}$ (transitions for the case that the top element is already known)

- $T_5 = \{\, \bar{u}_t^{con} \mid t \in$
  $T^* \wedge \exists (p, cs) \in F^*, c \in C^* : prod(t) = (p, cs) \wedge c = constr(p, cs)\,\}$ (transitions for the case that the constraint is not satisfied)
- $T_6 = \{\, u_{t,n} \mid t \in T^* \wedge 1 \le n \le 5\,\}$ (transitions used for attempting to apply a production rule)
- $T' = \{t^{init}\} \cup T \cup \bigcup\limits_{n=1}^{6} T_n$

Relations R' are defined by:

- $R_1 = \{(q, \bar{u}_t^{con}) \mid (q, t) \in R \wedge q \ne i\}$
- $R_2 = \{(i^{init}, \bar{u}_t^{con}) \mid (i, t) \in R\}$
- $R_3 = \{(q_d, \bar{u}_t^{con})$
  $\mid t \in T^* \wedge d \in D^* \wedge \exists (p, cs) \in F^* : prod(t) = (p, cs) \wedge d \in cs\}$
- $R_4 = \{(\bar{u}_t^{con}, q) \mid (t, q) \in R\}$
- $R_5 = R_3^{-1}$
- $R_6 = \{(q, \bar{u}_{t,\bar{q}_d}) \mid (q, t) \in R \wedge d \in D^* \wedge q \ne i \wedge$
  $\exists (p, cs) \in F^* : prod(t) = (p, cs) \wedge d \in cs\}$
- $R_7 = \{(i^{init}, \bar{u}_{t,\bar{q}_d}) \mid$
  $(i, t) \in R \wedge d \in D^* \wedge \exists (p, cs) \in F^* : prod(t) = (p, cs) \wedge d \in cs\}$
- $R_8 = \{(q_d, \bar{u}_{t,\bar{q}_d}) \mid$
  $t \in T^* \wedge d \in D^* \wedge \exists (p, cs) \in F^* : prod(t) = (p, cs) \wedge d \in cs\}$
- $R_9 = \{(\bar{u}_{t,\bar{q}_d}, q) \mid$
  $(t, q) \in R \wedge d \in D^* \wedge \exists (p, cs) \in F^* : prod(t) = (p, cs) \wedge d \in cs\}$
- $R_{10} = R_8^{-1}$
- $R_{11} = \{(q, \bar{u}_{t,(p,cs)}) \mid$
  $(q, t) \in R \wedge (p, cs) \in F^* \wedge prod(t) = (p, cs) \wedge q \ne i\}$
- $R_{12} = \{(i^{init}, \bar{u}_{t,(p,cs)}) \mid (i, t) \in R \wedge (p, cs) \in F^* \wedge prod(t) = (p, cs)\}$
- $R_{13} = \{(q_{(p,cs)}, \bar{t}_{u,(p,cs)}) \mid t \in T^* \wedge (p, cs) \in F^* \wedge prod(t) = (p, cs)\}$
- $R_{14} = \{(\bar{u}_{t,(p,cs)}, q) \mid (t, q) \in R \wedge (p, cs) \in F^* \wedge prod(t) = (p, cs)\}$
- $R_{15} = R_{13}^{-1}$

- $R_{16} =$
  $\{(q, \overline{u_{t,q_p}}) | (q,t) \in R \wedge p \in D^* \wedge q \neq i \wedge$
  $\exists (d,cs) \in F^* : prod(t) = (d,cs) \wedge d = p \}$
- $R_{17} = \{(i^{init}, \overline{u_{t,q_p}}) |$
  $(i,t) \in R \wedge p \in D^* \wedge \exists (d,cs) \in F^* : prod(t) = (d,cs) \wedge d = p \}$
- $R_{18} = \{(q_p, \overline{u_{t,q_p}}) |$
  $t \in T^* \wedge p \in D^* \wedge \exists (d,cs) \in F^* : prod(t) = (d,cs) \wedge d = p \}$
- $R_{19} = \{(\overline{u_{t,q_p}}, q) |$
  $(t,q) \in R \wedge p \in D^* \wedge \exists (d,cs) \in F^* : prod(t) = (d,cs) \wedge d = p \}$
- $R_{20} = R_{18}^{-1}$
- $R_{21} = \{(q, \overline{u_{t,q_{top}}}) |$
  $(q,t) \in R \wedge q \neq i \wedge \exists (p,cs) \in F^* : prod(t) = (p,cs) \wedge p \neq \underline{top} \}$
- $R_{22} = \{(i^{init}, \overline{u_{t,q_{top}}}) |$
  $(i,t) \in R \wedge \exists (p,cs) \in F^* : prod(t) = (p,cs) \wedge p \neq \underline{top} \}$
- $R_{23} = \{(q_{top}, \overline{u_{t,q_{top}}}) |$
  $t \in T^* \wedge \exists (p,cs) \in F^* : prod(t) = (p,cs) \wedge p \neq \underline{top} \}$
- $R_{24} = \{(\overline{u_{t,q_{top}}}, q) |$
  $(t,q) \in R \wedge \exists (p,cs) \in F^* : prod(t) = (p,cs) \wedge p \neq \underline{top} \}$
- $R_{25} = R_{23}^{-1}$
- $R_{26} = \{(q, u_{t,1}) | (q,t) \in R \wedge q \neq i \}$
- $R_{27} = \{(i^{init}, u_{t,1}) | (i,t) \in R \}$
- $R_{28} = \{(q_d, u_{t,1}) |$
  $t \in T^* \wedge d \in D^* \wedge \exists (p,cs) \in F^* : prod(t) = (p,cs) \wedge d \in cs \}$
- $R_{29} = \{(\overline{q_{(p,cs)}}, u_{t,1}) | t \in T^* \wedge (p,cs) \in F^* \wedge prod(t) = (p,cs) \}$
- $R_{30} = \{(\overline{q_p}, u_{t,1}) |$
  $t \in T^* \wedge p \in D^* \wedge \exists (d,cs) \in F^* : prod(t) = (d,cs) \wedge d = p \}$
- $R_{31} = \{(\overline{q_{top}}, u_{t,1}) |$
  $t \in T^* \wedge \exists (p,cs) \in F^* : prod(t) = (p,cs) \wedge p \neq \underline{top} \}$
- $R_{32} = \{(u_{t,1}, q_{(p,cs)}) | t \in T^* \wedge (p,cs) \in F^* \wedge prod(t) = (p,cs) \}$
- $R_{33} = \{(u_{t,1}, q_t^{app}) | t \in T^* \}$

- $R_{34} = R_{28}^{-1}$
- $R_{35} = R_{30}^{-1}$
- $R_{36} = R_{31}^{-1}$
- $R_{37} = \{(q_t^{app}, t) \mid t \in T^*\}$
- $R_{38} = \{(t, q_t^{suc}) \mid t \in T^*\}$
- $R_{39} = \{(q_t^{app}, u_{t,2}) \mid t \in T^*\}$
- $R_{40} = \{(u_{t,2}, q_t^{fin}) \mid t \in T^*\}$
- $R_{41} = \{(q_t^{suc}, u_{t,3} \mid t \in T^*\}$
- $R_{42} = \{(q_p, u_{t,3}) \mid$
  $t \in T^* \wedge p \in D^* \wedge \exists (d, cs) \in F^* : prod(t) = (p, cs) \wedge d = p\}$
- $R_{43} = \{(u_{t,3}, q_t^{fin}) \mid t \in T^*\}$
- $R_{44} = R_{42}^{-1}$
- $R_{45} = \{(q_t^{suc}, u_{t,4} \mid t \in T^*\}$
- $R_{46} = \{(\overline{q}_p, u_{t,4} \mid$
  $t \in T^* \wedge p \in D^* \wedge \exists (d, cs) \in F^* : prod(t) = (d, cs) \wedge d = p\}$
- $R_{47} = \{(u_{t,4}, q_p) \mid$
  $t \in T^* \wedge p \in D^* \wedge \exists (d, cs) \in F^* : prod(t) = (d, cs) \wedge d = p\}$
- $R_{48} = \{(u_{t,4}, q_t^{fin}) \mid t \in T^*\}$
- $R_{49} = \{(q_t^{fin}, u_{t,5}) \mid t \in T^*\}$
- $R_{50} = \{(u_{t,5}, q) \mid (t, q) \in R\}$
- $R_{51} = \{(q, t) \mid (q, t) \in R \wedge t \in T \setminus T^* \wedge q \neq i\}$
- $R_{52} = \{(i^{init}, t) \mid (i, t) \in R \wedge t \in T \setminus T^*\}$
- $R_{53} = \{(t, q) \mid (t, q) \in R \wedge t \in T \setminus T^*\}$
- $R_{54} = \{(t^{init}, \overline{q}_d) \mid d \in D^*\}$
- $R_{55} = \{(t^{init}, \overline{q}_{(p,cs)}) \mid (p, cs) \in F^*\}$
- $R' = \{(i, t^{init}), (t^{init}, i^{init})\} \cup \bigcup_{n=1}^{55} R_n$

The function *prod'* is defined by:
- *prod'*: $T' \rightarrow F \cup \{skip\}$ such that for $t \in T'$,
  $$prod'(t) = \begin{cases} prod(t), & \text{if } t \in T, \\ skip, & \text{if } t \notin T. \end{cases}$$

A stretched workflow model maintains a detailed administration about the information elements and production rules. For each information element d that is in fact used (D^*), there is a place that signifies the existence of a value for d (P_3) – the positive place of d – and a place that indicates the lack of such a value (P_4) – the negative place of d. Similarly, there are places for each used production rule (F^*) to signify whether it has been applied (P_1) or not (P_2), the positive and negative places for the production rules. These values are used to determine whether a task that incorporates a production rule (T^*) can be executed and – if so – what the result is of its execution. We distinguished five conditions that are to be met for applying a production rule when its corresponding transition is enabled. We also indicated that even when these conditions are met, the application of the rule does not necessarily succeed. The firing in the stretched workflow net of a transition $t \in T_1 \cup T_2 \cup T_3 \cup T_4 \cup T_5$ indicates that the production rule associated with t was not applicable. Firing of a transition $u_{t,1}$ indicates that the production rule associated with t is applicable. Actual firing of a transition $t \in T$ indicates a successful application of its production rule – if any. Firing of a transition $u_{t,5}$ indicates that t's production was not successful, although it was applicable.

To illustrate the notion of a stretched workflow model we will use the example of a workflow model used in Chapter 3, once more depicted in Figure A.2.

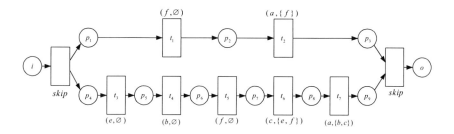

Fig. A.2. Workflow example

We will not present the entire stretched workflow model on the basis of the workflow example. It would result in stretched workflow model of more than 50 places and 80 transitions, with an intricate web of flow relations. For the sake of readability, we restrict ourselves to two interesting parts of the stretched workflow model.

In Figure A.3 the part near the source place of the stretched workflow model can be seen. The original source place is now the only input of the special transition t^{init}, which has as output places all the negative places of information elements and production rules. This is the initial situation of any workflow execution. Also, the special place i^{init} is an output place of t^{init}. In Definition A.1, the relations of this part of the stretched workflow model are given by R_{54}, R_{55}, and the elements (i, t^{init}) and (t^{init}, i) that are part of R'.

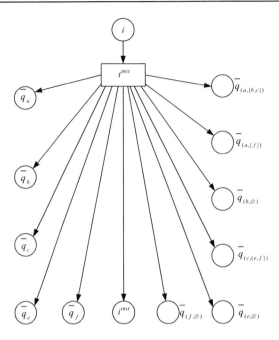

Fig. A.3. Start of stretched workflow

Next, we will consider the other characteristic part of the stretched workflow model, by focusing on the single transition t_6 in Figure A.2. It is characteristic for any translation of a transition in a workflow model to a stretched workflow model. To transition t_6, the production rule $(c, \{e, f\})$ is associated. In Figure A.4 the translation of t_6 can be seen.

The transition t_6 in the middle of the figure is the central transition in this part of the stretched workflow model. Its firing represents a successful application of the production rule $(c, \{e, f\})$.

The transitions on the left-hand side of the figure each express one of the five conditions that may not be met, so that the production rule is not applicable. We will briefly consider each of these. The transition $\overline{u}_{t_6}^{-con}$ is used to represent the situation that the precondition is not met, although all inputs are available (relations $R_1 \ldots R_5$ of Definition A.6). Transitions $\overline{u}_{t_6, \overline{q}_e}$ and $\overline{u}_{t_6, \overline{q}_f}$ represent the absence of a value for respectively e and f, so that the production rule is not applicable ($R_6 \ldots R_{10}$). Transition $\overline{u}_{t_6, (c, \{e, f\})}$ fires when the production rule $(c, \{e, f\})$ is already applied ($R_{11} \ldots R_{15}$). Transition $\overline{u}_{t_6, q_c}$ fires when a value for the output c has already been established ($R_{16} \ldots R_{20}$). Finally, transition $\overline{u}_{t_6, q_a}$ fires when a value for the top element a has already been established ($R_{21} \ldots R_{25}$).

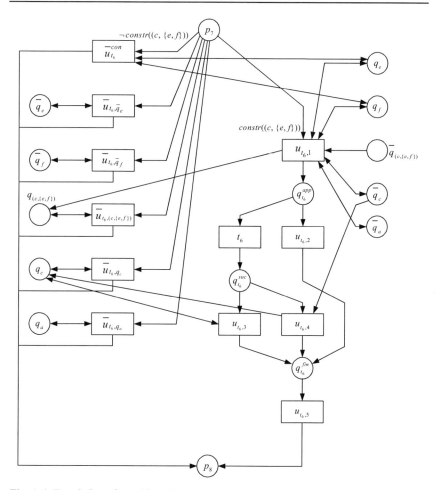

Fig. A.4. Translation of transition t6

The right-hand side of the figure is used to represent the situation that all five conditions are met, but that it still needs to be settled whether the application of the production rules is successful. Five special transitions $u_{t_6,1} \ldots u_{t_6,5}$ are used for its modeling, as well as three special places $q_{t_6}^{app}$, $q_{t_6}^{suc}$ and $q_{t_6}^{fin}$. Transition $u_{t_6,1}$ fires if all conditions are met for the production rule to become applicable ($R_{26} \ldots R_{36}$). In particular, it marks the place $q_{(c, \{e, f\})}$ to signify that it has been attempted to apply the production rule (R_{32}), which will prevent any following attempt. Then, either transition t_6 fires to represent the successful application of $(c, \{e, f\})$ (R_{37}, R_{38}) or transition $u_{t_6,2}$ to represent the opposite case (R_{39}, R_{40}). Transitions $u_{t_6,3}$ and $u_{t_6,4}$ are used to administrate that a value for c is now known, tak-

ing into account that it could have been updated (almost simultaneously) by another transition (R_{41}...R_{48}). The final transition $u_{t_6,5}$ properly ends this part of the
net (R_{49}, R_{50}).

All relations maintained by transitions of the original workflow net that do not
have a production rule associated with it, i.e., each transition $t \in T$ such that
$prod(t) = skip$, are preserved in the stretched workflow model (R_{51}...R_{53}).

Note that in the figure the precondition of $(c, \{e, f\})$ and its negation are also
depicted. They are not, however, a formal part of the stretched workflow model.
We will assume that the firing of transitions $u_{t,(p,cs)}$ and $\overline{u}_{t,1}$ for a transition t with
$prod(t) = (p, cs)$ nonetheless respect these conditions.

Before we proceed with the final part of defining the bottom-level workflow
model, we want to indicate some properties of a stretched workflow model.

Lemma A.1   **(Properties of the stretched workflow model).** If PM' = (P', T',
R', *prod*) is a stretched workflow model of the workflow model PM = (P, T, R,
prod) then:
a. (P', T', R') is a workflow net,
b. for each used information element, the sum of tokens in its positive and nega-
    tive places is equal to one for each reachable marking from $[\![i]\!]$ – excluding
    $[\![i]\!]$ itself; formally: for each $d \in D^*$ and for each reachable marking M from
    $[\![i]\!]$ in (P', T', R') holds that $M(q_d) + M(\overline{q}_d) + M(i) = 1$,
c. for each used production rule, the sum of tokens in its positive and negative
    places is equal to one for each reachable marking from $[\![i]\!]$ – excluding $[\![i]\!]$
    itself; formally: for each $(p, cs) \in F^*$ and for each reachable marking M from
    $[\![i]\!]$ in (P', T', R') holds that $M(q_{(p, cs)}) + M(\overline{q}_{(p,cs)}) + M(i) = 1$.

Proof a. The workflow net is defined in Definition 2.13. Inspection of Definition
A.1 yields that there is only one source place and one sink place. The source place
is the input place of the new transition t^{init}; the output place is the same as in (P, T,
R). All other places have at least one preceding and one succeeding transition. For
each node $n \in (P \cup T)$ holds that there is a path in (P, T, R) from i to o (conformance). For every node $n \in (P' \cup T') \setminus (P \cup T)$ there is a path to a node $r \in (P \cup
T)$ and a path from $s \in (P \cup T)$. Hence, the net is a workflow net.
b. Consider the workflow net system (P', T', R', $[\![i]\!]$) and let M be such that
$[\![i]\!] \xrightarrow{t^{init}} M$ for the special transition t^{init}. Then the claim holds for M on the basis of R' of Definition A.1. Corresponding to the definition of R', each other transi-
tion that removes a token from either a negative or positive place of a specific information element takes one token from exactly one of these two places. That
same transition puts one token back in either the positive or the negative place of
that same information element. Hence, the equality holds.
c. Similar to the proof of part b., respectively for the positive and negative places
of production rules. □

This result shows that the administration of the stretched workflow model of obtained information elements and executed production rules is proper. The stretched workflow model enforces a certain correctness property as well.

Definition A.2   (Limited soundness). A workflow net (P, T, R) is said to be limited sound with respect to a set $S \subseteq P$ if and only if:
- for every marking M reachable from marking $[\![i]\!]$, there exists a firing sequence leading from marking M to a marking M' which marks o. Formally:

$$\forall_M \left[\left([\![i]\!] \xrightarrow{\;*\;} M \right) \Rightarrow \exists_{M'} \left(M \xrightarrow{\;*\;} M' \wedge M'(o) \geq 1 \right) \right] \quad \text{(completion option),}$$

and
- for every marking M reachable from marking $[\![i]\!]$ which marks o holds that there is exactly one token in o and each other place that is marked by M is no part of S:

$$\forall_{M,p \in P'} \left[\left([\![i]\!] \xrightarrow{\;*\;} M \wedge M(o) \geq 1 \wedge M(p) \geq 1 \wedge p \neq o \right) \Rightarrow M(o) = 1 \wedge p \notin S \right]$$

(proper completion).

If we compare this with Definition 2.14, it is clear that the proper completion requirement is relaxed, i.e., in the end state tokens may reside in places outside S. The original requirement in the soundness notion of the liveness of all transitions is omitted. Practically, we do not require this notion, but it would be hard to verify whether it is satisfied for a given case.

Lemma A.2   (Limited soundness of stretched workflow model). If PM' = (P', T', R', *prod*) is a stretched workflow model of the workflow model PM = (P, T, R, *prod*) and PN = (P, T, R) is sound then PN' = (P', T', R') is limited sound with respect to $P \subseteq P'$.

Proof 'Completion option'. Let M be a marking of PN' such that $[\![i]\!] \xrightarrow{\;\rho\;} M$, where M does not mark o. Without loss of generality, we assume that for each $t \in$ T with $prod(t) \neq skip$ holds that neither q_t^{app}, q_t^{suc}, or q_t^{fin} is marked at M. (Clearly such a marking is reachable from any other marking that does not satisfy this property, because the translation of each transition in a stretched workflow model is a state machine that can always proceed until it marks the output places of that transition). Consider the mapping $M_{PN} = (M(p_1)...M(p_n))$ and the firing sequence τ, with $\tau = \rho|_T$, $\epsilon|_T = \epsilon$ and

$$(u\lambda)\|_{\mathsf{T}} = \begin{cases} t(\lambda\|_{\mathsf{T}}) & \text{if } u = \overline{u_t}^{-con} \text{ for } t \in \mathsf{T}, \\ t(\lambda\|_{\mathsf{T}}) & \text{if } u = \overline{u_{t,\overline{q}_d}} \text{ for } t \in \mathsf{T}, d \in D \\ t(\lambda\|_{\mathsf{T}}) & \text{if } u = \overline{u_{t,(p,cs)}} \text{ for } t \in \mathsf{T}, (p,cs) \in F \\ t(\lambda\|_{\mathsf{T}}) & \text{if } u = \overline{u_{t,q_d}} \text{ for } t \in \mathsf{T}, d \in D \\ t(\lambda\|_{\mathsf{T}}) & \text{if } u = u_{t,1} \text{ for } t \in \mathsf{T}, prod(t) \neq skip \\ u(\lambda\|_{\mathsf{T}}) & \text{if } u \in \mathsf{T}, prod(u) = skip \\ \lambda\|_{\mathsf{T}} & \text{if } u = u_{t,2}, u = u_{t,3}, u = u_{t,4}, \text{ or } u = u_{t,5} \text{ for } t \in \mathsf{T} \\ \lambda\|_{\mathsf{T}} & \text{if } u \in \mathsf{T}, prod(u) \neq skip \end{cases}$$

The firing sequence τ consists of transitions that are part of T only. The sequence τ contains the transitions of the original workflow model PM in the order that their production rules – if any – are considered for application in the firing of the stretched workflow, regardless of it actual application or success. Note that firing of the transition $u_{t,1}$ for any $t \in$ T with $prod(t) \neq skip$ is sufficient as an indication of its production rule to have been applicable. On the basis of the definition of the stretched workflow net (Definition A.1), we must conclude that $\llbracket i \rrbracket \xrightarrow{\tau} M_{PN}$ in PN. On the basis of the soundness of PN, there is a firing sequence σ in PN such that $M_{PN} \xrightarrow{\sigma} M_{PN}'$ and $M_{PN}'(o) \geq 1$. But then, on the basis of the definition of the stretched workflow net (Definition A.1), there is also a firing sequence θ in PN' with $M \xrightarrow{\theta} M'$ and $\sigma = \theta\|_{\mathsf{T}}$ such that $(M'(p_1)...M'(p_n)) = M_{PN}'$. Obviously, such a marking M' marks o.

'Proper completion'. Let M be a dead state in PN' such that $\llbracket i \rrbracket \xrightarrow{\rho} M$. Clearly, for no $t \in$ T, q_t^{app}, q_t^{suc}, or q_t^{fin} can be marked at M, as it is dead. Now suppose that there is a place $p \in P\backslash\{o\}$ such that $M(p)$ is marked or that $M(o) > 1$. Let $P = (p_1, p_2...p_n)$ for some $n \in \mathbb{N}$. Consider the mapping $M_{PN} = (M(p_1)...M(p_n))$ and the firing sequence τ, with $\tau = \rho\|_{\mathsf{T}}$. On the basis of the definition of the stretched workflow net, we must conclude that $\llbracket i \rrbracket \xrightarrow{\tau} M_{PN}$ in PN. But because we assumed that M is a dead state with either $M(p)$ marked for some $p \in$ P or $M(o) > 1$, the net PN cannot be sound. Clearly, this is a contradiction. We conclude that if M is a dead state in PN', $M(p)$ is marked for no $p \in$ P and $M(o) = 1$ on the basis of the soundness of PN. □

The limited soundness of a stretched workflow model guarantees us that the execution of a stretched workflow model is sound from a high-level perspective, the perspective of the overarching workflow model. The only tokens that reside in the net as soon as the sink place is marked have to do with the administration of information elements and production rules. When implementing the workflow as an operational way of working, the logistics of the workflow will be carried out correctly. Only information about the used information is still available, e.g., in the form of stored values in a database. It is now clear that it is possible to extend the definition of the stretched workflow model in such a way that *it is sound itself.* After all, "vacuum-cleaning" transitions could be added for each distribution of tokens over the administrative places which consume the remaining tokens. Obviously, the bottom-level workflow model would indeed be larger still, so we leave the subject here with this observation.

The final step for defining the bottom-level model can now be made, which adds the probability and timing logic to the stretched workflow model.

Definition A.3   (Bottom-level workflow model). If PM' = (P', T', R', *prod'*) is the stretched version of the workflow model PM = (P, T, R, *prod*) conforming to the extended product data model (*D, C, pre, F, constr, cst, flow, prob*), then the bottom-level workflow model OM = (P', T', R', W, *f*) of PM is a Stochastic Workflow net (see Definition 2.20) where:

 – for $t, u \in$ T' where *prod*(*t*) = (*p, cs*) $\in$ *F* and $\bullet t = \bullet u$, W(*t*) $\in$ ℕ and W(*u*) $\in$ ℕ are chosen such that W(*t*) / (W(*t*) + W(*u*)) = *prob*(*p, cs*),
 – for $t \in$ T' where *prod*(*t*) = *skip* and there is no $u \in$ T' such that *prod*(*u*) = (*p, cs*) $\in$ *F* and $\bullet t = \bullet u$, W(*t*) = 1,
 – for $t \in$ T',

$$f_t(x) = \begin{cases} 1 & \text{if } t = (p,cs) \in F \wedge x = flow((p,cs)), \\ 0 & \text{if } t = skip \vee \big(t = (p,cs) \in F \wedge x \neq flow((p,cs))\big). \end{cases}$$

The weights are assigned to a transition *t* in such a way that if the applicable place q_t^{app} is reached in the attempted application of a production rule (*p, cs*), then there is a probability *prob*(*p, cs*) that this application will succeed (and a probability of 1 - *prob*(*p, cs*) that it will fail). In Figure A.4, this is represented by the respective transitions t_6 and $u_{t_6,2}$. All other transitions have a weight equal to one.

Each transition *t* in the bottom-level workflow model that also occurs in the stretched workflow model with *prod'*(*t*) = (*p, cs*) will exactly last *flow*(*p, cs*) time units.

Note that we implicitly transfer the existing preconditions of the transitions in the stretched workflow model to the bottom-level workflow model. Once again, a formal definition could be given but this would result in elaborate definitions. The definition of the Stochastic Petri net (Definition 2.16) would need to be extended, and its firing rule would require a strengthening (Definition 2.19).

Note that the costs of production rules as specified in the product data model have not been incorporated in the bottom-level model. The reason is that the cost of a production rule has no consequence for the execution of the bottom-level workflow model. This in contrast to e.g., the success probability of a production rule and the flow time which is associated with it.

The bottom-level workflow model has the same structure as the stretched level workflow model. Although the structure of the bottom-level workflow model is not free-choice, the timing of the net will not obstruct a proper completion in the sense of the limited soundness we discussed. Although blocking may occur, most blocking conditions are lifted instantaneously. For example, checking a place for the existence of an information element by one transition may block that same checking by another, but this will only affect the ordering of transitions – not the timing of the net or a routing decision.

The bottom-level workflow model gives a more explicit semantics of actual executions of production rules than the workflow model it has been derived of. Although this is an advantage from the viewpoint of actually applying the design in practice or for analysis and evaluation purposes, a bottom-level workflow model quickly becomes quite large. This is why we preferred the use of the workflow model for the sake of analysis and presentation in Chapter 3. The bottom-level workflow model, especially because we have molded it into a Stochastic Workflow net is suitable for evaluation purposes.

We end this appendix with a definition of the interpreted firing sequence, which is informally defined in Definition 3.5.

Definition A.4   (Interpreted and factual firing sequences). If $OM = (P', T', R', W, f)$ is the bottom-level workflow model of the workflow model $PM = (P, T, R, prod)$ that conforms to the extended product data model $(D, C, pre, F, constr, cst, flow, prob)$ and induces a stochastic process $SP = \{ (X_n, Y_n, Z_n) \mid n = 0, 1, 2, \ldots \}$, then the sequence of production rules ρ is the interpreted firing sequence of PM, which can be recursively defined as $\rho = Y_1 Y_2 \ldots \|_{\{t \in T \mid prod(t) \neq skip\}}^{prod}$ with $\epsilon \|_B^f = \epsilon$ and

$$(a\sigma)\|_B^f = \begin{cases} f(a)(\sigma\|_B^f) & \text{if } a \in B, \\ \sigma\|_B^f & \text{if } a \notin B. \end{cases}$$

An interpreted firing sequence is an ordering of successively applied production rules. From this definition it can be seen how the exact semantics of the bottom-level workflow model can be used to derive a concept which is meaningful for the original workflow model. The interpreted firing sequence is used in the design phase of Chapter 3 to determine the expected cost of a workflow model.

This concludes the specification of the semantic of a workflow model.

B The Fourier Transform

To enable an efficient computation of the throughput time of the sequential and the iteration block in Chapter 4, the Fast Fourier Transform is applied. In this appendix a brief explanation of this algorithm will be given, based on an in-depth description by Cormen et al. (1990).

The convolution of two vectors $\vec{a}$ and $\vec{b}$ of length n - also denoted as $\vec{a} \otimes \vec{b}$ - yields a vector $\vec{c}$ of length $2n$, where for each of its elements c_j, $0 \leq j \leq 2n$, holds:

$$c_j = \sum_{k=0}^{j} a_k b_{j-k}.$$

Computing the convolution of two vectors of length n in a straightforward approach takes $\theta(n^2)$ steps. This effort can be reduced by taking a stepwise approach. The first step consists of efficiently determining the Discrete Fourier Transforms of the vectors involved; the next step consist of multiplying the resulting vectors, and the last step of determining the result by an inverse transformation.

Definition B.1 (Discrete Fourier Transform, inverse Discrete Fourier Transform) The Discrete Fourier Transform (*DFT*) of the vector $\vec{a} = (a_0, a_1, ..., a_{n-1})$ is given by the vector $\vec{y} = (y_0, y_1, ..., y_{n-1})$ with

$$y_k = \sum_{j=0}^{n-1} a_j \omega_n^{kj}, \text{ for } 0 \leq k < n \text{ and } \omega_n = e^{2\pi i/n}.$$

The inverse Discrete Fourier Transform (DFT^{-1}) of the vector $\vec{y} = (y_0, y_1, ..., y_{n-1})$ is given by the vector $\vec{a} = (a_0, a_1, ..., a_{n-1})$ with

$$a_j = \frac{1}{n} \sum_{k=0}^{n-1} y_k \omega_n^{-kj}, \text{ for } 0 \leq k < n \text{ and } \omega_n = e^{2\pi i/n}.$$

When the vector $\vec{y}$ is the Discrete Fourier Transform of vector $\vec{a}$ with length n we also write $\vec{y} = DFT_n(\vec{a})$. It is easy to verify that $DFT_n^{-1}(DFT_n(\vec{a})) = \vec{a}$. The elements $\omega_n^0, \omega_n^1, ..., \omega_n^{n-1}$ used to compute the *DFT* of a vector of length n are the nth roots of unity. It can be easily shown that if n is positive and even, then the squares of the nth roots of unity are the $(n/2)$th roots of unity. This implies that if all the nth roots of unity are squared, then each $(n/2)$th root of unity is obtained exactly twice. This result is known as the *halving lemma*.

H.A. Reijers: Design and Control of Workflow Processes, LNCS 2617, pp. 303-304, 2003.
© Springer-Verlag Berlin Heidelberg 2003

Now consider polynomials p and q in x, with coefficients $\vec{a} = (a_0, a_1, ..., a_{n-1})$ and $\vec{b} = (b_0, b_1, ..., b_{n-1})$ respectively. Let r be defined by $r(x) = p(x)\,q(x)$. Then r is a polynomial with coefficients $\vec{c} = \vec{a} \otimes \vec{b}$. Note that $DFT_n(\vec{a}) = (p(\omega_n^0), p(\omega_n^1),$ $..., p(\omega_n^{n-1}))$ and similarly for $\vec{b}$ and $\vec{c}$. On the one hand, due to $r(x) = p(x)\,q(x)$, we have $DFT_n(\vec{c}) = DFT_n(\vec{a}) \cdot DFT_n(\vec{b})$ where $\cdot$ denotes the pointwise product. On the other hand, due to $\vec{c} = \vec{a} \otimes \vec{b}$, we have that $DFT_n(\vec{c}) = DFT_n(\vec{a} \otimes \vec{b})$. This results in the following theorem.

Theorem B.1   **(Convolution theorem)** For any two vectors $\vec{a}$ and $\vec{b}$ of length n, where n is a power of 2,

$$DFT_{2n}(\vec{a} \otimes \vec{b}) = DFT_{2n}(\vec{a}) \cdot DFT_{2n}(\vec{b}),$$

where the vectors a and b are padded with 0's to length 2n and $\cdot$ denotes the componentwise product of two vectors.

The Fast Fourier Transform (*FFT*) computes the *DFT* of a vector by taking advantage of the halving lemma. Doing so, $DFT_n(\vec{a})$ can be computed in $\Theta(n \log n)$ time, as opposed to the $\Theta(n^2)$ time of the straightforward method. To determine $\vec{y} = DFT_n(\vec{a})$ with each of its elements y_k, $0 \le k < n$, with n even and positive, and $\omega_n = e^{2\pi i/n}$, the following equality is used:

$$y_k = \sum_{j=0}^{n-1} a_j \omega_n^{kj} = \sum_{j=0}^{n/2-1} a_{2j} (\omega_n^{kj})^2 + \omega_n^k \sum_{j=0}^{n/2-1} a_{2j+1} (\omega_n^{kj})^2 .$$

The problem of determining a point-value representation in the points $\omega_n^0, \omega_n^1, ..., \omega_n^{n-1}$ on the basis of n coefficients has now been reduced to evaluating two point-value representations in the points $(\omega_n^0)^2, (\omega_n^1)^2, ..., (\omega_n^{n-1})^2$ on the basis of $n/2$ coefficients and combining them according to the above equation. On the basis of the halving lemma, we know that the list $(\omega_n^0)^2, (\omega_n^1)^2, ..., (\omega_n^{n-1})^2$ consists only of $n/2$ distinct values. These values are exactly the $(n/2)$th roots of unity, with each root occurring twice. The original DFT_n computation has now been divided into two $DFT_{n/2}$ computations. At this point it is also clear that the convolution theorem requires n to be a power of two, so that an ultimate division of the computation effort can be accomplished. The *FFT* will perform the *DFT* and inverse *DFT* operations in $\Theta(n \log n)$ time.

C The Simulation of the Workbench

In Chapter 5, a so-called "workbench" of resource-extended SWN's has been used to investigate the effects of various resource allocation strategies. For the simulation of the workflows in question, the package ExSpect was used (Van Hee et al., 1989; Van der Aalst et al., 2000a). This appendix goes deeper into the technical details of the simulation.

For each of the workflows as described in Section 5.4, the effects of assigning either two or three additional resources has been studied. For this purpose, each incremental addition of one extra resource up to the total number of "free" resources was simulated. In Table C.1, for each workflow the information in the columns show the following:

- The number of resource classes.
- The total number of resources that can be freely allocated within the considered scenario.
- The number of different allocations with one, two or three extra resources over the available resource classes (if considered for the specific workflow).
- The total number of simulated, different resource allocations (excluding initial allocations).

From the table it follows that a total number 285 different resource allocations have been considered in the evaluation of the workbench, aside from the six initial allocations.

The approach to simulate each of the various different allocations was as follows. For each of the considered workflows, an ExSpect model was developed that represented its specific structure and timing behavior. The graphic representation of one such model can be seen in Figure C.1. Different shades of gray in this figure represent whether a transition requires a resource or not, and whether the transition is part of the original model or not. Some transitions were added for modeling reasons.

Aside from each of the workflow-specific ExSpect models, a generic framework has also been developed within ExSpect. This framework could incorporate any of the workflow-specific ExSpect models. In other words, one part of the framework could be parameterized with a specific model of one of the workflows.

If the general framework was instantiated with (a) one workflow-specific ExSpect model and (b) a specific initial resource allocation successively it took care of the following:

H.A. Reijers: Design and Control of Workflow Processes, LNCS 2617, pp. 305-308, 2003.
© Springer-Verlag Berlin Heidelberg 2003

Table C.1. Number of simulated allocations

	# res. classes	# total re- sources	# alloc. one extra re- source	# alloc. two extra resources	# alloc. three extra re- sources	# total simulated allocations
tandem net	3	3	3	6	10	19
N-construc-tion	4	3	4	10	20	34
parallel sequential	4	2	4	10	-	14
alternative sequential	4	2	4	10	-	14
handling appeals	7	3	7	28	84	129
money transfers	5	3	5	15	35	75

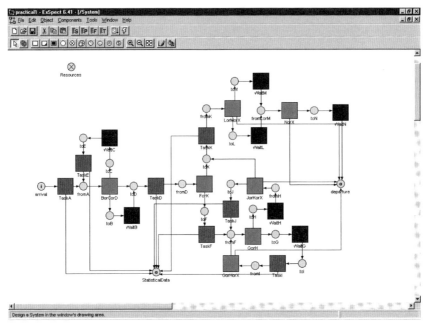

Fig. C1. ExSpect model of "handling of appeals" workflow

1. *Scenario creation*

   The instantiated framework created a scenario that could be used to replay a large set of the same executions of the specific workflow regardless of the exact allocation of resources; for a large number of executions, the scenario determined a partially ordered list of tasks that were executed and the service time of each transition.

2. *Scenario execution for initial and successor allocations*

   On the basis of an earlier created scenario, the instantiated framework simulated the execution of this scenario taking the available resources into account of the following:

   – The initial resource allocation.
   – Each resource allocation of a successor of the initial allocation, i.e., the initial allocation with one extra resource in one of the resource classes (see Section 5.3).

   To save effort in the creation of different models, the initial resource allocation and each of the successors was processed in parallel (but independently).

A graphic representation of an instantiated framework can be seen in Figure C.2. The box labeled "System0" contains the workflow-specific ExSpect model with the initial resource allocation. A transition labeled "SystemX" contains the workflow-specific ExSpect model with a resource allocation that extends the initial resource allocation with one additional resource in resource class X.

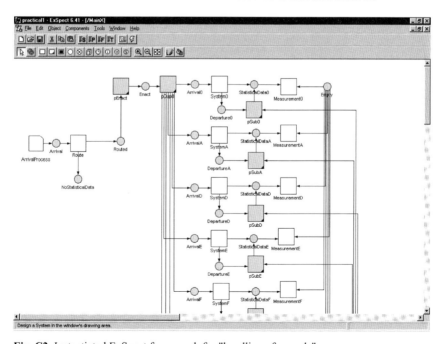

Fig. C2. Instantiated ExSpect framework for "handling of appeals"

As stated before, for each workflow the allocation of two or three additional re-sources was considered. After execution of an instantiated framework on the basis of the initial resource allocation of the workflow – which delivered the informa-tion on the effects of assigning *one* additional resource – each successor allocation itself was used as an initial allocation of an execution of an instantiated framework – which delivered the information on the effects of assigning two additional re-sources. This was analogously done for the scenario's where three additional re-sources were considered. For example, for the "handling of appeals" where the addition of three additional resources was considered, a total of 57 $(= 1 + 7 + 49)$ instantiated frameworks were executed. This approach obviously yields redundant results, but double results were used as checks.

Each simulated resource allocation for each of the simulated workflows was di-vided into 50 subruns of 20,000 time units each (simulation time), including 10 start runs. The duration of a simulation of an instantiated framework varied con-siderably, caused by the varying complexity of the different workflow models. The simulation of one instantiated framework for the "handling of appeals" (which, as explained, included all seven successors of an initial resource allocation including the initial allocation itself) took about one and a half hour on a PC sys-tem with a clock-speed of 1Ghz and 1024 Mb internal memory.

An interesting property of the described approach is that it is possible to evalu-ate more than the regular comparison of different simulation experiments. Because of the same scenario that underlies each simulation for the same workflow model, an analysis of the exact differences of two or more outcomes is also possible. The analysis as presented in Chapter 5 did not include such an analysis.

Also note that the sketched approach was only feasible because all used work-flow nets were free-choice. In other words, the set of tasks in an execution did not depend on the exact duration of each task's execution.

Lecture Notes in Computer Science

For information about Vols. 1–2539

please contact your bookseller or Springer-Verlag